CONCEPTUALIZING RELIGION

CONCEPTUALIZING RELIGION

IMMANENT ANTHROPOLOGISTS, TRANSCENDENT NATIVES, AND UNBOUNDED CATEGORIES

BY

BENSON SALER

Berghahn Books
NEW YORK · OXFORD

First published by E.J. Brill in 1993
Paperback edition with new preface published by Berghahn Books in 2000

Grateful acknowledgment is made to
Koninklijke Brill for permission to publish this edition.

Library of Congress Cataloging-in-Publication Data

Saler, Benson.
 Conceptualizing religion : immanent anthropologists, transcendent
natives, & unbounded categories / Benson Saler.
  p.   cm.
 Originally published : Leiden ; New York : E.J. Brill, 1993, in series:
Studies in the history of religions. With new pref.
 Includes bibliographical references and index.
 ISBN 1-57181-219-9
 1. Religion.   2. Ethnology--Religious aspects.   I. Title.
 [BL48.S255   1999]   99-41407
 200--dc21   CIP

British Library Cataloguing in Publication Data

A catalogue record for this book is available from the British Library.

Printed in the United States on acid-free paper.

To Joyce

CONTENTS

Preface ix

Acknowledgements xvii

Introduction 1

   I. Abjuring a Definition and Other Matters 27

  II. Holding a Definition in Abeyance and
      A Case for a Definition 70

  III. Monothetic Definitions 87

  IV. More on Monothetic Definitions 122

   V. Multi-factorial Approaches: Family
      Resemblance and Polythesis 158

  VI. A Prototype Approach 197

  VII. Ethnocentrism and Distanciation 227

References Cited 265

Index 277

PREFACE TO THE PAPERBACK EDITION

In this Preface I set forth the central argument of the book, shorn for the most part of complexities encountered in the text. In doing so, I call the reader's attention to a matter otherwise insufficiently emphasized: that the idea of "family resemblances" can be applied productively not only to the category religion and to denominated families of religions, but also to elements that scholars variously attribute to religion and to religions (e.g., theism, soul concepts, rituals and ritualizations, etc.). Finally, I address an omission in the text that was noted by a reviewer.

THE PROBLEM

Religion is a Western folk category that contemporary Western scholars have appropriated. As I put it elsewhere,

> Western scholars who study religion develop some understanding of what is meant by religion in their society long before they become scholars. This observation is so unremarkable, so obvious and seemingly trite, that I would be embarrassed to voice it were it not important. But it is important. Long before European scholars of religion become scholars of religion, they have fairly well developed ideas of what to look for in searching the world for religions. In large measure, indeed, their scholarly efforts to define or characterize religion are efforts to refine and deepen the folk category that they began to use as children, and to foreground what they deem most salient or important about religion. (Saler 1997:28)

For well over a hundred years, Western academics have labored at the task of refining and deepening the folk category, writing definition after definition and explication after explication. They have variously identified the essence of religion as the supposed fact of, or a special sensitivity to, or a belief in, or commerce with, the supernatural, the super-human, the spiritual, the sacred, the transcendent, the numinous, the wholly other, and the partially other (that is, the anthropomorphized). Or they have sought to locate religion's center of gravity in something special about people in their solitude, or people in their effervescent sociability, or people asserting self, or people projecting, or people otherwise engaging in therapy, or people symboling, or people being reflexive, and so on and so forth.

While these efforts have sometimes contributed to our understandings of the longings, hopes, ideas, expectations, and practices of our fellow human beings, the task of identifying the essence or universal core of religion has largely been a failure, considering the lack of consensus among scholars.

Some scholars, indeed, cite the lack of definitional consensus as supporting their contention that the term "religion" does not point to some universal phenomenon, to some one "thing," that can be recognized throughout the world. Religion, they maintain, is a term with discrete Euro-American associations and accreted and multiple meanings in the Western world, and it is therefore difficult, and perhaps inadvisable, to apply it cross-culturally. Some even explicitly recommend dropping the term. But arguments similar to those made for abandoning the word religion have also been made for such terms as kinship, marriage, property, law, belief, tribe, peasant, and so on. Indeed, virtually all of the analytical terms used by Euro-American social scientists have distinct Western associations and multiple meanings. Were we to drop all of them, social scientists could well be rendered speechless. (I hope that no one cheers at the prospect! In fairness to social scientists, we ought to admit that sometimes they *do* say things that are informative and interesting!) A less radical solution, I argue in this book, is to consider an alternative approach that neither seeks to do away with terms that have served as convenient tools for talking about things that interest us nor unduly attempts to restrict the range of those terms by creating narrow definitions.

SOURCES OF THE SOLUTION PROFFERED

The approach to conceptualizing religion recommended in this book draws on the philosopher Ludwig Wittgenstein's discussions of "family resemblances." Further, it supplements and complements the idea of family resemblances with selected insights derived from prototype theory in the contemporary cognitive sciences. While I hold that the idea of family resemblances offers great potential advantages for conceptualizing religion, I do not think that a family resemblance approach by itself is adequate for scholarly purposes. Something more is required. Prototype theory supplies that something more.

FAMILY RESEMBLANCE

The traditional theory of categorization endorsed by Western scholars holds that the members of a group comprehended by a category are mutually and equally members because they all share some one feature, or some conjunction of features, in common. Such features are called "distinguishing features" or "defining features." In the traditional theory, they define the category. And they serve as standards for determining whether or not some candidate should be admitted to the group comprehended by the category. According to the traditional theory, for instance, all things called "game" must share something in common — at the very least, one "distinguishing feature" — if they are properly labeled by the category term.

Wittgenstein disagrees. While he acknowledges that the instantiations of a category might share one or more features in common, it is not necessary for them to do so in order to justify being mutually labeled by the category term. It is sufficient that they are linked together by overlapping similarities of various sorts, just as the members of a human family may show overlapping similarities — "family resemblances" — in facial features, body build, hair color, and so forth, without all the members of the family sharing the very same features.

Indeed, in the case of some categories ("game," for instance), some instantiations (e.g., solitaire) will not share any discrete features with other instantiations (e.g., football). In such cases, however, there are typically still other instantiations of the category with which they overlap. Let us suppose that our category has three subsets of instances, A, B, and C. A and C share no features in common. Members of both, however, share some features with members of the subset B. Instances of B, therefore, serve to link instances of A and C, just as the central links in a chain connect the peripheral links on either end. Such linkages, the philosopher J.R. Bambrough suggests (see Chapter Five), provide an "objective" justification for the category and its instantiations.

I recommend that we think of "religion" in a similar way. The various instantiations of the category, popularly called "religions," need not all share some one feature, or some specific conjunction of features, in common.

We can deal with religion in terms of a pool of elements that we deem *typical* of religion, without supposing that any one element is *necessary* for the existence of a religion. These elements or "typicality features" (see the reference to Jackendoff in Chapter Seven) mutually pertain to our general model. But while all of them are formally predicated of "religion," not all of them will be found in all "religions." Thus, for instance, we tend to suppose that theism is typical of religion, and we predicate it of our general model. Yet while many religions encountered in the world do indeed accord central importance to "gods," some (e.g., Canonical Theravada Buddhism) do not. It is not necessary for all complexes of phenomena that we call religions to share the very same elements, even though such elements are typical of what we usually mean by religion.

In the text, I make it clear that this logic is also likely to apply to the different instances of some denominated religion. Thus, for instance, the doctrine of the dual nature of Christ — the doctrine that Jesus Christ is both fully human and fully divine — specifically applies to the Christian family of confessions. But not all Christians accept it. Monophysite Christians, for instance, reject it, maintaining that Christ has only one nature, the divine, which incorporates or assumes human attributes. This helps make the point that "Christianity" is not some monolithic religion. Rather, it is a family of religions, linked together by family likenesses. Although we can and should predicate the doctrine of the dual nature of Christ to our scholarly model of "Christianity," we cannot legitimately insist that it is found in all Christianities.

In the text, I suggest that this logic also applies to the elements or typicality features that we predicate of our general model of "religion" (see, for instance, my treatment of E.B. Tylor's discussion of the category "spiritual beings" in Chapter Three). In retrospect, however, I now think that I fail to emphasize the point adequately. So let me make amends in this Preface.

If we accept the applicability of the idea of family resemblances to what some authors call "religion in general" and to denominated families of religions, we should also deal with the likelihood that that idea will apply at an even more fundamental level. That is, the elements or typicality features that we predicate of our scholarly model of religion ("religion in general") are themselves likely to be organized by family resemblances. Numbers of anthropologists either recognize this or verge on doing so. Take, for example, "sacrifice," which many scholars associate with religion. Maurice Bloch (1992:25) writes that "I believe it is right to stress the great variety that exists among the various examples of 'sacrifice' as they have been described in the anthropological literature ..." Yes, it is right to stress this "great variety." The problem, however, is how best to deal with it.

PROTOTYPE THEORY

In the argument advanced in this book, insights derived from prototype theory suggest how we might deal productively with "great variety." And they help defuse a common complaint voiced about a family resemblance approach to religion: the complaint that, in the absence of a set of necessary features that distinguish religion from all else, a huge and bewildering array of phenomena can be assigned to the category, and this renders the category virtually useless as a scholarly analytical tool. That complaint calls in effect for sure borders erected by stipulating necessary features or conditions. Prototype theory, in contrast, induces us to celebrate central tendencies and peripheries rather than necessities and borders.

Prototype theory is not monolithic. Prototype theorists disagree among themselves on a number of issues. Prototype theory, nevertheless, can be narrowly described as attempts — attempts among which there are discernable family resemblances — to account for "prototype effects."

Prototype effects are differences in the effective judgments that people render about how well various instances of a category exemplify that category. Many persons, for instance, may judge robins and sparrows to be clearer or "better" examples of "bird" than penguins, or apples and oranges to be clearer or "better" examples of "fruit" than olives. These judgments may be explicitly given. Or they may be suggested by such things as the order in which people list examples of a category, or the differential alacrity that individuals manifest in citing examples or in responding to examples voiced by others. The clearest or "best" examples in judgments rendered are called "the prototypes" of their categories, or "the most prototypical exemplars."

Research accomplished by a diversity of persons suggests that prototype effects are widely encountered. The classical theory of categorization cannot account for that finding. That theory, it may be recalled, holds that all of the members of a group comprehended by a category are equally members by virtue of sharing some set of necessary features.

Now, while many categories are associated with prototype effects, prototype theorists do not hold that all categories enjoy the same structure. There are significant differences in the organizational principles hypothesized for different categories, and prototype effects must be accounted for in different ways, depending on the organizational structures of their respective categories.

I advocate that "religion" be conceptualized as a "graded" category, on the model of "tall person" or "rich person." Some tall persons are taller than others and some rich persons are richer than others. And while various individuals or public agencies may suggest guidelines, there are, insofar as I know, no sure, sharp,

and universally accepted criteria for marking off the tall from the
not tall, or the rich from the not rich.

As the scholarly literature on religion indicates, there are no
sure, sharp, and universally accepted criteria for marking off religion from not-religion. (Some scholars, indeed, have proposed
such labels as "quasi-religions" or "semi-religions" to indicate that
various complexes of phenomena resemble religions in some
ways, but not sufficiently in other respects to justify the unquali-
fied label "religion.") Further, some religions exhibit more of the
typicality features that we associate with our general model of religion than do others, and perhaps greater elaboration of these features than is the case elsewhere. Some religions, in a manner of
speaking, are "more religious" than others.

Religion, then, in my approach, is a graded category the instantiations of which are linked by family resemblances.

I further advocate that we acknowledge explicitly that for most
Western scholars the clearest examples of the category religion,
the most prototypical exemplars of it, are those families of religions that we call "Judaism," "Christianity," and "Islam." Those
families exhibit the greatest clusterings of typicality features that
we associate with religion. And, of course, those are the religions
that most of us, as children, first identified with the term religion.

Fairly early in life we learned to set religion off from other
things, though imperfectly. We learned, moreover, that just as
religion may help unite persons who participate in the same con-
fession, it can also divide them off from others.

As scholars, we seek to refine and deepen such understandings
in systematic ways. We use our understandings, indeed, to search
the world for other religions. We identify various verbal assertions
and other behaviors in non-Western societies as "religious" by
analogy to what we find in the West.

Now, while our most prototypical religions are important cognitive reference points, useful for purposes of orientation, illustra-
tion, and comparison, they do not immediately supply or fully
disclose our general scholarly model of religion. That model is
developed out of all that we have learned about religions, Western
and non-Western.

Our general model is, of course, biased by our experiences in
our own society. By recognizing such bias, however, we are in a
better position to correct for it in our own attending to the world.
We have some clear cases of what we mean by religion, and then
candidates that are increasingly less clear and more problematic.
But contrary to the charge that a family resemblance approach is

promiscuously inclusive, we find that as our typicality features diminish, there are fewer reasons to term peripheral candidates "religions." Our category, to repeat what was said earlier, rests on central tendencies, and centrality implies distance and periphery.

Peripheral cases are themselves extremely interesting. To the extent that they manifest elements or features that we associate with religion in our clearest or most central cases, they provide us with opportunities to study such elements or features as they may occur outside of the purview of what we unhesitatingly label religion. This, indeed, suggests that to some extent we can transcend "religion" while attending to a religious dimension in human life.

AN OMISSION

In the final pages of this book, I recommend that anthropologists selectively borrow non-Western categories and experiment with them "for probing and describing the cultures of people who do not employ them, just as we now use religion as a category for probing and describing the cultures of people who have no word and category for religion." In a review published in 1994 (p.179), the anthropologist Brian Morris registers surprise that in entering my suggestion I fail to note that anthropologists have long engaged in inter-cultural borrowing by using terms such as "mana," "taboo," and "totem." Morris is justified in expressing surprise. In conceding that, I take the opportunity to clarify my position.

Mana, taboo, and totem are examples of what I would hope to avoid if my proposals were enacted fully. Those terms were inadequately explored in their original cultural settings, and they have been applied dubiously elsewhere. Franz Steiner (1999) gives us reasons to conclude that Victorian anthropologists, and numbers of their successors, oversimplified what may be involved in "taboo." Roger Keesing (1984) indicates that established anthropological notions of "mana," going back to the writings of R.H. Codrington (1891), are confused and not to the point in certain ethnographic applications. And the term "totem," borrowed from the Ojibwa and imposed on various other populations, is hardly a unitary phenomenon, and totem as an "ism," Claude Lévi-Strauss (1962) argues, is an illusion fashioned by anthropologists.

Non-Western folk categories that might be borrowed as tools for cross-cultural analysis should be studied as thoroughly as possible in their own cultural settings. One ought to explore in detail, for instance, the uses to which the category terms are put among the populations that employ them. We might very well find that those

terms are polysemous, that the categories to which they pertain
are organized by family resemblances, an d that members of local
populations judge some instantiations of those categories to be
clearer exemplars than others. Indeed, the prescriptions given in
this book for conceptualizing religion might well apply to many
other folk categories, among both Western and non-Western populations. While the pages that follow have much to say about "religion," I use religion as a case study for exploring how we might
best conceptualize analytical categories in our efforts to study the
human condition.

Benson Saler, 1999

REFERENCES CITED

Bloch, Maurice. 1992. *Prey Into Hunter: The Politics of Religious Experience.*
    Cambridge: Cambridge University Press.
Codrington, Robert H. 1891. *The Melanesians: Studies in Their Anthropology and
    Folklore.* Oxford: The Clarendon Press.
Keesing, Roger M. 1984. Rethinking *Mana. Journal of Anthropological Research*
    5:137-56.
Lévi-Strauss, Claude. 1962. *Le totémisme aujourd'hui.* Paris: Presses Universitaires
    de France.
Morris, Brian. 1994. Review of Benson Saler, *Conceptualizing Religion. Method and
    Theory in the Study of Religion* 6(2):177-79.
Saler, Benson. 1997. Conceptualizing Religion: The Matter of Boundaries. In
    Vergleichen und Verstehen in der Religionswissenchaft, ed. Hans-Joachim Klim-
    keit, 27-35. Wiesbaden:Harrassowitz Verlag.
Steiner, Franz Baermann. 1999. *Selected Writings, Volume 1: Taboo, Truth, and Religion.*
    Edited by Jeremy Adler and Richard Fardon. New York: Berghahn Books.

ACKNOWLEDGEMENTS

Various persons have read and commented on early drafts of certain sections of this work. I am most grateful to them for doing so even though I have not always followed their advice.

Early drafts of the Introduction were read by George N. Appell and Abraham Rosman. Richard J. Parmentier read the section on structuralism.

The section on Paul Tillich in an early draft of Chapter Three was read by William A. Johnson.

Early drafts of Chapter Five were read by David F. Aberle, George L. Cowgill, Gerald D. Fasman, Sally A. McBrearty, and Rodney Needham.

Early drafts of Chapter Six were read by Stanley N. Kurtz, David W. Murray, and Melford E. Spiro. An early version of that chapter was presented as a lecture to the Department of Anthropology at Brandeis University, and another version was read and commented on by members of the Brandeis Center for the Humanities Seminar.

I very much appreciate the encouragement of E. Thomas Lawson. And I am very grateful to Elisabeth Erdman-Visser of E. J. Brill for her consistent interest in the progress of my writing and her gentle, tactful prodding to complete the work.

An enlarged version of my paper, "*Religio* and the Definition of Religion," *Cultural Anthropology* 2(3):395–399 (1987), is incorporated into Chapter One with the permission of the American Anthropological Association.

"Relativism certainly is self-refuting, but
there is a difference between saying that every
community is as good as every other and saying
that we have to work out from the networks we
are, from the communities with which we presently
identify. Postmodernism is no more relativistic
than Hilary Putnam's suggestion that we stop
trying for a 'God's-eye view' and realize that
'We can only hope to produce a more rational
conception of rationality or a better conception
of morality if we operate from within our tradition.'"

Richard Rorty, "Postmodernist Bourgeois
Liberalism," In *Objectivity,
Relativism and Truth*, 1991
[1983], p. 202.

INTRODUCTION

*What the fieldworker invents . . . is his own understanding; the analogies
he creates are extensions of his own notions and those of his culture,
transformed by his experiences of the field situation.*
Roy Wagner, *The Invention of Culture*, 1981, p. 12.

The general question that this work addresses is: How might we
transform a folk category into an analytical category that will
facilitate transcultural research and understanding?

The particular category discussed in what follows is "religion."
The general argument, though, is probably applicable to such
other categories as "kinship," "marriage," "law," "the state," and
so forth, categories the suitability of which has been called into
question with respect to the analysis and description of non-
Western social and cultural phenomena (e.g., Needham 1971,
Schneider 1984). I do not attempt, however, to extend my
argument explicitly to those categories in the ensuing pages.

In posing the question above, I assume the great importance
of categories in human cognizing. I also recognize the widespread
use of the category term religion in the conversations of both
the contemporary social sciences and humanities and the larger
populations that support them. Although various scholars have
questioned the analytical powers of the category religion, and
some have proposed that the term religion be dropped from
research vocabularies or that employment of it be limited, many
academics and the public-at-large continue to talk about religion
freely. It seems that we are more or less stuck with religion, both
as term and as category, at least for the foreseeable future. That
confers practicality on a critical discussion of how religion has
been conceptualized — and of how it might be conceptualized
for certain purposes.

THE "WE" AT INTEREST

A problem that must immediately be faced — one that I return
to in various chapters — is this: Who are the "we" in this work
who are interested in transforming folk categories into utile analytical ones? "We," most particularly, are cultural anthropologists.
But the "we" can be extended, I think, to sizeable numbers of
persons who take an interest in cultural anthropology, especially
with respect to how cultural anthropologists go about conceptualizing and studying religion in a wide diversity of societies.

The various chapters of this work will describe how certain

anthropologists (and some others) have variously conceptualized religion. Here, however, I want to generalize about orientations that numbers of cultural anthropologists more or less share, and certain considerations relevant to those orientations. Since contrast can heighten understanding, I begin by briefly contrasting anthropologists to fellow academics in departments of religious studies in Canadian and U.S. universities. The contrast, though not applicable in all respects to all anthropologists and to all members of departments of religious studies, is nevertheless fairly well marked.

Members of departments of religious studies often describe themselves as historians of religion or students of comparative religion. In recent years some of them have carried on a lively debate among themselves as to whether or not religion should be said to be an "autonomous" or "*sui generis*" phenomenon (e.g., Dawson 1987, 1988, 1990; Pals 1986, 1987, 1990a, 1990b; Penner 1989; Segal 1983; Segal and Wiebe 1989; Wiebe 1981, 1983, 1984, 1988, 1990).

According to various disputants, the central argument over "autonomy" has to do with whether religion should be subjected to the perspectives and methods of the social sciences, with the likely consequence that it would be theorized about in so-called "reductive" socio-cultural and psychological terms, or whether religion should be "interpreted" rather than "explained," or perhaps "explained" in distinctly "religious" terms. Those who champion the latter course tend to claim that religion pivots on something irreducibly "religious," such as a consciousness of "the transcendent" or "the sacred" (e.g., Eliade 1958:xi).

The idea of autonomy, Wiebe (1988, 1990) argues, relates to the original establishment and subsequent histories of departments of religious studies. The faculties of those departments, he maintains, partially justified membership in secular universities by undertaking in their professional work to bracket judgments about the truth of religious claims, devoting themselves solely to the scholarly or "scientific" study of religion. But in maintaining the integrity of their subject matter, many of them resisted theorizing that might seem to explain religion away by rendering it epiphenomenal to psychodynamic forces, economic determinants, political power plays, or other factors exogenous to religion as fairly narrowly conceived.

Efforts to assert and maintain the autonomy of religion, Wiebe suggests, are distinctly agreeable to those members of departments of religious studies who are personally committed to some religion. This is particularly so if they deem their religion to be ultimately founded on some "transcendent" or "supernatural" truth. According to Pals (1990a:6), "a strong majority" of persons who undertake studies of religion "under the banner of the American Academy [of Religion] and its affiliates," the scholarly organizations to which many members of departments of religious studies belong, are themselves either religiously committed (mainly to Christianity) or they have had significant educational and other experiences in contexts marked by such commitment. And some of these students of religion, Wiebe (1990:28) charges, insinuate theology into religious studies, thus conferring a certain academic legitimation on "a variety of crypto-theologies."

How do cultural anthropologists contrast with many of their fellow academics in departments of religious studies?

First, anthropologists generally seem uninterested in raising (or attending to) arguments claiming autonomy for religion. Many treat religion as a sort of department of culture. Or, to invoke a phrasing popularized by Clifford Geertz (1966), they discuss it as a "cultural system." As such, they regard it as pertaining to a larger fabric of meanings. While holding that religion may vitalize, support, or constrain much else, many anthropologists also conceive it to be nourished, motivated, and patterned in part by the weaving of more inclusive designs.

It is the case, of course, that some anthropologists strongly resist reductive arguments advanced by sociobiologists or other utilitarians, arguments subversive of perspectives that accord a certain autonomy to *culture* (see, for example, Sahlins 1976a and 1976b). Numbers of other anthropologists, however, are attracted to utilitarian theorizing. Few in either case, however, would contend that religion is "*sui generis*" and ought not to be understood and perhaps accounted for by relating it to events and eventualities that are not themselves conventionally described as religious. For many anthropologists, religion has an imputed categorical distinctiveness but not an autonomous or *sui generis* existence.

Second, I suspect that it would be erroneous to say that "a strong majority" of those who study religion and belong to the American Anthropological Association (which is quite distinct from the American Academy of Religion and its affiliates) are personally religious in any conventional Euro-American theistic or "supernaturalistic" sense. Such, at any rate, is my impression, an impression gained from years of talking to fellow anthropologists in various contexts and reading their works. Some anthropologists, indeed, are personally hostile to what they conceive to be religion, or, at least, selectively disapproving of what they take to be examples of religiosity.

But perhaps a substantial number of anthropologists who study religion — I know of no reliable studies of this and I am extrapolating from my own introspections — do so because, among other things, they are fascinated by it in two rather special, related senses. Having no consciousness of any strong conventional religious commitment on their own part, they are intrigued by persons who appear to make such commitments. Why, they may sometimes in effect ask, do so many people invest themselves in religion? And, though they do not usually phrase it as an explicit question reflexive to themselves, some anthropologists may also occasionally wonder if they are missing something of value because of their irreligiosity, something that they might perhaps come to understand vicariously through scholarship.

INTERPRETATION AND EXPLANATION

The above discussion indirectly conduces to a debate within anthropology respecting "interpretation" (viewed as an emphasis on meaning) and "explanation" (viewed as an emphasis on causality). This debate relates to, among other things, how and why one studies religion. A similar debate occurs among members of departments of religious studies. Ultimately, however, the opposition between explanation and interpretation (which derives to some extent from Dilthey's distinction between explanation and understanding) deserves to be dismissed as specious, for explanation is nothing if not an exercise in interpretation.

In any case, some anthropologists maintain that cultural anthropology is one of the humanities and not a science. In their view, anthropology's major concern should be the attempt to understand, insofar as possible, "the native's point of view." Cultural anthropology, in this perspective, is a hermeneutical or interpretive discipline. The hope of explaining socio-cultural phenomena, particularly if that means accounting for those phenomena in deductive-nomothetic fashion, is held to be chimerical. Those who subscribe to this point of view are critical of efforts to "discover" or adduce cultural universals and to incorporate them into "totalizing" explanatory theories.

Other cultural anthropologists claim, in one fashion or another, that anthropology can be a science: that it can and should frame testable hypotheses, establish universals, and formulate powerful (and, in principle, refutable) explanatory theories. Some persons of this persuasion all-too-easily dismiss the work of interpretivists as anarchic subjectivism. Others, however, recognize the importance and inevitability of interpretation, and some of them call for an anthropology where hermeneutical and explanatory efforts will complement each other — or where, even better, we will not encumber it with that particular dualism.

Still other cultural anthropologists, chary of realist epistemology, skeptical about the possibilities of realist-representational ethnography, and dissatisfied in one way or another with early forms of interpretivism (such as, for example, that of Geertz 1973), espouse perspectives that can be very broadly — and very tentatively — called "postmodernist." Clifford (1988:425) refers to "the many contesting definitions of postmodernism." Postmodernism, to be sure, is difficult to characterize, albeit somewhat easier to caricature.

Hassan (1985:123–124, reproduced in Harvey 1989:43) provides us with a number of stylistic oppositions between modernism and postmodernism, the latter being viewed as an alternative to, and something of a rejection of, the former. Harvey (1989:42) deems those stylistic oppositions "a useful starting point" for an exploration of postmodernism. He acknowledges, however, and credits Hassan with acknowledging, the dubiousness of listing simple polarizations to convey complex relationships. In Hassan's schema, modernism tends to emphasize (among other things) "semantics," "genre/boundary," "paradigm," "interpretation/ reading," "signified," "determinacy," and "transcendence." Postmodernism, in contrast, tends to emphasize (among other things) "rhetoric," "text/intertext," "syntagm," "against interpretation/ misreading," "signifier," "indeterminacy," and "immanence" (Harvey 1989:43).

This book has been influenced to an extent by both interpretivist and postmodernist points of view, the former emphasizing contextuality in constructing interpretations, the latter noting ironically that interpretations are contingent, that they might be otherwise. (I retain a certain sympathy for postmodernism's anti-transcendental, anti-authoritarian stance despite occasional encounters with transcendentally-committed authoritarians who call themselves postmodernists.) Yet while sympathetic to some of the positions taken by interpretivists and postmodernists, I am not on that account opposed in principle to "explanation." Indeed, I welcome two recent and very different books — Preus 1987 and Lawson and McCauley 1990 — that make impressive cases for the importance of explanatory theory in the study of religion.

In developing its point of view, a point of view that draws from a diversity of sources, this book also borrows and adapts ideas advanced by certain theologians to the effect that, for any human subject, any human alter is a "transcendent" (Kaufman 1965, 1972) or "relatively occult" (McLain 1969) being. (This work also describes anthropologists as professionally "immanent," in a dictionary sense of immanent: "remaining or operating within a domain of reality or realm of discourse.")

Human alters are "transcendent" for each of us, Kaufman maintains in some early essays, because we have no knowledge of their thoughts, attitudes, or feelings except as they "reveal" them to us. That is an interesting idea, although, as McLain points out, it is overdrawn, for there are "public," observable aspects to persons that are crucial to our understandings of their personhood. Others, McLain suggests, are "relatively occult" rather than fully so. But when, I hasten to add, others do give us some indications of their thoughts, feelings, and attitudes, perhaps including those that we somehow provoke them into revealing, they do not unambiguously and fully "unveil" themselves. We are obliged to interpret their self-disclosures in order to render them meaningful for ourselves. In interpreting, however, we cannot hope to fill in all of the experiential associations, the rich and shifting experiential contexts, from which alter derives meanings. To some extent alter's thoughts, feelings, and attitudes remain elusive — which is to say "transcendent."

We may suppose, moreover, that interpretation would be erratic, shallow, and unsatisfying in the absence of tacit explanatory theories about human behavior. Interpretation, in any case, does not occur in a void. Rather, it relates to and is supported by (and may reflexively alter) numerous unvoiced assumptions. Such assumptions sum in effect to existential and causal theories about human beings and their proclivities to operate in various ways in various worlds. Interpretation, moreover, makes use of (and may refine or extend) established categories. Those categories, heuristics in research and springboards for analogies, themselves relate to, and express, theoretical structures.

Take, for example, the study of theism (which brings the discussion back to a matter raised in the preceding section of this Introduction). Many persons, or so ethnographies affirm, not only *believe that* Gods or "superhuman" personages exist, but they *believe in* those beings — that is, they are committed to them in one way or another. For the reflective cultural anthropologist who does not believe that any Gods or "superhuman" beings exist except in the imaginations and conventions of human beings, that could be a staggering affirmation. It is usually not that, however.

How does a disbeliever accommodate to the apparent fact that many (perhaps most) human beings not only believe that Gods or superhuman beings exist but that those beings affect human life in significant ways, ways relating to human aspirations, expectations, and behavior? S/he accommodates by means of theory, tacit or explicit, of why people might believe in Gods or superhuman beings. Theory, that is, *about human beings* that renders belief in Gods or superhumans broadly plausible whenever it is encountered (but that, given the disbeliever's disbelief, ought not to entail that theistic belief will be found among all persons without exception). A powerful theory, I might add, should go beyond trivial statements to the effect that people learn about Gods or superhuman beings as they grow up and often accept what they learn. The persistence of theistic commitments requires better attempts at explanation than that (see the Preface to Spiro 1978 for a cogent theory that builds on pre-linguistic, pre-cultural experiences). In short, the anthropologist's interpretive efforts are supported and colored by tacit theories about human beings and how they operate in their worlds. While neither interpretivists nor postmodernists will convert those theories into formal hypothetico-deductive statements in the service of nomothetic goals, such theories function to underwrite the plausibility of many interpretations.

THE CATEGORY RELIGION

In dealing with the category religion, anthropologists tacitly assume things about religion that suggest particular explanatory theories. By so doing, they rule out other, rival explanatory theories, theories that might affect ethnographic interpretations in imaginable ways. Few anthropologists, for example, appear to subscribe to the theory that humanity has religion because it was originally given or established by God. Rather, most account religion to be a variable cultural creation. So conceiving of it, of course, relates to a host of assumptions about human life and history as viewed from a number of perspectives.

Now, in recognizing the general proclivity of anthropologists to conceive of religion as a variable cultural creation, it must also be noted that many anthropologists have studied religion in non-Western settings (although there were always some who studied it in Euro-American contexts as well). Yet the category "religion," a category commonly used by anthropologists in transcultural research in non-Western societies as well as in research conducted in the West, is itself a relatively recent (Enlightenment and post-Enlightenment) Euro-American creation (Cohen 1964, 1967; Despland 1979; Preus 1987; W.C. Smith 1963 [1962]; Wax 1984). So, too, is the category "culture" and the category and discipline "anthropology."

In short, the practitioners of a mostly Western profession (anthropology) employ a Western category (religion), conceptualized as a component of a larger Western category (culture), to achieve their professional goal of coming to understand what is meaningful and important for non-Western peoples. This privileging of Western categories, it might seem, constitutes or betokens ethnocentrism, a matter that I discuss at some length in Chapter 7 but begin to consider here.

ETHNOCENTRISM

In 1977 anthropologists from a diversity of countries established The Association of Third World Anthropologists. The declared goal of that organization is to make "anthropology less prejudiced against Third World peoples by making it less ethnocentric in its use of language and paradigms" (quoted in Kim 1990:196). I, and most other anthropologists, certainly endorse the idea of reducing whatever prejudice there may be against Third World (and other) peoples. That point remains a potent moral commitment, and I need say no more about it here. But the matter of ethnocentrism requires comment.

Ethnocentrism continues to be a bugbear for many anthropologists, and for some it represents the very heart of darkness. One could, I suppose, argue that there is a certain irony in that. Ethnocentrism is deemed a matter of destructive consequence, and is warned against in distinctive ways, in the culture or subculture to which contemporary anthropology pertains. Indeed, that culture is perhaps unique among the world's cultures with respect to its sensitivity to ethnocentrism and the weight it assigns to vigilance against falling into "ethnocentric traps." In consequence, it could be claimed, an anthropologist's strong concern with ethnocentrism is itself ethnocentric.

In any case, by ethnocentrism I mean understanding, and perhaps judging, the professed convictions and other behaviors and cultural products of persons in other societies in terms of the categories and standards of one's own. Doing so can of course lead to consequences that anthropologists generally deplore, clearly with specific respect to misunderstanding and misjudging.

But rather than intone a blanket condemnation of ethnocentrism and all its works, we might better seek to tame it. For some amount of ethnocentrism is probably unavoidable as a cognitive starting point in the search for transcultural understandings. In English — to indulge in a bit of ethnocentrism — we commonly say that we wish "to arrive at" understanding and knowledge, a phrasing that implies a journey. And journey, as I ethnocentrically understand it, involves a starting point. Ethnocentrism is not necessarily a fatal contaminant when we constitute a starting point, for it enables us initially to identify problems that we deem interesting, and it furnishes us start-up categories with which to embark on a journey toward greater understandings.

Ethnocentrism, however, betokens insensitivity, derivativeness, and lack of creativity if we fail eventually to transcend it to some productive extent on our transcultural journeys. Misunderstandings of what is significant and important to other people, and the reification of one's own categories and constructs, are the likely consequences of failing to confront ethnocentrism and lighten its load.

Our conceptualization of the problem of ethnocentrism, moreover, might be broadened. The declaration of The Association of Third World Anthropologists, it may be remembered, calls for rendering anthropology "less ethnocentric in its use of language and paradigms." This could be rephrased as rendering anthropology less parochial and rigid, and more pluralistic and supple, in its uses of language and paradigms. Both Third World anthropologists and anthropologists from other Worlds can contribute to the advancement of that goal.

Up until now, however, the contributions of non-Western anthropologists, though valuable in terms of conventional research, have been relatively modest with respect to enriching and rendering more flexible the languages and concepts used by the world community of anthropologists. But as anthropology grows both as an academic discipline and as an applied profession, and as non-Western anthropologists draw increasingly on their own rich cultural heritages (see Chapter 7), the florescence of a more pluralistic, a more intellectually exciting, anthropology is likely to occur. In the meantime, however, anthropology remains saliently Western, both demographically and culturally. Most of the world's professional anthropologists are of Euro-American backgrounds. And most professional anthropologists of non-Western backgrounds now largely conceive of problems, and employ Western-derived analytical categories, in much the same ways that native Euro-American anthropologists do.

Contemporary academic anthropology has been, and for the time being largely remains, a Western invention. As such, it has been, and continues to be, influenced in complex and sometimes subtle ways by various Euro-American intellectual and, broadly put, social developments. Like the Western societies that nurture it, anthropology is heterogeneous and dynamic. And in various ways it has shared certain of the perspectives and concerns localized in those societies as they developed at different times in association with class, ethnic, or other particularized interests. Critics within the profession, indeed, charge that some anthropologists, and the anthropologies that they constructed, have sometimes served colonialism, capitalism, or other special interests of segments of the larger societies that funded or otherwise supported anthropology.

It is almost trite to say that Western societies have given rise to diverse ideas and theories, synchronically as well as diachronically, and that they are heterogeneous in other ways. But until quite recently, and despite their heterogeneity, many of their citizens have been strongly marked — as have the various anthropologies that some of them supported — by a decided fondness for essentialism. To a great extent, indeed, essentialism probably remains an unexamined commitment for large numbers of persons in contemporary Euro-American societies. And despite the inroads of postmodernist skepticism, irony, and criticism, it may still command allegiance from numbers of anthropologists — especially in the conceptualization of categories such as "religion.".

ESSENTIALISM AND NOMINALISM

Essentialism pivots on the notion of "essence." As the idea developed in Western metaphysics, the essence of something is conceived to be the unchanging and necessary qualities or properties of that object: that by which it is what it is, including inherent developmental potentialities that can be realized or actualized in a world of change. Conceived as such, essence is distinguished from "existence" (having being, being real) and from "accident" (contingent features that may be associated at times with the object but are not necessary to its existential identity).

In the development of standard (two-valued) Western logic, essence has traditionally been conceived to refer to some set of properties that a candidate for class (or species) inclusion must have if it is to be accurately ascribed to that class (or species). (In the Aristotelian tradition, a genus is a class divisible into smaller classes called species. This tradition is expressed in part by the conceptualization of "natural classes" in logic and "natural kinds" in biology — see Chapter 5 — and by the method of "genus and difference" for constructing definitions).

The philosopher Karl Popper uses the term essentialism to refer to a generalized anti-nominalist theory, regardless of whether that theory be constituted in "realist" or "idealist" forms (1957: 26–27). Classical essentialists maintain that we can properly use the same name or expression (e.g., "human being," "religion," "blue," "larger than") for different things (e.g., particular human beings, particular religions, particular blue things, particular cases of being larger than something else) because those general terms correspond to objects, properties, or relations whose existence and persistence transcends their particular instantiations. That is, there is some "form" or "universal" for humankind, religion, blueness, or being larger than that exists somewhere (e.g., in a realm of eternal forms, in God's mind, in nature, and/or innately in the human mind).

Nominalists, in contrast, claim that such putative forms or universals do not have a mind-independent or "objective" reality, nor do they have an innate, universal existence in our minds. Rather, the nominalist maintains, only particular, individual objects, features, and relations exist. So-called "universals" are names or expressions that people assign on the basis of conventional groupings and discriminations. Such assignments are human contrivances for customarily ordering the world. In an extended nominalist view, people not only order the world by local human conventions rather than in accordance with divine or natural design, but "The worlds in which different societies live are distinct worlds, not merely the same world with different labels attached" (Sapir 1949 [1929]:162).

Essentialism, in my view, is itself one kind of realization of something more fundamental: a culture-stimulated proclivity to digitize, a proclivity that supports conceptual and social dualisms as well as essentialism. Dualisms or binary schemas are apparently motivated by numbers of cultures (Maybury-Lewis and Almagor

1989), including those of the classical Greeks (Lloyd 1966) and those of the contemporary West. It is probably the case, however, that all cultures support digital, analog, and analogical approaches to ordering and analyzing the world, but some may emphasize one in certain conceptualized domains over the others. Appell (1983), in comparing different ethnic groups in a region of Borneo, found that certain populations appeared to stress either digital or non-digital means for managing and storing particular sorts of information. In the West, certainly, digital and non-digital modalities are used (as my discussion of anthropological and folk conceptualizations of religion will demonstrate later in this Introduction). Yet digitizing, although by no means relied upon exclusively in Euro-American logic, metaphysics, and epistemology, has clearly been popular among Euro-American logicians, metaphysicians, and epistemologists.

DIGITIZING

Digitizing, an engineer might say, is an activity that has to do with coding information in numerical digit form (the relay switch, with its binary on/off positions, provides a simple model for how that might be done). As popularly understood by numbers of computer users, purchasers of compact discs, and so on, to digitize is to express the presence or absence of features in a code of ones and zeros.

In this work I use the terms "digitize" and "digital" in extended and much broader ways, particularly with respect to categories and categorizing. In doing so I follow the lead of Eleanor Rosch (1975:179), who writes that "The overwhelming preponderance of American studies [of category use and learning and cross-cultural comparisons of categories], in attempting to treat categories scientifically, have defined and treated them as though they were 'digital,' that is, as though they were composed of discrete 'units' which are 'either-or' in nature" (see also Rosch and Mervis 1975:573).

The long-standing popularity in the West of "digitizing" in my extended sense of the term is attested to by essentialism's "categorical" ("yes" or "no") analyses and orderings of the world (i.e., analyses and orderings whereby something is conceived to be either a member or not a member of a denominated class or group). The analytical disposition to conceptualize reality digitally, moreover, has undoubtedly supported something rather more complex and subtle: various cultural propensities to cast thematic relevancies in dualistic form. While digitizing in human cognizing is clearly expressed in essentialist analytical procedures, dualism is more a matter of conceptual content. Some dualisms are preponderantly antagonistic (e.g., good and evil in Manichaean conventions). Others are notably complementary, perhaps constitutive of a whole (e.g., yin and yang in some varieties of Chinese thought). And some, or so structuralist analyses suggest, appear to be transcended in the creation of superordinate structures in narratives of various sorts.

The proclivity to digitize long nurtured in Euro-American societies is more than cognitively instrumental, a means for conceptually creating and maintaining a tidy (and thus perhaps more manageable) world by imposing sharply bounded distinctions. It is also loaded with strong moral overtones. Those are based in part on commitments to the effect that order is morally positive in contrast to disorder and that order is "natural" (or, according to some, God-given). This perspective by no means rules out the conceiving of analog scales (representations of information in continuously variable fashion). It often allows the conceptualization of, and the attachment of importance to, intermediary states or values between contrastive poles. And it does sometimes endorse "golden means." Yet it also tends to foster the evaluation of some intermediary states as wishy-washy or otherwise less than praise-worthy:

> I know thy works, that thou art neither cold nor hot: I would thou wert cold or hot. So then because thou art lukewarm, and neither cold nor hot, I will spue thee out of my mouth. — Revelation 3:15–16.

STRUCTURALISM

Digitizing in anthropology, some may suppose, is most clearly and powerfully expressed in structuralism, which assigns great importance to "binary oppositions." More than two decades ago, indeed, one heard this effort at drollery from various North American anthropologists: Claude Lévi-Strauss, anthropology's structuralist Grand Master, was so impressed by a digital computer that he supposed that the human mind operates in much the same way, and he built a major anthropological enterprise on that supposition. Just imagine, the wags who related this buffoonery added, what Lévi-Strauss might have accomplished had someone shown him an analog computer!

Putting aside the silly business about computers, this attempt

to encapsulate a profundity in a joke may well have suggested
to some auditors that Lévi-Strauss's structuralism is based entirely
on digital processes. But if that is what it suggested, then its
humor is vitiated by its inaccuracy. Lévi-Strauss is not anthropology's Prince of Digitizers. Let us look at certain important
facets of his theorizing.

Lévi-Strauss apparently committed himself early in his career
to various themes that now underwrite the structuralist perspective. In *Tristes Tropiques*, for example, he tells us that when he
read philosophy at the Sorbonne and later, he found phenomenology "unacceptable, in so far as it postulated a continuity
between experience and reality." And he resisted "the trend of
thought which was to find fulfilment in existentialism" because
it seemed to him "the exact opposite of true thought, by reason
of its indulgent attitude towards the illusions of subjectivity" (1961
[1955]:61–62). There exists "beyond the rational," he affirms, "a
category at once more important and more valid: that of the
meaningful," and in retrospect he criticizes his teachers who "never
so much as mentioned its name" (1961:59).

For the mature Lévi-Strauss, meaning is to be found in structure, in relations among elements in cultural systems, as, for
example, in myths. (Structuralist analyses of myths arguably afford
the most rounded examples of the structuralist perspective in
action.) It is the relations obtaining among elements that render
those elements meaningful. And these structures reveal the
workings of mind in culture. In the case of myths, for example,
we are confronted by narratives that, from the structuralist's perspective, have more to say about the nature of thought than
about the nature of the world. A primary task of the structuralist is to foreground cultural categories for thinking and show how
they both organize, and are organized in, systems of thought.
The structuralist program is thus of considerable interest to
students of religion and, more inclusively, to students of categorization and classification.

Basic to the structuralist's search for intelligibility in cultural
systems is the identification and analysis of pairs of "opposites"
(e.g., up/down, forward/backward, north/south, us/them,
marriageable/not marriageable, life/death). Then, the particular values of various pairs are related to the specific values of
other pairs. In certain sections of a myth or corpus of myth
variants, for example, up might be associated with north, while
down might be associated with south. These and more inclusive
structures are likely to be transformed into different structures,

in consonance with a variety of factors or circumstances. Meaning is found at the level of so-called "binary oppositions" ("thick" has meaning when contrasted with "thin"), at the level of discovered arrangements and rearrangements in the associations of the values of different "binary opposites," at the level of more inclusive structures and their transformations, and in the attempted transcendence of paradox or contradiction (various religious structures, for example, may work toward some resolution of the implicit 'contradiction' between life and death).

Of great importance to working out meanings, and of crucial significance for describing how the mind works, are so-called "homological relations" (see Chapter 5 for a discussion of disagreements respecting uses of the term "homology" in the biological sciences). These relations are found in structures more inclusive than that of a single pair of binary opposites. They take the form a:b::c:d, which is read "a is to b what c is to d" (Lévi-Strauss 1969 [1964]). In Aristotelianism, that is a classic statement of analogy: the relation between a and b is analogous to the relation between c and d. That formulation of 'analogy' (from the Greek ana, 'according to', + logos, 'proportion'), proposes a meaningful relation among four elements. Such a semantic relation of resemblances, as employed by Lévi-Strauss and other structuralists, pertains to a different conceptual domain than does "digital" in the sense of referring to the presence or absence of a feature.

While Lévi-Strauss attaches great importance to binary phenomena, thus affirming the significance of "digitizing" in the workings of mind and the constitution of cultural systems, he also suggests that human thought, as we can study it in the classificatory edifices it has created, is to a considerable extent analogical.

The above described attributions of importance to both digital and analogical processes imply and express a larger theoretical framework. Structuralism, which some of its practitioners conceive of as a scientific undertaking, a "science of relations" revelatory of the orderly nature of culture and the rationality of the human mind, is far more than a method. It is a wide-ranging theory about "communications" of various sorts that encompasses diverse assumptions and postulates.

An important postulate in a sizeable portion of Lévi-Strauss's writings, for example, is the opposition of nature and culture. Culture, in contrast to nature, is conceived to constitute a domain distinguished by the imposition of human laws or rules (as in the incest tabu, recipes for cooking food rather than consuming it raw, and so on). This nature/culture opposition, though perhaps most strongly impressed upon Lévi-Strauss's sensibilities through his readings of ethnographic materials constructed by Arthur Maurice Hocart and other anthropologists, may nevertheless strike some of us as reminiscent of such Greek conceptual distinctions as those of *phusis* ('nature') and *technê* ('art') and *phusis* and *nomos* ('usage', 'custom', 'human law'). As employed by Lévi-Strauss, the culture/nature distinction becomes an arresting theme in works of extraordinary analytical dexterity, a postulate in glistering commentaries on human creativity in conceptualizing and classifying. As employed by legions of would-be Lévi-Strauss imitators, however, the distinction all too often appears to be a cliché that prompts tedious sortings of assertions into boxes labelled "nature" and "culture."

Certain of the larger contributions of structuralism — analytical sensitivities to structural analogues, inversions, and transformations, for example — continue to influence the work of numbers of anthropologists. Some anthropologists, moreover, convinced that "societies all over the world organize their social thought and their social institutions in patterns of opposites" (Maybury-Lewis 1989:1), continue to concern themselves with "finding" and analyzing dualisms in the organizing principles employed by different peoples (see, for example, the collection of papers edited by Maybury-Lewis and Almagor 1989). Doing so is justified in part by available ethnographies (although we ought to remember that ethnographies are strongly colored by our own cultural assumptions and culturally-induced sensitivities). It also has a certain justification conferred on it by analogical extrapolations from our own society where digitizing and dualism are accorded a multiplicity of important places. Questions remain, however, as to the place of digitizing in formulating the analytical categories of anthropologists — questions now raised to some extent even within anthropological circles concerned with "thought and society in the dualistic mode" (e.g., Seeger 1989).

Enthusiasm for structuralism within anthropology, in any case, has diminished in recent years. In part this stems from a mounting suspicion that structuralism by itself has no place to go: that unalloyed structuralism would lead to repetitive, endless — and, except for virtuoso performances, ultimately boring — analyses of myths and other cultural artifacts, without any cumulative payoff.

Diminished enthusiasm for structuralism can also be attributed in part to the attractions of other perspectives. Some of these perspectives selectively borrow from structuralism while rejecting the structuralist's disjunction between reality and experience and disdain for subjectivity (e.g., various brands of hermeneutics). Or they claim to supplant structuralism as a more powerful heir and successor (e.g., recent extensions of Saussurian, as distinguished from Peircean, semiotics).

A diminished enthusiasm for structuralism, moreover, can be attributed in part to specific criticisms of structuralism, whether they be offered in support of a rival perspective or mainly as deficiencies noted of the structuralist orientation and program. With respect to the latter, I have heard two major criticisms voiced over and over again by anthropologists. First, numbers of them complain that structuralism by itself is incapable of dealing with change in cultures. And second, that in viewing cultural products such as myths as related to, and motivated by, the contradictions or paradoxes of human social life, a focus on relations among elements without explicitly tieing them to a serious consideration of cognizing and intention-laden human subjects is bloodless and unproductive. But additionally, and perhaps most fatally of all with respect to the weaknesses of structuralism, deconstructionists have "put in question the binary oppositions through which structuralists describe and master cultural productions" (Culler 1982:220).

Facile digitizing in analytical realms is increasingly called into question by post-structuralist, postmodernist skepticism and irony. Increasingly, moreover, critics give anthropologists reasons for doubting, or at least re-examining, comfortable old paradigms (see, for example, Marcus and Fischer 1986). This work attempts in part to further such criticism by examining some major efforts on the part of anthropologists and certain others to conceptualize "religion."

RELIGION AS A PROBLEM IN ETHNOGRAPHIC FIELD WORK

The need to conceptualize religion in one way or another can become a critical problem in ethnographic field work. If an ethnographer sets out to study possible non-Western analogues of what is conventionally designated religion in Euro-American societies, s/he may run into certain hurdles. First, the ethnographer may discover that the local people have no word corresponding to our "religion." Second, they may not conceptualize religion as a department of culture. Indeed, those of their expressed convictions and other behaviors that remind the ethnographer of what is called religion back home may not be organized into a coherent bundle. Rather, they may be so diffused throughout local lifeways and conceptions that the ethnographer will find it difficult in various instances to disentangle what s/he might like to call religion from something else.

How then does the ethnographer proceed? How does s/he come to understand what is meaningful for local people? According to Wagner (1981), the fieldworker proceeds by "inventing" culture. The act of invention involves the use of meanings known to the ethnographer, his/her own and those of his/her culture, to construct

> an understandable representation of his subject matter. The result is an analogy, or a set of analogies, that "translates" one group of basic meanings into another, and can be said to participate in both meaning systems at the same time in the same way that their creator does. (Wagner 1981:9)

That which the ethnographer calls "religion" is likely to constitute part of the meanings upon which s/he builds in the effort to invent understandings — that is, to create analogies. And if one builds on some conceptualization of religion, then the structure and content of that conceptualization become important.

Ideally, one's conceptualization of religion ought to be serviceable enough to facilitate the creation of warrantable and productive analogies in field work. Or, at any rate, it ought not to be so rigid as to inhibit the invention of analogies in favor of creating equivalence through the imposition of some digitized and presumptively transcultural definition of religion.

The latter strategy, to be sure, is attractive to many who desire a neat and tidy world (for anything in the cosmos then either is or is not religion). But it is likely to erect boundaries in unproductive ways, ways that choke off valuable information. And the equivalences it produces may well be dubious. This position need not be argued solely with respect to non-Western and seemingly exotic field situations. It can sometimes be even more effectively illustrated when the anthropologist grapples with Euro-American cultural phenomena.

HEALTH FOOD AND COMMUNISM

Consider the following:

(1) Jill Dubisch, an anthropologist, argues that an analysis of

the "symbols and the underlying world view" associated with certain uses of "health foods" in the contemporary United States "reveals that, as a system of beliefs and practices, the health food movement has some of the characteristics of a religion" (1989 [1981]: 69). Drawing on Geertz's (1966) characterization of religion as a cultural system, she attempts to describe the "religious dimension" (1989:76) of the "movement" (1989:76).

First, Dubisch writes, there is "a system of symbols . . . based on certain kinds and qualities of food," foods that symbolize a world view "concerned with the right way to live one's life and the right way to construct a society." She maintains, moreover, that followers of the movement distinguish between pure and impure food, and that "Concepts of mana and taboo" guide their choice of foods. Further, they patronize "temples" in the form of health food stores and certain other establishments; they are guided by "rabbis" or experts; they utilize "sacred and instructional writings;" they imagine a "golden age" when people ate "natural foods" and were not afflicted by the evils of "junk foods;" and individuals entering the movement "may undergo a process of conversion" (1989:76). Though the world view of the health food movement does not center around beliefs in "supernatural beings," Dubisch states, it nevertheless does posit "a higher authority — the wisdom of nature — as the source of ultimate legitimacy for its views" (1989:77).

(2) Ward H. Goodenough, another anthropologist, remarks that "In my work as an anthropologist I have found little use for the Western notion of religion." He then goes on to say that "with Marx as its prophet, socialism provided a creed for the emergence of communism as one of the great religions of modern times" (1989:6).

It is important to recognize that while Goodenough clearly states that communism is a religion — a religion because it meets his stipulated definition of religion (see the section on Goodenough in Chapter 3) — Dubisch does not make quite the same claim for the health food "movement." Rather, she views it as having "some of the characteristics of a religion." By attributing to it a "religious dimension" without actually calling it a religion, she in effect is suggesting two things. First, that we can better *understand* the health food movement by recognizing that certain of its elements are similar to those that we conventionally associate with religions. Second, that by doing that, we are in a better position to *appreciate* the health food movement as something other than an insubstantial, trivial fad.

Dubisch and Goodenough confront us with two discernably

different positions on cultural phenomena in Euro-American societies. Both suggest that we can understand the phenomena
discussed — the health food movement and communism, respectively — by viewing them within a religious frame. But when
Goodenough claims that communism *is* (by his definition) a
religion, he implies that it is just as much of a religion as Roman
Catholicism or Islam. In the essentialist perspective, candidates
for admission to a group comprehended by a category either
must be admitted or rejected. If they possess the necessary and
sufficient features for admission, then they are admitted, and
each admittee is as good a member as any other. Dubisch, on
the other hand, in stating that the health food movement has
"some of the characteristics of a religion," strikes me as implying
that it is either not quite a religion or that, if a religion, it is
less of one than, say, those that incorporate beliefs about
"supernatural beings."

While Goodenough offers us a "digital" approach (in my
extended sense of digital) to categorizing, the specific content
of his definition mandating that communism be included under
the rubric religion, Dubisch in effect presents us with both an
analog and an analogical approach to understanding the health
food movement. An analog approach takes account of continuously variable possibilities. And an analogical approach expresses
or implies analogies, judgments that there are resemblances in
some respects between objects that otherwise differ. While a digital
approach to religion insists that the health food movement either
is or is not a religion, analog and analogical approaches are less
severe and more comparative: the health food movement can be
judged less a religion than certain things, and more so than
others.

The reader's experiences may induce him/her to feel that
Dubisch's approach makes sense not only with respect to thinking about the health food movement but with regard to communism as well. One might think of communism as 'religion-
like' in several respects (e.g., a foundational canon, a concern
with 'salvation', an eschatology, etc.) while yet recognizing that
many communists identify themselves as atheists who, in all probability, would reject "religion" as a label for their ideology and
political commitments. Communism may seem like a religion in
certain respects, but many readers are likely to stop short of
agreeing that it *is* a religion — or, at least, they are likely to stop
short of claiming that it is *as much* of a religion as varieties of
Christianity or Islam.

Despite whatever predilections or cravings that we might have for clear definitions and sharp boundaries, many of us, anthropologists and non-anthropologists alike, sense that the world as we experience it often falls short of the precision given by dictionaries and experts to various of the folk and professional categories through which we claim to know it. Cognitive scientists, moreover, give us reasons to doubt that our everyday conceptualizations and ways of speaking conform to essentialist theory (Lakoff 1987; see also Chapter Six).

In both the anthropological profession and in the larger societies that support it, digital, analog, and analogical conceptualizations coexist. We have seen that that is so with respect to anthropological conceptualizations of communism and the health food movement relative to a religious frame. We can see something similar when we turn to "folk" approaches to conceptualizing religion in the contemporary United States. (By "folk" approaches I mean approaches current among persons who are not professional anthropologists or other academics engaged in disciplinary analytical activities.)

RELIGION AS A FOLK CATEGORY IN THE CONTEMPORARY U.S.

A serviceable, explicit definition of religion would seem to be a practical necessity for certain public agencies in the United States. It is most obviously so in the case of the courts that are called upon to interpret and uphold constitutional restrictions on the government with respect both to establishing a religion and to prohibiting the free exercise of one. But it would also seem to be an operational desideratum for various other civil organs. Some Americans would like to think, for example, that the Internal Revenue Service routinely employs a fairly clear formulation of religion when it evaluates petitions for tax-exempt status advanced on behalf of organizations claimed to be religious associations. Public agencies are in principle formally accountable, and they may be obliged on occasion to justify certain of their decisions by citing some specific acceptation of "religion" or "religious."

Private citizens, in comparison, generally have less need for an explicit definition. If they use the word religion in ways that accord with the usages of their fellows, that is usually sufficient to establish and maintain a universe of discourse. To the extent that they may voice a definition at all, they are likely to emphasize belief — "belief in," traditionally, a "Supreme Being" or a "God" or

"Gods" — and, quite possibly, "worship" (the Latin word for which is *cultus*).

Both private citizens and public agencies in the United States have tended to make theistic "belief" central to their conceptions of religion. Doing so is in keeping with hoary Western traditions that dispose them to convert religious imaginings and sensitivities into systems of propositions. Those traditions were stimulated by a respect for Greek philosophy on the part of many Western religious thinkers, they were fired by the identification and condemnation of "heretics," they were given new impetus and wide currency by the sectarian doctrinal controversies of the Reformation and Counter-Reformation (thanks in part to roughly contemporary technological breakthroughs in printing), and they were further shaped and emphasized by the Enlightenment's optimistic celebration of human reason.

At the same time, however, there is a long-standing Western proclivity to look for the embodiment of theistic belief in rites and in moral communities, in *cultus* and in 'church'. Tieing theistic belief to *cultus* supports such dictionary definitions of religion as "Action or conduct indicating a belief in, reverence for, and desire to please, a divine ruling power; the exercise or practice of rites or observances implying this" (*Oxford English Dictionary* 1971:2481) and "The service and adoration of God or a god as expressed in forms of worship" (Webster's New Collegiate Dictionary 1961:715).

In recent years, however, there has been an increasing tendency in U.S society to render non-theistically phrased matters of conscience the public equivalents of traditional religious convictions. The accelerating acceptance of that tendency in many circles is one of a number of things that signal increased judicial recognition and public toleration of certain expressions of pluralism in social identities and moral idioms. At the same time, moreover, affirmations of theism have increasingly been reduced in several areas of the public domain: organized prayers are no longer permitted in public schools, fewer creches are erected on public lands, and so forth.

Some people, furthermore, occasionally employ "religion" as a label for complexes of affirmations and other behaviors that are not constituted or supported within a theistic frame. Certain advocates of religious instruction in public schools, for that matter, have adopted the tactic of declaring that "secular humanism" is a "religion." They argue that because "secular humanism" is "taught" in the schools, the principle of equity demands that other religions — in effect, their religion — be taught as well. Thoughtful laymen who ponder the variable and at times confusing semantic inclusiveness of the word "religion" as used among contemporary sub-populations in the United States may thus encounter problems in conceptualizing religion that are analogous to those faced by cultural anthropologists when they attempt to characterize religion cross-culturally.

In brief, public agencies, lawyers, and others may resort to essentialist definitions of religion in specific contexts, but segments of the general public and persons pursuing special agendas often extend the use and inclusiveness of the term beyond conventional dictionary acceptations and supporting conceptualizations. *But when they do so, they are usually understood by others in the contemporary United States.* Among the "folk," as among the anthropologists, there are digital and non-digital approaches to conceptualizing "religion."

AN OUTLINE OF WHAT FOLLOWS

The first five chapters of this book review different strategies and tactics proposed by anthropologists and certain others for conceptualizing religion.

Chapter 1 is largely concerned with evaluating Wilfred Cantwell Smith's advice (1963 [1962]) to drop the term religion from our investigative vocabulary. He recommends that we substitute "cumulative traditions" and "faith" for it. While I do not regard it as either necessary or practical to excise the term religion from scholarly discourse — indeed, in later publications (e.g., 1984) Smith bows to the pervasiveness of the term and uses it himself — much of what Smith says is extremely valuable and commands my respect. In discussing some of the points that he raises, I take the opportunity (thereby lengthening and complicating the chapter) to demonstrate that anthropologists have also recognized their importance and have done some interesting things in addressing them.

Chapter 2 deals with the advice of various persons to refrain from offering an explicit definition of religion, at least until substantial preliminary work is accomplished to prepare the way, as it were, for such a definition. I note that those who proffer this advice nevertheless typically operate with some conception of religion. I explore why that is so. Some readers may wonder why we need a definition at all. I supply some reasons, but observe that definitions — at least of the sort that have been conventionally offered in the past — do have their costs.

Chapters Three and Four critically discuss certain essentialist or "monothetic" definitions encountered in the literature. Essentialist definitions constitute the great majority of definitions explicitly proffered. They typically gravitate toward one of two poles, the substantive ("religion *is* such and such") or the functional ("religion is that which *does* this and that"). Both sorts (or intermediaries on a continuum between the poles) pose problems for transcultural research.

Substantive definitions may depend on categories that are not cognitively salient among various peoples (as, for instance, in definitions that are tied to the Western category "supernatural"). Or, more broadly, they require the analyst to identify and circumscribe some domain in native representations and experiences that fits, however problematically, the definition (as, for example, in definitions that rest the essence of religion on "the sacred" or on a hypothesized "feeling of utter dependence on the infinite").

Essentialist conceptions and definitions of religion that gravitate toward functional considerations may prove even more problematical in actual applications. They tend to be so elastic — universal applicability is typically purchased by decreasing the specifics of content — that it is sometimes difficult to be certain what they actually exclude. When, for example, they identify religion as, in essence, a way of coping with broadly conceived emotional or existential concerns, it is hard to limit what can then be assigned to the rubric "religion." This compromises the analytical utility of the category religion as a research tool.

Chapter Five is concerned with a more recent strategy for conceptualizing religion: multi-factorial approaches, where no one "feature" or element is deemed essential to the conception of religion. Two specific multi-factorial conceptualizations are discussed, one offered by a philosopher, the other by an anthropologist. They are inspired, respectively, by Wittgenstein's discussion of "family resemblances" and by numerical phenetics and so-called "polythetic classification" in the biological sciences. While I endorse the employment of Wittgenstein's perspectives, I furnish several reservations respecting the suitability and utility of "polythetic classification" for achieving the understandings that cultural anthropologists desire.

In Chapter 6 I present what I favor as a practical and productive solution to the problem of conceptualizing religion (and perhaps various other traditional anthropological categories). My proposed solution derives from the idea of family resemblances, particularly as it is elaborated on in prototype theory, as that has been developed by cognitive scientists of several disciplinary affiliations.

It must be emphasized, however, that while my preferred solution is influenced by prototype theory, which itself is hardly monolithic, it also deviates in certain respects from the theorizing of some leading advocates of that theory. The research basis of prototype theory is built on studies of natural language usage — how people actually use the category terms of everyday speech and the judgments they make about goodness of fit between phenomena and category, as studied mainly by some psychologists, linguists, anthropologists, and computer scientists. I am only partly concerned, however, with natural language usage. I go beyond it to *prescribe* how I think anthropologists should use religion as an *analytical* category.

My proposed solution not only drops demands for necessary conditions or "features" for recognizing instances of religion, but it dispenses in principle with any *a priori* requirement for sufficiency as well. It seeks, moreover, to profit from the biases of many anthropologists by recognizing those biases and, with critical deliberation, employing them within an analytical framework that does not entail a hard-and-fast boundary between "religion" and "non-religion." The conceptualization so produced is ineluctably comparativist, for (with apologies to some theorists!) it renders religion an affair of more or less rather than, as in the digitized constructs employed by essentialists, a cate gorical matter of "yes" or "no." Unbounded categories, I argue in Chapter Seven, can prove to be productive connectives for bridging (but not closing) the gap between "immanent anthropologists" and "transcendent natives."

Chapter Seven, the concluding chapter, defends my proposed solution from the anticipated charge that it is ethnocentric, that it privileges Western concepts. In defending my position, I consider the seeming antinomy between "alienating distanciation and participatory belonging" (Ricoeur 1981:131), and I relate that consideration to a more substantial treatment of ethnocentrism and ethnography than that offered in this Introduction.

Finally, Chapter 7 advances two suggestions for improving the anthropological enterprise — not only with respect to the study of religion, but with regard to other matters as well.

First, because Western folk categories continue to serve anthropology as sources for analytical categories, I recommend that anthropologists learn more about the cultural-historical matrices in which some of those categories were developed and applied. Doing so would expand understanding of their complexities and subtleties. Further, sophistication gained through the exercise of exploring those categories in their Euro-American settings might sharpen the anthropologist's sensitivities and sensibilities for attending to other peoples' categories.

Second, I recommend that increased efforts be made to experiment with alternative concepts and categories in order to move anthropologists toward novel and nuanced understandings. One way to do so is to draw upon non-Western as well as Western conceptualizations and perspectives. An imaginative, creative, and pluralistic anthropology could benefit from selectively experimenting with some of them.

CHAPTER ONE

ABJURING A DEFINITION AND OTHER MATTERS

Nominalists see language as just human beings using marks and noises
to get what they want.
— Richard Rorty, "Is Derrida a Transcendental Philosopher?,"
in *Essays on Heidegger and Others*, 1991, p. 127.

I. RELIGION AS A DUBIOUS ANALYTICAL CATEGORY

Some authors voice reasoned doubts about the analytical utility of "religion" as a category for transcultural research. They doubt that common acceptations of the word refer to some universal set of phenomena that may be isolated among the diverse branches of mankind. They are skeptical, moreover, of the likelihood of scoring any perduring success in attempts to frame a technical, cross-culturally applicable definition that would prove to be a significant instrument for furthering our understandings of humanity.

Needham and the Nose of the Camel

Yet while ultimately dubious of efforts to shore-up religion as an analytical category, some skeptics nevertheless accord a limited utility to the popular, Western concept. Thus, for instance, after declaring that "There are indeed many grounds on which to conclude that the notion of 'religion' is altogether too polysemous, indistinct, and malleable to serve any steady analytical purpose," Rodney Needham (1981:73) goes on to say that:

> If we cannot rely on the concept for any precise task of comparison or interpretation, it still possesses certain odd-job connotations that make it somewhat useful in the preliminary assortment of social facts and in general descriptions.

Using some concept of religion for "preliminary" purposes and "general descriptions," of course, accords a measure of intellectual value to that concept. Unless one is very careful, however, such employment may be like the proverbial admission of the nose of the camel into one's tent. In fact, where the concept is not adequately explicated, we invite in the camel at night. Although onlookers may agree about the beast's general shape or outline, they are unlikely to reach consensus respecting its particular features or how it may resemble, and differ from, other creatures. Philip Bock provides us with an example.

Bock's Beast

In order to emphasize a pedagogic point, Bock does something that was once unusual in organizing an introductory textbook in anthropology: he refrains from writing a chapter about religion. As he puts it,

> I have not treated the topic of religion in any one place in this book. Religious roles, techniques, and beliefs have been discussed, respectively, in relation to the social, technological, and ideological systems of which they are a part. This is somewhat unconventional, but it has been done to stress the point that, in most societies, religion is not a separate category of experience and action. There is, rather, a *religious dimension* to every part of social life, and the Western contrast between "natural" and "supernatural" is simply not relevant to the understanding of many societies. (1969:380)

Bock's statement that "*in most societies*, religion is not a separate category of experience and action" (italics added), accords with the views of numbers of anthropologists. His statement is ethnographically founded, and it might give pause to scholars who maintain that religion is phenomenologically "autonomous" or "*sui generis*" (as distinct from arguing that it is autonomous because it is the constituted object of study of a discipline).

Arguments about phenomenological autonomy are not clearly and directly supported by the ethnographic corpus. One can, nevertheless, draw analogies from contemporary Euro-American societies, where various factors have promoted the crystalization of "religion" as a category, to certain ethnographically described features of non-Western societies. The claim could be advanced that religion is to be found by analogy even where it is not a category meaningful to the natives. But even if one might identify religion by analogy, this does not render it phenomenologically "autonomous." Indeed, even in Euro-American societies religion is tied to much else, and it could be argued that in those societies as well as in others religion can be best understood by viewing it in larger cultural and social contexts.

Bock performs a valuable service by calling his readers' attention to an important conclusion based on ethnographic research in a wide range of societies. His text, however, does not render his observation the sort of strong, unambiguous support it deserves.

Thus, for example, while an argument can be made for Bock's claim that "the Western contrast between 'natural' and 'supernatural' is simply not relevant to the understanding of many societies," some writers who enter this or a similar claim — Émile Durkheim (1965 [1912]:39–43), for example — are not deterred on that account from writing about, and defining, religion. It is of course the case that many anthropologists tie their definitions of religion to the "supernatural" (Saliba 1976:182–183, 191–193). But there are definitional approaches that avoid doing so, and in discounting the power of the Western natural/supernatural distinction for transcultural understandings, Bock by no means subverts definitional efforts that do not depend on it.

As a matter of fact, even though he prefers to write about "Religious roles, techniques, and beliefs" rather than about "religion," Bock clearly *operates* with some concept of religion. He not only claims (in italics) that there is a "religious dimension" to human social life, which might be construed as suggesting some implicit notion of religion, but he invokes "religion" explicitly on the very same page:

> Concepts and practices derived from the world *religions* [he writes] often exist side-by-side with aboriginal customs . . . For example, . . . it is not at all unusual to find Jesus, Mary, and various saints incorporated into a Maya or Aztec pantheon and worshipped alongside of native gods, while in parts of India we find many tribal peoples who have added the Hindu concept of reincarnation to their otherwise distinctive *religion*. Such syncretisms are also found in the "higher" *religions*, as anyone familiar with the origins of the Christmas tree or the Easter bunny will recognize. (1969:380, emphasis added)

In short, concepts of "religion" and of different "religions" evidently inform Bock's assertion that a religious dimension pertains to "every part of social life." But while Bock tells us that he does not rest such concepts cross-culturally on the "supernatural," we are left to infer as best we can from a reading of his sizeable text what they may include and, perhaps more importantly, exclude.

Still and all, suppositions about a "religious dimension" are intriguing. One might attribute it to culture, or, as Bock does, to human social life. A somewhat different strategy, however, is to predicate it of (some) human beings.

The strategy of predicating religion of human beings need not entail the insistence that all human beings "have" or are characterizeable by a religious dimension. Nor need it maintain that those who are "religious" express their religiosity in the same ways, or with the same intensities, as other religiously inclined members of their society. But it does suggest — and this is the crucial point — that human beings rather than religions be clearly taken as the primary phenomenal realities. One consequence might be the deflection of scholarly emphasis from the noun "religion" to an adjective ("religious") and an adverb ("religiously"). The problem, then, would be how to make a convincing case for the utility of the adjective and adverb while downplaying, or even expressing doubts about, the analytical usefulness of the noun.

II. ABJURING A DEFINITION OF RELIGION:
W.C. SMITH'S PERSPECTIVE

Such a perspective, and an interesting attempt to solve the problems that it poses, are found in Wilfred Cantwell Smith's *The Meaning and End of Religion* (1963 [1962]). Though not an anthropologist, Smith, who received degrees in Islamic studies and in theology, is an historian and a comparativist with wide-ranging scholarly interests.

Our term *"religion,"* Smith points out, derives from the Latin *religio*. But while popular, contemporary usages of religion refer primarily to certain sorts of *beliefs*, and by extension to communities of believers, those meanings were developed largely during and after the Enlightenment. Prior to the Enlightenment *religio* and its derivatives in other European languages were accorded other primary acceptations at different times (a subject treated later in this chapter). There was no cultivated concept of religion as a sort of institutional department of human life that could be studied as if it were a bounded phenomenon in its own right.

Contemporary attempts to define religion in general or religions in the particular, Smith maintains, are often animated by a commitment to the idea of "essence." Such commitment supports, and is manifested in, the search for definitions that presumptively point to unchanging constituents or features of things. But in the case of what is commonly called religion and religions, Smith argues, the quest for essences is misdirected and yields reifications.

The religious person, the person of faith, in Smith's view, does not participate in an entity, a thing, called religion. He or she participates in "transcendence," in "something" or "Someone" beyond the self. The object of Christian faith, for example, is not Christianity but Christ. To reify Christianity or any other so-called religion by asserting that it has an essence consisting of a certain creed (and perhaps a set of rituals, a liturgical corpus, and the like), Smith argues, is to engage in a doubly misleading enterprise.

First, in reifying religion and specific religions, insufficient attention is likely to be paid to the role of transcendence in human experience. Even if one supposes that apprehensions of, and sensitivities toward, the transcendent are wholly products of human cultural and psychological processes, it must nevertheless be acknowledged that those awarenesses and feelings have had great power in human life. To slight the experiential dimension, the personal religious factor, because attention is rivetted on certain of its overt expressions, would be to impoverish our understandings of religiosity in human history.

Second, the quest for essences is likely to compromise appreciation of the dynamic character of religious traditions. The attempt, for example, to capture the essence of Hinduism in a definition — to state what is distinctive of Hinduism in comparison, say, to Christianity or Islam — constitutes an effort to describe some cluster of traits presumably found in all forms of "Hinduism" over some long period of time. But what we popularly call religions, Smith reminds us, change: they have histories. *At any one point in time, moreover, there are likely to be multiple forms of any one so-called religion.*

What is called Hinduism, for instance, is so richly variegated, so much a "growing congeries of living realities," that it cannot be defined as some "systematic intellectual pattern." "'Hinduism'", Smith declares, "refers not to an entity; it is a name that the West has given to a prodigiously variegated series of facts" (1963:144). Indeed,

> there is no *a priori* reason, and perhaps no historical evidence, for believing that all instances of 'Hinduism'...or 'Taoism' or 'Buddhism' must have something in common. It is both logically and historically possible that two quite different things can both be Hindu. (1963:149)

"Neither religion in general nor any one of the religions," Smith contends, "is in itself an intelligible entity, a valid object of inquiry or concern either for the scholar or for the man of faith" (1963:12). The scholar should be concerned "not with religions, but with religious persons" (1963:153). One might well dispense with the noun religion in both the singular and the plural. Its adjectival and adverbial forms, nevertheless, are useful analytical tools in that "living religiously is an attribute of persons" (1963:195).

How, then, are we to advance our study of the religious dimension in human life? What intellectual tools might we use? Were scholars to drop the term "religion" from their investigative vocabulary, doing so would leave a serious void. A responsible person who advocates dispensing with the term religion in scholarly research ought to suggest some alternative. Smith is responsible. While numbers of students of the religious dimension in human life may not endorse his alternative (perhaps concluding that some conceptualization of religion is likely to pose fewer problems than what Smith offers in replacement), one can appreciate his efforts to go beyond mere nay-saying and provide an option worthy of consideration. He recommends that we employ two major constructs: "cumulative tradition" and "faith."

Faith, as Smith conceives it, is personal faith. He characterizes it as the individual's inner experiences as they relate to what Smith terms the "impingement" of the transcendent on the person (regardless of whether or not we deem the transcendent to have a reality independent of human conjectures and sentiments). It can be distinguished from "belief," an analytical point that Smith addresses in greater detail in a later book (1979). Faith as inner experience is not directly amenable to our observations. But the faith of individuals has operated in history and has been manifested in a diversity of ways: in expressed beliefs, rites, art, architecture, communal life, and so forth. Scholars must do their best to discover what such statements "meant to the man who first uttered them, and what they have meant to those since for whom they have served as expressions of their faith" (1963:183).

By cumulative tradition Smith means the entire mass of phenomena amenable to observation, the "historical deposit" (1963:156) of human religiosity. Although religious persons may share various expressions of their religiosity with others, the world's cumulative traditions exhibit much diversity. Those traditions, Smith maintains, are linked to faith through living persons. Faith, as he describes it, denotes an inner reality for many men and women while cumulative traditions, he tells us, constitute outer realities for those same persons.

In evaluating W.C. Smith's approach to "the religious dimension" in human life, I focus on three facets of his argument: (a) the important (and, in the writings of anthropologists and historians, variously handled) fact that there is typically synchronic as well as diachronic variability in cumulative traditions and in the faiths of individuals; (b) Smith's emphasis on the importance of "the transcendent" in personal religious experience; and (c) his utilization of a brief semantic history of the word religion to undermine from yet another angle the category religion (and so obviate any genuine need to define the category label).

These points in Smith's argument serve as convenient springboards for discussing some similar or, as the case may be, divergent views proffered by anthropologists and others in their efforts to grapple with the religious dimension in human life. My inclusion of the problem orientations and theorizing of selected others relative to points raised by Smith complicates and lengthens this chapter. But by making the first chapter, so to speak, double in brass, my intention is to situate the general problem of conceptualizing religion in a fairly complex intellectual matrix, and to do so as early as possible.

III. SYNCHRONIC VARIABILITY

Virtually all anthropologists would concede that at any one moment in time persons who seemingly pertain to the same religious community may nevertheless entertain significantly different understandings, attitudes, and aspirations. Perhaps some anthropologists suppose that this is most markedly so in the case of what are conventionally called "world" or "historical religions" (Buddhism, Islam, and others), religions whose numerous and geographically dispersed adherents speak various languages and have different ethnic backgrounds. Numbers of anthropologists, however, recognize that it may also be the case, if to a lesser extent, among those who support so-called "primitive," "tribal," or "primal religions." In a classic ethnographic monograph, for example, James Owen Dorsey scrupulously records instances where his chief informants (Two Crows and Joseph and Frank La Fleche) either doubt (1884:231, 232, 237, 240, 251, etc.) or explicitly deny (1884:217, 227, 232, 234, 237, etc.) what other Omaha Indians affirm.

In dealing with something so obviously complex as "Hinduism," anthropologists sometimes employ a distinction between the "Great Tradition" (widely respected sacred texts, accreted theological and philosophical commentaries, and broadly diffused ritual observances: the religion, in short, that is usually described in textbooks in comparative religion) and the "Little Tradition" (local folk variants of the Great Tradition, generally held to be characterized by admixtures of local concepts and practices and a reduction or absence of some of the Great Tradition's textual and other features). There has been much deserved criticism of this distinction. Yet, like many other analytical constructs in anthropology, it does amount to an important conceptualization, although in certain respects it may prove to be misleading.

The Great/Little Distinction and Religious Dualism

The Great Tradition/Little Tradition distinction was nurtured within anthropology by the development of so-called "community studies." These focused on the local community as, putatively, the smallest social entity that is likely to bear a supposedly "complete" culture. But, as is the case with the distinction between Great and Little Traditions which it supports, the community study approach suffers from boundary problems.

First, what should we mean by "a local community"? In Mesoamerica, for instance, where both the community study approach and the Great/Little distinction were mutually stimulated by Robert Redfield's work in Yucatan (1941, 1955; with Villa Rojas 1934), there are various kinds of non-urban, local populations. Some reside in widely dispersed households, others in relatively compact aggregates of different sizes and structures. Which, if any of these, is appropriate for studying "a culture"? Various answers to that question — as well as questions about the suitability of the question itself — have been hotly debated within anthropology.

Second, considerable research amply demonstrates that populations at relative remove from urban centers are unlikely to be insulated from the larger world. In Mesoamerica, for example, even very rural *municipios* (a certain sort of administrative unit) generally have mail service, tax collectors, and residents who leave for a time and then return, as well as a variety of visitors (medical personnel, police inspectors, merchants, missionaries, etc.), that serve as two-way channels in communication with the larger world.

Somewhat analogous considerations affect the neatness and utility of the Great/Little distinction. First, as Tambiah (1970:3–4, 370) and others point out, "Great Traditions" themselves are typically heterogeneous in important respects (a point emphasized by W.C. Smith, though in a somewhat different vocabulary). Major traditions evolved over long periods of time. Though cumulative in certain respects, they are also marked by internal sub-traditions reflective of innovations and other developments. Second, fractionating religion into two-tiers — an overarching,

literary tradition associated with an elite *versus* local traditions associated with the folk — may mislead us in our efforts to understand religion among villagers or other non-elite
populations.

Claiming that village or local religion is simply Little Tradition
religion may well be simplistic. Marriott (1955), in an effort to
counter such a naive, monocular perspective with respect to rural
religiosity in India, argues that elements of both the Great
(Sanskritic) and Little Traditions are present among Hindu
villagers. The Sanskritic tradition becomes meaningful to many
villagers both through a reductive process of "parochialization"
and the alignment of local elements with it through a process
of "universalization." But while Marriott thus posits a complex
situation involving transformative processes for much of village
religion in India, his way of doing so supports the distinction
between the two traditions.

Dumont and Pocock (1957, 1959) judge the Great/Little
dualism to be analytically unsuitable for comprehending the
religiosity of Hindu villagers. They maintain that villagers apperceive but one religious system on the local level. A system, of
course, is composed of heterogeneous elements. Yet while Hindu
villagers may accord greater prestige to Sanskritic elements, the
Sanskritic tradition, Dumont and Pocock suggest, is generally used
to express concerns and ideas similar to those addressed by extra-
Sanskritic elements. Structural principles underwrite the system
and generate coherence in meanings in what might strike some
outside observers as out-and-out diversity in Hindu religiosity.

Tambiah, in a study of religion in north-east Thailand, also
attacks the idea of "two levels in religion — the high Literary
and the lower Popular" (1970:370). As is the case in many places
elsewhere in Southeast Asia, Tambiah's Thai not only identify
with Theravada Buddhism, but they engage in religious activities
that scholars of literary Buddhism do not generally assign to that
tradition. In presenting a synchronic view of religion as studied
on the ground, Tambiah attempts to show how four distinct "ritual
complexes" are both different from one another and yet are
linked together in what he calls "*a single total field.*"

Spiro offers an analytical alternative to Tambiah's single "field"
solution to the problem of conceptualizing religious diversity
among persons conventionally associated with Theravada Buddhism. He claims that "despite differences in terminology"
between Tambiah and himself, he and Tambiah both actually say
much the same things respecting the actual relationships between

Buddhism and other local religious traditions in Thailand and
Burma (Spiro 1978:xxxv). He maintains, nevertheless, that there
is a fundamental and consequential dissonance in their analytical
approaches.

Tambiah (1970:339–340) declares that "The systematic arrangement and structuring of the religious field as such has to be
sought not at the level of the individual actor but elsewhere —
at the level of collective representations composed of religious
ideas and formalized rituals." "On this point," Spiro (1978:xxxv)
remarks, "Tambiah and I are in complete disagreement." Spiro
holds that "the religious field — and, for that matter, any other
— is best understood when it is studied" at two "levels," culturally
and psychologically (that is, to borrow and adapt Tambiah's words,
"at the level of the individual actor" as well as at the level of
"collective representations"). In so attempting to study religion,
Spiro produces a complex and, with respect to his "two religions"
thesis and some other matters, a controversial analysis of religious diversity in Burma.

First, Spiro maintains that Buddhism in Burma includes several
distinct sorts: "Nibbanic Buddhism," a "religion of radical salvation;" "Kammatic Buddhism," a "religion of proximate salvation;"
"Apotropaic Buddhism," a "religion of magical protection;" and
"Esoteric Buddhism," a "religion of chiliastic expectations" (1982
[1970]). Kammatic ('Karmic') Buddhism, he argues, is actually
the predominate form of Buddhism among Burmese villagers
even though they accord great prestige to Nibbanic ('Nirvanic')
Buddhism, the Buddhism, basically, of the Pali Canon. Spiro's
analysis of the various forms of Buddhism is arguably compatible
with a highly abstracted conception of the Great Tradition/Little
Tradition distinction — indeed, he subtitles *Buddhism and Society*,
the book in which he presents it, *A Great Tradition and Its Burmese
Vicissitudes.*

Second, in a separate book (1967, enlarged edition 1978), Spiro
breaks with those anthropologists who habitually posit syncretism
in conceptualizing the relationships between a world religion and
the enduring elements of a local religious tradition that ante-
dates the introduction of the world religion. In Burma, contemporary expressions of such an ancient tradition pivot on the
conviction that certain superhuman and largely malevolent beings
called "Nats" exist and play significant roles in human affairs. An
ancillary supposition holds that by propitiating the Nats human
beings may forestall or perhaps reverse misfortune. Spiro does
not maintain that Nat animism and Buddhism have combined

syncretistically to produce a new religion. Nor does he claim that instead of two distinct religions there are diverse religious elements ordered by "structural relations of hierarchy, opposition, complementarity and linkage" into a "single total field," as does Tambiah (1970:377) for north-east Thailand. Rather, he insists that there are actually "two religions" and that they exist side by side.

Each religion, according to Spiro, has its own history. Each is served by its own religious specialists. And each is invoked or utilized by largely the same people for different purposes. While, for example, the Buddhist doctrine of *karma* might be taken to account for why one's child is seriously sick, and while the textually inscribed teachings of the Buddha may serve to reconcile one to the prospect of the child's death, if a Burmese villager wants to do something in the hope of effecting a cure, s/he might give a gift (a propitiation or bribe) to one of the Nats.

In summary, Spiro's analytical solution to the problem of recognizing and describing religious diversity in Burma is to emphasize, on the one hand, that Buddhism is not a monolithic religion, a single entity, but a family of related Buddhisms — a point of view that, as a generalization, accords with the position espoused by W.C. Smith. And, on the other hand, Spiro argues that Buddhism and the ancient Nat cultus are discrete religions utilized by the same people for different needs and purposes. This latter view is known as "religious dualism," as distinct both from often invoked notions of religious "syncretism" and some newer ideas about religious "fields" or "cultures."

Some other anthropologists have also also argued for religious dualism in specific cases. Thus, for example, Goulet (1982) maintains that a Dene-tha population in Northwestern Alberta supports two religions, Christianity and a native Athapascan faith.

Tedlock (1983), though not adopting a dualistic interpretation in the manner of Spiro and Goulet, nevertheless comes close to that point of view. She rejects a syncretistic "Christo-paganism" characterization of religion among Maya-Quiché in the *municipio* of Momostenango (Guatemala) in favor of what she describes as "a phenomenological approach" to comprehending the dynamics of local religiosity. Her approach incorporates what she calls a "dialectical" perspective that recognizes the cultural distinctiveness of an enduring Mayan tradition in more than four centuries of creative interactions with Christianity.

Tedlock attributes an out-and-out "dualistic" view to some catechized Indians who have been taught that they must choose

between being "true Christians" or remaining in the company
of native priest-shamans. This use of the concept of dualism,
however, differs from that of Spiro and Goulet. Their analytical
employment of the term points to a religious richness that the
Burmans and Dene-tha can avail themselves of without fearing
that by participating in one tradition they invalidate their participation in the other. The Momosteco catechumens as described
by Tedlock, however, are faced with an either/or situation. In
their case, it seems, they hold that choosing Christianity as taught
by a Catholic priest must henceforth prevent them from access-
ing certain Mayan traditions.

Conceptualizing religious dualism in the style of Spiro and
Goulet is a welcome enrichment of our appreciation of religious
diversity if only as an analytical alternative to formulaic invocations of syncretism. This is not to say that syncretism does not
occur — there is too much evidence for it in various places (e.g.,
Mexico) to assert so extravagant a claim. Nor does it mean that
dualism and syncretism are necessarily irreconcilable opposites.
It may well be the case that where we have grounds to argue
for religious dualism we also have grounds to argue for religious
syncretism, for the distinct historical traditions that co-exist may
have influenced and colored one another in interesting ways.

Other Dualisms

Another way of acknowledging and attempting to sort out religious diversity, overlapping to some extent with the Great
Tradition/Little Tradition distinction, is phrased by Leach as a
"distinction between philosophical religion and practical religion"
(1968:1). The former, he maintains, is "philosophic theology" as
derived from sacred texts and found in "the theology of the higher
philosophers," whereas the latter refers to "the religious principles which guide the behaviour" of ordinary religionists (Leach
1968:1). As is the case with many such dualisms in an irremedially
analog world, much occurs between the described poles. Leach's
conceptual polarity, however, does touch on something of interest even if religionists sometimes blur its sharpness.

Some distinction of this general kind has long been posited
by scholars (to say nothing of inquisitors, missionaries, and others).
But Leach offers some interesting comments about how the
distinction has been used in academic circles and how it might
be most profitably employed.

Until fairly recently, Leach states, Western scholars concerned with Buddhism based their interpretations of that tradition almost exclusively on studies of ancient sacred texts and modern, sophisticated commentaries. They paid relatively little attention to the Buddhism of the folk. Such Western scholars, indeed, tended to suppose that "pure" Buddhism is represented by what can be derived from the sacred texts, while regarding those local elements of religious practice not justified by the texts as debased folk accretions. Their distinction between "pure" and "impure" forms of Buddhism supported their claim that Buddhism, "properly understood," is an ascetic, monastic religion that becomes the concern of ordinary villagers only in very special contexts (contexts mainly associated with death).

Leach declares that by using the term "practical" to describe the religion of ordinary folk, he is emphasizing his "distrust of all distinctions" of the "pure"/"impure" kind. But while eschewing that sort of distinction, and while rejecting assertions to the effect that a religious tradition such as Buddhism must be properly understood as pertaining to some special set of religionists, Leach does assert what he deems to be a significant dualism in religious concerns. "Theological philosophy," he writes, "is often greatly preoccupied with the life hereafter; practical religion is concerned with the life here and now" (Leach 1968;1).

Utilizing distinctions of one kind or another, of course, is fundamental to the analytical enterprise, and Leach and other anthropologists, in rejecting some, clearly support others. And, as the material thus far presented on Great/Little and philosophical religion/practical religion distinctions suggest, the discriminations made are often coded in digital form.

It is worth noting at this juncture (lest we go on and on with the distinctions offered by anthropologists) that the Great Tradition/Little Tradition duality, or some avatar or cousinly rival of it, has been invoked outside of anthropology as well as within it. Historians and sociologists, for example, have variously distinguished — in dual format — between universal religion and folk or local religion (Mensching 1964, Christian 1981), official religion and common religion (Towler 1974), official religion and popular or non-official religion (Vrijhof 1979:688), and so forth.

Although the expression "popular religion" has been used to refer to the religion of the folk or lower classes in distinction to the elite, in some usages it became transformed into an analytical construct for *transcending* various elite/folk distinctions and avoiding some of the dubious understandings that crude employment of such dichotomies may nurture. Davis supplies us with an example.

Davis notes that historians minimally agree to conceive "popular religion" to be "religion as practiced and experienced and not merely as defined and prescribed" (1982:322). There may well be commonalities, she observes, in the actual practices and experiences of laymen and clergy in some area during a given time period. If that be the case, Davis holds, then the historian can discern an overarching, dynamic tradition of popular religiosity that embraces and to some extent unites laymen and clergy, though they be divided by other things (1974). Bell (1989:38) remarks that as "a revisionist term," Davis's use of popular religion "was most useful for suggesting the existence of social attitudes and practices that cut across the categories of previous analyses."

In some applications, Bell points out, the term "popular religion" is used to indicate the very basis of cultural unity rather than signifying an elite/non-elite dualism. It may be characterized, she writes, as some set of basic values, practices, and attitudes that *span* class and regional differences or as a "distinct set of social organizations that have come to mediate elite and peasant worldviews" (Bell 1989:42). But other authors use "popular religion" in ways approximating to divisive employments of "Little Tradition."

O'Neil (1986:222) calls our attention to the "many contradictory meanings" of "popular religion." Davis (1982:322) remarks that because of "so much ambiguity in usage" some distinguished historians have advised their colleagues not to employ the expression "popular religion" at all. For this and other reasons, she has come (1982) to favor the construct "religious cultures," a construct inspired by the anthropologist Clifford Geertz (whose seminal 1966 paper, "Religion as a Cultural System," is discussed in Chapter 3).

The Great Tradition/Little Tradition dualism, and its avatars or cousins by the dozens, do have one endearing value despite their faults and failings in actual applications: they point to religious diversity, however misleadingly or inadequately that diversity may be analyzed and characterized. The likelihood that diversity may be bridged or organized in various ways, as numbers of persons suggest, does not obviate its significance in our attentions to religiosity and much else in human life. Indeed, the very notion of bridging or organizing implies that there is something heterogeneous to be bridged or organized. How best to conceptualize diversity for different purposes remains a fundamental problem in the social sciences.

Other Approaches to Diversity

In addition to analyzing religious diversity through the modality of constructs such as those described above, anthropologists employ numbers of others. While Great Tradition/Little Tradition distinctions were largely invoked to emphasize cultural differences, some anthropologists foreground social diversity. This is often the case in studies of "religious factionalism," especially as such factionalism may be related to economic, political, and educational disparities. And some anthropologists accord importance to psychological or temperamental variables. Paul Radin (1957 [1937]), for example, proposes that we recognize an interpersonal gradation in the continuity and intensity of religious interests and feelings in all populations: "the truly religious, the intermittently religious, and the indifferently religious" (see Chapter 3). In these and in other ways anthropologists conceptualize, and attempt to deal with, synchronic variability.

At the same time, however, some of our primary sources of data, the ethnographies that detail religious convictions and practices, confront us with more or less monolithic portraits of religion. We are all too often given the impression that the natives, or most of them, "believe" the same things with the same intensities and that, allowing for differences in social identity and status, they are mutually committed to, and support, some traditional body of rituals.

One sometimes wonders to what extent some ethnographic accounts may be superficial montages constructed of snippets from different informants — dogmas from Tom, speculations from Dick, and anecdotes from Harry — and a medley of observations and reports about ritual. Even if, as I suspect, numbers are montages, they usually downplay or ignore heterogeneity of sources and perspectives in favor of a homogenized description of "the" native point of view and ritual schedule. If examples of variability are given at all in numbers of older ethnographies, they are usually tied to traditional differences in social identities (as typically structured by age, sex, and other factors that recur in each generation) or they are directly connected to salient culture change.

Within the social sciences generally there is the perennial problem of how far to go toward abstracting a monolithic portrait — or, alternatively put, how far to go in emphasizing interindividual variation and heterogeneity. Digitizers sometimes term this the problem of lumping versus splitting.

It is my impression that anthropologists have been lumpers to a much greater extent than splitters in describing the religious dimensions of the populations that they have studied. Today there is something of a swing toward the splitting pole, prompted in significant measure by intense discussions of "the making of eth-nographic texts" (Clifford and Marcus 1986:vii), discussions that generally recognize the vital role of the individual in fashioning his or her understandings in interactions of various sorts. I regard that as a very welcome swing, and I think that Wilfred Cantwell Smith's book might be usefully employed to further it.

Smith recognizes considerable diversity within "religions" conventionally labeled "Hinduism," "Christianity," and the like. His insistence on appreciating diversity both with respect to culture ("the traditions") and with respect to the individual ("faith") is a welcome improvement over the disposition to homogenize and standardize. But how to do so — how best to conceptualize and relate similarities and differences — remains problematical, as the following case suggests.

Diversity in Cumulative Traditions: "Hinduism"

There is, it is true, no single "Christianity." Christianity is a label that we apply to a family of religions differentially supported by a wide variety of religionists. We can justify the label by invoking "family resemblances" (see Chapter 5) and prototype theory (see Chapter 6). But in any case, we need to go beyond "Great Tradition" justifications of the following sort: Since the end of the second century, we are told,

> nearly all Christians ... have shared three basic premises. First, they accept the canon of the New Testament; second, they confess the apostolic creed; and third, they affirm specific forms of church institution. (Pagels 5 1979:xxii–xxiii)

The problem that immediately arrests our attention is con-tained in the phrase "nearly all Christians." Today, as in the past, there are undoubtedly many persons who are more or less ignorant of the canon and apostolic creed and perhaps indiffer-ent to (or resentful of) church institution, yet nevertheless think of themselves as "Christians" and are deemed such by others. It comes as no great surprise to read in a U.S. newspaper that

> Half of the nation's Christians ... do not know who delivered the Sermon on the Mount, [George Gallup, Jr.] said, citing a poll by his organization. "We revere the Bible, but don't read it," he said. "We believe the Ten Commandments to be valid rules for living, although we can't name them. We believe in God, but this

God . . . does not command our total allegiance." — *The Boston Globe*, 6/2/90, p. 27.

"Hinduism" is at least as problematical — and will serve us as the setting for a case study of some interesting efforts to grapple with diversity in what is conventionally labeled "a religion."

Numbers of writers, although aware of diversity, have maintained that certain widely diffused concepts, structures, or considerations serve to link or relate the many practices and professed convictions that they attribute to "Hinduism:" a hierarchical social structure (the caste system) that is generally accepted but sometimes openly rejected; certain famous concepts (e.g., *dharma, karma, samsara, mokśa*), however poorly understood or parochially interpreted they may be on the local level; various widely distributed though not universally honored rituals; idealized but imperfectly realized life-stages (student, householder, forest-dweller, and renouncer); and, in a huge and diverse population where many are illiterate, an early, sacred (*śruti*, 'heard') literature of great prestige (the Vedas, Brahmanas, Aranyakas, and Upanishads) and a later, diverse (*smriti*, 'remembered') literature that relates to the *śruti* literature in complex ways. Or, in a fascinating and challenging approach that is closer to W.C. Smith's emphasis on personal experience and meaning, some writers foreground overlapping ideas, attitudes, feelings, and etiquettes respecting expectations about, and realizations of, experiences of embodied divinity (Eck 1981, Waghorne and Cutler 1985).

The idea of a sacred literature as a unifying factor despite considerable diversity has been favored by a number of Western scholars, as my earlier discussion of "The Great Tradition" concept suggests. Recently, Brian K. Smith has offered a very interesting version of a "canonical" approach to detecting unity in Hindu diversity. His perspective is all the more engaging in that it is generalized to all "religions," including, he maintains, "Marxism" and "Freudianism" (1987:53–54).

Smith begins by offering what he terms "a working definition" of Hinduism, one that touches on a unifying process (rather than an essence) within Hinduism and that distinguishes it from other Indic religions such as Buddhism and Jainism. "Hinduism," he writes, "is the religion of those humans who create, perpetuate, and transform traditions with legitimizing reference to the authority of the Veda" (1987:40, italics omitted).

The Veda is the sacred canon; other sacred literatures are related to it in various ways and are said to be authoritative to the extent that they are held to restate, simplify, extend, prove equivalent to, or in other respects resemble the Vedas. This is so, B.K. Smith says, even though "in post-Vedic times the subject matter of the Veda is largely unknown by those who define themselves in relation to it" (1987:45). It is not, he writes, the "essential nature" of the Veda, nor what it may "symbolize," that is of defining significance. Rather, "it is the particular relations Hindus establish and maintain with it" (1987:51). The Brahmins derive their authority from their special connections to the Vedas. And Hindus regard Buddhists and Jains as heretics because they refer to other canonical sources for legitimation (1987:41).

B.K. Smith claims that his conception of the unity of Hinduism resembles that of many Hindus. He asserts, however, this crucial difference: that while Hindus usually present their religion as a perpetuation of enduring verities, for Smith "it is not timeless, static, or changeless" but is "a series of creations and transformations" (1987:45).

Going beyond Hinduism, Smith writes that "it is arguable that all religions, by definition, must have a fixed canon (although not necessarily a written one) and a ruled set of exegetical strategies for its interpretation" (1987:41). Religion, he suggests, "is defined by its rules of discourse," rules that mandate a return to some authority, some "canon," whether it be texts or a text, an oral tradition (e.g., myths), the sayings of some founding figure, or, equivalently, "any other absolutely authoritative source of legitimation" (1987:53). It is the requirement for a return to the canon, and not the nature of the canon itself, that is definitive of religious traditions.

Smith holds that we can advance the humanistic study of religion by "exorcising the transcendent and postulating working definitions of religions in terms of their rules or strategies vis-à-vis canonical authority" (1987:55). This approach subsumes Marxism and Freudianism under the rubric religion because, in Smith's view, they are dependent on canonical authority.

B.K. Smith's advice to exorcise the transcendent runs directly counter to the advice offered us by W.C. Smith.

The approach to conceptualizing religion advocated by B.K. Smith is attractive in a number of respects. By conceiving of religion as discourse reflexive to some canon, Smith sidesteps problems posed by conceptualizations that depend on "beliefs," problems noted by W.C. Smith (1963, 1979) and the anthropologist Rodney Needham (1972) in their respective ways. His approach also avoids some of the problems that would be posed by a dependency on "the transcendent" (see the discussion of transcendence later in this chapter). Yet conceptualizing religion in terms of relations with some canon is hardly unproblematical. We can begin to appreciate some of the difficulties by first considering Smith's approach with respect to Hinduism, and then voicing some broader considerations.

Smith (1987:38) mentions in passing "major movements and entire traditions normally regarded as Hindu" that have rejected both Brahmanical authority and the legitimacy of the caste system. He does not specifically tell us, however, to what extent persons of these and various other persuasions "normally regarded as Hindu" may relate to the Vedic tradition — with what degree of awareness and commitment. The rejection of Brahmanical authority, for instance, might — or might not — imply rejection of Vedic authority, for in other branches of Hinduism Brahmanical authority is underwritten by the Vedas. While conscious acceptance of, and reference to, the Vedas may indeed be the touchstone of what Smith calls "Hindu orthodoxy" (1987:50), what does one do with persons who, to one degree or another, may be heterodox in that respect? If some do not really resort to Vedic authority for legitimation, a strict reading of Smith's definition of "Hinduism" would exclude them even if certified Hindus (by Smith's definition) accept them as co-religionists in contrast, say, to Muslims, Buddhists, and Jains.

Perhaps, however, some persons in India, although not resorting to Vedic authority for legitimation of their world views and lifeways, nevertheless regard the Vedas as a part of their cultural heritage. In that case, we might say that the Vedas function as a symbol of belonging, and, contrary to what Smith says, we might opine that such people are indeed Hindus, regardless of what they otherwise reject. But this would reduce the Vedic canon in such cases to a factor making for, and an emblem of, social identity. If the canon has no other meanings for the Hindus imagined here, in what sense is it a crucial component in their *religion?*

The notion of canon deserves some discussion. A single named canon may constitute in effect a multiplicity of canons in some populations. This is because different people may situate or reposition themselves with respect to a named canon in different ways, and how they do so has a good deal to do with the meanings of the canon for them. A named canon may well mean very different things to different people, which can be taken as meaning that it is not the same canon for everyone. In short, there may be very wide latitude in how people relate to — and distance themselves from — some named canon, and the analyst might well resist the temptation to over-homogenize populations relative to canons.

It is also germane to note that Smith's conceptual and definitional approach includes under the rubric "religion" phenomena that many persons (e.g., numbers of theists as well as communists and Freudians) do not conventionally group together. This in itself is no reason for withholding endorsement from that approach. Some other authors, for that matter, also explicitly frame their definitions in ways that render "Freudianism" and/or "Marxism" religion, often on functional grounds (see, for example, the discussion of Ward Goodenough's characterization of religion in Chapter 3). But Smith's approach is potentially as sweeping — and as equalizing — as the most inclusive of any of those — and that does give reason to withhold endorsement.

B.K. Smith's approach to conceptualizing and defining religion is sweeping because of his very broad explication of "canon" with respect to legitimating authority. And it is equalizing because it is essentialist. Human beings turn to many sorts of authority in their efforts to construct meaningful worlds and to deal with a host of concerns. We can identify numerous legitimating "canons," in Smith's elastic sense of canon, that are implicated in their efforts to do so. In consequence, and as is the case with some of the definitional approaches discussed in Chapter 3, Smith's conceptualization of religion encompasses so much that its analytical powers are compromised.

Religion ceases to be very interesting if an enormous number of disparate phenomena are equally grouped together as religions because, in one way or another, they mutually can be said to implicate some "fixed canon (although not necessarily a written one) and a ruled set of exegetical strategies for its interpretation." Smith's essentialist definition renders anything that meets that definition as much of a religion as anything else that is comprehended by the definition. Communism, for example, is by definition as much of a religion as Islam.

What B.K. Smith has actually identified is a genre of authoritarianism in human life. Canonical reflexivity (conceiving "canon" broadly) would seem to be an important aspect of the religious dimension, as Smith contends. It is also, however, important in much else. Smith explicitly mentions Marxism and Freudianism. And he is justified in doing so. But while that may make Marxism and Freudianism religions according to Smith's definition, I have trouble in thinking of either one of them as being as clearly a "religion" as "Hinduism" or "Christianity."

Even though Marxism and Freudianism resemble Hinduism and Christianity in ways additional to their reliance on a canon (e.g., both include moral prescriptions, both endorse special rituals, and both embrace their own versions of *telos* with respect to hoped for transformations in human beings and social orders), they also differ in significant respects.

Unlike Devotional Hinduism and Christianity, for example, Marxism and Freudianism, so-called, do not attribute Mind (will, purpose, and the ability to receive and send complex messages) to extra-human agencies. Some authors (e.g., Argyll 1884, 1896:23; Guthrie 1980:189) deem such attribution a crucial factor for identifying what they regard as religions. Further, Marxist and Freudian canons, as I read them, emphasize reason over faith and, in effect, they reject divine revelation and hermetic teachings in favor of accessible, "naturalistic" theories.

Many other authors who identify Hinduism largely in terms of a sacred literature, or some other feature or combination of features, also acknowledge that there are great internal diversities among Hindus. Many tend, nevertheless, to emphasize the spirituality of that religious life. Hinduism, as presented in Western text-books, is often identified with a quest for salvation, a quest ideally and ultimately fulfilled in the transcendental self's liberation from illusion and from a cycle of repeated bodily deaths and incarnations.

Not all authors, however, subscribe to that characterization. Nirad C. Chaudhuri, for example, who is himself a Bengali, asserts that:

> As to the notion of salvation, it is wholly unreal and unattractive — a mere talking point, as indeed the verbiage about it shows. Salvation is never the object of the religious observances and worship of the Hindus. The main object is worldly prosperity . . . (1979:10)

Even discounting the words "wholly," "mere," and "never" in the above statement, it challenges the emphases that various other writers have put on soteriological themes in "Hinduism." Chaudhuri's overriding view of Hindu religious life seems to emphasize what Mandelbaum (1966) terms the "pragmatic" as analytically contrasted with the "transcendental" aspects of religion, and what Leach (1968) calls "practical religion" as distinguished from "the theology of the higher philosophers." "Hinduism in its fundamental aspect," Chaudhuri maintains, "is a civilized amplification of the primitive man's way of living in the world . . . " (1979:21). Though it "succeeds in converting religion into philosophy," that philosophy, he warns us, should not be regarded "as the true Hindu religion" (1979:147).

What Chaudhuri says about the goal of worldly prosperity is a monochromatic rendering of a profusion of colors. One thinks immediately of renouncers and other sorts of dedicated holy persons — minorities, to be sure, but often respected in certain ways by the masses. They are the most dramatic examples of Hindus moved by what some people call spiritual concerns, but there are many other Hindus who, at least on occasion, are also so moved. The philosophy to which Chaudhuri refers, moreover, is a significant aspect of the religious dimension of numbers of persons whom we call "Hindus," though it may be of lesser or very little importance to others whom we label with that term. And Chaudhuri's reference to "the true Hindu religion" strikes me as more invidious than scholarly.

Franklin Edgerton is one of many students of Hinduism who supply us with alternative and more temperate perspectives (although, of course, perspectives open to the criticisms of their fellow Indologists). Edgerton suggests that "Hinduism" includes alternative philosophical programs. In Indian culture, he writes, there are "two radically different norms of human life and conduct, both at least tolerated, indeed in some sense accepted and approved, each in its own sphere" (1942:151). One, expressed in effect by the great majority of Hindus, he calls the "ordinary" norm: the pursuit of a responsible and fulfilling life in the world, in accordance with what Hindu texts say about *dharma* ('propriety'), *artha* ('profit' in the sense of worldly success), and *kama* ('love'). The other norm, which Edgerton calls "extraordinary," guides a small but sometimes reverenced minority. It extols the achievement of salvation in the sense of release from the round of births and deaths, and "It involves rejection of ordinary human aims; a denial, in theory at least complete, of the generally accepted cultural pattern" (1944:153).

This dualism deserves further discussion. "Hinduism," as I understand it, is credited with simultaneously endorsing both "norms." Not only that, the weight of Hindu traditions indicates that both support the fundamental monism upheld by the dominant schools of Hindu philosophy. Yet, if taken out of context, they appear to be antithetical.

Hindus attempt to resolve this particular paradox in different ways. Thus, by way of one example, *dharma, artha,* and *kama,* on

the one hand, and *mokṣa* ('release') on the other, are related
sequentially: that is, in the first two idealized life-stages (student
and householder), people are supposed to participate in the world
and maintain the social order, whereas in the last two (forest
dweller and renouncer) they are supposed to turn progressively
away from normal social life. Or, to cite a related but more general
example, while the great mass of people are accepted as participating in, and so maintaining, the social order, a smaller number
are admired for turning away from it in keeping with their special
spiritual sensitivities. These conceptualizations (among others)
help dissolve paradox — although an analyst might still claim
that it flourishes here or elsewhere in Hinduism.

Chaudhuri, for example, views Hinduism as pivoting on
understandings that suggest "a social contract between two
acquisitive communities," the Gods and human beings (1979:14).
At the same time, however, he allows that some Hindus manifest
what can be regarded as profound spiritual sensitivities and
strivings. He recognizes, moreover, great diversity within what is
called Hinduism — "Another intellectual failure," he writes, "is
to seek any kind of unity in Hinduism" (1979:145) — while he
also declares that "Despite its all too-obvious inconsistencies,
Hinduism is one whole" (1979:1). Its wholeness, he suggests, can
be comprehended by invoking "certain images from the world
of plants, where vegetation relentlessly proliferates and expands"
(1979:146). Hinduism's very diversity and richness, he in effect
suggests, is itself a salient factor that sets Hinduism off — in
degree if not in kind — from various other religions. Hinduism,
in this view, consists of numerous accreted and still extant pro-
liferations from common roots.

Despite blemishes in the form of overstatements, what
Chaudhuri writes about "Hinduism" is valuable for the reader
who reflects on his text. The paradoxes in his account are
themselves instructive, for they suggest the complex and refrac-
tory untidyness of "Hinduism" — and perhaps, by extrapolation
and analogy, of "Buddhism," "Christianity," "Islam," "Judaism,"
and much else.

While our analytical efforts may discern centers of gravity in
named "world religions," centers of gravity documented by
apperceived overlap in the understandings and observances of
their respective adherents, we ought not to overlook divergencies
in views and practices and the apparent paradoxes to which they
may give rise.

In summary, W.C. Smith's concept of "cumulative traditions"

is easily accommodated to the anthropologist's conceptualization of religion as a cultural system. And W.C. Smith's emphasis on diversity in traditions accords with important if not entirely successful efforts made by anthropologists to grapple with such diversity. The recognition and analyses of diversity within conceptualized religious traditions is, as Smith suggests, a very important aspect of our efforts to explore the religious dimension in human life.

IV. "THE TRANSCENDENT" IN PERSONAL RELIGIOUS EXPERIENCE

Central to W.C. Smith's discussion of personal religious experience is an assumption that is also basic to William James's Gifford Lectures: that "feeling is the deeper source of religion, and that philosophic and theological formulas are secondary products, like translations of a text into another tongue" (James 1929 [1902]:422). Smith focuses his treatment of personal religious experience on faith, and he ties faith to an experience of, and response to, "the transcendent."

Smith's treatment of "the transcendent" keys into (and is in all probability inspired by) long established Western religious traditions. It is necessary to establish this point at the outset, for the terms "transcendent" and "transcendence" have been applied in numbers of different ways by a variety of authors pursuing different interests and addressing different questions. Indeed, some authors have developed highly technical applications, especially in philosophy and theology. Transcendent is commonly defined in dictionaries as "crossing a boundary" or "exceeding usual limits." Etymologically, it derives from the Latin *trans* + *scandere*, 'to climb across'.

Transcendence and the Axial Age

Schwartz (1975:3) claims that he comes close to "the etymological meaning of" transcendence when he characterizes it as "a kind of standing back and looking beyond — a kind of critical, reflective questioning of the actual and a new vision of what lies beyond." He favors this derivation for a specific purpose: that of describing a vital aspect of "certain major spiritual, moral, and intellectual 'breakthroughs'" — what Karl Jaspers (1945) calls the "axial age" — in several Old World civilizations of the first millenium before Christ (Schwartz 1975:1).

The axial age encompassed the development of prophetic

Judaism and the beginnings of rabbinical Judaism in Palestine, the rise of Zoroastrianism in Persia, a transition from Vedic religion to later forms of Hinduism and the emergence of Buddhism and Jainism in India, the florescence of Confucianism, Taoism, and the "hundred schools" in China, and the rise of pre-Socratic and classical philosophy in Greece. Schwartz maintains that a common impulse underlying these axial movements was "a strain toward transcendence" (1975:3), as he characterizes transcendence. Eisenstadt endorses Schwartz's conceptualization of transcendence and maintains that "Axial Age revolutions," revolutions that constituted profound movements away from what Dumont (1982) calls "holistic orders," were crucially defined by "the emergence, conceptualisation and institutionalisation of a basic tension between the transcendental and mundane orders" (1983:2–3).

In pre-axial, "pagan" civilizations, Eisenstadt writes, transmundane orders were "symbolically structured according to principles very similar to the mundane or lower one" (1983:3). But in axial age civilizations "there is an emphasis on the chasm between the transcendental and the mundane order and a conception of a higher moral or metaphysical order" (1983:3). The possibility of some continuity beyond "this world" is "usually seen in terms of the reconstruction of human behavior and personality. This reconstruction would be based on the precepts of the higher moral or metaphysical order through which the chasm between the transcendental and mundane orders is bridged . . . " (1983:4). This conceptualization of a distinctly structured transcendental order, and the institutionalization of a conceptualized tension between it and the mundane order, Eisenstadt suggests, laid the basis for subsequent, and varying, conceptualizations of transcendence and the transcendent in "several major civilisations," including those of the West.

Transcendent in Postmodernist Criticism

Today an interesting application of the term transcendent is sometimes made in critical discussions within contemporary philosophy, literary studies, and anthropology. Postmodernist critics generally maintain that it is not possible to achieve and successfully maintain a culture-free, "transcendent" posture for evaluating philosophical positions, literary works, or anthropological theories. They decry the notion that formal logic or any rigorously constructed analytical system might provide a "neutral

ground," a content-less and authoritative position, from which
to discern and judge universally. Attempts at establishing transcendent analytical and evaluative systems, they say, are themselves contextually contingent: they are cultural creations that
some persons elevate to privileged positions while mistakenly
supposing them to be neutral.

W.C. Smith's Transcendent

W.C. Smith's interest in "the transcendent" is not allied to the
critical tradition referred to above. Rather, in his schema, the
transcendent is *something* or *Someone* that "impinges" on — that
has an effect on, that makes an impression on — persons of faith.
His usage of transcendent harmonizes better with the perspectives of the Axial Age than with those of postmodernism.

There is no such thing, Smith maintains, as *the* Christian (or
Islamic, or Hindu, etc.) faith. Faith is personal and varied. *All*
persons of faith, he avers, do nevertheless share something. That
something, he says, is neither a tradition nor their personal faith.
Rather, it is "that to which they respond, the transcendent itself"
(1963:192). The transcendent is "abiding and ideal" (1963:153).
Referring to it as "God," a term that is commonly applied to
it in the West, Smith compares its abidingness and universality
to the mutability and particularity of cumulative traditions and
faith: "The traditions evolve. Men's faith varies. God endures"
(1963:192).

Now, what Smith says about "the transcendent" makes a certain
sense to Western readers, for it is well grounded in old and still
persisting Western imaginings and idioms. Gordon Kaufman
points to a

> fundamental metaphysical-cosmological dualism found in the Bible
> (as well as in traditional metaphysics) and in virtually all Western
> religious thought. There is the division of reality into "earth" and
> "heaven" — that which is accessible to us in and through our
> experience and in some measure under our control, and that beyond
> our experience and not directly open to our knowledge or mani-
> pulation. (1972:42)

Western religious traditions generally presume an ultimate
reality, an order, that is not accessible to the routine exercise
of the senses and that cannot be apprehended directly by the
unaided human mind. In a religious frame, that order, broadly
put, is "the transcendent." Western religious traditions, moreover, normally represent it to be an authority of some kind: the

ground and reason for the origin and continued existence of the world, the ultimate guarantor of the moral code, the external source of an internally experienced impulse to a higher existential state, or something of the sort.

Western religious concepts of the transcendent characteristically fulfill authority functions. They implicate and express conceptions of enduring and ultimate truth, that which finally matters. These functions, however, do not preclude their occasional employment as instruments for challenging or overthrowing established social orders. Notions of the transcendent sometimes have played important roles in achieving social reorderings just as they sometimes have served to legitimate and preserve long established social interests and forms.

W.C. Smith's transcendent is in the Western religious tradition. He appears to suppose, moreover, that a longing for the authority of the transcendent is natural to humanity and that some realization of that longing is experienced by many — perhaps most — human beings. He writes that the "impingement" of the transcendent is a universal constant in man's otherwise diverse and dynamic religious experiences, and he would almost certainly endorse Johnson's (1974:1) opinion that "The impulse to move from the ordinary dimension of life to the extraordinary is not one invented by the theologian but is one which appears to spring from the deepest levels of consciousness itself."

Difficulties, however, interpose between our culture-bound understandings of Smith's statements about "the transcendent" and the anthropologist's acceptance of them as guides or tools for research.

There are, for example, various conceptual problems noted by some Western analysts in attending to traditional ideas about "the transcendent" in Euro-American cultures. These should be of interest to the anthropologist both because anthropology is grounded in Western traditions and because analogous problems may sometimes be apperceived by the ethnographic fieldworker in non-Western settings.

Kaufman, it will be recalled, points to a traditional Western metaphysical and cosmological dualism. That dualism, he suggests (1965, 1972), supports the idea of God as a reality that transcends all of our experiences. But modernist Western intellectuals, he observes, are likely to be strongly attached to a monistic conception of reality. Reality, in the secular modernist view, is integral: there is only one reality. To the extent that we may know it, it is because it is accessible to our experiences. This

perspective insists that statements about reality that are meaningful and worthy of our attention must refer to, or connect with,
some aspect or dimension of experience. Such a world view cannot
easily be reconciled with the idea of a reality that transcends all
of our experiences.

That which is beyond all our experience, some proponents of
secular modernist Western world views have opined, is open to
the charge of being devoid of meaning.

W.D. Hudson, a philosopher sympathetic to religion, writes of
what he calls "logical transcendence" (1977:225), which he
contrasts with what he terms "empirical transcendence" ("that
overplus of some property or properties which always seems to
distinguish god from man"). Logical transcendence relates to the
languages in which religious ideas and commitments are expressed. The expression of some religious ideas and commitments, Hudson notes, may well strain or bend the usual, work-
a-day meanings of words and phrases to the point where, in the
critical judgment of a Western analytical philosopher, religious
statements are likely to seem logically odd. Hudson avers that
"philosophical difficulties about religion always have to do with
how much strain ordinary language can bear before the point
of unintelligibility is reached" (1977:235).

Numbers of contemporary Western theologians are sensitive
to that issue and seek to deal with it. Some of them construe
the problem to be epistemological as well as semantic: how can
we know, and, eschewing non-sense, *talk about*, a mysterious and
infinite reality that transcends our experiences, experiences that
are all finite and that reflect our existential human finitude?

A popular — but hardly unproblematical — strategy is to try
to demonstrate that there is some meaningful and non-trivial
sense of transcendence in our ordinary, finite lives. That is, a
transcendence the referents of which are in our experiences and
that might serve as a useful model for analogous conceptions of
transcendence in a theological sense.

That enterprise is subject to a general criticism of all such
efforts at analogical conceptualization (a criticism that will cast
its shadow over the recommendations contained in Chapter 6):
In proceeding from the relatively well known to the relatively less
known by an analogical leap, we necessarily distance the concepts
and categories of the relatively well known from their nurturing
contexts. It is their contexts that support their meanings, and
if the leap is too great — if conceptualizations are wrenched
from their contexts without adequate consideration and compen-

sation — the analogy may be too far-fetched to be convincing.

Kaufman and McLain

Gordon Kaufman, a theologian, supplies us with an interesting (and not noticeably far-fetched) analysis in his efforts to conceptualize divine transcendence by analogy to human experiences. Although he later altered his views somewhat (see the Preface to Kaufman 1972), in some early essays he calls our attention to two possibilities.

One model, "teleological transcendence," is based on a human proclivity to set goals and then organize one's life to achieve them. A targeted end transcends one's present experiences. Indeed, Kaufman suggests, it is because the goal is not present that "the self" works toward it (1972:75). In goal seeking, of course, some goals may be attained eventually. But others are perpetually experienced as transcendent because we do not fully achieve them. Kaufman avers that this model of transcendence, in theological adaptation, conduces to a relatively abstract theology of *Being*. In that theology, ultimate reality is conceived to be an unmoved good that teleologically moves all else. The framers of such theologies (see, for example, the discussion of Tillich in Chapter 3) generally attempt to conceptualize ultimate reality in non-anthropomorphic fashion. But doing so, many theologians recognize, raises problems respecting the traditional Judeo-Christian-Islamic view of a personal God who acts in history.

Another model of transcendence is based on our experiences of communicating with, and attempting to know, other human beings. Those experiences figure in the theorizing of various theologians (e.g., Barth, Bultmann, Brunner, and Niebuhr) (McLain 1969:158). Kaufman, in developing his model of interpersonal transcendence, argues that other human beings are actually transcendent for us in certain respects. They are forever beyond our full knowledge and understanding. Their thoughts and feelings are inaccessible to us except in moments of "revelation:" indications that they give us of how they may think and feel (Kaufman 1972:75). This model, theologically adapted, conduces in Judeo-Christian-Islamic traditions to the idea of a radically transcendent, personal, and self-revealing God. Conceptualized as an autonomous anthropomorphic agency, that God is deemed capable of genuine free acts as distinguished from mere activity (Kaufman 1972:78).

F. Michael McLain, drawing on the philosopher P.F. Strawson's book, *Individuals: An Essay in Descriptive Metaphysics* (1963), criticizes Kaufman's interpersonal model, particularly with respect to its theological suitability for conceptualizing radical transcendence. The human self, McLain argues, cannot be construed as a radically transcendent reality known to us only through self-disclosures (1969:167). Our primitive notion of the self, he says, is that of an embodied reality. The public and observable side of the self, he argues, is intrinsic to the concept of a person and not merely adventitious to the self as a hidden subject. The self is thus not radically transcendent, and so the interpersonal model offered by Kaufman is not adequate for conceptualizing a radically transcendent divine reality. But for all that, McLain allows that persons "are relatively occult, and it is a contingent fact that we know some things about them only because they choose to reveal them" (1969:167). What Kaufman's analysis gives us, he suggests, is a model of "revelation" and an account of our sense of "otherness" (1969:167).

McLain favors a modified teleological model for conceptualizing God. Kaufman, in offering a teleological model, focuses on the ends or goals that transcend our immediate experiences. McLain suggests that this focus be altered, and that our attention be directed to the agent who chooses those ends (1969:170). This yields what he calls an "agent-act model." God is to be understood as one who acts, who realizes his intentions and purposes in history. This model, McLain states, accords well with the Bible and with mainstream Christian faith.

The above models of transcendence, it is worth reiterating, are *experientially* based. We are conscious experientially, says Kaufman, of our own finitude, our own limitations. Transcendence, he argues, relates to an understanding or recognition of our ultimate experiential limits. God-talk in Western traditions, he suggests, is a way of confronting the duality between concrete experiences and the limits of our knowledge and experience. For Kaufman, McLain (1969:174) points out, the idea of God is the idea of something we do not know but apprehend as a limit.

The Transcendence or Relative Occultism of the Natives

Kaufman's two models of transcendence, one based on human intentionality and transcendent goals, the other based on human interpersonal relations and the transcendence of alter (or, as McLain would have it, the relative occultism of alter), will remind anthropologists of discussions and debates now being conducted within the profession.

Questions are asked about intentionality and about whether or not elemental notions or consciousness of self and person are transcultural universals. And questions about our efforts to understand the conceptions and behaviors of others, questions raised by past generations of anthropologists, are now being given intense, and in certain respects novel, airings. Criticism, for example, is currently directed against styles of ethnographic writing that present cultural descriptions as if their authors were transcendent — as if the ethnographers had achieved what Hilary Putnam terms a "God's-eye view," rendering understandings, as it were, from a neutral place, one of God-like dispassion and wisdom.

The ethnographer's understandings are negotiated and developed — invented, as Wagner puts it — in interactions with the local people. And the natives, in their interactions with the ethnographer, are to an extent "transcendent" in the manner suggested by Kaufman — or they are "relatively occult," to borrow McLain's more accurate phrasing. In addition to attending to the "public" or most accessible aspects of native life, the anthropologist is likely to attempt to provoke individual informants into various sorts of self-disclosures by dialogues of various sorts. But any "revelations," such as they may be, are not unambiguous and complete in themselves. There is always something of a veil between the ethnographer and the natives. The ethnographer is obliged to interpret what s/he construes as disclosures and to construct his/her own understandings.

Some theologians make somewhat similar statements about what they conceive to be divine revelations. William Temple (1934), for example, maintains that the locus of divine revelation is not in the divine word but, rather, in the relation between a "divinely guided event" and humanity's "divinely guided apprehension" of it. Shorn of theological language, an event must be apprehended, which is to say, 'grasped with the understanding', to be meaningful. It is a matter of faith for numbers of theologians that the interpretive act of apprehending divine revelation is transcendentally guided for at least some interpreters: those who are given grace. But the ethnographer, though guided by the natives (who are transcendent beings in Kaufman's sense), ought not to assume grace. The ethnographer must beware not only of apotheosizing research methods and attractive theories but of apotheosizing the natives. That can come about, in effect, by failing to appreciate that the significance of native utterances depends on their assimilation into a body of constructed understandings.

There are some interesting parallels between the ethnographer's efforts to understand human alters and those of theologians with respect to what they conceive to be a divine alter. Transcendence, broadly conceptualized, can be invoked in both cases. For the ethnographer, moreover, whatever ideas the natives may have that suggest analogies to what Westerners call transcendence can also be important. Some fairly clear initial understanding of how persons in the ethnographer's society talk about transcendence would be helpful in sensitizing the ethnographer to the possibilities of constructing productive analogies. But when we look closely at Euro-American discourse respecting transcendence, we apperceive a certain elusiveness in it.

The Elusiveness of Transcendence

As the philosopher Wyschograd (1981) notes, much Euro-American talk about transcendence and the transcendent involves metaphors of spatial exteriority (e.g., "beyond" or "above" the world). The general imagery is of something outside of a boundary or limit. But as Wyschograd (1981:59–60) observes,

> whatever transcends, whether conceived as unlimited in the absolute sense or as unsurpassable by any other being, acquires its meaning by virtue of its elusiveness. For if the object has been obtained, a limit has been transgressed. What is exterior has been incorporated into a totality and what transcends now lies elsewhere.

Some persons have recognized that talk about the transcendent, talk that initially depends on conceptualized boundaries, if continued to the point of specifying what is beyond the boundary may actually become boundary-transgressing. And some have used that recognition to construct more inclusive systems. Thus, for example, Horace Bushnell, a nineteenth century American Protestant theologian, sought to revise and transcend a distinction between nature and the supernatural that was current in his day, and he entitled his book on the subject *Nature and the Supernatural as Together Constituting the One System of God* (1858). (The supernatural, Bushnell declares, "meets us in what is least transcendent and most familiar, even in ourselves . . . The very idea of our personality is that of a being not under the law of cause and effect, a being supernatural" [1910:31].) But most people, I suspect, do not recognize the boundary-transgressing possibilities of common talk about the transcendent. Such talk is meaningful for them, even if for the logician it may sometimes seem elusive or even incoherent.

Transcendence and Religion

But even if we encounter in non-Western societies talk that, by analogy with speech conventions in our own society, strikes us as talk about what we would call transcendental ("supernatural" or "superhuman") beings, such talk does not necessarily point to a religion that pivots on the transcendent. Nor does it, by itself, indicate profound concern for the transcendent. We might well allow that even where *talk* about transcendence can (by analogy) be discerned, *concern* may be elsewhere.

Consider, for instance, an interpretation that challenges W.C. Smith's assertion that personal religious sentiments are universally oriented to the transcendent. Max Weber maintains that among so-called "primitive" peoples "The most elementary forms of behavior motivated by religious or magical factors are oriented to *this* world" (1963 [1922]:1). Talcott Parsons, in explicating Weber's thought on the subject, describes as "particularly important" Weber's

> insistence that the conception of a supernatural order does not imply any "transcendental" goals or focus of interest for man. The aid of the supernatural is sought, so far as "primitive man" is concerned, entirely in the interest of mundane, worldly concerns: health, long life, defeat of enemies, good relations with one's own people, and the like. (1963:xxviii)

But what are we to understand by "*this* world," "a supernatural order," and "transcendental" goals? We might suppose that we understand quite a lot about them, since they are perduring and important concepts in our own cultural history. We may be mistaken, however. Our understandings might be shallow. A superficial acquaintance with those expressions in our own traditions is perhaps a factor promoting the sometimes glib — and quite possibly misleading — application of them to the constructs and categories of other peoples.

This does not mean that anthropologists should drop "transcendence" and "transcendent" from their analytical vocabulary. That would be hard to do in any case because those terms have wide currency and are very much a part of both the working vocabulary and every-day vocabulary of many social scientists. Proscribing terms, moreover, is not something that ought to be recommended lightly.

A more productive approach is to examine various uses of "transcendence" and "transcendent" in the larger society in the hope of finding some senses that can be employed in transcultural analyses and descriptions with maximal comprehension and minimal difficulty. Let us look at the term "transcendent," a term utilized by W.C. Smith in explicating his proposed substitutes for "religion," and the related word "transcendence."

The elemental meaning of transcendent in Anglo-American discourse is broad — and, in a religious context, it is often associated with beings that are conceived of as human-like in various ways:

> Surpassing or excelling others of its kind; going beyond the ordinary limits; pre-eminent; superior or supreme; extraordinary. (*Oxford English Dictionary* 253)

This general sense can probably be applied in descriptions of non-Western world views with a minimum of problems. For even where the ideational expressions of various non-Western peoples include (from the anthropologist's perspective) "anthropomorphic" Gods or spiritual beings that do not appear to stand outside of the world, such beings are nevertheless often pictured by native informants as 'transcending', as being superior to, human beings in various traits, qualities, or capacities. They exceed at least some of the existential limits that the natives — and often the ethnographer as well — ordinarily associate with humanity.

Ideational systems, moreover, often entertain the prospect that humans may transcend in one way or another their own normal life conditions, perhaps through the agency of other-than-human personages. Transcendence in this case refers to passage from an initial state to another that is deemed superior, a state that surpasses or excels what is regarded as ordinary for human existents or for much of human existence. As Johnson (1974:3) notes, "Transcendence can also be related to a description of the humanistic objective of becoming something other than one is at present."

If the instrumental aspects of religiosity be given the prominent place that they deserve in our explorations of the religious dimension in human life, then an important topic for study is the widespread conviction — and hope — that human beings may transcend their ordinary state with (though sometimes without) the assistance of beings superior to them in various qualities and capacities. In saying this I recognize that religious strivings are often directed to the *maintenance* of states rather than their alteration. I acknowledge, moreover, that modalities that we may not choose to construe as religious are sometimes invoked in the hope of changing what are supposed to be humanity's ordinary conditions of existence. Still and all, a consideration of transcendence in its elemental meaning should prove useful for comparative investigations. Whether they have a word for it or not, many peoples have ideas about transcendence in that sense.

A sense of transcendence that represents a leap from the sense given above, one utilized by numbers of Westerners, is exemplified by the qualitative separation of the Judeo-Christian-Islamic God, the Creator, from all that he created. This is not the superiority of one variety of something over "others of its kind." Nor is it the superiority of something over things otherwise like it in many or most respects. Numbers of religious Westerners conceive it to be, rather, the overwhelming superiority of something that is radically different *in nature* from that which it is superior to. Distinct superiority in powers and achievements in this case betokens and inheres in ontological superiority, as Job is reminded when God speaks to him out of the whirlwind:

> Where wast thou when I laid the foundations of the earth? Declare, if thou hast the understanding. Who determined the measures thereof, if thou knowest? Or who stretched the line upon it? Whereupon were the foundations thereof fastened? Or who laid the corner-stone thereof, When the morning stars sang together, And all the sons of God shouted for joy? (Job 38:1–7)

The two senses of transcendence referred to above should be kept in mind lest unrecognized slippages from one to the other mar the anthropologist's analyses of what people say. The contents of religious statements reflecting one as compared to the other may well exemplify different metaphysical asssumptions, and perhaps significant differences in expectations and aspirations as well. They may also differ with respect to their relative intelligibility within some more inclusive world of language conventions. Broadly put, the greater the presumed differences between human beings and other-than-human beings, the more unlikely it would seem that predicates accepted for the former could be applied coherently to the latter.

Conceptualizations of transcendence and the transcendent of the sort suggested above may prove utile in interpreting particular world views for the audiences for which anthropologists write — provided, at a minimum, that two conditions be met.

First, the audience must be told how the anthropologist understands himself/herself to be using those terms. Sophistication in doing so will be increased by reading widely and deeply in the literatures where the peculiar problems of transcendence are most rigorously discussed: namely, philosophy, theology, and religious studies.

Second, the anthropologist might explicitly address the question of whether or not his/her usages of transcendence and the transcendent approximate to native conceptualizations as s/he has come to understand such conceptualizations.

In addition to the two senses of transcendence and the transcendent discussed above, senses useful for describing and analyzing the world views of populations that anthropologists study, there is a third utile sense, one that often overlaps with the second when applied to other-than-human beings. It does so because beings that are conceptualized as radically different in nature from human beings (the second sense) may be regarded as posing an epistemological conundrum. They may be held to be "beyond" understandings grounded in routine experiences. So conceiving them would constitute a discriminable third sense of transcendence.

In many Euro-American theological discourses God is described as radically transcendent, a being beyond human experiences, and thus human understandings, save as the deity selectively reveals itself in history. Some theologians, it may be recalled, argue that other human beings are also "transcendent" in parallel but less radical ways, and that they serve as experiential models that ground concepts of radical transcendence as applied to deity. As I indicated earlier, I deem talk about human alters as "transcendent" an interesting way of conceptualizing a basic problem: that of attempting to understand, to relate to our experiences, the thoughts, attitudes, and feelings of other persons who do not fully reveal them to us experientially — who, in fact, never do so.

W.C. Smith's discussions of transcendence and the transcendent contribute to our efforts to become aware of various complexities and subtleties that may attend the use of those terms. Smith, indeed, makes us aware of certain difficulties that attach to talk about transcendence.

In a recent lecture entitled "Transcendence," Smith speaks of many things that he deems "transcendent": e.g., music (1988:12), truth (1988:12), reality (1988:13), and much else. He sees transcendence and immanence, moreover, as "two facets of the same diamond" (1988:11). Thus, for example, "Harvard University transcends Harvard College, but is immanent within it . . . The English language transcends every English sentence, and is immanent within it. The community of which any individual is a member transcends each of its members, and to varying degrees is immanent within each," and so forth (1988:11).

Smith avers, nevertheless, that, as a conception, "Transcendence is not to be comprehended though it is to be apprehended" — indeed, "Transcendence is a mystery, . . . and the point of mystery . . . is that it is not to be clarified yet is to be explored" (1988:10). Of great importance to his perspective is the sense of human movement toward the transcendent. The "inherent significance" of transcendence, he says, is "*going* above and beyond; this is quite different from simply being above and beyond . . . This matter of movement is crucial; as is the point that it is human beings that move. Central to an understanding of the universe, of humanity, and of transcendence itself as a principle, is that the three are interrelated, intimately — and dynamically" (1988:11).

Transcendence, as Smith views it, is a principle at work in human understandings and aspirations, and "the transcendent" is something that expresses or crystallizes those understandings and aspirations. What he has to say about it is stimulating, but his formulation of it is not suitable for conversion into an analytical category of use to cultural anthropologists. Transcendence and the transcendent in Smith's usages are too broad, omnipresent, and, on Smith's testimony, mysterious, to serve us analytically. Further, Smith's designation of the presumed "impingement" of the transcendent as a universal feature shared by all persons of faith is not likely to appeal to many anthropologists.

In his 1963 book Smith was vague about the ontological implications of "impingement." He tried to leave the matter as open as possible (and so provoked numerous calls for clarification, which he finally answered — but only in part — in his 1988 lecture). But what he says both in 1963 and in 1988 is quite compatible with the agency view of transcendence favored by many contemporary Christian theologians and philosophers ("whatever is god," says the philosopher Hudson [1977:224–225], "is conceived as agency . . . allowing for variations, what god does, or refrains from doing, is taken in all religions to make some difference to the believer").

Impingement suggests an impinger. Smith, like many other historians and comparative students of religion, attempts to bracket personal theistic and theological commitments. But they are there, nevertheless. Since analytical categories are components in, and affirm, more inclusive conceptual structures and strategies of research, many anthropologists (the present author included) would prefer to avoid those that implicate perspectives that they do not share.

In summary, elemental conceptions of transcendence and transcendent may sometimes be productively employed by the ethnographer in constructing analogies and "inventing" cultures. Such conceptions, indeed, may prove promising in a variety of undertakings, including the conceptualization of human alters as "transcendent" or "relatively occult" beings. But W.C. Smith's vague presentation of "the transcendent," and his emphasis on its universal "impingement" on persons of faith, are very unlikely to appeal to cultural anthropologists. Most anthropologists, I think, would be more comfortable in employing "religion" as a category, even if they recognize various of the problems it poses for transcultural research, than W.C. Smith's "faith."

V. A Semantic History of Religio

Smith furnishes a brief semantic history of the Latin term *religio*, and he uses that history as another source of reasons for casting doubt on the analytical utility of the category religion.

In his consideration of the semantic developments of *religio* and *religiosus* among pagan Romans, Smith recognizes that those words sometimes were used to refer to presumptive subjective states or dispositions. He weights his discussion, however, toward applications that point to public behavior and to socially recognized obligations. He does so, I think, partly to stress differences between meanings indicated by Roman usages of *religio* and popular, contemporary acceptations of the word "religion" that focus on "systems of beliefs." In so doing, he calls our attention to some ambivalent features of Roman usages:

> To say that such-and-such a thing was *religio* for me meant that it was mightily incumbent upon me to do it (alternatively, not to do it: both are found, as is not unusual with 'mana', 'tabu', the holy, the sacred). Oaths, family proprieties, cultic observances and the like were each *religio* to a man; or, showing the ambivalence, one could easily say that to break a solemn oath is *religio* . . . (1962:20)

Smith also notes that "ritual ceremonies themselves were designated *religiones*," and that "The *religio* of a specified god could . . . designate the traditional cultic pattern at his shrine" (1962:20–21).

Other authors give greater play to usages that refer to subjective feelings or attitudes. Fowler, in consonance with those Latinists who opine that the elemental meaning of *religio* in early usages was 'scruple', imagines that it may have stood for "a doubt or scruple of any kind, or for anything uncanny which creates such doubt or scruple" (1908:170). He notes that the word is not found in the *Corpus Inscriptionum*, where we should expect to find it if it had had a technical or legal sense (1908:170). He remarks, moreover, that the Romans never personified *religio* as a deity, an honor that they conferred on *Pietas, Sanctitas*, and other virtues. He concludes that *religio* was not deemed a virtue but was regarded as a *feeling* to which human nature is susceptible under certain circumstances (1908:171). Eventually, he supposes, the word was credited with meanings having to do with the forms of cults and the entertainment of scruples respecting accurate performance of mandated rites.

Wilt (1954), in an unpublished dissertation, also emphasizes subjective feelings or dispositions. The novelty of his thesis rests on etymological speculations. Much of the scholarly literature directs our attention to two candidates from which *religio* may have derived: *legere*, 'to gather together', 'to arrange', a proposed derivation that we associate with Cicero, and *ligare*, 'to tie together', 'to bind', a possibility recognized by Lucretius and favored by the Christian writers, Lactantius and Tertullian (Fowler 1908:169, Benveniste 1969:268). Wilt, however, rejects the *re-* compounds of both *lego* and *ligo* and hypothesizes "a *re-* compound of a simplex verb etymologically identical with the Greek verb *alegō*, meaning 'care for', 'have regard for'" (1954:113).

Émile Benveniste, after remarking that *religio* did not originally mean "religion," tells us that early in its traceable history it meant having a scruple, and that that usage was constant in the classical period (1969:269). *Religio* in that sense, he says, denominated "a hesitation that holds back, a scruple that impedes . . . ," and the adjective *religiosus* often meant "scrupulous with regard to cult, having a case of conscience regarding rites" (1969:270).

Benveniste argues impressively that *religio* derives from *legere*, 'to collect'. He concludes that that derivation yields "to re-collect," that is, "to take up again for a new choice, to reconsider a previous step:"

> To begin again with a choice already made, . . . to revise the decision that results from it, such is the proper sense of *religio*. It indicates an interior disposition and not an objective property of certain things or an ensemble of beliefs and practices. (1969:272)

Benveniste also states that "*superstitio*" in the sense of "contemptible religious beliefs" was a "contrary" of *religio* that was recognized as such by the Romans themselves (1969:272): that *superstitio* was in 'opposition' ("*il s'oppose*") to *religio* (1969:273). He argues that *superstitio* derives from *superstes* in the latter's sense of 'witness' — but not 'witness' as conveyed by *testis*. *Superstes*, rather, referred to a 'witness' who claims to attest to past events not by having been present but by 'seeing' them, as it were, by virtue of a sort of second sight or 'gift of presence'.

Superstitio, Benveniste maintains, suggested in its early usage such a gift, or the quality of being a witness 'who has his being beyond' the empirical hère and now. But numbers of Romans, though generally respectful of their traditional augurs, became contemptuous of other diviners (many of whom were foreigners or associated with foreign cults). *Superstitio*, often associated with the word *hariolus* ('seer'), took on distinctly pejorative connotations. It was used, Benveniste indicates, in reference to divination, sorcery, and other magical practices that were regarded as puerile and the practitioners of which were often despised as charlatans. Various assertions associated with such practices were deemed unworthy of reasonable minds: "contemptible religious beliefs," Beneveniste terms them, in an effort to approximate fairly to Roman sensibilities in words that we commonly utilize.

Not surprisingly, Benveniste does not address the possibility that *religio* may itself have been employed in some contexts to mean what we normally understand by *superstition* and what the Romans, on his testimony, sometimes understood by *superstitio*. In an earlier work, "Remarks on the Function of Language in Freudian Theory" (1956), Benveniste expresses opposition to the possibility that a word 'includes' two contradictory senses in the same language, a possibility that he distinguishes from the possible operation of "cultural conditions" that may determine "two opposed attitudes" toward an object described by that word (1971 [1956]:70). He maintains that language "operates on a world considered to be 'real' and reflects a 'real' world," and that language categories tend to be consistent. "It is thus a priori improbable — and an attentive examination confirms it —," he states, that ancient or archaic languages — or any other examples of what he calls "organized" languages — "escape the 'principle of contradiction' by using the same expression for two mutually exclusive or simply contrary notions" (1971 [1956]:71).

Benveniste's remarks, we note, are focused on certain ideas expressed by Freud in his 1910 paper, *Gegensinn der Urworte* ('The Antithetical Sense of Primal Words'). Freud maintains in that work that the apparent insensitivity to contradiction found in dreams matches a peculiarity in certain ancient languages described in a study by Karl Abel — a peculiarity consisting in the use of a single expression to state both one thing and its opposite. But while Benveniste vigorously attacks "the etymological speculations of Karl Abel that intrigued Freud" (1971 [1956]:69) and the uses that Freud made of them in the 1910 paper, he makes no explicit reference to Freud's 1919 essay, *Das Unheimliche* ('The Uncanny'). The latter work, drawing on a range of literary materials, makes an interesting case in support of the idea that words can sometimes be invested with logically related but seemingly opposite meanings.

In the case of *religio*, at any rate, there is some evidence that points to distinct and perhaps 'opposable' uses (contemporary semantic theories may persuade us on occasion to regard a word in one determined sense as constituting "a marked form" of that same word credited with some other sense). Caesar (*De Bello Gallico* VI:37), for example, employs it in a way that puts us in mind of superstition — the more so since he combines it with a suggestive verbal construction, *fingo* in association with *sibi*, 'to conjure up in the mind'. This stirs our memory of the relation between *superstitio* and disvalued mantic arts noted by Benveniste in distinguishing *superstitio* from *religio*. Caesar relates that when some Germans suddenly attacked a Roman fortification located on a site that many of its garrison deemed unlucky, there was panic among the defenders, most of whom conjured up *novas religiones*, which we may gloss as 'fresh superstitions' or 'fresh superstitious dreads', regarding the place (*"plerique novas sibi ex loco religiones fingunt"*).

In later periods *religio* and its derivatives in various European languages took on other meanings: piety, a life lived in accordance with suppositions about God's will and ordinances, absorption in spiritual concerns (the monastic life during much of the Middle Ages was termed *religio*), cultic observances, and so on.

The fact that *religio* could and sometimes did mean different — and differently valued — things testifies to its semantic suppleness. One enhances one's appreciation of that by turning to the entry on *religio* in the triple columns of *The Oxford Latin Dictionary* (pp. 1605–1606). One finds there a number of usages subsumed under ten senses, and the evidence unmistakably points to a certain complexity and subtlety of meanings for *religio* both diachronically and (most clearly in late Republican and subsequent periods) synchronically. *Religio*, indeed, was at least as multivocal among the later Romans as "religion" is among us. Those who demand some unitary, stable, and comprehensive sense of religion, and who despair of obtaining it from contemporary social scientists, are thus unlikely to find what they require by tracing out the roots of the word among the Senate and the Roman People.

An inquiry into the history of *religio* is one of a multitude of inquiries that might serve to disabuse us of a longing for the authority of pedigree in the fashioning of our analytical categories. Many of the constructs and terms that anthropologists employ in the study of religions are taken from cultural traditions where meanings are not only multiplied and accreted over time, but where their impacted complexities and subtleties are preserved for us by texts and by the diligent labors of generations of humanist scholars. Yet while a cultivated appreciation of their histories enlarges our understandings and heightens our sensibilities, the anthropologist's analytical categories must be pointed to the issues at hand.

The power of religion as an analytical category, anthropologists might well affirm, depends on its instrumental value in facilitating the formulation of interesting statements about human beings, the phenomenal subjects of anthropological research. To borrow an adjective from the Romans, the anthropologist needs to be *religiosus* — 'scrupulous', 'conscientious' — in the shaping of cross-cultural instruments. While we should be knowledgeable about words, we must also struggle against a facile surrender to their authority, an authority that all too often turns out to be unstable or evanescent when probed.

Should We Drop the Term Religion?

However polysemous the word religion may be, it nevertheless is employed by millions of people today. That employment, moreover, undoubtedly relates to how some of those people may conceptualize or experience "the transcendent." This militates against following Smith's 1963 recommendations to drop the word from investigative vocabularies. The fact that not all peoples have an expression or concept approximating to what contemporary Westerners generally mean by "religion," and the multivocality of terms for it among those who do utilize such terms, might be regarded as subverting the suitability of a transcultural analytical category labeled religion. But even so, scholars must nevertheless confront its considerable powers among the millions who do employ it.

One must also take cognizance of the fact that many (probably most) anthropologists show little inclination to dispense with the term religion. They use it often, authors of introductory texts usually attempt to define it, and, as later chapters indicate, there is no dearth of proffered, explicit definitions in the literature intended for professional anthropologists.

Anthropologists seem to be rather conservative with respect to traditional categories. Though some have published interesting criticisms not only of "religion" (e.g., Needham 1981) but of such other traditional categories as "kinship" (e.g., Needham 1971, Schneider 1984) and "marriage" (e.g., Rivière 1971), invocations of the respective category labels continue to be common. While numbers of anthropologists appear to favor, on general principles, refining or reforming well used categories, I detect little in the way of a groundswell for dropping those categories.

Until anthropologists are offered an appealing substitute (or appealing substitutes) for the term religion or, indeed, for the discourses in which that term is embedded, they are likely to continue to use religion as a traditional way of talking about certain sorts of phenomena that interest them. Religion is part of current anthropological discourses, and to jettison it entirely would probably require something very much more radical than the excision of a word or two. In the meantime, though anthropologists would do well to refine their conceptualizations of the category labeled by the term, they can draw comfort from the nominalist's view of language as characterized by Rorty (1991 [1989]:127): language, in that view, is "just human beings using marks and noises to get what they want."

CHAPTER TWO

HOLDING A DEFINITION IN ABEYANCE AND A CASE FOR A DEFINITION

Is an indistinct photograph a picture of a person at all? Is it even
always an advantage to replace an indistinct picture by a sharp one?
Isn't the indistinct one often exactly what we need?
— Ludwig Wittgenstein, *Philosophical Investigations* I:71

The preceding chapter ended by concluding that the term "religion" can be usefully retained. But do anthropologists need to define it and the category to which they connect it?

The testimony of various ethnographies affirms that people do not need a category and term for religion in order to "have" a religion or to be religious in ways that accord with notions of religiosity entertained by anthropologists. And members of speech communities that employ the English word religion or some cognate do not usually require an explicit definition; using the term in ways that accord with the speech conventions of their fellows appears to suffice in many cases for maintaining discourse.

But what about research workers and teachers? If they are going to study religions, or teach courses that deal with religions, don't they need an explicit definition? An argument can certainly be made for the utility of a definition in those cases.

At the same time, however, we ought to recognize that a definition might mislead students. It could do so by being so narrow and didactive that it is egregiously ethnocentric and, in companionship with other definitions and word uses, miscasts other cultures into a Western mold, thereby misrepresenting them. Or it could do so by being so speciously inclusive that things that might otherwise be usefully distinguished are now mutually made "religion" and virtually everyone is rendered "religious."

An explicit definition might also prove unfortunate for some persons embarking on research. Acceptance of an explicit definition without much reflection would constitute *de facto* conformance to an established conceptual mold. Such conformance might blind researchers to valuable information, information beyond the purview of the established conceptualization, and inhibit the development of fresh perspectives.

The danger that an explicit definition might prematurely

channel and determine research and theorizing has prompted
some authors to counsel holding such a definition in abeyance,
at least until substantial groundwork is accomplished. That advice
may also be motivated in some cases by rhetorical considerations
relative to enhancing the likelihood that one's point of view will
be accepted. Consider the following three assertions:

> to define "religion," to say what it *is*, is not possible at the start
> of a presentation such as this [a long section on the sociology of
> religion within a still larger work]. Definition can be attempted,
> if at all, only at the conclusion of the study. (Weber 1963 [1922]:1).

> To obtain objectivity in the study of primitive religions what is
> required is to build up general conclusions from particular ones.
> One must not ask 'What is religion?' but what are the main features
> of, let us say, the religion of one Melanesian people; then one must
> seek to compare the religion of that people with the religions of
> several other Melanesian peoples who are nearest to the first in
> their cultures and social institutions; and then after a laborious
> comparative study of all Melanesian peoples, one may be able to
> say something general about Melanesian religions as a whole. One
> can only take the long road. There is no short cut. (Evans-Pritchard
> 1954:8-9)

> Leaving aside all conceptions of religion in general, let us consider
> the various religions in their concrete reality, and attempt to
> disengage that which they have in common; for religion cannot
> be defined except by the characteristics which are found wherever
> religion itself is found. (Durkheim 1965 [1912]:38).

Postponing a definition in these and similar cases is possible
because the authors are operating with tacit understandings until
explicit characterizations are presented. As Spiro (1966:90–91)
points out, ". . . when the term 'religion' is given no explicit ostensive definition, the observer, perforce, employs an implicit
one." This observation is of great importance for the perspective
championed in this work.

Weber, Evans-Pritchard, and Durkheim explicitly talk about
"religion," yet they maintain that it should be defined later in
the course of the research that concerns them rather than at the
beginning. Yet the respective research in each case has to do with
"religion."

The three authors cited are able to maintain their stand in
sanity and good conscience. They can do so because they correctly assume that their readers will have some general understanding of "religion," an understanding that they and their readers
more or less tacitly share. Where does that shared tacit understanding come from? From, I think, similar experiences that

Weber, Evans-Pritchard, Durkheim, and many of their readers
have had in Euro-American societies, from their common culturally-induced inclinations to regard "Judaism" and "Christianity" as religions, and from their common culturally-supported dispositions to deem those religions clear exemplars of what they
mean by "religion." (These are matters that I explore in more
detail elsewhere in this work, particularly in Chapter 6.)

Thus, for instance, in studying Melanesian religions the Western
anthropologist can heed Evans-Pritchard's counsel to refrain from
initially asking "What is religion?" The anthropologist already has
some idea of an answer to that question, based on an acquaintance with religions in Euro-American societies and in the anthropological and ancillary literatures. If this were not the case,
then what Evans-Pritchard says would be absurd. For how could
one possibly heed that author's advice to ask "what are the main
features of . . . the religion of one Melanesian people" without at
least a tacit understanding of what Evans-Pritchard probably means
by "religion"?

One can do as Evans-Pritchard bids by finding cultural analogues among one Melanesian population to what is conventionally recognized as constituting religion in Western societies and
in Western scholarly literatures. One can do the same, of course,
for a number of Melanesian societies and then compare those
societies with respect to their analogues to Western religiosity.
Whether or not this is the best way to procede is an open question.
But it is at least an intelligent way of acting. In any case, one
can rescue Evans-Pritchard from the charge of non-sense by
assuming an understanding of his tacit understandings.

Depending on tacit understandings, it must also be noted, can
be tactically advantageous in advancing one's own point of view
in certain styles of argument. Durkheim (1965), for example,
first describes various theories of religion that are rivals of his
own, and then immediately attempts to demolish them, one by
one. These theories pivot on various conceptualizations of religion, and they support certain definitions. To the extent that the
reader deems Durkheim's attacks on rival theories, conceptualizations, and definitions successful, s/he is softened up for the
acceptance of Durkheim's own theory and its attendant conceptualizations and definitions when they are eventually presented.

Durkheim's definition — "A religion is a unified system of
beliefs and practices relative to sacred things, that is to say, things
set apart and forbidden — beliefs and practices which unite into
one single moral community called a Church, all those who adhere

to them" (1965 [1912]:62, italics deleted) — is a "theoretical definition." That is, it is a definition that is offered as "a theoretically adequate characterization of the objects to which it is applied" (Copi 1961:105). As Copi (*ibid.*) notes, "To propose a theoretical definition is tantamount to proposing the acceptance of a *theory*." That, of course, is probably what Durkheim intends, after first weakening the reader's possible attachment to any of a number of alternative theories.

DIFFICULTIES IN FORMULATING A DEFINITION

In addition to its potential advantages as a rhetorical tactic, deferring a definition of religion may also signal the recognition of substantial difficulties in formulating a definition.

Anthropologists who have engaged in fieldwork in small-scale societies have often remarked on the difficulty of abstracting what they are prepared to recognize as "the religion" of the natives from larger social and cultural fields. Opinions and practices that text-books instruct us to label "religious" often overlap with opinions and practices that might be assigned on other grounds to other analytical domains.

If we decide to define religion narrowly, we may end by excluding from our analysis of local religion various matters that relate to native conceptions and experiences, a knowledge of which would add to our understandings. On the other hand, if we conceive of religion broadly and reach out to include a diversity of social and cultural factors in our portrait, we may well raise the problem, as someone once put it, of identifying the religious element in religion. Ethnographic mariners who want to steer a prudent course between this particular Scylla and Charybdis may be tempted to cut their motors and coast silently for as long as possible — to operate, that is, with tacit rather than explicit definitions until they feel secure.

There is a closely related problem that may further stimulate us to postpone a definition or even to operate entirely with a tacit one. I refer to difficulties encountered in attempting to juggle context-specific categories and purportedly universal ones.

Usages in natural languages often engage us with meanings that are context-related and that depend on communities of unexpressed understandings. Some anthropologists, however, hope to develop a "scientific language" — a presumptively "neutral" (non-ethnocentric) language the terms of which would retain semantic constancy when applied analytically across

cultural and sub-cultural boundaries and whose meanings would
depend only minimally (if at all) on unexpressed understandings. That, I suspect, is an aspiration that may be impossible to
achieve. It strikes me as especially chimerical when the procedure is to take a multivocal folk term such as religion and define
it anew — and monothetically — in the hope of transforming
it into a universal analytical term that can be successfully applied
transculturally.

Religion, of course, is a category term in the natural languages
that most anthropologists grow up speaking, and the usages made
of it and of associated terms such as "sacred" and "supernatural"
are complex, nuanced, and historically variable. Such terms are
heavily laden with associations in Western cultural traditions, and
attempting to convert them into cross-cultural instruments would
be difficult enough even when the anthropologist has a good
grasp of their social and semantic histories and complexities. But
when the anthropologist has a foggy understanding and superficial
appreciation of their careers and subtleties in his/her own cultural
traditions, the problem may well be exacerbated by the
anthropologist's lack of sophistication.

Electing a conceptualization of religion that is neither intellectually simplistic nor transculturally inappropriate is not a simple
matter. But if we suppose that there is indeed a dimension of
human life that can be described as "religious," and if we further
suppose — as most anthropologists seem to do — that there is
likely to be some worth in cross-cultural applications of the noun
most closely related to that adjective, then we must explore our
conceptual options.

THE PRACTICALITY OF HOLDING A DEFINITION IN ABEYANCE

One option is to hold an explicit definition in abeyance. In many
cases, indeed, we can successfully operate with tacit rather than
explicit understandings. Doing so is attractive in some ways.

By avoiding an explicit commitment to a definition — which
is what the failure to offer or endorse an explicit definition
amounts to — we retain a certain flexibility.

Explicit definitions are explicit heuristics: they guide or impel
us in certain directions. By doing so they tend to divert our
attention from information beyond the channels they cleave, and
so choke off possibilities. That can sometimes be something of
an advantage, since it facilitates focused and orderly attention to
one set of possibilities at a time. But it is only an advantage if

heuristics are evaluated and compared relative to situational applications. If heuristics are not deemed provisional, subjected to criticism, and compared to alternatives, they may well become stultifying conventions.

Flexibility is further retained by avoiding the specious sharpness that explicit definitions may sometimes impose. In grappling with the complex phenomena conventionally referred to by the term religion, much remains obscure or indistinct in the anthropologist's research. Given the difficulties and problematics associated with ethnographic research, a portrait that is soft in certain respects is inevitable. It can also, however, be serviceable and inviting.

Achieving an ethnography is sometimes regarded as a two-fold task of research followed by writing. But in point of fact, writing is itself a kind of research. In constructing an ethnography, the ethnographer usually writes about his/her understandings of native understandings in a language that the natives would not understand. In doing so, s/he must weigh words. Care with words is the burden of any conscientious writer. But for the really good ethnographer, it is a particularly heavy burden.

The ethnographer, in the course of fieldwork, has come to have some understanding and appreciation of concepts unmatched fully by any shared by the audience for whom the ethnography is written. The problem is how to be true to one's own understandings and appreciations in conveying them. This is not a matter of preserving "truth value" in "translation." It is a matter, rather, of attempting to overcome a lack of adequate context, vocabulary, and conceptualizations in an effort somehow to convey to readers what has hitherto been beyond their experiences and understandings. In a manner of speaking, it is an effort to render the transcendent less transcendent, to make it intelligible in a discourse to which it was formerly alien and unknown. This calls for creativity — artistry — in writing an ethnography.

In the creative work called for to cap productive fieldwork, commitments to precisely phrased monothetic definitions can prove to be hindrances. They impose limits, boundaries, that may seem to render the ethnographic account sharp. But that sharpness might be specious, for in attempting to capture the ethnographer's "inventions" of native culture the category boundaries imposed by explicit definitions may need to be blurred or transgressed. Wittgenstein allows that a photograph that is indistinct may sometimes be just what we need. To a certain extent, and especially where category boundaries are concerned, that might sometimes be the case for an ethnography as well.

A CASE FOR A DEFINITION

Spiro makes a strong case for a definition of religion. I will focus my remarks on what he says, both because I have been influenced by several of his points and because by doing so I can construct a more compact discussion than otherwise might be the case.

While "a definition cannot take the place of inquiry," Spiro (1966:90) writes, "in the absence of definitions there can be no inquiry — for it is the definition, either ostensive or nominal, which designates the phenomenon to be investigated." He allows that the investigator's definition may not be explicit: "Indeed," he says, "when the term 'religion' is given no explicit ostensive definition, the observer, perforce, employs an implicit one" (1966:90). But he clearly prefers an explicit definition.

The claim that a definition marks out a subject matter or field of study by designating what is to be investigated is a practical point in favor of definitions. I would add to it another consideration: Some of what passes for theoretical disagreements over religion pivots on, or sometimes reduces to, tacit disagreements about how to use the word religion and how to conceptualize the category. Making definitions explicit with respect to theorizing could contribute to exposing hitherto unexpressed assumptions and interests, assumptions and interests perhaps partially hidden even from those who act on them.

In any case, in advancing his argument in favor of an explicit definition, Spiro makes three points that I deem especially valuable. These have to do with (1) universalism, (2) intuitivity, and (3) controversy over what religion "really is."

(1) Universalism. Spiro suggests that definitions in anthropology need not aim for universality. He holds, in fact, that an "insistence on universality in the interests of a comparative social science is . . . an obstacle to the comparative method" (1966:86). It is such, he contends, because it leads to continuous alterations of definitions in light of newly encountered cases that may seem anomalous with respect to established definitions. Ultimately, moreover, in order to accomodate the diversity recognized, anthropologists committed to universal definitions are likely to construct definitions so vague or abstract as to be "all but useless" (1966:86). Further, such definitions appear to imply that certain

institutions (e.g., religion, kinship) are universal "rather than recognizing that universality is a creation of definition" (1966:87).

(2) Intuitivity. Inasmuch as religion, says Spiro, "is a term with historically rooted meanings, a definition must satisfy not only the criterion of cross-cultural applicability but also the criterion of intra-cultural intuitivity; at the least, it should not be counterintuitive" (1966:91). That is, the definition that we settle on ought to allow place to conventional cultural meanings already associated with the term — or, at a minimum, it ought not to contradict major established meanings. I would add that inasmuch as religion is a Western category, and inasmuch as anthropologists write largely for Western audiences, Spiro's advice has practical worth. Resonance with established meanings, when coupled with careful attention to discourse, can be expected to facilitate communication between anthropologist and audience.

(3) Controversy over what religion "really is." Fruitless controversy, Spiro suggests, can stem from opting for "real" definitions. "Real" definitions, as he characterizes them, "are conceived to be true statements about entities or things" (1966:86). Spiro regards essential definitions, definitions that "stipulate what the definer takes to be the 'essential nature' of some entity," as a "kind" of real definition (1966:86). He does not elaborate on the notion of essence. He argues, however, that essential definitions are "necessarily vague and almost always non-empirical" (he cites Durkheim's stipulation of the "sacred" as an example; he also remarks that "Most functional definitions of religion are essentially a subclass of real definitions . . . ") (1966:89). Vagueness (which, in my opinion, is ironic because of the efforts of some essentialists to be precise) and an inability to test essential definitions empirically, according to Spiro, render such definitions unsatisfactory and conduce to endless and unproductive debate about what religion "really is."

Spiro also maintains that most definitional controversies concerning religion are really "jurisdictional disputes over the phenomenon or range of phenomena which are considered to constitute legitimately the empirical referent of the term" (1966:87). Such definitional controversies are disagreements over "ostensive definitions." "To define a word ostensively," he states, "is to point to the object which that word designates" (1966:87). Controversy arises, he says, from disagreement respecting "the phenomena to which the word 'religion' *ought* to apply" (1966:87, italics in original).

Spiro nevertheless calls for "an ostensive or substantive

definition." Unless religion "is defined substantively," he avers (albeit he does not specifically define "substantively" or "substantive"), "it would be impossible to delineate its boundaries" (1966:90). "In sum," he declares, "any comparative study of religion requires, as an operation antecedent to inquiry, an ostensive or substantive definition that stipulates unambiguously those phenomenal variables which are designated by the term" (1966:91). Such a definition, he adds, will "at the same time" be a nominal definition because some of its designata are likely to strike other scholars as arbitrary. This will not remove the term religion from "the arena of definitional controversy," but by encouraging the formulation of empirically (cross-culturally) testable hypotheses, it should remove the term "from the context of fruitless controversy over what religion 'really is'" (1966:91).

I agree with Spiro, subject to certain considerations to be voiced later, about the instrumentality of definitions of religion for marking out a subject matter or field of study (although I suspect that I am rather more sanguine about implicit definitions than he). I also agree that such definitions ought not to be "counterintuitive." And I agree that we ought to avoid fruitless essentialist arguments about what religion "really is." But I diverge from Spiro's position as expressed in his 1966 essay in two ways: I prefer another vocabulary for talking about definitions; and I do not deem it either necessary or desireable to so arrange things as to "delineate . . . boundaries" for what the term religion will cover.

My second point of divergence, the matter of boundaries, is addressed in subsequent chapters (especially in Chapter 6, where an argument in favor of conceptualizing an *unbounded* category denominated "religion" is advanced at some length). Suffice it here to discuss the matter of vocabulary for talking about definitions.

Talking about Definitions

The vocabularies utilizied by Euro-American logicians, theologians, anthropologists, and others for talking about definitions are not carved in stone. They are, in fact, fairly variable and often somewhat vague in various particulars. Numbers of Western authors have long held that definitions help partition our cognized worlds. But they differ among themselves about how this is done or should be done, and their vocabularies reflect somewhat divergent orientations and senses of precision. Thus, for example,

Euro-American philosophers disagree to some extent about what they mean by, and the significance they assign to, "ostensive definitions" (Copi 1961:115–116).

It is an illusion to suppose that definitions can be utterly precise. As Popper and others have noted, definitions, if we take them too seriously, can involve us in infinite regress. In definitions as popularly conceived, one attempts to specify the meaning of some word or expression (technically, the *definiendum*) by other words or expressions (technically, the *definiens*). But various of what are popularly regarded as words given in the *definiens* are themselves likely to be ambiguous or vague. A quest for precision might induce the definer to define them as well. And the words used to define them might next be defined. If a halt isn't called, terms in each generation of a *definiens* will be converted into *definienda* to be defined in their turn, producing expanding definitional chains that go on forever and ever, amen! A neurotic fantasy perhaps, but, in any case, a situation that would clearly mark a non-productive investment of time and energy.

How might we avoid unproductive commitments to definitional tasks? First, by relaxing with respect to definitions. Any proffered definitions of categories such as religion, law, the state, kinship, and marriage are likely to be problematic in one way or another — though they may nevertheless be useful in their own limited ways. Second, by taking account of the fact that our conceptualizations and definitions depend on larger theoretical perspectives. The kinds of conceptions of definitions that we prefer or are persuaded to adopt themselves constitute theoretical commitments, all the more so if we claim that certain approaches to definitions serve us better than others.

In talking about definitions, I deem it useful to employ a term not found in Spiro's essay: "monothetic" (from the Greek, 'one capable of placing'). A monothetic definition, as I conceive it, stipulates a single feature or a set of conjunctive features that specifies what a category term basically means, for by so doing it specifies a set of necessary and sufficient features or conditions for identifying instances of the group of objects comprehended by the category. If any one stipulated feature or condition is missing with respect to some candidate for inclusion in the group, that candidate cannot be properly admitted.

Monothetic definitions, as I conceive them, are of three sorts: substantive, functional, and mixed. A substantive definition of religion tells us what religion fundamentally *is*, what it is composed of (for example, beliefs of a certain sort, or beliefs of a certain sort plus certain kinds of behaviors). A functional definition of religion states what religion *does*, what consequences it has, for individuals and/or culturally organized human social groups (for example, it expresses and facilitates coping with existential concerns, or it promotes social solidarity). Mixed definitions combine substantive and functional conceptualizations in various ways.

Substantive monothetic definitions imply commitment to an ancient and influential idea in Euro-American cultures: that a category is to be conceptualized and defined in terms of the features or properties shared by the members of the group comprehended by that category. Functionalist monothetic definitions imply basically the same commitment, although what is shared by the members is now couched in a language of consequences.

Commitment to the idea of a set of necessary and sufficient features or functions generally signals commitment to a more inclusive traditional perspective. As characterized by Lakoff, the larger framework avers that "reason is abstract and disembodied" and that "meaningful concepts and rationality are *transcendental*, in the sense that they transcend, or go beyond the physical limitations of any organism" (1987:xi). Modern efforts to vivify this perspective, moreover, often embrace assumptions to the effect that the symbols manipulated in rational thought get their meaning by corresponding with a world objectively construed, and that symbols arranged in correspondence with that objectively construed world are to be viewed as representations of reality (Lakoff 1987:xii).

Against that traditional perspective Lakoff opposes a perspective that he calls "experientialism." The latter view affirms that "Human reason is not an instantiation of transcendental reason; it grows out of the nature of the organism and all that contributes to its individual and collective experience: its genetic inheritance, the nature of the environment it lives in, the way it functions in that environment, the nature of its social functioning, and the like" (Lakoff 1987:xv).

The perspective that informs this work, as the reader probably suspects, is closer to experientialism than to objectivism.

In my way of conceptualizing and talking about definitions, all monothetic definitions, whether they be substantive, functional, or mixed, are essentialist definitions. I intend "essentialist" to be a broader term than "essential" as used by Spiro with reference to some "real definitions."

By attributing to phenomena certain properties or functions that presumably endure, and which those phenomena must share or manifest in order to be labeled properly by the term defined, the framer of a monothetic definition comes close to classical metaphysicians. Essence, classically, is conceived to be that which is necessary and enduring in some class of objects, and thus crucial for identifying individual members of the class.

I have taken some pains to establish "monothetic" and "essentialist" as part of my vocabulary for talking about religion for two reasons. First, monothetic (essentialist) definitions are legion (I discuss some examples in Chapters 3 and 4). Second, it is important to establish what I turn away from in favor of an approach that I deem more productive. I do not want to seem to imply that essentialist definitions are devoid of utility. They depend on their framers' culturally mediated experiences, and they often suggest, in one form or another, qualities deemed significant and special about what is called religion in their framers' cultures. Ultimately founded on cultural conventions, they guide recognition of analogues in other cultures. But I think that we can improve on them, particularly in light of the ethnographer's need for conceptual flexibility in transcultural research.

Ad Hoc Definitions

"Objects," the philosopher Karl Popper writes, "can be classified, and can become similar or dissimilar, only . . . by being related to needs and interests" (1962:47). In this view, the analytical discriminations and groupings that we make are neither fortuitous nor dictated by the natural order of things. They are shaped with reference to our interests and sense of problems and possibilities.

We need to make distinctions in the very course of inquiry, and attending to that need may give rise to conceptual and definitional novelties. These are never "entirely" new. They represent, rather, a re-working or modification of existing concepts and definitions (implicit or explicit) in the process of attempted problem-solving. I call them *ad hoc* in recognition of their fabrication with respect to some specific line of inquiry. In some cases they may be generalized later to other areas of interest. But I want to direct attention to their initial development with respect to a specific sense of problem.

Working out ad hoc conceptualizations and definitions can be decidedly useful in ethnography. That includes ethnographic writing as well as fieldwork (the former is a form of learning or research and ought not to be rigidly separated from the latter). The ethnographer seeks to describe and make use of native conceptions and distinctions, and, usually, to do so in a language unknown to the natives and for the benefit of a non-native audience. Comparison is always implicit in the ethnographic task, and the imaginative, supple, and skillfull ethnographer will search for analogies, develop metaphors, and creatively describe or define relative to native and disciplinary distinctions that s/he deems it important to communicate.

In that regard, Stanley Kurtz (Personal Communication) recommends

> something like what Louis Dumont does with India and the West. He attempts to understand India in terms of its thoroughgoing "holism" and "hierarchy," and he notes that what we intuitively call religion cannot usefully be sharply distinguished from "social structure" (i.e. caste) in the Indian case. Then India is contrasted with the West in terms of a distinction between Indian holism and hierarchy on the one hand, and Western individualism, and differentiated domains on the other. Thus, comparative analytic categories are developed which cross-cut our usual distinctions between religion and other domains, and which, in fact, help us to clarify the concommitants of Western distinctions between domains (e.g. domain distinction is related to our individualism).

Kurtz's point is well taken. Dumont, as Kurtz notes, has indeed developed "comparative analytic categories . . . which cross-cut our usual distinctions," and those categories, I might add, are unusually powerful and persuasive. But that does not rule out efforts to clarify and recommend conceptualizations of religion, kinship, law, marriage, the state, and other major categories that anthropologists might usefully share.

Dumont himself speaks of

> the need to preserve, at the level of major categories, a common language for the profession, an indispensable condition for an already badly eroded consensus. Kinship is, *pace* Schneider, a scientific category in the making! (1980: xxxiv)

We need, Dumont goes on to say, "a medium of our own conceptions that must be preserved if we do not wish to find tomorrow as many anthropologies as anthropologists" (1980:xxxv).

The development of cross-cutting categories, of course, requires other categories to cross-cut. Let us take a look at some of Dumont's contributions by way of coming to appreciate how, "at the level of major categories," a common professional language might actually facilitate the development of cogent and culture-referential analytical categories. I take the category "hierarchy," as Dumont (1980, 1986) presents it to us with respect to India.

Many North American speakers of English who voice the term "hierarchy" probably use it to mean, very broadly put, 'a graded or ranked series'. Roman Catholics and some others may particularly associate it with sacerdotal authority organized into superordinate and subordinate ranks, that is, "the hierarchy of the Church." (*Hiereus* in Greek means 'priest', and *archē* means, among other things, 'rule'.) But our popular acceptations of "hierarchy" reflect pallid (and, for India, somewhat misleading) conceptualizations when they are confronted by the complexity and profundity of the category developed by Dumont.

Dumont speaks of "our misunderstanding of hierarchy. Modern man" (i.e., the contemporary Euro-American), he claims, "is virtually incapable of fully recognizing it" (1980:xlvii). In order to describe it for India, he analyzes several distinctions relevant to understanding that civilization (e.g., distinctions between "status" and "power," "purity" and "impurity," and "the encompassing" and "the encompassed").

It would require too long a digression to describe these and Dumont's other conceptual discriminations here. The reader unfamiliar with his work can gain some appreciation of the distinctiveness of what he means by hierarchy by considering brief quotations from two of his books. In the Postface to the revised English edition of *Homo Hierarchicus* he states that hierarchy is "a relation" that can succinctly be called "the encompassing of the contrary" (1980:239) and "hierarchial opposition" is "the relation between encompassing and encompassed or between ensemble and element" (1980:243). And in the glossary to his *Essays on Individualism*, he characterizes hierarchy in these words:

> To be distinguished from power, or command: order resulting from the consideration of value. The elementary hierarchial relation (or hierarchial opposition) is that between a whole (or a set) and an element of that whole (or set) — or else that between two parts with reference to the whole. It can be analyzed into two contradictory aspects belonging to different levels: it is a distinction within an identity, *an encompassing of the contrary* . . . Hierarchy is thus bi-dimensional . . . (1986:279)

Now, in his classic *Homo Hierarchicus* Dumont uses the terms "religion" and "religious" freely. They are clearly important terms in the construction of his argument, but he does not offer explicit definitions of them. In discussing problems Indologists have had in conceptualizing the relationship between caste and profession, for example, he remarks that "Much of the difficulty disappears if one admits, with Hocart, that caste and profession are linked through the intermediary of religion, which is obvious in the case of the ritual specialists like the barber and the washerman" (1980:93). Elsewhere he offers the interesting observation that "in every case in which caste is taken [by Western scholars] as an extreme form of something which exists in the West, the religious aspect of the system is considered secondary" (1980:27). In these and in other passages, Dumont appears to assume that his readers' understanding of what is generally meant by "religion" and "religious" is adequate to the task of understanding what he writes.

Dumont thus joins Durkheim, Evans-Pritchard, Weber, and others who use the term religion — at least initially — without explicitly defining it. Dumont invests his analytical energies in developing, and explicitly describing, distinct conceptualizations of "hierarchy" and certain other categories. His failure to devote equal attention to religion, coupled with the fact that his invocation of it is important in the specification of what he means by "hierarchy," suggests to me that Dumont probably regards religion as one of those major categories that anthropologists presumeably share.

Some Concluding Considerations

In many cases, to summarize some of what was said earlier, implicit conceptualizations of religion suffice, and there is no pressing need for an explicit statement of what we mean by religion. In certain respects, indeed, there are genuine advantages to not offering an explicit definition. Implicit conceptualizations and definitions, of course, cannot immediately be rejected in substance. The potential critic must first raise the question, and receive some answer or figure out as best s/he can, "What is meant by religion here?"

But over and beyond that point, tacit conceptualizations protect us from prematurely narrowing or widening the conceptual field. If we define religion explicitly by saying that it is, essentially, this or that — "belief in spiritual beings," for instance —, then we focus on beliefs of a certain kind, and by so doing we possibly exclude from direct consideration other beliefs, and much else, that might otherwise be considered productively under the rubric of religion. On the other hand, an explicit definition, particularly of the functionalist sort, might prematurely so widen the field that the rubric religion is stretched beyond useful instrumental shape.

It sometimes happens, however, that it is worth the effort to grapple with our conceptualizations and offer explicit definitions. *Whether or not we need an explicit definition is a situational matter.* It depends on who "we" are, what our needs may be, and strategic and tactical considerations that relate to serving those needs. Penner (1989:7) maintains that, "Given the ambiguities and various uses of the term [religion], it is imperative that we clarify what we mean by the word." Yet while I am sympathetic to his point, I judge his statement to be too strong. Nothing about religion, least of all defining it essentially (as he does, 1989: 7), strikes me as imperative.

It can be useful for scholars, particularly those who study religion transculturally, to clarify what they understand by religion. But usefulness is relative to recognized research needs and the difficult art of communicating with an audience. Further, I do not think that even when we posit need for an explicit definition it suffices merely to formulate such a definition. We also ought to give some indication of how that definition can be used — and used productively.

Spiro states a major reason for defining religion: it marks out a field of study and facilitates inquiry. There is an additional reason: some of our disagreements over theory may pivot on, or perhaps reduce to, variant definitional commitments. Some authors, moreover, view definitions of religion as veritable theories in miniature about religion (e.g., Pals 1987:272, Dawson 1990:42). Definitions, in any case, relate to and partially express larger perspectives. For just as meanings are always meanings within some context, so definitions are always definitions within some encompassing perspective. Those who subscribe to one perspective or another, however, may not be aware of some of the components that enter into it.

Forcing ourselves to conceptualize religion explicitly may help bring into the foreground background assumptions and interests. This is so whether we opt for traditional monothetic definitions or, as I advocate, break with them and avoid essentialist definitional commitments in favor of a family resemblance approach to the category religion. In either case, it will profit us to ask ourselves why we are interested in religion? What is it about religion, as we conceive it, that we especially wish to probe? Why? Those are worthwhile questions, questions not about religion but about us.

There is another question that ought to be raised: Does our way of conceptualizing religion suggest an adequate theory about the structures and uses of categories? That large question, as well as the others posed, will be considered in the chapters that follow.

CHAPTER THREE

MONOTHETIC DEFINITIONS

So just as the beauty of language is achieved by a contrast of opposites . . . the beauty of the course of the world is built up by a kind of rhetoric, not of words but of things, which employs the contrast of opposites.
— Alexander of Hales, *Summa Theologica* 2.4.2.2.1.1.3. 452

A monothetic definition, it may be recalled, stipulates one or more distinguishing features that must be present if something is to be recognized as pertaining to the class conceptualized and bounded by the definition. The features are held to be both necessary and sufficient for recognition, and a class so conceptualized is called monothetic because its "defining set of features is unique" (Sokal and Sneath 1963:13).

At first glance, monothetic definitions may seem attractive. Ideally, they ought to specify what is distinctive of the phenomena defined, what separates them out from all other phenomena. If in fact they did so successfully — I shall argue that they do not —, they would in effect "digitize" the phenomenal world in each definitional instance. Each monothetic definition would create (or "affirm," some might say in some cases) two contrasting groups, one composed of phenomena included by the definition, the other composed of all other phenomena excluded by the definition. Such a "contrast of opposites," were it sustainable, would work to resolve or obviate problems of ambiguity and vagueness.

Ambiguity stems from the fact that in common usage words often have more than one meaning. While verbal and non-verbal contexts usually suggest which of two or more senses is applicable, sometimes there is doubt. Some persons, indeed, may prefer to settle the matter of which meaning is intended before employing a term in certain applications.

Vagueness has to do with uncertainty about what a word covers in actual usage. Someone may use a term in a way that strikes us as vague: we are not clear about what is included and excluded. Or while we ourselves may apply a term in various situations without any misgivings, we may occasionally encounter other situations that render us uncertain about the term's suitability, perhaps even as metaphor. We may seek clarification in either case. In Euro-American societies there is a good chance that efforts at clarification will take the culturally established route of devising, or accepting on someone's authority, monothetic definitions.

Yet monothetic definitions actually often fail to do away with either ambiguity or vagueness. In attempting to specify which of more than one sense of a word applies, the ensemble of words used in the definition may itself engender new ambiguities and suggest a need for further clarification. And while a monothetic definition may be devised as a remedy for, or a prophylactic against, vagueness — vagueness is probably more of a goad to definition-making than ambiguity —, it may actually facilitate the propagation of new examples of vagueness. It can do so, ironically enough, by appearing to establish boundaries. For boundaries make possible so-called "borderline" cases. Borderline cases, by appearing to transgress or threaten the very boundaries that create them, are themselves veritable specters of vagueness for those who would tidy-up language and the world with monothetic devices.

Monothetic definitions can nevertheless be useful even if we do not accept them. They usually indicate what their formulators and endorsers regard as significant about some facet of the phenomenal world as they conceive it, and that can be useful to know. We can appreciate this aspect of monothetic definitions, as well as come to discern their deficiencies, by critically examining a number of monothetic definitions of religion.

Tylor's "Minimum Definition"

Edward Burnett Tylor's famous "minimum definition" of religion, "the belief in Spiritual Beings" (1970 [1871]:8), is both useful and problematic.

It is useful because it is exemplary. It renders explicit and succinct, and clearly foregrounds, key elements in the conceptualizations of many 19th and 20th century Euro-Americans. Religion as popularly conceived is above all a matter of belief, and particularly belief in beings termed "spiritual" or "supernatural." Tylor's definition, moreover, is more or less replicated by, or it otherwise resonates with, numbers of other substantive monothetic definitions offered by various scholars (see, for example, definitions by Horton [1960], Goody [1961], Spiro [1966], and Wallace [1966], quoted in Chapter 4).

Not only does Tylor's definition emphasize belief of a special sort as the essence of religion, but the larger theorizing to which his definition pertains is, as Preus (1987:133) puts it, "relentlessly focused" on religion's "cognitive element . . . to the neglect of the entire social and functional side [of religiosity] that Comte's work had opened up." Tylor does what Talal Asad charges Clifford Geertz with doing: he formulates "a universal, a-historical definition" (Asad 1983:238), a definition that makes religion "essentially a matter of meanings linked to ideas of general order" (Asad 1983:245).

But while Tylor emphasizes the cognitive aspects of religion, his concern with belief and rationality does not *necessarily* rule out interest in other facets of religion. "To a person brought up in the Quaker tradition," Paul Radin (1970:xi) suggests of Tylor, "reason and a mystical experience could be easily combined." Tylor himself declares that "Even in the life of the rudest savage, religious belief is associated with intense emotion, with awful reverence, with agonizing terror, with rapt ecstasy when sense and thought utterly transcend the common level of daily life." This may be even more the case, he opines, "in faiths where not only does the believer experience such enthusiasm, but where his utmost feelings of love and hope, of justice and mercy, of fortitude and tenderness and self-sacrificing devotion, of unutterable misery and dazzling happiness, twine and clasp round the fabric of religion" (1970:445). Yet in his own research and theorizing, "the intellectual rather than the emotional side of religion has . . . been kept in view" (1970:444–445). And numbers of other anthropologists have followed in his footsteps.

Tylor's footsteps, however, provide unsure purchase for traversing religion's undulating terrain. Let us look again at "belief" and "spiritual beings."

Many of Tylor's readers are likely to begin his book while entertaining a notion to the effect that "spiritual beings" are essentially "immaterial" or "incorporeal." If a spiritual/material dualism is what they bring with them from their 19th and 20th century Euro-American cultural backgrounds, they may take some of what Tylor says as confirming the idea that the spiritual is opposed to the material. Tylor writes, for example, of "the deep-lying doctrine of Spiritual Beings, which embodies the very essence of Spiritualistic as opposed to Materialistic philosophy" (1970:9). And he avers that "The divisions which have separated the great religions of the world into intolerant and hostile sects are for the most part superficial in comparison with the deepest of all religious schisms, that which divides Animism [the doctrine of spiritual beings] from Materialism" (1970:86).

Yet Tylor indicates that both "souls" and "other spiritual beings" are sometimes conceptualized as immaterial/incorporeal and sometimes as having a "vaporous materiality" or being "ethereal-material" (1970:41). The former conceptualization, he supposes, appears to have developed "within systematic schools of civilized philosophy" whereas the latter is more likely to be found "Among rude races" (1970:41). Tylor indicates, moreover, that there was disagreement about the materiality or immateriality of souls and other spiritual beings in Graco-Roman and early Christian thought. Epicurus, he relates, is credited with the assertion that "they who say the soul is incorporeal talk folly, for it could neither do nor suffer anything were it such" (1970:xxx). And the Christian writers Tertullian and Origen, he remarks, supposed angels and demons to be composed of "thin yet not immaterial substance" (1970:284).

In Tylor's account, in short, "spiritual beings" do not consti-tute a homogeneous class based on substance. They pertain to the same category more because of function than because of sub-stance. Even so, *the category spiritual beings is analogically constituted.* Spiritual beings have the function of animating, yet there are notable differences among them with respect to that function. Souls animate human bodies (and, by conceptual extension, other bodies). But spiritual beings such as Gods, viewed by Tylor as "personified causes" (1970:194), animate nature. The latter, on Tylor's account of human intellectual developments, are concep-tualized analogically to the former.

Animism, Tylor tells us, "divides into two great dogmas, form-ing parts of one consistent doctrine: first, concerning souls of individual creatures . . . ; second, concerning other spirits, upward to the rank of powerful deities" (1970:10). Conceptions of the second sort of spirits, Tylor speculates, developed out of primi-tive conceptions of the human soul as "an ethereal surviving being:"

> It seems as though the conception of a human soul, when once attained to by man, served as a type or model on which he framed not only his ideas of other souls of lower grade, but also his ideas of spiritual beings in general, from the tiniest elf that sports in the long grass up to the heavenly Creator and Ruler of the world, the Great Spirit. (1871:110)

Tylor's "minimum definition" appears at first glance to be a straight-forward, substantive monothetic definition. But when we unpack his conception of the crucial component "spiritual beings," those of us who may have supposed that such beings are immaterial discover unexpected complexity. All spiritual beings are not iso-substantive or iso-functional. Rather, they are analogically related. The category "spiritual beings," on a close reading of Tylor, is not based on simple essentialist digitizing. To apply it as if it were would be to ignore interesting subtleties in Tylor's conceptualization of animism.

It might almost seem that it would be a relief to turn now from "spiritual beings" in Tylor's definition to "belief." After all, though many of us don't make spiritual beings a daily topic of conversation, we do make frequent use of the word belief. It is a familiar and, we might suppose, unproblematic friend. But that happy supposition begins to dissolve when we look more closely at belief.

Although the expressions "believe that" and "believe in" are freely used by speakers of English, philosophers continue to argue about how to conceptualize belief. They disagree, for instance, about whether belief should be deemed a mental state, act, or event, or a disposition to act or feel in certain ways under certain conditions, or perhaps something else. And they raise questions about the relation of belief to knowledge, the status of so-called unconscious beliefs, and various other issues.

Many anthropologists employ the term belief with apparent abandon. A small number, however, wrestle explicitly with problems attendant on using that word. Among those who do, Rodney Needham is the most radical of any whom I have read. Needham argues that

> there are in fact conditions which can be regarded as normal and as specific to mankind. Gauged against these standards, the notion of a state or capacity of belief stands out as a quite idiocratic concept. It is not the recognition of a bodily phenomenon, it does not discriminate a distinct mode of consciousness, it has no logical claim to inclusion in a universal psychological vocabulary, and it is not a necessary institution for the conduct of social life. Belief does not constitute a natural resemblance among men. (1972:151)

He concludes that "Anything that we might please to say, and which in common speech is usually hung on to the handy peg of 'belief', will be better said by recourse to some other word; and if we are clear about what we want to say, we shall find that it can be said clearly only by another word" (1972:229).

Large numbers of anthropologists, insofar as I am aware, have not embraced Needham's position, or perhaps even read his book. Some who did read it seemed to have difficulty in following it. Indeed, none of the seven or eight published reviews that I have read, my own included (Saler 1974), now impress me as having done justice to Needham's complex argument. I do not want to re-open debate about that argument here, however. Readers interested in pursuing the subject of belief might start with an overview afforded by the philosopher H.H. Price (1969b) and then go on to read Needham's *Belief, Language, and Experience.* Suffice it for my purposes to say that debate over the status of belief ought to prove troubling for the easy acceptance of Tylor's minimum definition of religion — and, for that matter, any other definition that makes belief essential to religion and does not provide a cogent account of the significance of "belief" beyond particular cultural and linguistic conventions respecting its use.

Finally, a problem with Tylor's definition that he himself was aware of is its narrowness. Whatever different students of religion may variously deem religion to be, many would probably agree that it is complex. There are social and emotional aspects to it as well as intellectual ones, for example. And the experiential dimension of religiosity may be as important as the philosophical, or it may perhaps even overshadow it in some respects.

As noted earlier, Tylor admits that he says little about "the religion of vision and passion" (1970:445). The reason he gives for slighting what he himself regards as an important aspect of religion is this:

> Scientific progress is at times most furthered by working along a distinct intellectual line, without being tempted to diverge from the main object to what lies beyond, in however intimate connexion . . . My task has been here not to discuss Religion in all its bearings, but to portray in outline the great doctrine of Animism, as found in what I conceive to be its earliest stages among the lower races of mankind, and to show its transmission along the lines of religious thought. (1970:445).

Tylor's "minimum definition," one might conclude, is actually a definition of animism rather than of a more complex aggregate of phenomena termed religion. Tylor, of course, holds that "early" animistic thought is transformed and incorporated into what he supposes to be "higher religions," and so remains essential to religion.

Taken as a definition of animism, and putting aside any trepidation respecting "belief" (a can of worms that many anthropologists do not seem to recognize as a can of worms!), Tylor's definition facilitates exploring his larger theoretical framework. Although Tylor applies the category label "spiritual beings" both to somewhat different "soul" concepts — in human history, he remarks, the "doctrine of souls" has "assumed" "various phases" (1970:83) — and to variously conceived "other spirits," the category is not a jumble. It is a *manageable category* even if all conceptualized souls and other spirits do not share the same set of distinguishing features, a matter that I return to in Chapters 5 and 6.

Geertz: Religion as a Cultural System

In an essay much admired among anthropologists and other students of religion, Clifford Geertz characterizes religion as

(1) a system of symbols which acts to (2) establish powerful, pervasive, and long-lasting moods and motivations in men by (3) formulating conceptions of a general order of existence and (4) clothing these conceptions with such an aura of factuality that (5) the moods and motivations seem uniquely realistic. (1966:4)

Marvin Harris (1975:546) maintains that Geertz's definition is so broad that it includes "the entire ideological sector of cultural systems. . . ." Harris adds that while he himself does not object to the inclusion of capitalist or communist ideologies under the rubric "religion," along with ceremonies such as stockholders' meetings and May Day parades, he does object to the extension of the term to science. "Unlike religious beliefs," he writes, " . . . scientific beliefs are held only provisionally and are or ought to be deliberately and perpetually the subject of an unremitting attempt by those who hold them to prove themselves wrong" (1975:547).

But while a case for Harris's supposition — that if we accept Geertz's definition we would be obliged to extend it to science — might be built were we to isolate the few lines of the proffered characterization, it is clearly otherwise when we examine them within the context of the essay in which they appear. Most of the essay is an explication — Geertz describes it as "an extended unpacking" (1966:4) — of the definition, and a "religious perspective" is explicitly distinguished from what Geertz terms "common-sensical," "scientific," and "aesthetic" perspectives.

Common sense, in Geertz's view, is a mode of "seeing" that accepts objects and processes as being what they seem to be, and that encompasses a wish to master the world for one's own purposes or, if that proves impossible, to achieve adjustment to it (1966:26). In the scientific perspective, the common-sensical "givenness" of the world disappears, and the pragmatic motive, Geertz maintains, is suspended in favor of "disinterested observation" and efforts to analyze the world by utilizing formal concepts (1966:27). The aesthetic perspective also suspends the "naive realism" and "pragmatism" of common sense. But unlike the scientific perspective's concern with raising questions about the credentials of everyday experience, it ignores that experience, Geertz avers, and dwells eagerly upon appearances; it is absorbed "in things, as we say, 'in themselves'" (1966:27).

The religious perspective, Geertz declares, differs from all of these. Unlike common sense, it reaches out beyond the realities of everyday life, and its "defining concern" is with the acceptance of wider realities, with faith in them, rather than with acting upon them (1966:27). Like the scientific perspective, it, too, questions the realities of everyday life. It does so, however, not out of institutionalized skepticism but because of what it considers to be non-hypothetical truths that go beyond everyday realities (1966:27). And unlike the aesthetic perspective, it does not seek to effect disengagement from the question of factuality in favor of deliberately creating "an air of semblance and illusion." Rather, it is profoundly concerned with fact, and it endeavors to fashion an aura of thoroughgoing actuality. "It is this sense of the 'really real'," Geertz writes, "upon which the religious perspective rests and which the symbolic activities of religion as a cultural system are devoted to producing, intensifying, and so far as possible, rendering inviolable by the discordant revelations of secular experience" (1966:28).

Geertz's mixed definition emphasizes functions, as does his explication of that definition. Religion, described substantively as "a system of symbols," is characterized largely with respect to what that system "acts" to do. But while numbers of functionalist definitions simplistically characterize religion in terms of what *it* is held to "do" for the individual or for society, Geertz begins to transcend many such efforts in the complexity and subtlety of his vision. He attempts to sketch what *human beings*, threatened by the realization of their own analytical, emotional, and moral limits, might nevertheless *do for themselves* through the modality of religious symbols. But he does not sustain that perspective consistently. As Asad (1983: 241) notes, "Occasionally, in his essay, it is people who do things with symbols; more often it is symbols that do things to people."

Conceiving of religion as a cultural system, Geertz includes it within his overall conceptualization of culture: "an historically transmitted pattern of meanings embedded in symbols, a system of inherited conceptions expressed in symbolic form by means of which men communicate, perpetuate, and develop their knowledge about and attitudes toward life" (1966:3). Sacred symbols, he maintains, function to synthesize a people's ethos — the tone, character, and quality of their life, its moral and aesthetic style and mood — and their world-view — the picture they have of the way things in sheer actuality are, their most comprehensive ideas of order . . . Religious symbols formulate a basic congruence between a particular style of life and a specific (if, most often, implicit) metaphysics, and in so doing sustain each other with the borrowed authority of the other. (1966:3–4)

Geertz's approach to religion (and much else), it is worth pointing out, is founded on a crucial assumption about human beings: that human beings not only spin webs of meaning and act within or against their contexts, but that human beings *need* to create meanings. This prepossessing assumption amounts to a notion about human nature that subserves an explanatory function in suggesting why human beings create religion and other cultural systems. Though Geertz recommends "interpretation" and appears to be more than dubious about "explanation," there is an explanatory thread — a conviction about human beings — that runs through (and connects) many of his works.

Talal Asad: A Critical Evaluation of Geertz's Text

Geertz's 1966 essay, Talal Asad writes, "is perhaps the most influential, certainly the most accomplished, anthropological definition of religion to have appeared in the last two decades" (1983:237). A critical evaluation of it might therefore throw into relief biases that have colored a major contemporary anthropological approach to religion — and that are perhaps shared by numbers of other anthropologists.

In attempting a critical evaluation, Asad declares, he is not so much concerned with judging the soundness of specific points as "in trying to trace how and why historically specific forms of 'religion' have come to be presented, mistakenly, as having a paradigmatic status" (1983:237). Geertz's definition, Asad suggests, has been influential in promoting and strengthening "what appears to anthropologists today to be self-evident, namely that 'religion' is essentially a matter of meanings linked to ideas of general order (expressed in either or both rite and doctrine) and that it has universal functions" (1983:245). This view, Asad maintains, "has a specific Christian history. From being a concrete set of rules attached to specific processes of power and knowledge, 'religion' has come to be abstracted and universalised" (1983:245).

Asad trys in different ways to support his claim that universalist anthropological definitions of religion, as exemplified by Geertz's definition, are rooted in "Christian" historical processes. He asserts, for example, that "the earliest systematic attempts at producing a universal definition of religion" were made in seventeenth century Europe, and he refers specifically (albeit briefly) to contributions made by the celebrated deist, Edward, Lord Herbert of Cherbury (1983:244–245). Subsequent developments, Asad suggests, provided further impetus to the formulation of universalist definitions. The historical component of his essay, however, is neither detailed nor systematic.

Asad's argument is developed for the most part through an analysis of elements in Geertz's overview, followed by efforts to connect them to what Asad identifies as "Christian" points of view. Thus, for example, he avers that "Geertz's treatment of religious belief, which lies at the core of his conception of religion, is a modern, privatised Christian one because and to the extent that it emphasises the priority of belief as a state of mind" (1983:247).

Asad quotes Geertz's statement that "the basic axiom underlying . . . 'the religious perspective' is everywhere the same: he who would know must first believe." Although it might have strengthened his argument, Asad does not note the similarity of that assertion to one made by Augustine: "Understanding is the reward of faith. Therefore seek not to understand that thou mayest believe, but believe that thou mayest understand." ("No Greek philosopher," Étienne Gilson [1938:17] opines, "could ever have dreamt of making religious faith in some revealed truth the obligatory starting point of rational knowledge.") Rather, Asad argues that the qualities of belief differ with context. He maintains that "the form and texture and function" of medieval Christian "belief" differ from those aspects of "belief" in contemporary Western society, and he concludes that what Geertz terms "the basic axiom" underlying the religious perspective "is *not* everywhere the same" (1983:248). In discussing "belief," I might add, Asad adverts to Needham 1972 in an endnote (1983:256, n. 29), but he does not engage that radical work on "belief" in the body of his text.

Now, although I would argue the case differently, I agree with Asad on some points.

I agree, for instance, that Geertz's 1966 definitional effort is within what I prefer to call a Western (rather than specifically "Christian") tradition (see Chapters 6 and 7). I would add, however, that its cultural character, accurately described by Asad as universalist in orientation and ambition, is not surprising. Geertz, after all, was a Western intellectual of 1966 writing largely for an audience of his fellow Western intellectuals. Today numbers of anthropologists and others are more aware of, and more interested in, non-universalist, non-essentialist conceptual strategies than was the case then (see Chapters 4, 5, and 7 for discussions of "the problem of universals").

I also agree with Asad that the "form and texture and function" of "belief" is very likely to differ in different socio-historical settings. Asad broadly contrasts religious belief in medieval Western Europe to religious belief in contemporary Western Europe, and numbers of other authors make parallel contrasts for that area of the world (e.g., MacIntyre 1970:72–77) or for elsewhere. In a book that deals with religious developments in Indonesia and Morocco, for example, Geertz himself does so. He deftly suggests that in both countries an important shift from what once obtained to what is now the case is intelligible in terms of the difference "between being held by religious convictions and holding them" (1968:61).

Granting that there are likely to be significant differences in the qualities and consequences of belief, we might then question, as does Asad, the putative universality of Geertz's axiom respecting the "religious perspective." This might lead us either to reject Geertz's axiom as the universal distinguishing feature of religion or, were we to accept it as such, to question the universality of religion.

In addition to the above matters, Asad voices thoughtful questions about the adequacy of Geertz's conceptualizations of symbols. And he takes an analytically sophisticated and important position on faith: "for the anthropologist to explain 'faith'," Asad writes, "must be primarily a matter of describing a dependence on authoritative practices and discourses, and not of intuiting a mental state lying beyond them said to be caused by ritual" (1983:249).

At the same time that I endorse certain of Asad's points, I find myself out of sympathy with others. Most significantly with respect to the subject matter of this book, while I support Asad's claim that Geertz's definition derives from traditions that Asad calls "Christian" and that I more broadly term "Western," Asad and I differ on what to do about it. Thus, although Asad and I are critical of efforts to formulate and employ purportedly universal definitions of religion, we differ on the alternatives that we recommend.

Asad eschews universal-essentialist conceptions of religion in favor both of asking "how does power create religion" and of "trying to explore concrete sets of historical relations and processes" (1983:252). I also eschew universal-essentialist conceptions of religion, and I certainly favor exploring historical relations and processes. But I also recommend that we take certain culture-parochial phenomena and explicitly treat them as the clearest exemplars of an unbounded category denominated religion. I elaborate on my preferences in Chapter 6. Here I want to take a closer look at Asad's position.

Asad criticizes Geertz for failing to treat the "connection" between religious theory and practice as fundamentally one of power,

> of disciplines *creating* religion, interpreting true meanings, forbidding certain utterances and practices and authorising others. Hence the questions that Geertz does not ask: how does religious discourse actually define religion? What are the historical conditions in which it can act effectively as a demand for the imitation, or the prohibition, or the authentication of truthful utterances and practices? How does power create religion? (1983:246)

In his emphasis on meaning, Asad asserts, Geertz treats religious symbols as if they were *sui generis* (1983:250). Geertz, that is, does not explicitly devote attention to how different religious symbols may come to be socially shared and invested with authority. Asad protests such an approach. He advises that, "Instead of approaching religion with questions about the social meaning of doctrines and practices, or even about the psychological effects of symbols and rituals, let us begin by asking what are the historical conditions (movements, classes, institutions, ideologies) necessary for the existence of particular religious practices and discourses. In other words, let us ask: how does power create religion?" (1983:252).

Asad maintains that Geertz's definition derives its initial plausibility from its resonance with privatized forms of religion in our society where, for the most part, power and knowledge are no longer generated in significant degree by religious institutions. Geertz, he charges, sees the connection between religious theory and practice as essentially cognitive, and thus "as a means of *identifying* religion from a neutral place" (1983:246) This strikes him as "a modest view of religion," a "product of Geertz's recurrent desire to define religion in universal terms" (*ibid.*).

Universal definitions of religion, Asad contends, are likely to hinder the systematic investigation of what we should be study-ing, namely, "the ways in which, in each society, social disciplines produce and authorise knowledge, the ways in which selves are required to respond to those knowledges, the ways in which knowledges are accumulated and distributed" (1983:252). Uni-versal definitions are ill-equipped to assist such studies, he suggests, because they are concerned with identifying essences rather than exploring "concrete sets of historical relations and processes" (1983:252).

Ironically enough, considering Asad's criticisms of Geertz, Asad and Geertz parallel each other in a certain way with respect to key terms. Asad's repetitive use of the word "power," that is, is just as rooted in Western conceptualizations as is Geertz's use of "religion." While the proximate literature to which it pertains is that of poststructuralism, it has other antecedents in Western traditions as well.

Asad's general argument and particular use of the term "power" strike me as owing much to Michel Foucault (1980, etc.), al-though no reference to any of Foucault's works appears in his bibliography. The sorts of questions that Asad deems important — "how," for example, "does religious discourse actually define religion? . . . How does power create religion?" — are reminis-cent of the kinds of questions that Foucault raises, questions con-nected to a perspective that nurtures extended uses of the term "discourse" (Foucault 1972 [1969], Dreyfus and Rabinow 1983, Bové 1990). These are questions that mark a turning away from the focus on meaning emphasized in the kind of interpretivist perspective that Geertz had been so influential in shaping and diffusing within anthropology some years ago. Asad's "evaluation," as he calls it, of Geertz's essay is an attempt both to account for Geertz's conceptualization of religion and to champion a set of questions that would shift emphasis away from the questions that Geertz favored in 1966.

In any case, "power" is inadequately explicated in Asad's essay. While Asad privileges "power" as a high order abstraction, he does not say enough about what he means by it to inform his readers.

Although the word "power" may have decidedly negative connotations for some readers — Bové (1990:58) suggests inhibition, repression, and domination — , for many poststruc-turalists it has other values as well (Foucault uses it in several senses). As Bové puts it,

it must always be seen as "a making possible," as an opening up
of fields in which certain kinds of action and production are brought
about. As power disperses itself, it opens up specific fields of
possibility; it constitutes entire domains of action, knowledge, and
social being by shaping the institutions and disciplines in which,
for the most part, we largely make ourselves . . . What Foucault means
when he says that power acts upon actions is precisely that it regulates
our forming ourselves. (1990:58)

This conceptualization of "power" relates to poststructuralist
usages of "discourse." The latter is an organizing concept, one
that is conceptualized as implicating power relationships and as
functioning to organize and maintain various power structures.
A discourse generates meaningful questions and legitimates certain
sorts of answers to those questions. According to various poststruc-
turalists/postmodernists, empowered discourses constitute and
authorize truths. Statements within a discourse are judged true
or not relative to the structure and logic of that discourse.

The complexity and (if I may put it this way) the power of
the above described concept of power might be better appreciated by extensive consideration of other concepts such as
"discourse" and "genealogy" in poststructuralist writings. In any
case, it is a Western intellectual resource on which Asad draws,
as developed in the works of Nietzsche, Foucault, and others.

The irony of Asad's criticism of Geertz's "Christian" (Western)
anchorage aside, a specific criticism of Asad's position can begin
with a slight elaboration on a simple point made in Chapter 2:
that we are unlikely to investigate anything in efficient fashion
unless we have some idea of what we are investigating.

We are unlikely, for example, to explore "concrete sets of
historical relations and processes" with much sophistication unless
we are aware of, and can reflect critically on, the criteria that
we employ in recognizing objects or events by assigning them
to meaningful contexts and subsuming them under meaningful
categories. If we are to trace how "power realities" may have
stimulated the development of certain "meanings" while inhib-
iting the florescence of others, as Asad advises, we can do so only
to the extent that our conceptualizations enable us to identify
and intellectually assimilate both "power realities" and other sorts
of "meanings." And if we are to ask in any seriousness "how does
religious discourse actually define religion?" (Asad 1983:246), we
must have some idea of facilitating uses of "discourse" and
"religious." We can turn to Foucault to learn about the former.
But where would Asad have us go for the latter?

When we come upon matters that we determine to probe, we

do so initially through the mediation of our context-situated "privatized" categories, just as we initially conceptualize problems through their instrumentality. Those categories are categories framed by a discourse, a discourse that constitutes different objects of knowledge. We do not begin, in short, with "concrete sets of historical relations and processes," but with perspectives and mediating categories — and, if we are lucky, our perspectives are flexible and adaptive enough to warrant describing them as "a modest view."

I do not understand how Asad conceptualizes the historical relations and processes to which he seems to attach so much importance. He is vague about their ontological status. In some poststructuralist perspectives, in any case, allowance is made for what might be called the "real." It consists of ('is constitued by') objects/events that are described in statements that can be adjudged true or false. But, it must immediately be pointed out, truth and falsehood are held to be relative to the authority of empowered discourses (Bové 1990:59). From that point of view, historical relations and processes are not concrete things that we bump into (or that themselves go bump in the night). Account of them, that is, is created rather than taken.

Geertz opines that "The anthropological study of religion is . . . a two-stage operation: first, an analysis of the system of meanings embodied in the symbols which make up the religion proper, and, second, the relating of these systems to social-structural and psychological processes" (1966:42). Asad terms this "mistaken" (1983:250). "If religious symbols," he writes, "are understood, on the analogy with words, as vehicles for meaning,"

> can such meanings be established independently of the form of life in which they are used? If religious symbols are to be taken as the elements of a sacred text, can we know what they mean without regard to the social disciplines by which their correct reading is secured? If religious symbols are to be thought of as the patterns by which experience is organised, can we say much about that experience without considering how it comes to be formed? (1983:251)

Asad declares that "The two stages which Geertz proposes are, I would suggest, one" (1983:251).

I very much agree with the theoretical import of Asad's remark respecting the importance of a "form of life" (a construct that I associate with Wittgenstein), but I think that his criticism of Geertz on this point is unfair. Geertz, in recommending "two stages," is attempting to call attention to the need for the analysis of systems of meaning. Much social anthropological research on religion up to the time that he presented his essay, he contends, tended to neglect symbolic analysis in favor of what he calls "the second stage." Hence, in his opinion, there is need to highlight the importance of symbolic analysis in addition to socio-functional and psychological analyses.

Geertz, I think, would be very unlikely to suppose that the meanings of religious symbols could be "established independently of the forms of life in which they are used." His published works on Java, Bali, and Morocco indicate that his understandings are strongly rooted in socio-historical analyses. Although Asad interprets his 1966 essay as suggesting that religious symbols are *sui generis*, conceptualizing symbols in that way would not be in keeping with much of the rest of Geertz's work.

Asad's essay, however, can be read as an outline for developing trenchant criticisms of the views of persons who do maintain that religious symbols, if not precisely *sui generis* themselves, nevertheless symbolically represent that which, in their opinion, is *sui generis*. These are persons not actually mentioned in Asad's essay. They are nonetheless more deserving of Asad's full critical sweep than Geertz, and the reader has it in his/her power to read Asad's essay as the beginnings of a poststructuralist attack on their views.

I have in mind Mircea Eliade and like-minded others. Those students of religion maintain that religion indicates irreducibly "religious" sensitivities, such as a consciousness of "the sacred" or "the transcendent." Religion, they claim, is universally distinguished from all else by its references to, and representations of, that irreducibly religious element. Asad's essay, read with the views of those people in mind, raises issues and makes points that could be incorporated into a major criticism of the idea that religion is "autonomous."

Geertz and Individual Differences

One wonders how widely and how profoundly Geertz's characterizations apply to the actual understandings, feelings, hopes, aspirations, and expectations of individual men and women whom we conventionally term "religious." It is probably the case that there are numbers of persons in many societies who support views approximating to what Geertz characterizes as the religious perspective. But there are also some who do not, their ritual behavior notwithstanding.

Many people in a wide variety of societies perform rituals that we tend to identify as religious. Some do so so frequently, or with such careful regularity, that we may suppose them to be pious. But are such persons actually moved by "powerful, pervasive, and long-lasting motivations" of the sort that Geertz has in mind? Do they really concern themselves with "the really real" (Geertz 1966:28)? Are their thoughts directly, powerfully, and regularly affected by "conceptions of a general order of existence," conceptions clothed with "an aura of factuality"?

How did Geertz finally arrive at his conception of religion? Broadly put, and allowing for the cultural background out of which it derives, it would seem to be the end product of a complex analytical process of the sort that Paul Tillich (1957:21) terms "a conceptual analysis." A concept so attained, Tillich maintains, "is by no means the description of an always actualized state of the mind."

In fairness to Geertz, however, we must note that he registers his disagreement with "the surely untrue proposition" that all persons in all societies are religious in some meaningful sense of that word (1966:43,n.3). He remarks, moreover, that "if the anthropological study of religious commitment is underdeveloped, the anthropological study of religious non-commitment is non-existent," and that "The anthropology of religion will have come of age when some more subtle Malinowski writes a book called 'Belief and Unbelief (or even "Faith and Hypocrisy") in a Savage Society'" (ibid.).

Geertz allows, furthermore, that *those who do take a religious perspective are not continually locked into it.* There is "movement back and forth," say, "between the religious perspective and the common-sense perspective" (1966:36). One of the failings of some students of humankind, Geertz avers with specific reference to what he deems the different but equivalently extreme views of Lévy-Bruhl and Malinowski, is a failure "to see man as moving more or less easily, and very frequently, between radically contrasting ways of looking at the world, ways which are not continuous with one another but separated by cultural gaps across which Kierkegaardian leaps must be made in both directions" (1966:36–37).

The weight of Geertz's essay, nevertheless, maintains that when people do think religiously — when, as he puts it, they take (for however long) "a specifically religious perspective" (1966:36) — their moods, motivations, and thought, abstractly characterized, are much as he describes them. *Indeed, if they are not, then, according to Geertz, they are not really religious!* He maintains, for example, that "any religious ritual," regardless of how conventional or seemingly automatic it may appear, involves the "symbolic fusion of ethos and world-view" that he describes — and that "if it is truly automatic or merely conventional," if it does not involve the crucial fusion of ethos and world-view that he describes, "it is not religious" (1966:28).

Some, however, may prefer a more narrowly behavioral means of initially identifying what we conventionally call religion and religious actors. (Behavior includes the affirmation of "beliefs.") When, for example, we find persons behaving in ways that remind us of our most familiar examples of religious behavior (see Chapter 6), we may wish to recognize that behavior as religious without insisting that the moods and motivations of all actors necessarily conform to Geertz's didactic characterizations. (All the more so, I might add, in view of the likely difficulty of determining moods and motivations.) While for some persons, William James observes, religion is "an acute fever," for others it "exists . . . as a dull habit" (1929 [1902]:8).

If, then, we decide to call behavior religious because it *reminds us* of other behaviors that we have called religious, then — to approach this issue from a different direction than that taken by Asad — Geertz's characterization of "the" religious perspective probably does not point to some actualized state of mind among *all* religious actors, even when those persons are "in the midst of ritual."

Geertz's generalizations would seem to fit the perspectives and motivations of some persons better than those of others. They appear to correspond best to the postulated perspectives and motivations of individuals whom Radin calls "the truly religious." This is an ideal type that Radin contrasts to two others, "the intermittently religious" and "the indifferently religious" (1937; 1960 [1953]:68–104). I call them "ideal types," invoking an analytical expression made famous by Weber. Radin, however, treats them as real.

Radin's Types

The "truly religious," Radin writes, are individuals who can easily call up "a far more than normal sensitiveness to certain customs, beliefs, and superstitions." Such persons, he asserts, "have always been few in number" (1937:9).

The "intermittently religious," he says, comprise two groups:

"those who may be weakly religious at almost any moment; and those who may be strongly religious at certain moments, such as tempermental upheavals and crises" (1937:10).

The "indifferently religious," in effect, are a species of those who are at best weakly religious at any moment. They include persons who at times "fall into a vague scepticism" or who even deny the powers and efficacies of what others take to be divinity. Radin maintains that the indifferently religious "can be said to have little inherent capacity for religion," and that they "live primarily on the religious experience of others" (1960:94).

Without accepting Radin's typology in precisely the way that he phrases it, it seems reasonable to suppose that there *are* significant differences among the members of many populations with respect to religion. Our appreciation of Geertz's characterization of what it means to be religious might be tempered accordingly. Further, some populations may have significantly larger proportions of persons who seem religiously attuned and committed than others.

Some persons whose *behavior* at times may strike us as religious in terms of our conventional stereotypes of religious behavior might not be moved by *motivations* that we would conventionally deem "religious." They may act out of greater concern for the good opinions of their neighbors than for the approbation of the Gods or because of gratitude to them, love for them, or fear of them. Ritual actors, moreover, may be more aware of their ritual activities as matters of the moment than as segments of what Geertz terms some general order of existence. And their seemingly religious verbal affirmations may constitute cultural clichés the meanings and social significance of which should be investigated rather than gratuitously assumed to be appreciable and profound.

In short, a concern with ultimates and overarching orders, the different formulations of Geertz and Paul Tillich notwithstanding, may well be more characteristic of both many intellectuals who study religion and some religious persons than it is of the rank and file of the world's ritualists, persons often preoccupied with — and perhaps relatively secure in — their parochial daily routines.

Ultimate Concern

Tillich, a theologian and philosopher of religion (the distinction takes on special significance within the framework of Tillich's perspectives: see Adams 1969:17), allows that some people may be more intensely or noticeably concerned with ultimates than others. He maintains, however, that "one cannot admit that there is any man without an ultimate concern or without faith" (1957:106), faith denominating "the state of being ultimately concerned" (1957:4). He argues that "ultimate concern is the integrating center of the personal life," and that living without such concern is "being without a center." While one might approach a state devoid of ultimate concern, one does not reach it fully, for a person completely deprived of a center would no longer be a human being (1957:106).

Since everyone experiences some sort of ultimate concern, everyone to that extent is turned toward religion, for, according to Tillich, "Religion is the state of being grasped by an ultimate concern, a concern which qualifies all other concerns as preliminary and which itself contains the answer to the question of the meaning of our life" (1963:4).

Some social scientists have attempted to base their own monothetic definitions of religion on "ultimate concern." Thus, for example, William Lessa and Evon Z. Vogt, in the first three editions (but not the fourth) of an anthology that they edited (*Reader in Comparative Religion: An Anthropological Approach*), identify religion as:

> a system of beliefs and practices directed toward the "ultimate concern" of a society. "Ultimate concern," a concept used by Paul Tillich, has two aspects — meaning and power. It has meaning in the sense of ultimate meaning of the central values of a society, and it has power in the sense of ultimate, sacred, or supernatural power which stands behind these values. (1st edition 1958:1)

The sociologist J. Milton Yinger, who judges Tillich's approach to religion in terms of ultimate concern "a good starting point for a functional definition," (1970:6), defines religion as "a system of beliefs and practices by means of which a group of people struggles with . . . ultimate problems of human life" (1970:7).

Although the authors quoted above cite Tillich, and by so doing affirm a connection to his thought, the connection strikes me as superficial. Messrs. Lessa, Vogt, and Yinger take the most 'up-front' expression of Tillich's overview and immediately re-cast it into the terminology of the culture theory (values, coping strategies) that, respectively, appeals to them. In doing so, I think, they were influenced by other invocations of ultimates as well as by Tillich's (the period between the two world wars seems to have nurtured such talk).

The sociologist Talcott Parsons, for example, makes important use of the idea of "common ultimate-value attitudes" (Parsons 1937:433) in his own theorizing. Although Lessa and Vogt explicitly cite Tillich, they appear to be closer to Parsons when they stress religion's role in the expression and explanation "of the ultimate values of a society." They describe religion as having integrative functions for individual personalities and for groups of persons as well as defensive functions in the management of tensions and anxieties (Lessa and Vogt 1958:1).

Yinger's functionalist orientation inspires this usage of ultimacy:

> the level of technology affects religion by influencing the kinds of problems that will be regarded as ultimate. If the food supply is precarious — not occasionally but endemically — its protection is an ultimate concern. Men will not leave such protection to an unreliable or patently insufficient technology . . . but will bring into play their most sacred beliefs and practices. (1970:351)

In attending to these approaches, I am concerned with two questions. Have Lessa and Vogt and/or Yinger accurately applied Tillich's position on ultimate concern? And, regardless of the answer to that question, is the notion of ultimacy that they employ (and represent as being inspired by Tillich) useful for the comparative study of religions? My answer to both questions is "No." I take each in turn.

Paul Tillich's Position on Ultimate Concern

Anything even approaching a full exposition of Tillich's points of view is out of the question here, not only because it is unnecessary to the purposes of this work, but also because such an undertaking would be as daunting as it is digressive. Tillich was very productive in his writing and in his lecturing. His views, moreover, shifted somewhat over time, so that one might more accurately speak of his viewpoints in the plural than in the singular. Further, or so it seems to me, he was not always clear in what he said. And, if that were not enough, the expositor should be familiar with the intellectual currents that nurtured Tillich — and those were diverse, including not only the mainstreams (and various rivulets) of Christian worship and theology, but also existentialism, German phenomenology, and much else.

For my purposes, it must suffice to sketch what Tillich meant by "ultimate concern." Some of his statements about it, when taken by themselves, may not prove very helpful in advancing our understanding: e.g., "ultimate concern is concern about what is experienced as ultimate" (1957:9). But one can build on such statements.

Tillich conceives of ultimate concern as passionate (1957:106) and as something that "grasps" a person (1963:4) and to which the person responds (W.C. Smith's similar ideas about "the Transcendent," referred to in Chapter 1, may have been influenced to some extent by Tillich). The words of Deuteronomy 6:5 ("You shall love the Lord your God with all your heart, and with all your soul, and with all your might"), Tillich tells us (1957:3), are "what ultimate concern means . . . They state unambiguously the character of genuine faith, the demand of total surrender to the subject of ultimate concern."

Tillich allows that people may elevate such things as nationalism or the pursuit of "success" to what is *experienced* as ultimate concern and thus by definition *is* ultimate concern. Such a concern is prepossessing, for "whatever concerns man ultimately becomes god for him, and, conversely, . . . a man can be concerned ultimately only about that which is god for him" (1953:Vol.1, 234). All other concerns are subordinated or sacrificed to it and it is experienced as promising "total fulfillment." And since "Religion is the state of being grasped by an ultimate concern" (1963:4), nationalism or the pursuit of success may become the religions of some persons. But such concerns, according to Tillich, are falsely ultimate and idolatrous. The religions that they engender are consequently inauthentic: they are "quasi-religions" rather than "religions proper" (1963:11).

Tillich claims that "a critical principle was and is at work in man's religious consciousness, namely, that which is really ultimate over against what claims to be ultimate but is only preliminary, transitory, finite" (1957:10). One can distinguish between "true and false ultimacy" (1957:11). While there are "many degrees in the endless realm of false ultimacies," all are marked to some extent by a subject-object cleavage, whereas in truly ultimate concern there is "disappearance of the ordinary subject-object scheme in the experience of the ultimate, the unconditional" (1957:11).

The object of true ultimate concern, according to Tillich, is "the Unconditional," conceptualized ontologically as "Being Itself," the ground of being on which we all depend. Authentic religion for Tillich is "directedness toward the Unconditional" (1969:59, italics omitted).

Tillich allows, however, that the falsely ultimate objects of falsely ultimate concerns may symbolically hint at or point to something truly ultimate and a truly ultimate concern for it. Truly ultimate concern is grounded in the human existential situation, a situation characterized in part by an awareness of death and an anxiety about non-being. Concerns that are falsely ultimate are nevertheless meaningful, and the creation and affirmation of meaning is a way of coping with the threat of non-being.

In subtle fashion, then, Tillich disallows genuine ultimacy to some of the "ultimate concerns" that Lessa and Vogt in their way, and Yinger in his, are willing to recognize. If the object of concern is not truly ultimate, neither is the concern for it (although the experience is genuine enough, and the concern is to that extent experientially ultimate). But Tillich goes even further. He does so, indeed, in a way that is likely to estrange any genuinely relativistic social scientists who take the trouble to read him carefully. For in considering humanity's manifold "religions," Tillich suggests that some may be superior to others.

Tillich sometimes uses the word "religion" broadly: he applies it to a focus on, and responses to, any concern that is *experienced* as ultimate. This suggests, monothetically, that what is essential to all "religions" (those conventionally listed in our textbooks and many more besides) is such a concern and its ramifications in human experience. But since true ultimate concern is concern for the "Unconditional" *as it is manifested and expressed symbolically,* any prepossessing concern the symbolic object of which lacks the attributes of the Unconditional — that is, any concern the symbolic object of which is finite, transitory, and preliminary — is falsely treated as ultimate. Concerns falsely treated as ultimate engender religions, but the devotions inspired by such religions are directed to false Gods, whether their chief symbols be noble declarations about humanity-at-large or only parochial golden calves, silver BMW's, iron crosses, and the like.

Those religions (i.e., "quasi-religions") are inauthentic in two senses.

First, as already noted, the concerns on which they are based, though experienced as ultimate, are nevertheless falsely ultimate.

Second, they are existentially inauthentic with respect to human needs and potentialities. Human beings can and do make the passionate choices of which Kierkegaard spoke, passionate choices that Kierkegaard regarded as crucial for an authentic existence. Sadly enough, however, people often choose wrongly and lavish their concern on unworthy objects and symbols. When they do so, they act inauthentically with respect to their own nature. Tillich regrets such inauthenticity.

Far from unconditionally supporting pluralism or relativism, Tillich calls for a redirection of concern to what is truly ultimate: the Unconditional, Being Itself, or, to use a more common term, God. (Though Tillich does not endorse the notion of a personal God, he regards the God of traditional Judaism and Christianity as *symbolically* suggesting or pointing to Being Itself.) His line of argument is in keeping with his employment of "false" and "true" for characterizing different sorts of ultimate concern. Those usages are examples of what Stevenson (1944:210) calls "persuasive definitions:" attempts, whether fully recognized by their authors or not, to persuade us to embrace certain attitudes and values. Tillich's attempts at persuasion go even further than what I have summarized thus far.

Many religions, Tillich suggests, only hint at a concern for Being Itself in highly disguised symbolic fashion. But even among those that are founded on an explicit metaphysical sensitivity to the Unconditional, some, in Tillich's view, are superior to others. Their superiority is judged in terms of their central symbols.

The Unconditional cannot be grasped and responded to as a thing-in-itself. It is apprehended and incorporated into human experience through the modality of symbols. Yet there is a shadow cast upon such symbols by the human mind. Tillich agrees with Calvin in supposing that the human mind is a veritable factory for the unceasing production of idols (1957:97). There is therefore the ever-present danger that our minds will transform symbols for expressing the ultimate into ultimacies themselves — into idols. True faith must be served by symbols that are not idolatrous.

The most adequate religious symbol, Tillich opines, is one that "expresses not only the ultimate but also its own lack of ultimacy" (1957:97). He maintains, moreover, that

> Christianity expresses itself in such a symbol in contrast to all other religions, namely, in the Cross of Christ. Jesus could not have been the Christ without sacrificing himself as Jesus to himself as the Christ. Any acceptance of Jesus as the Christ which is not the acceptance of Jesus the crucified is a form of idolatry. The ultimate concern of the Christian is not Jesus, but the Christ Jesus who is manifest as the crucified. The event which has created this symbol has given the criterion by which the truth of Christianity, as well as of any other religion, must be judged. The only infallible truth of faith, the one in which the ultimate itself is unconditionally manifest, is that any truth of faith stands under a yes-or-no judgment. (1957:97–98)

Tillich goes even further. He suggests that not only is Christianity superior to other religions, but that at least some forms of Protestant Christianity are superior to other forms of Christianity. This is because of what Tillich calls "the Protestant principle": "the principle that no church has the right to put itself in the place of the ultimate" (1957:98). This principle is generalized to exclude the elevation of any human symbology of the ultimate — the Bible, for instance — into the ultimate itself. The best religion, in short, is one in which the central symbols nullify their own candidacies for ultimacy and take their significance only as manifesting and expressing Being Itself, which alone is properly deemed ultimate.

The above exposition of Tillich's point of view — one compressed to the point of glossing over certain statements in his writings that might soften it a bit — is faithful enough to suggest that while Lessa and Vogt and Yinger make use of some of Tillich's terminology, they (and others like them) do so outside of an authentically Tillichian theoretical framework.

It is a complex matter as to whether or not — and if so how and to what degree — Tillich's perspectives might be fruitfully combined with those of social scientists. John Morgan has explored and compared certain of the works of Tillich and Geertz, and he opines that they "do not appear to be inexorably antipathetic" (1977:367). Both authors are concerned with "meaning," and Tillich, Morgan suggests, adds an ontological dimension to our understanding of culture that is absent in Geertz's writings (*ibid.*). But Morgan's essay strikes me as being only a very preliminary assault on a very complex topic. It remains to be seen whether a dialogue between anthropologists and theologian-philosophers such as Tillich will prove substantially productive for either or both beyond yielding a certain mutual satisfaction over the broadmindedness suggested by the dialogue itself.

Lessa and Vogt, and Yinger

Now, while Lessa and Vogt's, and Yinger's, expressed ideas about "ultimate concern" do not reflect Tillich's perspectives in any profundity, that in itself certainly does not render them nugatory or otiose. Their utility can be evaluated independently of Tillich's theorizing. In doing so, I find a conceptual softness that gives me reason to regard those ideas as dubious instruments for the exploration and comparison of religions.

Concerns (marked interests or regards), whether ultimate or not, can be viewed as having existential loci in individual psychology. To the extent, however, that an observer is able to apprehend with fair accuracy another person's concerns, it is because such concerns are expressed in accessible symbolic idioms, idioms familiar to a community of persons. Their identification by the anthropologist requires learning the language, interviews, case studies, the assembling of life histories, and the other procedures of ethnographic fieldwork.

Social scientists such as Lessa, Vogt, and Yinger seek to learn about concerns formulated in communal idioms. They are far less likely to devote their research to what some people imagine to be genuinely private or idiosyncratic concerns. They tend to be conscious of the aims of their research because of their disciplinary interests in learning about the *culture* of some population. It is likely, however, that their interest happily coincides with a necessity (even if they do not recognize it as such). For can there be entirely idiosyncratic private concerns? Concerns, that is, that are distinguishable from mere *personalized* concerns — the concerns of a particular person — which are couched and to some extent reworked in a cultural idiom? I think not, on analogy to the reasons given in Wittgenstein's argument against the notion of a private language (*Philosophical Investigations* I:243–363).

In any case, the formulation of concerns in communal symbolic idioms does not automatically render those concerns easy to recognize. The observer often makes interpretive leaps in order to speak about them.

Socially approbated or expected concerns are not necessarily isomorphic with personalized concerns even if they are both formulated in much the same symbolic idiom. An individual, indeed, may develop concerns that others, if they became aware of them, would find intelligible but not admirable or socially acceptable. Individuals who develop such concerns may come to re-work and express them in more socially acceptable forms (see, for example, Obeyesekere 1981).

The normal human being (i.e., a person whose mental functioning is not severely incapacitated) is likely to experience numerous concerns during his or her lifetime. In some relatively brief time period, the individual may have multiple concerns, some of which will be invested with greater cognitive and affective intensity than others. The contents and mix of concerns, moreover, will shift over time. To some extent concerns are likely to reflect different stages in the life-cycle as well as a diversity of situational factors. Religions may well address these variable, multiple concerns, stimulating and enhancing their significance for the individual and perhaps affirming conventionalized denouements.

But what is the individual's *ultimate* — "extreme," "utmost," "finally reckoned" — concern? Tillich suggests that we are all ultimately troubled by recognition of the possibility of non-being, and that in attempting to cope with our anxiety over non-being we adopt and address various concerns that directly or indirectly reflect that anxiety and associated anxieties ("meaninglessness" and "condemnation"). Attempting to overcome those anxieties, he declares, indicates our "courage to be."

I suspect, however, that one could interpret virtually any concern expressed in what appears to be a self-affirming posture as doing so. A multitude of concerns would seemingly echo rumors of ultimacy, and actions that appear to serve those concerns could ultimately be interpreted as religious.

According to Tillich, however, the symbolic contents of some concerns are more adequate or appropriate for dealing with ultimate anxiety than the symbolic contents of others. But unless social scientists adopt this or an analogous position (they need not embrace Tillich's specifics), they are encumbered by a multiplicity of individual concerns (assuming, of course, — and it is a problematical assumption — that one might recognize them accurately). Some concerns may be dominant (and so seem ultimate) in adolescence, others in middle age, some in sickness, some in health, some for Tom, others for Dick, still others for Harry, and so on. Further, even if we suppose that two or more people share the same concern, we ought to admit that they might express it differently and seek resolution or fulfillment in different ways.

Methodological and theoretical difficulties attendant on studying ultimate concerns on the level of individuals, it might be supposed, could be bypassed to some extent by directing research to such concerns on the "textual" level. One would analyze rituals, myths, and other materials, and try to find what concerns they emphasize. Different interpreters, however, might report somewhat different concerns. But even were there a considerable overlap among interpreters, it is likely that there would be disagreement over the relative rankings of concerns. Which is ultimate and which are less than ultimate? Which are perduring and which are passing? Even assuming that one settles on answers that strike the analyst as persuasive, there still remains the problem of relating a ranking of "textual" concerns to the personalized concerns of individuals.

Some social scientists may argue that it is not necessary to relate them. Culture must be analyzed as if it were a text, they might say. Interpretive efforts should be directed to cultural concerns, just as certain literary critics attempt to understand the concerns expressed by (rather than in) works of literature. The object of study is culture, not the individual.

I do not endorse that suggestion across-the-board. While I think that the focus on culture that it encourages can stimulate worthwhile studies, such studies are likely to be most engaging when they are relevant to specific problems. When it comes to working toward a global perspective on religion — and the larger understandings to which a knowledge of religions conduces — a focus on culture, though valuable, is insufficient.

Why do we study religions? Many would probably agree that one of several intellectually compelling reasons is this: whatever the human situation may be, religion in much of human history has been a part of it, and the study of religions can contribute to our understanding of resemblances among human beings.

One can find value in that statement, however, without maintaining that religion is indispensible to human life even if its cultural distribution has approached universality. One can do so by appreciating religions as highly imaginative expressions of human creativity the study of which might enrich our understandings of important human capacities. But although people may creatively give voice to collective concerns through the modality of religion, they can also do so in virtually every other department of culture that our analytical traditions induce us to conceptualize and name. Different individuals, moreover, are likely to interpret those concerns somewhat differently, and to cathect or fail to cathect them in accordance with their personal situations.

Ultimate concerns of the sort conceived by Lessa and Vogt and Yinger are frail points on which to pivot religion.

In the first place, Lessa and Vogt and Yinger seem to assume gratuitously (at least in the case of so-called primitive societies) that ultimate cultural concerns are also mutually understood and equally cathected by most of the people sharing the culture. Were this an hypothesis rather than a facile assumption, I suspect that the process of testing it would lead us to a better appreciation of the complex and flexible relationships between cultural and personalized concerns.

In the second place, analysts might well disagree as to what are the ultimate cultural concerns of some population as expressed in their myths, rituals, and other "texts." And when it comes to exploring concerns on the level of individuals, it is likely to be even more problematical as to which concerns may be ultimate — and when and for how long and for whom.

Finally, by resting religion on ultimate concern — and doing so without Tillichian subtleties that allow one to deem various concerns as ultimate in one sense while judging them falsely ultimate in another —, it happens that whatever is claimed to fulfill the function of being an ultimate concern signals the presence of a religion — a religion that, on this level of abstraction, is equivalent to any other religion.

Lessa and Vogt explicitly (and Yinger implicitly) circumscribe to some extent the potential multiplicity and variability of what will be accounted "religions" by stipulating (or implying) that in religion the values expressed by ultimate concerns are generally conceived to be underwritten by some "ultimate, sacred, or supernatural power which stands behind these values" (Lessa and Vogt 1958:1). This power appears to be not so much a symbol of Tillich's "Being Itself" as a defining factor borrowed from numerous traditional essentialist definitions of religion. It serves, if not all that effectively, to rescue Lessa and Vogt's definition (and, implicitly, Yinger's) from some of the vagueness attendant on a superficial conceptualization of "ultimate concerns." It does so by bringing in the Gods (or their equivalents). A *deus ex machina*, in short, is invoked to do for definitions what others have made it do for heroes.

Ward H. Goodenough's Definition

An interesting variant of an ultimate concern approach is offered by Ward H. Goodenough (1974). Goodenough had not read Tillich when he wrote "Toward an Anthropologically Useful Definition of Religion," but he is willing to entertain the possibility that Tillich may have exerted an indirect influence on his thought through the writings of his father, Erwin R. Goodenough (W.H. Goodenough, Personal Communication). The senior Goodenough is the author of *The Psychology of Religious Experience* (1965) and a number of other works dealing with religion.

Goodenough begins his essay by relating that "The late Erwin Goodenough used to say that if we wish to understand what religion is about, we must study man praying, not what he is praying to" (1974:165). He notes that although that epigram, like most others, oversimplifies, it nevertheless "underscores what has been a major problem in the study of religion: a primary focus on the content of belief and relatively little concern with the believer" (1974:165).

Goodenough maintains that whatever else may be associated with religion, religion has to do with how humans handle important problems relating to the definition and achievement of self-goals (1974:169). His essay is peppered with the word "concern," and he views religion as fundamentally related to "the universal human concern with self-maintenance and self-realization" (1974:181). Seemingly like Tillich, his solution to the definitional problem is "to define religion in terms of human problems of being, in a psychological (i.e., spiritual) as distinct from a material sense" (1974:182).

In invoking "being," however, Goodenough is not waxing metaphysical. Unlike Tillich, he does not offer us an ontological dimension to add to our contemplation of religion. He is not concerned with some ultimate "ground" for our existence nor with arguments that implicate the idea of "Being Itself." His phrase, "human problems of being," expresses an existential position couched in the language of ego psychology.

Goodenough begins with an effort to decide "what kinds of human problems are to be regarded as religious" (1974:167). This, he says, is what the problem of defining religion is all about. He suggests that a good starting place is the "packet of problems to which the term 'salvation' refers."

Goodenough stipulates that salvation in his essay means "the achievement of an idealized state of being — whether that achievement is associated with the human condition before or after death" (1974:167). Salvation in his usage "involves goals for the self" (*ibid.*). A consideration of such goals is complicated by various problems, problems that Goodenough discusses with great analytical skill. He connects his focus on "problems relating to the definition and achievement of goals for the self" (1974:169) to ritual and to other matters, and he illustrates his point of view by drawing on his knowledge of the Trukese, a Micronesian people among whom he did fieldwork.

By making ego-problems his central point of reference, Goodenough expands the inclusiveness of "religious life" well beyond the bounds loosely or implicitly assigned to it by many anthropologists. He acknowledges early in the essay that he does so: "If concern with salvation is a religious concern, then I cannot dismiss Marxist definitions of it from the domain of religion because they eschew reference to spirits" (1974:168). In a later publication, he makes a bolder statement: ". . . with Marx as its prophet, socialism produced a creed for the emergence of communism as one of the great religions of modern times" (1989:6).

Like most anthropologists, Goodenough would probably be unwilling to opt for a Tillich-like solution (e.g., judging concerns for salvation defined in Marxist terms to be falsely ultimate). While anthropologists hardly eschew value-laden interpretations (despite what some might mistakenly affirm on that score), they generally shy away from any so brazen as the example taken from Tillich. Goodenough recognizes that his approach entails consequences that may not elicit enthusiasm from various anthropologists (including numbers who are Marxists), and he attempts to cope with one potential criticism.

To describe how people both express and try to deal with their major emotional preoccupations, particularly those that center on their concerns with "the cultivation and maintenance of the self in the social and symbolic millieus in which they live," Goodenough maintains, is "to describe their religious life" (1974:182). But some critics, he supposes (correctly), may deem his approach to open the door "too wide, so that almost everything becomes religion" (*ibid.*). He confesses himself untroubled, however, "That religious concerns pervade much of human activity," he writes, "seems to me no more troublesome in this regard than the well accepted idea that economic concerns do so also" (*ibid.*). Indeed, he finds it "Particularly attractive to me as an anthropologist . . . that, in this view, there is no man without a religious life, without religious concerns, and without some way of expressing them and dealing with them that together constitute something we can consider to be his religion" (*ibid.*).

I have no trouble with the idea that religious as well as economic concerns may pervade much of the activity of many persons. Were we to adopt Goodenough's definition, however, how might we disentangle religion from certain of our other traditional analytical categories? Given, for example, the universality and pervasiveness that Goodenough assigns to both economics and religion in human life, can we consistently tell them apart (assuming that we deem consistency to be an analytical desideratum)? It would seem that if economic concerns are involved in our major efforts to cultivate and maintain the self, they are "religious concerns" by application of Goodenough's criterion.

Failure to maintain a sharp boundary between "religion" and "non-religion," as Chapter 6 makes clear, is not something that troubles me — quite the contrary, in fact. But many proponents of monothetic definitions seem to hope that we can avoid blurring our analytical categories in attending to the phenomenal world. Goodenough himself has been a major voice in anthropology calling for clearly marked, universal categories — but his exercise in defining religion does not strike me as successfully implementing that summons.

Why define religion so broadly that it applies to virtually all human beings? There are two major reasons that either singly or in combination inspire diverse authors to formulate such definitions.

One reason is to defend religion by rendering everyone religious, whether people previously thought that they were or not. An implication of claimed universal distribution is that religion is a "natural" or, at any rate, an integral aspect of the human condition, and in that sense existentially immune to calls for its extirpation. Friedrich Schleiermacher (1958 [1799]), for example, characterizes religion in such a way that even its "cultured despisers" might seem religious.

Eschewing cognitive and ethical definitions, two of the leading kinds of definition in his time, Schleiermacher attempts to depict religion as autonomous by describing it as based on a special feeling: a feeling of absolute dependence, the dependence of a finite being on the 'infinite'. This particular approach provoked Hegel to offer the droll observation that if we were to accept Schleiermacher's characterization, dogs would be rendered more religious than many Christians. (In my capacity as the caretaker of a Wirehaired Fox Terrier, however, I am convinced that Hegel overstated the case; only some dogs would be more religious.)

Another reason — the professionally operative one in Goodenough's case — is to define religion and much else (e.g., property, kinship, marriage, etc.) in ways likely to advance the systematic study of humanity. By analytically positing universal categories that reflect our observations of broad similarities among diverse human populations, we might seem to be in a good position — or so Goodenough supposes — to explore, and to attempt to account for, particular social, psychological, and cultural differences.

In addition to its alleged methodological and analytical utility, a utility explicitly championed by Goodenough, allegiance among anthropologists to the assertion of universals may sometimes reflect certain ideological biases: among them the desire to affirm the essential oneness of humanity, and the ancillary disposition to realize that desire analytically. My colleague Robert Hunt (Personal Communication) suggests that some anthropologists may also partially be motivated to endorse such a position because of their repugnance for racism and/or their ideological commitment to affirming a great divide between human beings and all other animals.

In any case, Goodenough's essay on religion is in large part a continuation of his 1968 Lewis Henry Morgan Lectures at the University of Rochester. As he puts it in the introduction to the published version of those lectures, *Description and Comparsion in Cultural Anthropology*,

> we have to find some set of terms that will enable us to describe other cultures with minimal distortion from ethnocentric cultural bias. And we need some set of universally applicable concepts that will enable us to compare cultures and arrive at valid generalizations about them. (1970:2)

When anthropologists compare religion, or kinship, or property relationships in two cultures, Goodenough asks, what are the criteria that they employ for deciding that something can be called by one of those terms? The criteria that they utilize, he avers, "do not pertain to the content of cultural forms but to the roles these forms play in people's lives — to the conscious and unconscious ends for which people seem to use them (or to try to use them) as means, and to the kinds of outputs that seem to result from their use in the conduct of affairs. These terms, in short, reflect functional considerations" (1970:120).

One of Goodenough's critics argues that in the 1970 book resulting from the Morgan Lectures, a book that largely illustrates its argument by dealing with the anthropologist's traditional categories of kinship, descent, and marriage, Goodenough puts his definitions of various aspects of kinship (e.g., motherhood, fatherhood) "in strictly formal, not in functional terms" (Schneider 1984:151). Goodenough is charged, that is, with supplying essentially jural definitions, though "the domain of kinship itself is defined in functional terms, in terms of the universal problem of reproduction, as well as [in] formal terms as the system of relative products derived from marriage and parenthood . . ." (Schneider 1984:151–152). In Goodenough's later paper dealing with religion, however, functional concerns are clearly — and consistently — central to the definition and its explication.

In summary, Goodenough's approach is to formulate a universal definition of religion by attempting to define it "in relation to certain problems of human existence" (1974:166). He starts, that is, with abstractly phrased, presumptively universal existential problems in defining and achieving self-goals, especially as they relate to self-maintenance and self-realization. He views religions as humanity's attempts to deal with those problems both in their universal aspects and in their variegated, socially relevant particularities. His strategy, in short, is to begin with something that many of us do not ordinarily describe as religious, and to end by labeling humanity's efforts to deal with that something "religion."

In attempting to make "terms," category labels, "reflect functional considerations," Goodenough would seem to be committed to keeping his categories distinct. Yet the boundaries of his category religion are not clearly given. Where does religion leave off and other categories begin? How, indeed, can essentialist analytical categories be bounded so that they will prove mutually exclusive?

The question of boundaries plagues all efforts to establish universal categories by monothetic definitions, whether the definitions be weighted toward functional considerations, as in Goodenough's case, or toward substantive ones. Ideal essentialist definitions would supply unambiguous, un-vague boundary-creating and boundary-maintaining statements so that phenomena could be confidently sorted (digitized) into those that are covered by the definition and those that are not. Yet all of the monothetic definitions that we have examined thus far fail to do so. They fail because of vagueness in some of the terms composing the definitions and/or because we encounter so-called borderline cases.

Monothetic definitions that are heavily weighted toward presumptively universal human concerns generally reflect some global theory of human nature. The category terms, moreover, are usually hand-me-downs, terms that have been in use for some time, now to be given fresh meanings with respect to the identified concerns. Fresh meanings, but not entirely new meanings. Religion still has something to do with people praying or engaging in other rituals, not necessarily often, but often enough. And economics still has something to do with economizing choices and goods and services and their production, distribution, and consumption. And there's one of the rubs! For the heady wine of some newly celebrated, important, and widely distributed concern is likely to splash into different old category bottles.

Further, universal functional monothetic definitions —

Goodenough's is a good example — tend to be very elastic. Universalism, whether sought after substantively or functionally, is typically purchased by decreasing the specifics of content. Functional definitions, however, are likely to be significantly more elastic than substantive ones. When, as is usually the case, they identify religion as, in essence, a way of coping with broadly conceived emotional or existential concerns, it is hard to limit what can then be assigned to the rubric religion.

In his effort to construct a universal functional definition, Goodenough includes so much under that rubric that the category as he conceives it is not only counter-intuitive for many persons (numbers of Marxists would probably protest being dubbed "religious"), but of uncertain, problem-plagued application as well. By rendering everyone religious and myriads of things religions, Goodenough renders the category religion too inclusive to serve as a useful analytical instrument.

A useful analytical instrument would not only facilitate the postulation of interesting similarities or parallels, but it would also facilitate the drawing of sobering discriminations. It ought not to dispose us to lump all sorts of things together in such a way as to render them equivalent despite the disapproving whispers of our intuitions. On the other hand, it ought not to inspire sharp discriminations in obedience to some one criterion or rule the application of which separates phenomena that might usefully be grouped together on other grounds. Goodenough's approach to characterizing religion, an approach rooted in a quest for universal analytical categories and incorporating elements of a highly abstract psychological theory of the self, does the former. And Geertz's didactic insistence on a certain fusion of ethos and world view, a synthesis the lack of which condemns rituals or public shows of piety to be accounted less than authentically religous, comes uncomfortably close to doing the latter.

CHAPTER FOUR

MORE ON MONOTHETIC DEFINITIONS

... key terms are finally more important for their function, for their
place within intellectual practices, than they are for what they may be said
to 'mean' in the abstract.
- Paul A Bové, "Discourse," 1990, p. 51.

In a well known textbook, *Religion: An Anthropological View*, Anthony
F.C. Wallace describes Tylor's "belief in spiritual beings" as "a
still-respectable minimum definition of religion" (1966:5).
Wallace's own definitional effort expands on Tylor's:

> It is the premise of every religion — and this premise is religion's
> defining characteristic — that souls, supernatural beings, and super-
> natural forces exist. Furthermore, there are certain minimal cate-
> gories of behavior which, in the context of the *supernatural premise*,
> are always found in association with one another and which are
> the substance of religion itself. Although almost any behavior can
> be invested with a religious meaning, there seems to be a finite
> number — about thirteen — behavior categories most of which
> are, in any religious system, combined into a pattern that is con-
> ventionally assigned the title "religion." (1966:52)

I will not take the space here to describe and comment on
Wallace's thirteen minimal categories of behavior (Wallace
1966:53–67). I focus, instead, on what he calls the "*supernatural
premise*," which he regards as "religion's defining characteristic."

Wallace's free and seemingly untroubled use of "supernatural"
contrasts with strictures explicitly expressed by various others
respecting use of that word.

Hallowell, for example, declares that to describe the characters in the myths of the northern Ojibwa as "supernatural" would
be "completely misleading, if for no other reason than the fact
that the concept of 'supernatural' presupposes a concept of the
'natural.' The latter is not present in Ojibwa thought" (1960:28).
He opines that "It is unfortunate that the natural-supernatural
dichotomy has been so persistently invoked by many anthropologists in describing the outlook of peoples in cultures other than
our own" (*ibid.*).

Durkheim, to furnish another example, maintains that:

> In order to arrive at the idea of the supernatural, it is not
> enough ... to be witnesses to unexpected events; it is also necessary

that these be conceived as impossible, that is to say, irreconcilable with an order which, rightly or wrongly, appears to us to be implied in the nature of things. Now this idea of a necessary order has been constructed little by little by the positive sciences, and consequently the contrary notion could not have existed before them. (1965 [1912]:43)

Lienhardt (1961:28) refers to Durkheim in rejecting the natural-supernatural distinction for describing "the difference between men and Powers" conceptualized by the Dinka. Lévy-Bruhl (1936 [1931]:5), among others, endorses what Durkheim says about the sense of the "impossible," and Horton (1973:262) opines that Durkheim gives "a very cogent dismissal of the attempt to define religion in terms of the mysterious and the supernatural."

The word "supernatural" and various of its predecessors in Greek (*huperphuēs, huper phusin*) and in Latin (*supernaturalis, supra naturam rerum*), however, were in use well before the emergence of what Durkheim terms "the positive sciences" (de Lubac 1934, 1946). But Durkheim does not concern himself with earlier usages. Nor does he confront the fact that Western classical and medieval authors developed their own senses of the "impossible," although, of course, such acceptations were neither isopragmatic nor isosemantic with those cultivated by positivists. Tertullian, for example, declared of Christ's resurrection, "*certum est, quia impossibile est,*" "it is certain because it is impossible" (*De carne Christi* V,4).

I do not want to explore the development of concepts of the supernatural here. I am in the process of organizing materials for a work that will correct and expand my preliminary paper on the subject (Saler 1977). Suffice it to say for now that "supernatural" is a rather more complex matter, both diachronically and synchronically, than some seem to suppose.

Some anthropologists, aware of the Western identity of the category supernatural, think that it can be extended to roughly analogical conceptualizations among non-Western peoples (e.g., Hocart 1932a:59–61, 1932b; Harris 1975:514; Hultkrantz 1979 [1967]:10, n.2, 1983). I have a certain sympathy for that point of view, provided that those who attempt to use supernatural analogically take pains to spell out how they understand the term to be used in Western applications. Hultkrantz (1983) is exceptional in doing so, and the communicative powers of his efforts to generalize about supernaturalism in the religions of North American Indians are the better for it.

Still and all, I continue to harbor misgivings about employment of the term in anthropology.

For one thing, I suspect that by "supernatural beings" and "supernatural forces" many anthropologists fundamentally mean "imaginary beings" and "imaginary forces." If that is so, then supernatural is used to paper-over judgments that might better be confronted directly. Many anthropologists, while agreeing that sympathy and empathy are important in doing ethnography, nevertheless regard as unreal certain of the beings and forces that their informants deem real. This disagreement with their own informants must influence the ethnographies that they write, and its significance deserves serious evaluation.

For another thing, imposing a supernatural-natural dualism on peoples who do not themselves entertain that distinction is all the more problematical when the imposer may have rather fuzzy notions about the distinction in his/her own society.

Some years ago I administered questionnaires about the category supernatural to numbers of undergraduates at Brandeis University. Some students were simply asked to define the term supernatural. Others were asked to define both natural and supernatural. And still other students, after being asked to define supernatural, were supplied with descriptions of various items (God, angel, Dracula, Frankenstein's monster, etc.), and they were requested to label each as either "supernatural" or "not-supernatural" and to justify their labeling. Although the *definitions* and justifications that I received were varied and often vague, the respondents demonstrated a great deal of convergence in the *sorting* tasks.

It is my impression from reading a good deal of anthropology that professional anthropologists also show much convergence in the sorting task, although their definitions of supernatural, if given at all, are usually skimpy and somewhat vague. The worth of supernatural for them is to be assayed by its functions — by, to borrow words from Bové, its "place within intellectual practices" —, rather than by what it might "be said to 'mean' in the abstract."

Supernatural, in sum, is not a meaningful category for many non-Westerners. And it is a meaningful but fuzzy and often judgmental one for numbers of Westerners. While a case can be made for its analogical utility in transcultural research, the strength of such a case depends on how well the ground is prepared for the drawing of an analogy.

If we suppose that there is warrant to construct bridges of some sort to span the semantic chasms that separate us from others, we would do well to remember that bridges normally have two anchoring foundations, one on either side of what they span.

Much mischief, I think, has accrued from our failures to prepare the ground profoundly enough on *our* side of the divide. In the case at hand, if the ground is not prepared properly, and supernatural is simply asserted to be the essential defining attribute of religion, our biases are likely to be strengthened at the cost of increasing our knowledge and sensitivity.

OTHERS OF TYLOR'S HEIRS

Wallace's choice of supernaturalism as the distinguishing feature of religion is, as he explicitly acknowledges, an extension and refinement of Tylor's minimal definition. Numbers of other anthropologists can also be accounted among Tylor's heirs when it comes to defining religion, although they may disagree among themselves about the specifics of their definitions. I turn now to the respective contributions of four more of them, Jack Goody, Robin Horton, Melford E. Spiro, and Stewart Guthrie.

Jack Goody

Much of Goody's widely-cited 1961 essay, "Religion and Ritual: The Definitional Problem," is given over to a review of selected definitional approaches in the social sciences. Goody is particularly concerned to "reject Durkheim's assumption that the sacred profane dichotomy is a universal feature of people's views of the human situation" (1961:155). He argues that such dyads as sacred-profane and natural-supernatural are external to the operative semantic categories of many peoples and are supplied by the observing anthropologist (1961:156). He contends, more broadly, that criteria utilized by anthropologists to isolate phenomena that they label "ritual," "sacred," or "magico-religious" derive not from the non-Western actor's point of view but from the outside observer's "assessment of what is intrinsic" (1961:157). Those terms do not necessarily refer to universal categories grounded in panhuman experiences. Nor should we reify them into existential objects of study. They should be recognized, rather, as analytical devices whose worth is to be evaluated pragmatically.

Goody's overall view is much the same as the one that pervades this book and that will be discussed at some length in Chapters 6 and 7: *We need analytical concepts; but once we recognize where they come from, perhaps we might be more thoughtful, responsible, and productive in how we use them.* Goody and I give expression to that viewpoint in somewhat different fashion, however.

Goody sees continuing value in various terms as employed by

E. B. Tylor and other nineteenth century anthropologists. He calls for the partial rehabilitation and refinement of those usages in sorting out what we might most productively mean by terms such as "religion," "ritual," and "ceremonial."

Goody notes that in a famous work, *Nuer Religion* (1956), the twentieth century anthropologist E.E. Evans-Pritchard fundamentally defines "his field of discourse in Tylorian terms." Tylor, as noted previously, suggested that we can minimally define religion as "belief" in "spiritual beings."

This definition, Goody opines, "appears to offer the nearest approach to a resolution of our problem" despite what he considers to be its limitations (1961:157). He offers some suggestions about overcoming certain of those limitations and the problems that they pose (e.g., the problem of drawing a boundary between "spiritual beings" and "spiritual forces," a problem impressed on our awareness by R.R. Marett's [1909] efforts to distinguish what he called "animatism," belief in "impersonal spiritual forces," from Tylor's usage of the term "animism" to refer to belief in "spiritual beings"). Goody's essay attempts in part to clarify monothetically the use of several Western-derived terms in order to render them serviceable analytical tools and thus advance the comparative sociology of religion.

Robin Horton

Horton also analyzes various definitional approaches to religion. Definitions, he states, are "mere tools towards the discovery of empirical regularities" (1960:201). He distinguishes three general approaches to the definitional problem:

(1) The view that the term religion, exceedingly hard to define, covers an area of human activities that lacks sharp and clearly delineated boundaries. Where this view prevails, he declares, we are likely to be asked to accept as "religious" whatever some author selects for treatment under that label.

(2) The view (which owes something to Durkheim's influence) that religion refers to "a class of metaphorical statements and actions obliquely denoting social relationships and claims to social status."

(3) The view that the term religion is best treated as referring to commerce with some specified class of objects such as "spiritual" or "supernatural" beings (1960:201).

Horton contends that all of these approaches are unsatisfactory as they stand. After criticizing each, he offers us what he describes as an alternative definition. If we are to accept a definition, Horton advises, it should be able to satisfy two considerations: it must "conform as closely as possible to the usage of common sense" (by which I take him to mean commonly experienced usage in anthropology and in Western society at large); and "we must look for [and presumably find] the *universal* aspect of the phenomena commonly denoted by the term: for a culture-bound label [he contends] is of no use in cross-cultural comparisons" (1960:211, emphasis added).

The last quote given above appears in effect to recommend that we conceptualize religion by identifying its universal essence. Horton, to be sure, speaks of a *term* that "commonly" denotes certain phenomena. That is, a verbal expression that points to phenomena conventionally associated with it. But although thus allowing for convention, Horton nevertheless seems to suppose that the postulated phenomena do have their "universal aspect," which presumeably might explain why they are "commonly denoted" by some term.

Put another way, Horton seems to suggest that a universal inheres in, or is shared by, the phenomena themselves, and that a good definition is one that captures or makes explicit that universal. In short, Horton seems to veer in the direction of supporting a "real" definition of religion.

Horton, in any case, holds that "Religion can be looked upon as an extension of the field of people's social relationships beyond the confines of purely human society" (1960:211). In an effort to exclude pets from being rendered religious objects by definition, he adds the rider that the extension of the field of social relationships is one in which humans regard themselves as being in a dependent position vis-à-vis non-human alters (shades of Schleiermacher!). He notes that an obvious consequence of defining religion in this way is to suppose that variables found useful in the analysis of social relations among human beings will also prove productive in the analysis of "man-to-god relationships" (1960:212). He takes what he regards as "one of the most important of such variables," and he explores it to gauge its utility in furthering our comprehension of religious phenomena.

The variable that Horton chooses for exploratory purposes is described in terms of two values, "pure communion" and "pure manipulation." In a pure communion relationship, "ego's action is directed entirely towards obtaining certain responses in alter which he values intrinsically and towards giving certain responses to alter whose discharge is of similar intrinsic value to him." In a pure manipulation relationship, in contrast, "ego values intrinsi-cally neither his own nor alter's responses, alter being treated as a mere means of arriving at a goal which can be defined without reference to the behaviour included in the relationship" (1960:212).

Horton treats these values as two poles framing a continuum of adjustments in the relative importance of communion and manipulation in human relationships. "The majority of religious relationships likely to be studied," he writes, "will have both communion and manipulation aspects and any comprehensive analysis and interpretation must reckon with both" (1960:213).

Horton's thinking about the communion-manipulation contin-uum was stimulated in part by S.F. Nadel's 1954 monograph on the religion of the Nupe, a West African people. Nadel, acquainted with William James's 1902 discussion of religion based on European and American case materials, was struck by how different Nupe religion is in contents and ends from what is found in James's cases.

The materials employed by James, Horton states, are mainly "drawn from religious relationships of an extreme character in which sheer communion with God is stressed to the virtual exclusion of benefits accruing either in life or after death." Nupe religion, in comparison, "lays emphasis almost exclusively on the mainipulation of God for his worldly benefits of health, wealth, and increase" (1960:212).

Horton's remarks, however, strike me as raising a serious question about the appropriateness of comparing and contrast-ing the contents of James's culled cases with Nadel's understand-ings of the manipulative character of Nupe religion. James, after all, is concerned with what he calls "religious geniuses" (1929 [1902]:8), admittedly extreme cases in the general populations to which they belong. Unlike Nadel, James is not concerned with attempting to characterize the religious dispositions and expe-riences of a whole people. James's cases, moreover, may not lie quite as unambiguously close to the communion pole as Horton suggests.

James, of course, views communion as basic to religion. He maintains that "interior prayer" (a special kind of communicative effort) distinguishes religion from all else; wherever we find it, he avers, we find "living religion," even If there be a lack of doctrine (James 1929 [1902]:454). This could be construed as supporting Horton's interpretation of James's materials. One might argue, however, that Horton overinterprets James's case studies. James's communicants, as James describes them, appear to derive various direct benefits from communion, benefits which they themselves apperceive, not least among them a certain peace of mind and assurance in this world.

Horton's understanding of the Nupe situation as presented by Nadel, however, is less subject to critical debate, for Nadel makes such summary statements as the following:

> Nupe doctrine does not teach that the universe is benevolent or that the universe is closely concerned with human fate . . . The self-abandonment of the mystic or visionary is utterly foreign to the Nupe. (1954:273)
>   The acts of worship do not leave any vivid awareness of the achieved communion with the deity nor any lasting sense of the holy. There is nothing of "religiosity" in the Nupe character. (1954:277)

In any case, and despite my reservations, comparison between the religious involvements depicted by James in his case materials and those presented for the Nupe by Nadel does have a certain heuristic value. Nadel, Horton writes, seems to have been surprised by the differences in "the two cultures" with respect to the relationships between human beings and the Gods that they recognize, "but he is too good an ethnographer to have squeezed Nupe religion into a Jamesian mould and has left us instead with some stimulating, if unsystematic, comparisons" (1960:212).

Horton's perspectives and lines of inquiry both in the 1960 paper and in subsequent essays (e.g., 1962, 1964, 1967, 1971, 1973, 1982) impress me as highly stimulating contributions to the study of religion and, more generally, to the comparative study of modes of thought. They are imaginative probings into religiosity and into humanity's needs both to have some understanding of the world and to cope with it. Indeed, the analytical weight that Horton assigns to the communion-manipulation polarity might prove to be especially useful in coming to understand contemporary and future transformations of religiosity in our own society.

Thus, for example, while Anthony F.C. Wallace predicts that the evolutionary fate of religion (which he identifies as "supernaturalism") is inevitable extinction — extinction as a cultural trait throughout the world in consequence of "the increasing adequacy and diffusion of scientific knowledge and of the realization by secular faiths that supernatural belief is not necessary to the effective use of ritual" (1966:264–265) —, Horton suggests otherwise:

> Julian Huxley (1957) . . . and most other workers in the non-human
> sciences have tended to assume that as a wider and wider field of
> phenomena was covered by scientific explanation, so the field of
> the relevance of the gods would shrink, eventually to nothing.
> Certainly, if we look at the purely manipulative aspect of religious
> relationships, this seems a likely outcome . . . However, to infer from
> this the eventual demise of religion is to overlook the communion
> aspect of religious relationships, which is not directly affected by
> the advance of science. As this advance continues, it seems likely
> that the manipulative significance of our religious beliefs will be
> continuously eroded while communion remains. (1960:222)

Finally, because the ideas of both communion and manipulation are likely to be relevant to understanding religiosity and
conceptualizing religion, they provide a useful corrective to an
over-emphasis on what religions may *say* about "ultimate meanings" or "the really real." Devoting serious attention to the
possibility that religious *persons* may crave the emotional satisfaction of personal relations, or vicarious personal relations, with
non-human alters, and that they may wish to manipulate those
alters for their own ends, is likely to work for a better balance
in our overall understandings of religion. Such understandings
ought to be ultimately founded on a theory of human beings,
particularly as they express themselves through modalities that
we label religious. And once we firmly fix our attention on human
beings, we have to take account of their complexity and multi-
dimensionality.

One of the problems that seems to attend the study of religions by intellectuals is the danger of over-intellectualizing religious persons and their religions. Analysis of myth narratives
and other phenomena associated with religions may yield world
pictures of great interest to academics. But while religious persons
may situate themselves with respect to such cosmic schemata,
they might have rather imperfect understandings of them, and
perhaps relatively little interest in them. For religious persons,
religion may be a great deal less — or perhaps a great deal more
— than a system of coherent convictions about ultimate reality.

Melford E. Spiro

Horton's conceptualization of religion as an extension of social
relations outside of the purely human sphere finds a genre
complement in Spiro's definition: "an institution consisting of
culturally patterned interaction with culturally postulated superhuman beings" (1966:96). Spiro argues that belief in the exis-

tence of *superhuman* beings — he declines, he says (1966:91), to "muddy the metaphysical waters with 'supernatural'" — and in their powers to harm or to assist human beings, "is the core variable which ought to be designated by any definition of religion" (1966: 94). He notes, moreover, that Horton (1960) and Goody (1961) reached similar conclusions (Spiro 1966:94).

Spiro observes that it does not necessarily follow from his core variable that religious behavior, in comparison, say, to magical behavior, is "other-worldly" in orientation. Nor does it necessarily mean that religious behavior is fundamentally "spiritual." "The beliefs in superhuman beings, other-worldliness, and spiritual values," he writes, "vary independently" (1966:95).

Spiro emphasizes that religion is a "cultural institution." As such, it is part of the cultural heritage of human social groups. This means, he adds, "that the variables constituting a religious system have the same ontological status as those of other cultural systems: its beliefs are normative, its rituals collective, its values prescriptive" (1966:97). He interprets Durkheim to have this in mind when he insists that there can be no religion without a "church" (Spiro 1966:97). Treating religion this way, moreover, satisfies a desideratum pursued by Goodenough and numerous other social scientists: to study religion as part of the heritage of culturally organized human social groups, on a par with economic institutions, political institutions, and the like. Disagreement among social scientists who take this tack is largely occasioned by opinions respecting how — on the basis of what criteria — one might differentiate religion from other institutions.

Spiro declares — and, differences of phrasing notwithstanding, Goody and Horton are in substantial agreement — that "viewed systematically, religion can be differentiated from other culturally constituted institutions by virtue only of its reference to superhuman beings" (1966:98).

Not everyone accepts that position. Durkheim's (1965 [1912]) well known rejection of theistic definitions of religion, based largely on his understandings of Buddhism, would appear to apply to definitions that emphasize "superhuman beings" as well. And Southwold (1978) explicitly attacks Spiro's position and Spiro's defense of it, going beyond Durkheim in repudiating theism as a necessary element in religion (see Chapter 5).

Anthropomorphism and Stewart Guthrie

Xenophanes of Colophon (d. 470 B.C.E.?) is famous among some social scientists for suggesting that human beings are inclined to envision Gods in their own image: that the Ethiopians imagine their Gods to be black and flat-nosed while those of the Thracians are blue-eyed and red-haired (Diels 1951:133; Xenoph. B 16). But while this is "anthropomorphism," Xenophanes played with the idea that it might constitute part of a potentially more inclusive disposition among sentient life-forms. Speaking perhaps more as an ironist than as a naturalist, he is reported to have said that if cattle and horses had hands and could fashion works of art such as men can, then "horses would draw the forms of their Gods similar to horses, and cattle to cattle, imagining bodies for them in the shape which each of them possesses themselves" (Diels 1951:133; Xenoph. B 15).

Xenophanes, at any rate, clearly disapproved of the human tendency to anthropomorphize divinity. "Homer and Hesiod," he complained, "have attributed to the Gods all of the acts that are a disgrace and a shame to men: stealing, adultery, and deceiving one another" (Diels 1951: 132; Xenoph. B 11). He protested, moreover, human tendencies to suppose that Gods are generated and that they enjoy clothing and speech as well as shapes like human beings (Diels 1951:132; Xenoph. B 14). He himself conceived of a God that "is unlike mortals in either shape or thought" (Diels 1951:135; Xenoph. B 23). This God always remains "in the same place without moving" (Diels 1951:135; Xenoph. B 26), and it sets things in motion by the power of its thought (Diels 1951:135; Xenoph. B 25). (A notion voiced by Hyppolytus [*The Refutation of All Heresies* I:XII] and others to the effect that Xenophanes conceived his God to be spherical may embody a projection back to Parmenides of Elea who likened his own "One Being" to a sphere [Kerferd 1967:353].)

Interestingly enough, early Christian writers tended to regard Xenophanes as a perspicacious monist if not, indeed, one of the first monotheists among the Gentiles. Clement of Alexandria, for instance, congratulates him for "rightly teaching that God is one and incorporeal" (*Stromata* V:XIV). Aristotle, of course, had identified Xenophanes as "the first monist" among several named pre-Socratic theorists (*Metaphysics* A.5, 986b 22–23), albeit he did not esteem him as a natural philosopher, dismissing his views as "somewhat too crude" (*Metaphysics* A.5, 986b 25–27). Werner Jaeger describes him as "an intellectual revolutionary" (1947:41), an instrumental figure in establishing universalism as a basic assumption in Greek theology by nurturing the philosophical conception of a deity who relates to nature and the universe rather than to the polis (1947:48; 213, n. 45).

Xenophanes was one of the first Western writers to emphasize analytically — and to criticize — anthropomorphism as a facet of what we would call religion. He himself saw it as a complex phenomenon. It is not only the tendency to imagine the Gods as embodied in forms like our own, but also to assign them human attributes such as speech and clothing, and to suppose them to be moved by emotions and aspirations akin to those that move us.

Later writers who discuss anthropomorphism, and who are impressed largely by Judeo-Christian-Islamic traditions of religiosity, sometimes stress the attribution of speech, intelligence, will, and purpose over use of human body images. George Douglas Campbell, the Duke of Argyll, for example, deems it necessary to distinguish between "anthropomorphism" and what he calls "anthropopsychism." The former term, he writes,

> is in itself a misrepresentation of the fundamental idea which it is employed to designate, and against which it is intended to raise a prejudice. Anthropo-morphism means literally Man-Formism, conveying the idea that it is, in some sense or other, the human "form" that is ascribed to the agencies which are at work in Nature. But this suggestion is altogether at variance with the truth. It is not the Form of Man that is in question. It is the Mind and Spirit of Man — his Reason, his Intelligence, and his Will. Nor is it even these under all conditions, or under any of the limitations, with which they are associated in us. But the question is of a real and fundamental analogy, despite all differences of form or of limiting conditions, between the Mind which is in us and the Mind which is in Nature. The true etymological expression for the idea, if we are to have any word constructed on the same model out of Greek, would be ... Anthropopsychism, which means not Man-Formism, but Man-Soulism. (1884:99–100).

Argyll argued against the position espoused by Lange in his *Geschichte des Materialismus* (1876/1877 [1865]): that science can only know one kind of mind, the human mind. The increasing acceptance of Darwinian theory in Argyll's time both betokened and contributed to the increasing acceptance of that position, for, as the historian Neal Gillespie (1979:108) puts it, "the touchstone of positive biology, at bottom, was not law or natural causes, but the absence of conscious contrivance or purpose, however these might be conceived." Argyll, in contrast, resisted the elimination of teleology in biology out of conviction that there is Mind other than human mind in nature: that there is intelligence, will, and purpose in the cosmos over and beyond human intelligence, will, and purpose. He thus put himself in opposition to a process that, to adapt an expression from Schiller, we might call the de–Godding or profaning of nature.

Argyll both emphasized the importance of "anthropopsychism" to religion and defended it as a reality in nature. More recently, the anthropologist Stewart Guthrie (1980) has proffered a sophisticated analogue to anthropopsychism. He calls it anthropomorphism, however, and he does not endorse Argyll's religious claim that nature is guided by nonhuman contrivance and purpose.

Guthrie explicitly declares it to be his intention to offer a substantive definition of religion (1980:181). In constructing such a definition he recognizes the similarity of what he proposes to the definitions given by Goody, Horton, and Spiro (among others). Religion, he maintains, "may be defined as systematic application of human-like models to nonhuman, in addition to human phenomena (e.g., in the discovery of 'messages' in plagues and droughts as well as in human language)" (1980:181).

The application of "human-like models" to nonhuman phenomena is "anthropomorphism." Guthrie readily acknowledges that anthropomorphism, broadly conceived, is a phenomenon frequently encountered in human life, and that not all anthropomorphism falls within the purview of religion. He suggests this perhaps unavoidably imprecise distinction in an effort to deal with that fact:

> "Religious" anthropomorphism is relatively systematic, generalized, and integrated, while "nonreligious" anthropomorphism is, like Lévi-Strauss's *bricoleur*, opportunistic, ad hoc, and idiosyncratic. When it is narrow and ad hoc, as when a commercial artist gives a candy bar a face, it may be unconvincing and not "true" in any extended sense . . . When it is careful, elaborate, and well thought out, however, anthropomorphism achieves what Geertz calls the "aura of factuality" and the "uniquely realistic" mood (1966:4) of religion. (1980:192)

In another context, however, he asks what "human-like models" might be, particularly with respect to religion. He then answers that question in an interesting way:

> A few characteristics seem most nearly to distinguish humans from nonhumans. These . . . are . . . language and symbolism generally and resulting capacities for formal and symbolic statements about, and using, social relations among other things. "Religion," then, means applying models to the nonhuman world in whole or in part that credit it with a capacity for language (as do prayer and other linguistic, including some "ritual," action) and for associated symbolic action . . . It is the use of language, then, vis-à-vis the nonhuman world that I think most characterizes religion. (1980:189)

By emphasizing that religious anthropomorphism, which he

conceives to be the central element in religion, is above all the attribution to nonhuman phenomena of capacities to use and respond to symbols, Guthrie shelters his conceptualization of religion under the umbrella of contemporary efforts to identify and understand the semiotic dimensions of human life.

Guthrie's definition illustrates both the fundamental strength and the basic weaknesses of the most thoughtfully constructed monothetic definitions.

The strength of such definitions reposes in the attention that they lavish on some aspect of religions that we intuitively agree, or can be persuaded to agree, is important to religion as we conventionally conceive it. Anthropomorphism is certainly an example. Indeed, many students of religion have explicitly remarked on it or have implicitly credited it with importance. Thus, for example, Frankfort and Frankfort (1946:4) maintain that "The fundamental difference between the attitudes of modern and ancient man as regards the surrounding world is this: for modern, scientific man the phenomenal world is primarily an 'It'; for ancient — and also for primitive — man it is a 'Thou'."

Numbers of Jewish, Christian, and Muslim theologians have warned that the application of anthropomorphic language to deity may perplex and mislead their co-religionists. For the most part, however, they have accepted the use of such language as virtually inevitable. Numbers of them, moreover, have even welcomed it because of their strong commitment to a personalistic conception of God (e.g., Marmorstein 1968 [1937]:1).

Guthrie's recognition of the likely importance of anthropomorphism is thus hardly new. What is new, however, is the extensive and sophisticated analysis he makes of it within the framework of a largely cognitive and semiotic approach to human religiosity.

The major weaknesses of a definitional effort such as Guthrie's are at least two-fold.

First, the feature(s) said to distinguish religion is (are) also found outside of what even the definer may wish to recognize as religion. Yet the definer feels obliged to establish a boundary that will separate religion from non-religion. Guthrie, as already noted, attempts in part to do this by distinguishing between systematic, elaborated applications of anthropomorphism and those that are "narrow and ad hoc." But this hardly draws a firm and precise boundary. (Guthrie also suggests that while "religion may be described as a system of postulated communication at a linguistic level, perhaps magic and divination similarly may be

described as postulated communication at the level of nonhuman animal call systems" [1980:190]).

Horton, as noted earlier in this chapter, also attempts to modify
the definition that he supplies, in his case so that it might exclude
pets from being religious objects. His patchwork, however, does
not impress me as being water-tight. And Spiro trys to characterize the "superhuman" beings of his definition in such a way
as to avoid boundary problems. He tells us that they are "believed
to possess power greater than man," to be able to help or harm
human beings, and to be open to human influence. As Guthrie
points out, however, numbers of religions maintain that some
"superhuman" beings are in certain respects virtually "infrahu-
man" and subject to being threatened, reviled, or tricked, whereas
some human beings, such as magicians, witches, and presidents,
may be credited with great and unusual powers while yet being
non-religious figures (1980:182). In short, substantive monothetic
definitions generally need patchwork in order to sustain the
boundaries that they appear to create, but such patchwork is
more likely to exhibit holes than the perfection of the holy.

Second, in focusing attention on one distinguishing feature,
or on the conjunction of a few, monothetic definitions (as distinct
from listing definitions that do not make any feature necessary)
typically fail to mention many aspects of religion that deserve
discussion. Guthrie, to be sure, has some appreciation of that
weakness, and he takes prophylactic action concerning it in a
footnote: "What I wish to claim is not exactly that religion is
'nothing but' anthropomorphism (nothing is 'nothing but'
something else), but that anthropomorphism is fundamental to
it and that if the various phenomena that have been called
'religion' have anything in common, it is this" (1980:181, n.4).
But that defense strikes me as inadequate.

In my original comments on Guthrie's essay, published simultaneously with his article (Saler 1980:197), I remarked that "what
really needs further exploration and explanation is, in a manner
of speaking, the incompleteness of anthropomorphism." Guthrie
recognizes that nonhuman phenomena remain nonhuman even
though anthropomorphized. The thrust of his essay, nevertheless, is to rivet our attention on their anthropomorphization. Doing
so effectively ignores their vital and often very dramatic or
mysterious nonhuman character. Yet for religious persons, the
transcendence of, or divergence from, our humanity may well
be the very aspect of Gods or other nonhuman beings that signals
their status as religious objects. In support of that point of view,

I quoted the classicist Erland Ehnmark with respect to Homer's description of the Gods:

> To a modern reader the most striking characteristic of the Homeric gods is their humanity; but this cannot possibly have been their chief attribute. What constitutes their divinity is not their likeness to man but the quality that distinguishes them from him. From our point of view the most important criterion for the distinction between gods and men is the fact that the gods only existed in the belief of their worshippers. Such a view, however, necessarily implies that one has ceased to believe in the gods in question; for a living religious faith the gods are just as real as anything else. If they are conceived anthropomorphically they must consequently possess some other quality which renders them divine and distinct from man. It thus follows that if Homer's description of the gods embodied a living religious faith, if it was genuinely felt to represent reality, the gods cannot have been regarded as wholly human and their human attributes must have been of secondary importance. If on the other hand the gods are human throughout it is definitely improbable that they were the objects of faith. (Ehnmark 1935:1)

The Intellectualist Program and Literalism

The works of Goody, Guthrie, Horton, and Spiro cited above exemplify or are congenial with an approach to religion that is called "intellectualist." This approach goes back to Tylor, who emphasizes the roles of curiosity and theorizing in the development of religion, and the efforts of religionists to affect their worlds as well as to render them intelligible. It also goes back to James G. Frazer (1890 I:222), who states that by religion he understands "a propitiation or conciliation of powers superior to man which are believed to direct and control the course of human life." So defined, Frazer points out, religion has both a theoretical aspect (a belief in powers superior to man that significantly affect human life) and a practical aspect (an attempt to propitiate or conciliate those powers).

Horton and Guthrie explicitly declare themselves to be in that tradition, though they offer their own versions of it. Goody can also be accounted as standing in that tradition. Spiro, however, is rather more complex. His theorizing, indeed, is unusually comprehensive. In addition to giving weight to cognitive and pragmatic aspects of religiosity, he assigns considerable importance to *unconscious* needs and processes. He posits, moreover, an important role for "pre-cultural" (pre-verbal) experiences in the acquiring and maintaining of religious suppositions. (While a scholarly appreciation of Spiro's point of view requires us to read many of his works, including some that are not mainly concerned with religion [e.g., 1961], the Preface to the expanded edition of *Burmese Supernaturalism* [1978] is a good place to start.) Still and all, Spiro's position, though complex, overlaps to a significant extent with the intellectualist program as that is described for us by John Skorupski (1976).

Skorupski, a philosopher who interested himself in theories of religion propounded by anthropologists, views the intellectualist research program as turning on certain answers to four questions (1976:9):

1. Why do human actors in various cultures perform certain sorts of *actions* (e.g., ritual actions)? Because, the intellectualist holds, certain *beliefs* can be imputed to those persons, and those beliefs constitute a rationale for performing the actions.
2. How do the actors initially acquire their beliefs? They are socialized into them.
3. Why do these beliefs persist? The intellectualist's answer is complex, but suffice it to say that s/he holds that there are various structural and attitudinal impediments to their falsification.
4. How did these beliefs first originate? They originated out of important human needs: needs both to understand and to control the world. Such beliefs are components of theoretical schemes that render the world meaningful and that serve as rationales for action, and they continue to serve those functions for many people.

Skorupski holds that the answer given to question 4 "constitutes the distinctive intellectualist thesis" (1976:10). He adds that some writers, who could not be termed intellectualists, are in general agreement with the cited answers to the first three questions posed but do not entirely embrace the last (he suggests that Evans-Pritchard is an example).

Various writers credit religious beliefs with "face value" and accept them as sincerely uttered (if mistaken) convictions about the world. And while some of those same writers suppose that people deploy their beliefs in order both to explain the world and to provide a set of working assumptions for controlling it, they contend that those goals are not the only ones that we need to take into account in order to understand traditional religious thought — that needs and preoccupations other than those of explanation and control influence the contents of such thought. Skorupski applies the term "literalism" to "the broader consensus" that accepts the answers cited for the first three questions while leaving open the answer to question 4 (1976:11).

Symbolism

An approach alternative to literalism and its extension in intellectualism is "symbolism." While Skorupski claims that he has identified a program that intellectualists generally subscribe to, he maintains that it is impossible to describe a single program that symbolists would mutually accept (1976:19). Broadly speaking, however, if the key concept in the intellectualist program be "theory," then the key concept for symbolists is "symbol" (1976:12).

The intellectualist views traditional religious thought as constituting theoretical structures that posit causal connections among phenomena. It will be recalled that Tylor, a founding father of the intellectualist approach, viewed so-called primitive peoples as moved by curiosity and as acting to make the world more meaningful. All peoples, the great intellectualist argued (1871, Vol.2), are puzzled by phenomena such as death, dreams, and trances, and they propound theories to explain why the world is the way that they suppose it to be. It is important, intellectualists maintain, to understand the native's beliefs as comprising components of a theory that guides behavior.

In comparison, the traditional symbolist (as distinct from some contemporary practitioners of symbolic analysis who are likely to call themselves "interpretivists") tends to treat asserted religious beliefs as symbolic statements about social relations and social structure. Though admitting that religious utterances have "literal" senses, the symbolist nevertheless holds that those statements must be understood on another level of meaning. Their ultimate significance — and their real interest for the anthropologist — transcends their so-called literal contents. They must be interpreted with regard to the social life of those who affirm them.

Thus, for example, Edmund Leach (1965 [1954]:182) maintains that certain spiritual beings who are talked about by the Kachin, a population in Burma, "are, in the last analysis, nothing more than ways of describing the formal relationships that exist between real persons and real groups in ordinary Kachin society." And he elsewhere (Leach 1966) argues that in certain societies verbal assertions and rituals that seem to suggest an ignorance of the necessary role of males (or, at any rate, of sperm) in procreating human children are not to be understood as revealing a defective biological theory (as the literalist and intellectualist might suppose). Rather, they should be interpreted as cultural dogmas that make sociological sense. Their significance is sociological rather than bio-theoretical: they are symbolic expressions and justifications of various realities in social structure and in social behavior.

The intellectualist and symbolist approaches are freighted with other differences in the treatment of utterances and other forms of behavior (see Skorupski 1976). It is actually the case, however, that no thoughtful anthropologist is one-hundred per cent "symbolist" or one-hundred per cent "literalist-intellectualist," despite occasional polemical excess. A reasonable symbolist, for example, would certainly subscribe to a reasonable point made by Skorupski:

> a metaphorically or symbolically expressed thought is a thought expressed in a form which *does* have a literal meaning: what makes it symbolic or metaphorical is just that (i) the literal meaning (if any) of the sentence is not the meaning to be understood, and (ii) the literal meaning of the words must be grasped if one is to 'decode' the meaning which *is* to be understood. (1976:13)

(By "literal" I take Skorupski to mean the most common or every-day acceptations of words when arranged into sentences: the literal is the experientially familiar.) And any sensible intellectualist recognizes that asserted convictions and other behaviors may have a range of meanings, some rather less accessible than others, and that our appreciation of them will be enhanced if we expand our interpretations as far as the data at hand seem to warrant.

A Wittgensteinian Approach

Now, in addition to literalism-intellectualism and symbolism, Skorupski (1976:13–15) recognizes a third approach: one deriving from the philosopher Ludwig Wittgenstein. This approach maintains that a system of thought is part of a mode of social life and must be understood as such, a contention that most symbolists embrace and that many intellectualists and literalists allow for. But while traditional symbolists, literalists, and intellectualists agree on the need to translate the natives' religious statements (with the symbolists calling for further interpretation of the translations in accordance with their hermeneutical perspectives), the Wittgensteinian would be likely to question whether or not those statements have the literal meanings that the others suppose them to have.

Do religious statements, the Wittgensteinian would ask, have the meanings in the language-games in which they are expressed that allegedly literal translations impute to them? Skorupski (1976:14) observes that "This line of thought has one obvious advantage, which accrues from its preparedness to be much more radical with translation than is the symbolist: the Wittgensteinian has no need to distinguish between levels of meaning, symbolic and literal, and hence avoids the grave difficulties to which this distinction leads."

Within a language-game — "the term 'language-*game*' is meant to bring into prominence the fact that the *speaking* of language is part of an activity, or of a form of life" (Wittgenstein, *Philosophical Investigations* I.23) — , there may be understandings akin to what others mean when they speak of "literal" senses of expressions. "Suppose," says Wittgenstein (in his "Lectures on Religious Belief"),

> someone, before going to China, when he might never see me again, said to me: "We might see one another after death" — would I necessarily say that I don't understand him? I might say [want to say] simply, "Yes. I *understand* him entirely."
> *Lewy:* In this case, you might only mean that he expressed a certain attitude.
> I would say "No, it isn't the same as saying 'I'm very fond of you'" — and it may not be the same as saying anything else. It says what it says. Why should we be able to substitute anything else? (Wittgenstein 1966 [1938]:70–71).

Yet although people who speak the same conventionally denominated language — English, German, whatever — may in some sense understand one another, they may also not understand one another to the point of not really being able to contradict one another. An example given by Wittgenstein has to do with an unbeliever being unable to contradict a religious believer regarding belief in Judgment Day:

> What we call believing in a Judgment Day or not believing in a Judgment Day — The expression of belief may play an absolutely minor role.
> If you ask me whether or not I believe in a Judgment Day, in the sense in which religious people have belief in it, I wouldn't say: "No, I don't believe there will be such a thing." It would seem to me utterly crazy to say this.
> And then I give an explanation: "I don't believe in . . .", but then the religious person never believes what I describe.
> I can't say. I can't contradict that person. (Wittgenstein, *op. cit.*, p. 55).

This case presumably occurs in twentieth century Western

society where religious commitment is likely to signal a special
"form of life," so that where religious conviction is concerned
the believer and non-believer — or so many suppose Wittgenstein suggests — have recourse to different language-games.
Hudson (1977:233) interprets Wittgenstein's example as indicating that Wittgenstein "thought religious discourse irreducible to
any other kind of discourse."

A Wittgensteinian approach to understanding religious utterances and other forms of behavior is probably best known to
anthropologists through certain of the publications of the
philosopher Peter Winch (1958, 1970). Religion, from Winch's
perspective, as one of his critics puts it, is to be understood "from
the inside" (MacIntyre 1970:66). Ritual statements, that is, must
be understood within their contexts of expression. There is no
general norm for intelligibility (Winch 1958:102). That is, one
should not expect to evaluate the intelligibility and rationality of
religious statements against some universal standard of judgment
but only against the standards contained in the "form of life"
in which they are expressed.

Indeed, what we may think of as criteria of logic arise out of
"modes of social life" and are intelligible only in the context of
those ways of living. "For instance," Winch writes, "science is one
such mode and religion is another; and each has criteria of
intelligibility peculiar to itself. So within science or religion actions
can be logical or illogical . . . But we cannot sensibly say that
either the practice of science itself or that of religion is either
illogical or logical; both are non-logical" (1958:100–101). But my
colleague David Murray suggests (Personal Communication) that
Winch may be departing somewhat from a faithful rendition of
Wittgenstein's position. Murray argues that "criteria of intelligibility" as utilized by Winch, and a commitment to understanding
"from the inside" as attributed to Winch by MacIntyre, constitute
mentalisms that Wittgenstein does not include in his philosophical position.

In any case, Wittgensteinian approaches to the philosophy of
religion and, by extension, to the ethnography of religion, have
been criticized on various points by a diversity of critics (see, for
example, several of the essays contained in Wilson 1970). I speak
of approach in the plural, for if there were one True and Holy
later Wittgensteinian approach (Wittgenstein's protests against
such notions notwithstanding), it has long been complicated by,
and refracted through, the different senses of problem and
multiple viewpoints of those who to one extent or another find

stimulation in Wittgenstein's thoughts. Thus, for instance, MacIntyre (1970:69), with some justification, treats Leach as having committed himself to a version of Wittgenstein's theory of meaning (albeit I doubt that Wittgenstein would be pleased by all aspects of it), while others (e.g., Horton 1960 and Spiro 1966, 1968), with at least equal justification, treat Leach as a sort of Arch-Druid of the symbolists. Though we may try to sort out various approaches, life in the form of eclectic anthropologists — to say nothing of polemical ones! — often defeats our efforts to produce neat and tidy classifications.

The various approaches sketched here — literalist, intellectualist, symbolist, Wittgensteinian, and plausible and implausible combinations of any of the aforementioned — have much to say about intelligibility, translation, and rationality, all of which are important issues for the study of religions. I shall have more to say in the next two chapters about one strand of the Wittgensteinian tradition as it relates to the problem of conceptualizing religion as an analytical category. Here, however, some additional remarks about symbolist approaches are in order.

Some Symbolist Efforts at Clarification

Definitions offered by symbolists vary. By and large, however, symbolists tend to conceptualize religion elementally in ways that are not saliently incompatible with intellectualist definitions. Thus, for example, J. H. M. Beattie, a well known symbolist anthropologist, writes that he uses the terms religion and religious in one of his essays

> to refer to what used to be called 'primitive' religion, that is to the belief, widespread in all cultures, in individual and 'personalized' gods and other non-human spirit powers, who can influence and be influenced by human beings, and to the rites associated with this belief. I do not intend to refer to the vastly more sophisticated and abstract theological concepts of, for example, some kinds of modern Western Christianity. (1970:240, n.2)

As pointed out earlier, symbolist (as distinguished from "interpretivist") approaches not only tend to treat such beliefs as ritual affirmations that have symbolic as well as "literal" meanings, but to maintain that the former meanings are sociologically more interesting than the latter. In fact, traditional symbolists tend to focus on ritual, even to the point of according a certain analytical primacy to the *uttering* of "beliefs" rather than to their apparent contents. They tend to regard the voicing of beliefs as one sort of ritual event, and to interpret such an event as "saying" much the same thing that is acted out in other kinds of ritual behavior.

One of the most extreme statements of this point of view is furnished by Leach, who dismisses arguments about the rationality or irrationality of the contents of belief as "scholastic nonsense." He declares that, as he sees it, "myth regarded as a statement in words 'says' the same thing as ritual regarded as a statement in action. To ask questions about the content of belief which are not contained in the content of ritual is nonsense" (Leach 1965 [1954]:13–14).

Beattie advocates a more moderate symbolist approach in his text-book, *Other Cultures* (1964). He begins by distinguishing between practical, commonsensical techniques and "ritual or 'magico-religious'" ways of doing things. He does so by attributing an "institutionalized symbolic element" in what is done to the latter while claiming that it is absent in the former (1964:202). He then goes on to argue that in some cultures magic and religion are not clearly distinguished (1964:212). Beliefs and practices that "are usually called religious" often contain elements of magic, and magical activities, so-called, may often make reference to spirits or Gods. "What is common to all these kinds of activities," he states, "is the ritual, symbolic element they contain. With this is combined the idea, implicit or explicit, that there is a certain kind of efficacy in the performance of the rites themselves" (*ibid.*).

Yet if we allow for the complexity of the social and cultural situations in any specific case, Beattie argues, we may draw a convenient, practical distinction between magic and religion. Though there will be difficult borderline cases, the eminent symbolist maintains, we may nevertheless follow Tylor (!) in distinguishing beliefs and practices that involve references to "personalized" spiritual beings from those that do not but imply instead some notion of impersonal or "unindividualized" power. The former point to religion, the latter to magic (*ibid.*). And though beliefs embodied in ritual may provide the natives with "acceptable explanations for events which would otherwise be inexplicable" (1964:206), "the essentially expressive character of ritual" must be understood in addition to whatever instrumental power the natives may attribute to it and in addition to whatever explanatory significance they may invest in the beliefs that it embodies (1964:204).

Beattie thus allows for the intellectual aspects of belief — and, by implication, the questions that anthropologists might raise and debate about the rationality of belief — while directing our attention to the expressive aspects of ritual and the beliefs associated with it. This strikes me as both fair-minded and potentially productive.

The More Inclusive Outlooks of Symbolists and Intellectualists

Both symbolists and intellectualists are likely to treat with religion on the most elemental level by offering, and/or operating with, a monothetic definition. Among both intellectualists and symbolists, moreover, such definitions constitute components of more inclusive theoretical outlooks. Those outlooks transcend a focus on "religion." They sum to general overviews on human beings and their culturally organized societies. They also implicate methodological positions on how we might most productively enhance our understandings of humankind.

The intellectualist, to paraphrase Horton (1964), tends to see ritual humans as a subtype of theory-building humans. The symbolist may not deny that view. But s/he emphasizes human propensities to code messages in symbolic form and to enmesh one's self and one's fellows in webs of meaning that assert and confirm social values and social possibilities. If we discount polemics and look on these two approaches from some distance, they are not as far apart on the immediate ethnographic level as some of the protagonists in either camp would have us believe. On more general levels of significance, however, they are sometimes made to serve different appraisals of what one might do with ethnography.

Intellectualists, by and large, have historically supported the idea of engaging in comparative studies in order to test various hypotheses about causal relations between religious variables and other sorts of variables.

Symbolists are harder to characterize on that point. They do sometimes compare cultural traditions (e.g., Turner 1962). The earlier symbolists, moreover, are much given to positing relationships between social variables and what they take to be symbolic statements of one kind or another. They often affirm that the latter refer to or express the former, such affirmations effectively positing causal connections. For the most part, indeed, the efforts of many symbolists have largely been directed to "decoding messages:" they attempt to show what beliefs and other presumptively ideational expressions say about social structure, and they are inspired to that task by some relatively optimistic (if dubiously sophisticated) assumptions about "decoding."

Greater subtlety and a more tempered optimism (sometimes so tempered as to suggest pessimism) distinguish in part a newer style of approach that seems to be supplanting — and to some extent emerging from — the older symbolic anthropology. Some proponents of this newer approach broadly term themselves and like-minded others "interpretivists."

Interpretivists

Numbers of interpretivists disparage the intellectualists' conceptions of, and interest in, comparison and causality. They maintain that anthropology must be an "interpretive" or "hermeneutical" rather than a "scientific" discipline. Epistemological considerations appropriate to the natural sciences, they assert, are inappropriate for cultural anthropology.

Contemporary interpretivists, however, do not constitute a monolithic group. There are significant differences among them. One may discern, nevertheless, certain themes or directions that have kindled the enthusiasm of some and in one way or another have made an impress on others. These include, for example, suggestions offered with respect to refining the very idea of interpretation. Various suggested refinements are intended to move contemporary hermeneutics away from such older brands as those marked by Schleiermacher's romanticism or Dilthey's psychologizing (Dilthey emphasized a distinction between certain conceptions of explanation on the one hand and understanding and interpretation on the other, conceptions now supplanted by others).

In an effort to adopt and further develop a hermeneutical approach with which they might feel comfortable in the ethnographic field as well as in the lecture hall — that is, an interpretive approach that seems to maximize the prospects of an open texture —, some anthropologists turned to thinkers such as Michel Foucault and Paul Ricoeur. This introduced into anthropology novel and contextually related conceptualizations that attach to words such as "discourse," "text," "reading," and "appropriation" as well as, of course, "interpretation." It also introduced novelly-phrased suggestions for conceptualizing creative engagements with the objects of our scholarly concerns, as in the following statement:

> To read is, on any hypothesis, to conjoin a new discourse to the discourse of the text. This conjunction of discourses reveals, in the very constitution of the text, an original capacity for renewal which

is its open character. Interpretation is the concrete outcome of conjunction and renewal. (Ricoeur 1981:158)

These developments stimulated increased discussions of what is involved in the production of ethnographic texts. Anthropologists have long debated various issues in the doing of ethnography in the field. Now, however, in addition to enhanced considerations of ethnographer-native interactions and possible 'misreadings', increased critical attention is directed to a diversity of issues attendant on the writing of ethnographies and the interactions of readers with the texts produced (see, for example, Clifford and Marcus 1986). And, as one might expect, the problem of universals and other problems respecting categories arise in such discussions.

Are there human universals on which we can base analytical categories that might be defensibly used across ethnographies? Or should each ethnography be constructed largely by employing native categories? And if we elect the latter course, how do we avoid contaminating native categories with our own or in other ways encumbering the discourse of our text in the effort to make it intelligible to non-native readers?

Some contemporary anthropologists, sometimes identified by their colleagues as "poststructuralists" or "postmodernists," are especially outspoken in professing a marked preference for the particular. They endorse the suggestion, reiterated by Rorty (1979:43), that universals may well be "*flatus vocis*," mere words. They are very likely to be inhospitable to the notion that religion is a *sui generis* universal (see the discussion of Asad in Chapter 3). More or less critical of representationalist theories of language, they espouse a relativism that not only affirms the uniqueness of each interpretive effort, but holds that the published product of such an effort can be read in multiple ways — that, in fact, interpretations must be interpreted, and that they are likely to be interpreted in diverse fashion by different readers. They are, in a manner of speaking, *against interpretation* to the extent that it may be formulaically conceived, seemingly apodictic, and the product and servant of what some of them call "encompassing" or "totalizing" theories.

The interpretivist agenda, still evolving, has much to recommend it. Nurtured by various streams of literary criticism and Continental philosophy, and influenced by much else besides, it confesses itself to be anti-authoritarian. In principle, at least, it welcomes many kinds of experiments in the writing and reading of ethnographies. According to James Clifford (1983:133), "Interpretive anthropology, by viewing cultures as assemblages of texts, loosely and sometimes contradictorally united, and by highlighting the inventive poesis at work in all collective representations, has contributed significantly to the defamiliarization of ethnographic authority."

Contemporary anthropological interpretivists tend to emphasize ambiguity, multivocality, and paradox in what people say and in culture as condition or context for what people say. They question old paradigms for bounding and comprehending cultural phenomena. They try (not always successfully) to avoid following in the footsteps of those older anthropologists who portrayed the natives as abstract and a-historical. And they are often self-conscious about the roles of authors — and readers — in working towards some understanding of concretized and historicized others. I find all of this attractive and promising. But there are some features of the interpretivist agenda — it is still too early to speak of a program, and some interpretivists in any case would repudiate the very notion of a program — that dampen somewhat my enthusiasm for it.

While I recognize that "interpretivists" call themselves that to emphasize that their approach is "hermeneutical" rather than "scientific," and that their claims about cultures are to be regarded as interpretations, *constructions*, rather than objective recordings of "data" given by the world, I nevertheless regret their appropriation of the word "interpretation," even allowing for the refinements they have attached to that term. *All of us*, after all, are *inevitably* interpretivists in a broad sense of the word, for, as Popper (1962:38, n.3) points out, all of our observations "*are interpretations in the light of theories.*" Observations, Popper suggests, are perceptions that have been prepared in some way by our theories or biases. They thus constitute low-level interpretations. Since we all make, and are dependent on, observations, we all engage in and proffer interpretations. A cardinal problem — at least for some of us — is how to render our interpretations responsible. Are we not accountable to some canon? Or does anything go?

To their credit, numbers of interpretivists are sensitive to that problem. They generally recognize that observations are in some sense guided or colored interpretations, in the most common acceptation of the word interpretation. While the relativist position espoused by many of the postmodernists suggests that full interpretive consensus is unlikely — that, indeed, two ethnographers may come to radically different understandings of the cultural expressions of some population and in a profound sense both may be right —, many interpretivists nevertheless explicitly or implicitly endorse general standards for research.

Hard work, which is likely to include serious efforts to learn the local language, and personal sensitivity and honesty, interpretivists generally acknowledge (as do other anthropologists), are professional obligations. Professional standards, in short, are given wide consensual endorsement within the discipline.

In practice, however, attempts to implement the interpretivists' agenda sometimes eventuate in claims that critics may regard as unsubstantiated. In fairness to interpretivists, however, it must be acknowledged that this is not peculiar to them. Other sorts of ethnographers may also leave their readers with the impression that there is something of a gap or inconsistency between so-called "data" (low-level interpretations) and imaginative higher order interpretations. But over and beyond that problem, there is the seeming lack of cumulative payoff in extreme forms of the interpretivist approach.

As I understand it, extreme varieties of that approach would have us spend our lives in generating interpretations, without overtly formulating and testing transcultural theories. But even if we could avoid developing and evaluating such theories — even, that is, if it were possible to immunize our minds against transcultural conjectures and comparisons — , should we want to do so?

In actuality, of course, the problem does not arise, for we are perforce transcultural comparativists and theorists, whether we like it or not and whether we admit it or not. Our culture's categories, themes, and nurtured sensitivities are not exorcised from our minds when we immerse ourselves in the study of some other culture. Rather, our understandings (including what some might call our "misunderstandings") of our own culture affect the ways that we attend to, and interpret, the cultural creations of the natives. So, too, do any of our other cross-cultural experiences and understandings, including the reading, discussing, and intellectual assimilation of ethnographies.

In the absence of formal articulation and testing of our transcultural theories, we tend to impose them without adequate controls. We are all guilty of doing that to one degree or another. Some of our theoretical suppositions and categorical allegiances are so fundamental to our thinking that we are either not fully aware of them or in other respects are not inclined to test them. Still others are deemed deserving of testing, at least in some circles, but we never seem to get around to doing so. Some interpretivists, as is the case for some other anthropologists, occasionally appear to be quite casual about relating assertion to evidence and critically reviewing their own interpretive leaps.

That might seem to be ironic, for "criticism" is virtually a sacred word among contemporary anthropological interpretivists. Not only do they call for the use of our knowledge of non-Western others to criticize our own society, but they endorse, and often practice, criticism of the rhetorical styles and analytical efforts of other anthropologists. Further, contemporary interpretivist anthropologists are on record as calling for rigorous self-criticism: criticism of one's own categories, one's own rhetoric, one's own assumptions and interpretations. We would all be better anthropologists, and better students of religion, I imagine, if we were as self-critical as we sometimes advise ourselves to be.

Some contemporary interpretivists, in any case, tend to operate with tacit understandings of what they mean by religion rather than explicit monothetic characterizations, even of the sort given by Geertz in 1966. They prefer engaging native categories and constructing "thick descriptions" rather than investing time and energy in what some of them regard as "scholastic" essentialist exercises. In brief, they deem attempts to establish and characterize universal categories to be unnecessary and unproductive.

Universals

Horton, it may be recalled, remarks that in evaluating a definition, "we must look for the universal aspect of the phenomena commonly denoted by the term" (1960:211). Guthrie, who seems to agree with Horton on that point, writes of "the apparently universal anthropomorphism of religion" (1980:183) in justifying his own proffered definition.

These particular references to the universal do not advance the claim that religion is universally distributed among all human groups. Other anthropologists, however, make such a claim. Some who do, moreover, include religion (or something that falls within its conventionally conceived purview) in lists of so-called "cultural universals," resemblances in form that are claimed to be found in every culture (e.g., Wissler 1923, Murdock 1945, Kluckhohn 1953). Some anthropologists, moreover, stress the importance of achieving adequate definitions of universal categories of culture for comparative studies (e.g., Goodenough 1970). A cogent riposte to that point of view is given by Spiro:

insistence on universality in the interests of a comparative social science is, in my opinion, an obstacle to the comparative method for it leads to continuous changes in definition and, ultimately, to definitions which, because of their vagueness or abstractness, are all but useless. (And of course they commit the fallacy of assuming that certain institutions must, in fact, be universal, rather than recognizing that universality is a creation of definition . . .) (1966:86–87)

Horton and Guthrie use universal in a related but different way. They are concerned with some feature of religion that must always be present if religion is to be present: that is, to use Horton's words, "the universal aspect of the phenomena commonly denoted by the term" religion. Spiro in effect joins Horton and Guthrie when he insists that "the belief in superhuman beings and in their power to assist or to harm man . . . is the core variable which ought to be designated by any definition of religion" (1966:94). Not only that, but this belief "approaches universal distribution," although Spiro does not describe religion as a cultural universal on that account.

The use of universal in reference to a necessary feature or "aspect" of "phenomena commonly denoted" by the term religion touches on what philosophers have called "the problem of universals." That problem, as it developed in Euro-American philosophy and theology, is actually a congeries of related problems in metaphysics, epistemology, and the philosophy of language. Wolterstorff (1970:1) speaks of it as a "cluster of issues." Thus, for example, while universals are sometimes formulaically distinguished from particulars (or "substances") by application of a simplistic rule — universals can be predicated of particulars, but particulars cannot be predicated of universals — Bochenski observes that the term universal

> has been and is still used in regard to different levels or realms of reality and it seems to have a different meaning in each of them. At least five such levels have been quoted, namely that of linguistic symbols, of subjective mental entities, of objective meanings, of phenomenal realities and of transcendent entities. (1956:36)

At the risk of simplifying too greatly, formulations of the classical problem can be approached in terms of questions such as these: In addition to recognizing the existence of individual things, should we grant ontic status to species, properties, or relations? When we use general terms such as human being or religion, or when we say that something is blue, or that something is larger than someting else, do those expressions have correspondences in the "objective" world that support those words as labels for universals? What justifications might we claim for grouping singulars together under the same term? And if there are universals, what knowledge might we have of them and how do we account for that knowledge?

Philosophers discern several major approaches to that congeries of problems. Those approaches, each of which admits of varieties, are dubbed "realism," "conceptualism," "nominalism," "recurrence theory," and "resemblance theory" (Aaron 1967, Woozley 1967, Staniland 1972).

Realism holds that universals exist as mind-independent entities. For Plato, universals (Forms) exist self-sufficiently in their own realm. Aristotle, though believing in the reality of universals, denied the absolute reality, the total independence, attributed to them by Plato. He envisioned them, rather, as existing as common elements of form relative to, and "said of," particular things.

Conceptualisms of various sorts, associated in one way or another with philosophers such as Locke, Berkeley, and Hume, generally hold that only particulars exist in the objective world and that universals are mind-dependent. Our use of general terms is justified because such words relate to, or correspond to, concepts or ideas that we develop in our minds through experience. We build-up general concepts from particular ideas, according to Hume, by 'annexing' them to a general term.

Nominalism admits of a number of varieties. Generally speaking, nominalists hold that only particular or individual things exist in the world, and that universals are merely names or words. Universals have no independent reality of their own either within the mind (conceptualism) or outside of it (realism). In an extreme version of nominalism (one that scarcely anyone endorses), what is common to particulars called by the same name is simply that name, for human beings use general terms to group things in completely arbitrary ways. More moderate versions, while holding that only words are universals, attribute the groupings of things that people make to the apperception (perhaps culturally induced) of some resemblance between those things.

"Nominalism for me," Nelson Goodman writes (1956:16–17), "consists specifically in the refusal to recognize classes . . . Nominalism as I conceive it . . . does not involve excluding abstract entities, spirits, intimations of immortality, or anything of the sort; but requires only that whatever is admitted as an entity at all be construed as an individual." I have elsewhere cited Rorty's relaxed, pragmatic construal of nominalism.

Recurrence theory is mainly associated with the philosopher Richard I. Aaron (1952, 2nd edition 1967). He holds that our approach to universals should start with the fact that "our thinking rests in part on the observation of recurrences... The same features recur in different individual beings and individual things and we are aware of this fact" (1967:231). Both recurring similarities and identities are universals (1967:235), which suggests that recurrence theory is a variety of realism. But Aaron adds that principles of grouping are also universals:

> We cannot then simply say that a universal is a natural recurrence. Any principle of grouping is a universal and we cannot identify principle of grouping with natural recurrence. This is an avowal that the question 'What is a universal?' cannot be answered in one sentence, but needs two. *Universals are natural recurrences; universals are principles of grouping or classifying.* (1967:240)

Resemblance theories resemble moderate nominalism is certain ways, and on some accounts "nominalism must in the end reduce itself to a resemblance theory which, if acceptable, finally renders nominalism unnecessary" (Woozley 1967:204). Resemblance theories maintain that only individual things exist, and that they resemble and differ from one another in various ways. At the same time, however, those theories generally reject the supposition that if two objects resemble one another they can be said to be identical in one or more features. Not to reject that idea, Woozley (1967:204) points out, "would be to reintroduce the Aristotelian universal":

> Red objects are to be called red simply because they resemble each other in a way in which they do not resemble blue objects, or hard objects... Nothing is described by saying that the universal red is what is common to any pair of red objects which is not more accurately and less misleadingly described by saying that both are red — that is, resemble each other in respect of being each red. There is a similarity between the red of one and the red of the other, and the similarity might be anything from being virtually exact... to being only approximate and generic... The world is made up of individual things and events, with their individual qualities and relations, and with resemblances in different respects and of different degrees. (Woozley 1967:204)

Bertrand Russell (1912) holds that resemblance, which he identifies as a relation, must itself be a universal. If we admit it as such, he suggests, we have undercut the ground for denying that there are other universals, and we might as well go ahead and recognize others when and if it is convenient to do so.

Philosophers such as Price (1969a [1953]) and Woozley (1967), however, seek to avoid the force of Russell's suggestion by particularizing resemblances. That is, the resemblance that we posit between two individuals is as individual as the individuals themselves. And we may go on, if so inclined, to apperceive an individual resemblance between one resemblance relation and another, and so on. This, of course, constitutes a concession to regress. But it seems a tolerable one, for it allows us to avoid apotheosizing resemblance into a universal and so rendering ourselves captive to metaphysical commitments that we might prefer to avoid.

A case can be made for including Wittgenstein's "family resemblances" under the rubric of resemblance theory, and perhaps treating it as the "fruition" of that approach (e.g., Reese 1980:599). On the other hand, Wittgenstein's theorizing may perhaps be judged to deserve a special classificatory niche, especially if one gives credence to Bambrough's (1960/1961) claim that Wittgenstein has solved the problem of universals (see Chapter 5). In any case, Wittgenstein's construct plays important roles in the argument respecting the conceptualization of religion that is developed in the next two chapters, and additional remarks on the concept of family likeness will be deferred till then.

Suffice it for present purposes to observe that most past anthropological discussions of the problem of defining religion have tended to gravitate toward Aristotelian realism or to some form of conceptualism. Nowadays, however, the fashionableness of nominalism works against those gravitational pulls, at least among the fashionable. One wonders, however, how free of allegiances to universals most contemporary anthropologists actually are.

It is my impression that many anthropologists continue to assume that if various phenomena throughout the world pertain to a category the general term for which is "religion," it should be because those phenomena share some property, or some set of conjunctive features, in common. It is my further impression that numbers of anthropologists continue to assume that the general term "religion" is properly used, or is best used, when its usage corresponds with reality: that is, when it is used to refer to, and to construct representations of, what is "out there" in the world. Religion, as term or concept or existential reality, is still, for many anthropologists, assimilable to this dictionary definition of "universal" as a noun: "a general concept or term or something in reality to which it corresponds: ESSENCE" (*Webster's Ninth New Collegiate Dictionary* 1983:1291).

The dictionary definition of "universal" that follows immediately after the one quoted above reads: "a behavior pattern or institution (as the family) existing in all cultures." I have already alluded to the efforts of anthropologists to list "cultural universals." These are sometimes conceived of as common denominators of cultures (Murdock 1945), that is, similarities or identities in form (but not necessarily in content) claimed to be found in all cultures (e.g., religion, kinship, law, etc.). Those who list them generally regard culture itself as a human universal, although at a higher level of abstraction than its putative common denominators.

It is less fashionable today to publish such lists (albeit discursive, limited approximations to them are still encountered in introductory textbooks in anthropology). This tradition, nevertheless, a tradition that has constituted a salient aspect of the disciplinary emphasis given to concepts of culture, has doubtless reinforced the tacit or explicit allegiances that many anthropologists have given to the notion of universals. So, too, has the positing of "linguistic" or "language universals" and debate among linguists with respect to "formal" and "substantive" universals, "implicational" and "non-implicational" universals, "absolute" universals, and related issues (see, for example, Greenberg 1966, 1990 and Comrie 1989).

Frits Staal has recently used the term "universal" in a technical work in Indology "to refer to any feature, entity, or structure that is shared by all human beings but not by other animals" (1988:1). Staal's usage is reminiscent of an important traditional use of extended conceptions of universals: the celebration of what is variously held to be distinctive of human beings. This employment probably contributes to the attachment that many have for universals. And it may account in part for resistance to replacing them with family resemblances or other constructs. For some people, Rorty writes, "To suggest that there are no universals — that they are *flatus vocis* — is to endanger our uniqueness" (1979:43). It is to do so, that is, for persons who cannot divorce themselves from essentialism and its incapsulation in realist or conceptualist universals. There are, however, alternatives, and I consider some with particular respect to religion in the following chapters.

Finally, by way of a bridge statement to Chapters 5 and 6, I suggest that many scholars might be better off if they approached universals as a matter of costs and benefits rather than ontology. Numbers have quarreled over whether or not universals are (to borrow language from Geertz, who borrowed language from Plato) "really real." But do the benefits of talking about universals as if they have an objective or independent existence outweigh the costs (calculated in terms of metaphysical baggage)? Perhaps in linguistics and in some other fields the costs are slight or otherwise justifiable. For students of religion (kinship, law, etc.), however, the costs, in my opinion, are a needless extravagance. That is because everything worthwhile that scholars might hope to gain in such cases by affirming universals can be accomplished by positing resemblances.

In Summary: Some Benefits and Costs of Monothetic Definitions

Monothetic definitions have a certain utility. They can be pedagogically useful in initially marking out some domain of study for students. They can be heuristically utile, aiding in the learning process and stimulating thought and research along demarcated lines. And because they generally do capture at least some similar elements in similar areas of human experience, they can have orientational value as starting points for interesting inquiries. Their disadvantages for the establishment of analytical categories, however, overshadow their advantages.

Monothetic definitions typically narrow down whatever it is that they purport to define to one or a few variables. While this does not necessarily foreclose consideration of interesting complexities and subtleties in the case of religion, it does serve to concentrate interest, and so potentially deflect attention away from other matters. Over and above this general — though not in itself fatal — observation, there are others that deserve notice.

Thoughtful ethnographers are likely to judge substantive monothetic definitions of religion to constitute potential sources of distortion in some ethnographic applications. Such definitions sometimes explicitly depend on concepts that may not be cognitively salient among various peoples (as, for instance, in definitions that are tied to the Western category "supernatural"). Or, more broadly, they require the ethnographer to identify and circumscribe some domain in native representations or experiences that fits, however problematically, the definition (as, for example, in definitions that rest the essence of religion on a putative sensitivity to "the sacred," or on a concern for "the really real," or on a hypothesized feeling of "utter dependence on the infinite").

Because, moreover, substantive monothetic definitions are constituted by the specification of a set of necessary and sufficient conditions for determining "categorically" — that is, "digitally" in terms of "yes" or "no" — whether a prospective candidate belongs to the group comprehended by the definition, they establish overly rigid boundaries between religion and non-religion. This, in turn, sometimes gives rise to interminable arguments about so-called "borderline" cases — are they, or are they not, "religions"?

Monothetic definitions of religion that veer toward functional considerations may well involve us in even more severe problems when we try to apply them. When, for instance, they identify religion as a way of coping with presumptively universal existential or emotional concerns, it is hard to limit what can then be assigned to the rubric religion, and virtually everyone is rendered religious by definition. This in effect constitutes a rejection of Spiro's (1966:91) plea that our definition ought not to be "counter-intuitive." Religion is a word that has traditional meanings for us and for the audience for which we write, and by so widening or otherwise altering what it includes, it may well cease to have much utility as a research and literary tool.

In conclusion, monothetic definitions of religion are costly research devices. In effect, they both express and facilitate the concretization of analytical categories and terms, the dubious conflation of those categories and terms with presumptive "things out there in the world." Our word religion, monothetic definitions notwithstanding, has considerable functional utility, and it may well be given more if we desist from attempting to bound some abstract, universal meaning for it.

CHAPTER FIVE

MULTI-FACTORIAL APPROACHES:
FAMILY RESEMBLANCE AND POLYTHESIS

> *... arranging butterflies according to their types and sub-types is tautology. It merely reasserts something you already know in a slightly different form.*
> — Edmund R. Leach, *Rethinking Anthropology*, 1961, p.5

> *Although it is contrary to our intuition as taxonomists, we must adjust to the existence of a multitude of 'valid' taxonomic arrangements of the butterflies.*
> — Paul R. Ehrlich and Anne H. Ehrlich, "The Phenetic Relationships of the Butterflies: I. Adult Taxonomy and the Nonspecificity Hypothesis," *Systematic Zoology* 16(4):315 (1967).

Some students of religion have come to suspect or suppose that no single distinguishing feature, or no specific conjunction of distinguishing features, can universally be found in what, on various grounds, we may wish to identify as "religions."

William James, for example, remarks that "As there ... seems to be no elementary religious emotion, but only a common storehouse of emotions upon which religious objects may draw, so there might conceivably also prove to be no one specific and essential kind of religious act" (1929 [1902]:29). We are very likely to find, James (1929:27) suggests, "no one essence, but many characters which may alternately be equally important to religion."

In a similar vein, Raymond Firth observes that "resting the definition on a single criterion is like balancing a pyramid on its point — in theory it can be done, but it is an unstable position and not a very helpful exercise." He goes on to state that he prefers

> a demarcation of the field in more empirical terms, in configurational or multi-factorial fashion. This must allow for the possibility that in any one case not every element in the configuration will be present, and that every element present will not necessarily be there to the same degree. (1959:131)

In general agreement with the positions taken by James and Firth in the passages quoted, this and the following chapter are concerned with multi-factorial approaches to conceptualizing religion. Such approaches suggest how we might deliberately crystalize analytical categories suitable for furthering transcultural research and writing.

My exercise is addressed to this question: Given our various appetites for descriptive, historical, and comparative engagements, and taking "religion" as an example of traditional anthropological categories, how might we best conceptualize and use it?

Two conceptual approaches, brought to the attention of many cultural and social anthropologists by Rodney Needham (1972, 1975, 1980, 1983), command a certain attention. They are identified, respectively, as the concept of "family resemblance" and, with some demurs to be discussed later, "polythetic classification" (from the Greek, *poly*, 'many', *thetikos*, 'capable of placing').

J.Z. Smith (1982 [1980]:136, n.15) remarks that these two approaches "are built around quite different philosophical presuppositions," and he finds "the parallel" that Needham (1975) draws between them "somewhat superficial." Chaney (1978:139), in a more extensive treatment, makes an analogous point: that while "Needham's discussion of 'family resemblances' and his discussion of 'polythetic classification' are first-class, separately, ... his converging of them veils phenomenal differences."

I agree with Chaney, and concur with Smith regarding the different philosophical presuppositions around which the two are built. Considered pragmatically, however, both conceptualizations encourage us to think in anti-essentialist ways about definitions and their relation to the phenomenal world. In that respect, at least, Needham is right to argue that they indicate a certain intellectual convergence as understood against the background of the history of ideas; he does not claim identity for them.

Family Resemblance

"Family resemblance," as an established philosophical construct, is preeminently associated with Ludwig Wittgenstein's concept of philosophy as "a battle against the bewitchment of our intelligence by means of language" (*Philosophical Investigations* I.109).

Wittgenstein argues in his later work that the meanings of expressions — "'symbols', 'words', 'sentences'" (*Philosophical Investigations* I.23) — are to be found in their use. The use of an expression relates to a "language-game:" "the whole, consisting of language and the actions into which it is woven" (*Philosophical Investigations* I.7).

While a given expression may be employed to talk about various particulars, there need be no single quality or feature that links them all:

> Consider for example the proceedings that we call "games." I mean board-games, card-games, ball-games, Olympic games, and so on. What is common to them all?—Don't say: "There *must* be something common, or they would not be called 'games'"—but *look and see* whether there is anything common to all.—For if you look at them you will not see something that is common to all, but similarities, relationships, and a whole series of them at that. To repeat: don't think, but look! . . . And the result of this examination is: we see a complicated network of similarities overlapping and criss-crossing: sometimes overall similarities, sometimes similarities of detail.(*Philosophical Investigations* I.66)

Wittgenstein adds that "I can think of no better expression to characterize these similarities than 'family resemblances'; for the various resemblances between members of a family: build, features, colour of eyes, gait, temperament, etc. etc. overlap and criss-cross in the same way.- And I shall say: 'games' form a family" (*Philosophical Investigations* I.67).

Just as Wittgenstein maintains that what we call "games" are linked by family resemblances, so, too, do some persons inspired by him suggest the same for "religions." In this view, the phenomena for which we commonly use the word "religion" do not all necessarily share a feature in common, nor do they all necessarily resemble one another with respect to some one trait or quality. On inspection, however, they collectively reveal a multiplicity of "similarities overlapping and criss-crossing."

J.R. Bambrough

This approach is doubtless even more attractive for persons who agree with J. Renford Bambrough that "Wittgenstein solved what is known as 'the problem of universals'" (1960/61:207). Bambrough suggests that many philosophers have failed to recognize Wittgenstein's achievement because he talks to them in an idiom that diverges from their conventional academic discourse. "In his striving to find a cure for 'our craving for generality', in his polemic against 'the contemptuous attitude towards the particular case'," Bambrough writes, Wittgenstein "was understandably wary of expressing his own conclusions in general terms" (1960/61: 211–212). In avoiding generalities, he avoids the standard phrasings of problems and theories in philosophy: he speaks about "games," and "colors," and "families," and about reading, and understanding, and the like, but not about "the problem of universals" (1960/61: 212).

In support of his opinion that Wittgenstein solved the problem of universals, Bambrough paraphrases him in general terms that can be related to traditional philosophical theories. In doing so, of course, he states what he thinks that Wittgenstein is actually saying. Various other philosophers, Bambrough alleges, misinterpret Wittgenstein. Or they understand his concept of "family resemblances" in such a way as to restrict its range of application unduly (1960/61: 214), and so fail to obtain a clear view of what Wittgenstein has accomplished.

Bambrough's exposition of his understanding of Wittgenstein's position contrasts Wittgenstein to nominalists and realists. Both nominalists and realists agree that to justify objectively the application of a general term (such as, for example, "game") to its instances (in this example, "games"), those instances would have to have something in common over and beyond their mutuality in being instances. But having agreed to that point, they then diverge in their opinions.

The nominalist, Bambrough (1960/61:217) says, is right to claim that the instances lack a common additional element beyond mutually being instances of the general term. But the nominalist is wrong to conclude that the application of a general term lacks objective justification. "The nominalist says that games have nothing in common except that they are called games" (1960/61:217).

The realist, Bambrough opines (1960/61:217), is right to hold that there is some objective justification for our applications of general terms. But at the same time he is wrong to conclude that there *must* be a common element attributable to the instances of a general term that is additional to their being instances. With respect to the case of games, for example, "The realist says that games must have something in common, and by this he means that they must have something in common other than that they are games" (1960/61: 217–218).

"Wittgenstein," according to Bambrough, "says that games have nothing in common except that they are games" (1960/61:218). He

> thus denies at one and the same time the nominalist's claim that games have nothing in common except that they are called games and the realist's claim that games have something in common other than that they are games. He asserts at one and the same time the realist's claim that there is an objective justification for the application of the word "game" to games and the nominalist's claim that there is no element that is common to all games. And he is able to do all this because he denies the joint claim of the nominalist and the realist that there cannot be an objective justification for

the application of the word "game" to games unless there is an element that is common to all games (*universalia in rebus*) or a common relation that all games bear to something that is not a game (*universalia ante res*). (1960/61:218)

At this point some readers may grimace, or cry out, or perhaps renew their vows to Aristotle and his henchpersons (so to speak) in anthropology. At first blush one's composure might be rattled by the claim that Wittgenstein says that games *are* games, as distinct from merely saying that games are *called* games. Bambrough, in taking that position, is certainly not suggesting that Wittgenstein says this out of incredible naivete. Nor does he aver that Wittgenstein supposes that games are what they are because of the ineluctable workings of nature, or because games exist as ideas in God's mind, or anything of the sort. Yet, on Bambrough's testimony, Wittgenstein holds that the *only* thing that games have in common is that they *are* games, and that this *objectively* justifies our application of the general term game to them.

Bambrough, who fully agrees with what he thinks Wittgenstein is claiming, attempts to justify that claim. He may not, however, convince everyone, especially those persons who are initially dumbfounded by his assertion. What he does say, however, is very interesting. It relates, moreover, to my advocacy in Chapter 6 of conceptualizing religion as an unbounded or open analytical category. It also relates to the discussion in Chapter 7 of a connection between "ethnocentrism" and "objectivity," objectivity being there conceptualized as a positive relation between research and disciplinary canons. So let us look at what Bambrough says.

In evaluating the nominalist's claim that things called by the same name have only that in common, Bambrough imagines such a case. One could give a name — he chooses "alpha" — to a set of objects that have nothing in common except that Bambrough arbitrarily chooses to call them by the same name (e.g., his fountain-pen, the star Sirius, the color red, the Parthenon, the letter Z, and the number 5).

This case, however, sharply contrasts with a typical case of applying a general term to what we accept as some among many possible instances to which that general term applies. Bambrough chooses as an example the word "chair," and he points out that normal usage of that word does not parallel the arbitrariness of his selection of the objects that he calls alphas. "In giving a list of chairs," he observes, "I cannot just mention anything that happens to come into my head, while this is exactly what I do in giving my list of alphas" (1960/61:219).

Bambrough calls attention to the fact that his class of alphas is a *closed* class. Once he has given his list he has "referred to every single alpha in the universe, actual and possible" (1960/61:219). If he later adds or subtracts an object from his list, then he would be making a different use of the word alpha. But that is not the case for the general word chair. "There are," he says "an infinite number of actual and possible chairs," and he cannot aspire to enumerate completely all chairs; nor would the application of the word to a new instance produce a significant change in its use (1960/61: 219).

Further, Bambrough observes, he cannot teach others his use of the word alpha except by specifically listing each of the arbitrarily chosen items that are attached to it. An observer cannot conclude from watching him attach labels to objects that he calls alpha which other objects he is likely to call by that term. But this is not so when it comes to using the general term chair (1960/61:219).

Bambrough declares that "In teaching the use of a general word we may and must refer to characteristics of the objects to which it applies, and of the objects to which it does not apply, and indicate which of these characteristics count for the application of the word and which count against it" (1960/61:219). This talk of characteristics, however, is best understood in light of the idea of family resemblances, where the referents of a general term are linked by chains of "characteristics," characteristics that they may not all share.

In a later passage, Bambrough gives explicit recognition to the importance of exemplification in learning how to use general terms (I shall have more to say about exemplification in the next chapter). He writes that "The reference that we make to a finite number of objects to which the word applies, and to a finite number of objects to which the word does not apply, is capable of equipping the pupil with a capacity for correctly applying or withholding the word to or from an infinite number of objects to which we have made no reference" (1960/61:220).

The nominalist, Bambrough affirms, is right to say that human interests and purposes are of great importance in determining the choice of principles of classification (1960/61:220). The nominalist, moreover, is right to claim that there is no limit in principle to the possible number of classifications that human beings might make (1960/61:221). But the realist is right to say that any genuine classification of any set of objects (as distinct from an arbitrary system of names) "is objectively based on genuine similarities and differences" (1960/61:222). The trouble is that the nominalist, greatly impressed by the potential diversity of possible classifications, does not take cognizance of their objectivity. And the realist, impressed by the objectivity of genuine classifications, underestimates the possible diversity of such classifications (1960/61:222).

Finally, Bambrough cautions that

> In talking of genuine or objective similarities and differences we must not forget that we are concerned with similarities and differences between *possible* cases as well as between actual cases, and indeed that we are concerned with the actual cases only because they are themselves a selection of the possible cases. (1960/61:222).

Keith Campbell

Now, Bambrough's claim that Wittgenstein has solved the problem of universals is rejected by some philosophers. In a much read technical paper, for instance, Keith Campbell produces what he deems a "result in conflict with Bambrough's." He goes on to conclude that "the notion of family resemblance cannot of itself solve the problem of universals for any given linguistic context" (1965:243). He also states that

> in making a classification by a family resemblance predicate, we are making a division without reference to any natural ground it might have. For otherwise we would be classifying on that basis and all members of the reference class would have something in common, to wit, that which gives rise to the observed pattern of surface phenomena. For the discussion of human affairs, this is perhaps of no great moment. But it is our faith that all divisions in nature, save the most fundamental, have a ground . . . we should not rest content until family resemblance predicates, admittedly intelligible, have been banished from our sciences. (1965:244)

Students of religion, of course, are concerned mainly with "discussions of human affairs." Campbell's remark that it is "perhaps of no great moment" to make divisions in such discussions by recourse to family resemblance predicates relates to his earlier allowance (1965:243) that Wittgenstein himself has shown that "many psychological terms" conform to the family resemblance model and that "Many terms from natural history . . . and the discussion of human affairs" fit the requirements for family resemblance predicates (1965:243).

Wittgenstein, Campbell (1965:241) points out, contrasts the whole family to which a family resemblance predicate is applied with pairs of members of the family. While all the members of the former need have no one feature or quality in common, some pairs of members typically do have features or qualities in common, and their particular commonalities are predicable of them. Thus, for example, some games are ball games, some involve more than one person, some are competitive, etc., whereas none of those features can be predicated of *all* games, of every member of the "family" of games.

A family resemblance predicate, Cambell writes, "is not a family resemblance predicate *in any absolute sense, but only as relative to a given linguistic context embracing as variables the vocabulary, purposes, capacities, and choices of a language-using group*" (1965:243; emphasis added). Some persons might claim that that is the case for particular predicates applied to pairs within the family as well. Campbell, in any case, clearly views family resemblance predicates as *intelligible* relative to the variables that he lists.

Cambell's recognition of the relativity of family resemblance predicates, coupled with a consideration of them expressed in a format favored by Western logicians, supplies him with reasons for offering reservations about them. He finds family resemblance predicates to be "defective" in some respects (1965:244). This charge includes two related specifics, one having to do with borders, the other with natural grounds.

Family resemblance predicates, Campbell charges, are heir to a dimension of border problems that, he maintains, is not the case for defined predicates — predicate terms, that is, that are monothetically defined. "Where F is a family resemblance predicate," he writes,

> the generalization "All F's are G's" admits of exceptions even where G is a criterial mark for F. With defined terms this is not so. Accordingly, where we wish to make generalizations in the confidence that they admit of no exceptions, defined terms are to be preferred to family resemblance terms, other things being equal. (1965:244)

In the study of religions, however, it is hard to imagine when "other things" are clearly "equal." If we define our terms narrowly, the application of them to phenomena that we study is bound to generate borderline cases. Borderline cases relate to borders, which are created by monothetic definitions, and situations that we encounter in the study of religions often tend to transgress our neat boundaries. On the other hand, if we monothetically define terms so broadly that boundary problems are inhibited if not actually obviated, our definitions tend to be so broad that they are in effect vacuous.

Campbell's second major objection is that "in making a

classification by a family resemblance predicate, we are making a division without reference to any natural ground it might have" (1965:244). Cambell holds that that can be unfortunate. The traditional way of conceptualizing predicates, he suggests, "not only offered a model, it also held up as an ideal a system of classification which fits the grounded divisions of nature" (1965:244). He deems this important for science — so much so, indeed, that he would banish family resemblance predicates from "our sciences" (1965:244).

I shall soon turn to the testimonies of certain biological scientists respecting the matter of fitting "the grounded divisions of nature." At the moment, however, I answer Cambell out of a perspective entertained by some contemporary cultural anthropologists.

Numbers of contemporary cultural anthropologists are persuaded that nature does not confront us with clear divisions that are directly read off or represented (even in the case of local fauna). Rather, they generally hold that cultural factors, variable from society to society, are of crucial significance for classification. In this view, culturally cultivated sensitivities (and, I would add, insensitivities) mediate and variously reduce, treat as equivalent or distinct, or otherwise organize a huge diversity of stimuli in accordance with socially parochial interpretive principles (a somewhat different point of view respecting ethnobiological classifications will be discussed later). Consistent with that perspective, but carrying it beyond what many of its supporters explicitly endorse, some maintain that the contemporary natural sciences and their predecessors are themselves interpretive enterprises dependent on tropes. In keeping with that opinion, they deem what others describe as scientific revolutions to be "metaphoric redescriptions" of nature (Mary Hesse 1980, quoted in Rorty 1989:16).

It is my impression that numbers of anthropologists also regard the drawing of distinctions in "human affairs" as largely a matter of convention. In this view, those "natives" who (unlike Hallowell's Ojibwa) recognize a category of "the natural" tend to suppose that their local distinctions reflect "natural grounds," for what people take to be natural grounds is usually as conventional as anything else.

This view does not claim that such distinctions are entirely arbitrary. Nor does it allege that they are without constraints. It does not assert that the distinctions have no relevance to both possibilities and impediments conditioned by mind-independent realities. But it does hold that we do not take our classifications either directly from nature or from innate ideas. And it maintains that while there may be resemblances in the structures, contents, and indexicalities of human classificatory schemes, there are also interesting differences.

In growing up in our own society, we have learned how the general terms game, chair, and religion are applied in our language-games largely by noting their applications to actual cases, "a selection of the possible cases." And for us, but not *ipso facto* for others, games *are* games. They are such without it being necessary that they all share some discrete feature or set of discrete features. They *are* games because they are linked by overlapping or chain-like apperceived resemblances, and those linkages "objectively" support the practice of applying the same general term to them. Similarly, chairs *are* chairs, and (somewhat more problematically, especially in academia) religions *are* religions. They are such as part of the reality that we affirm whenever we conventionally resort to established general terms and the conventional sortings of similarities and differences that they invoke and to which they pertain.

Polythetic Grouping

In contrast to the idea of family likeness as utilized in natural language philosophy, the development of polythetic grouping is largely the work of biologists rather than philosophers — although the former freely borrowed concepts and sensitivities from the latter, just as the naturalists of yesteryear borrowed concepts of genus and species from logicians.

Polythetic taxa in the biological sciences are especially (though not exclusively) associated with an approach to classification once known as numerical taxonomy and now more generally called numerical phenetics. "Phenetics" refers to observable character states (including those that refer to such things as feeding habits, sexual behavior, and microbiological structures as well as what Western laypersons conventionally term "physical features"). "Numerical" indicates that this classificatory approach utilizes mathematical and statistical methods, including the coding of observed character states in numerical form.

Briefly characterized, numerical phenetics is classification by "overall similarity." It is ideally undertaken without any initial input from, or immediate reference to, discrete suppositions about the possible evolutionary histories of the life forms being classified. The purposes for making such a classification, however, normally include "the drawing of phylogenetic inferences from the data by statistical or other mathematical methods to the extent to which this is possible" (Sneath and Sokal 1973:4, emphasis omitted).

Numerical phenetics, according to its champions, offers biologists the hope of constructing taxa of high informational content, thus avoiding or minimizing problems posed by the employment of monothetic classifications (such as the possibility that an organism aberrant in one or another feature will be separated from its natural congeners even if identical with them in other features). This classificatory approach also offers the hope of obviating certain logico-philosophical embarassments (such as, for example, the circularity attendant on the application for taxonomic purposes of a categorically phylogenetic definition of homology, where morphological or biochemical correspondences are deemed homologous rather than analogous because they are held to be products of descent from a common ancestral stock, yet our primary evidence for such descent consists of those very correspondences).

Grouping in numerical phenetics "is generally based on a matrix of resemblances, in which taxa are constructed through various techniques designed to disclose and summarize the structure of the matrix" (Sneath and Sokal 1973:6). Entities are assigned to a polythetic taxon in recognition of overlapping features, "where no single feature is either essential to group membership or is sufficient to make an organism [or other taxonomic unit] a member of the group" (Sokal and Sneath 1963:14). Membership is accorded, that is, on the basis of sharing a sizeable number of defining attributes or "character states," but not necessarily all of them or, indeed, any particular one of them (Beckner 1959:22).

Specification of the principles governing the construction of polythetic taxa, however, does not rule out the possibility that the members of a taxon may actually share one or more attributes in common (Sokal and Sneath 1963:14). For that matter, according to Sneath and Sokal (1973:21–22), "natural taxa are usually not fully polythetic, since one can usually find some character states common to all members of a taxon," though for operational purposes biologists entertain the possibility of a taxon being "fully polythetic."

A polythetic taxon, in short, generally serves to group together taxonomic units that have the greatest number of *overlapping* attributes. By way of a highly simplified example, let us say that Unit 1 has "features" (character states) a, b, c, and d, Unit 2 c, d, e, and f, and Unit 3 e, f, g, and h. All three of these "units" (they could be organisms or sub-organic phenomena) might be assigned to the same group. Units 1 and 3 have no character states ("features") in common, but each, in its own way, partially overlaps in character states with Unit 2 (adapted from Beckner 1959). The group to which our three taxonomic units are assigned is "polythetic" because 'many features' (a, b, c, d, e, f, g, and h) govern admission to it and no one of those features is either necessary or sufficient for membership.

Sokal and Sneath counsel that "At least sixty" characters be used in classifying organisms, and they opine that "less than forty should never be used" (1963:51). A huge amount of information is generated when numerous *characters* (e.g., leaf margins in botany) and *character states* (e.g., whether the leaf margins are serrated, undulating, and so forth) are employed criterially for the sorting of a number of organisms or sub-organic taxonomic units (as in molecular biology and biochemistry). Processing such large amounts of data is feasible thanks to electronic computers, and the taxa produced are higher in information content, and in that sense more realistic, than monothetically defined taxa.

Judgments of Centrality

Significantly, as I shall remark with respect to religions, polythetic groupings do not necessarily exclude judgments of centrality, whether centrality be described in statistical or monothetic language (that is, as central tendencies in frequency distributions or as monothetic cores in polythetic taxa). While *a priori* no character has more weight than any other character in conceptualizing taxonomic groups before assignment of individual organisms or other taxonomic units begins, at later stages of taxonomic procedure analysts weight characters in constructing taxonomic keys and in identifying specimens (Sneath and Sokal 1973:109).

Furthermore, although all organisms or entities assigned to a taxonomic group are equally members, analysts may come to choose those that exhibit the character states most frequently encountered in experience as exemplars of the taxon for certain purposes; exemplars are useful reference points, and they do not indicate the limits of the taxon that they exemplify (Sneath and Sokal 1973:69). Anthony Kenny (1973:224), in quite another referential domain, makes an analogous point: " . . . the concept of family likeness leaves room for the notion of convergence on, and divergence from, a paradigm, in the way that natural numbers are the paradigm for the family-likeness concept of 'number'" (see Wittgenstein's *Philosophical Investigations* I.67).

Family Resemblance and Polythetic Classification Compared

Chaney (1978:139–140) points out that "'Family resemblances' have to do with how we use our words and concepts" whereas polythetic classifications, which he describes as "actuarial data summary," refer "to our data charts." To this distinction we can add a broader one. The family resemblance approach not only deals with how we use our words and concepts, but it implies the question of why we use them — for what purposes in what contexts? It focuses our attention on human activity and convention. The polythetic approach of the biological pheneticists, in comparison, represents a significantly different perspective and commitment. An operant empiricism in the service of a statistical realism, it is founded on the conviction that life forms can be apprehended, characterized, and grouped in their multiplicity. Yet despite referential and perspectival differences that separate so-called polythetic classification and Wittgenstein's family likeness, the practical consequences of those intellectual tools may turn out to be analogous when applied by some analysts to what we call "religions."

Applications to Religion

The likely practical convergence that I affirm can be documented by comparing a characterization of religion inspired by the family resemblance concept with one offered in support of polythetic classification. The philosopher William P. Alston provides us with the former, and the anthropologist Martin Southwold furnishes one that purports to be an example of the latter.

Alston and Family Likeness

Alston describes nine "religion-making characteristics:"

1. Belief in supernatural beings (gods).
2. A distinction between sacred and profane objects.
3. Ritual acts focused on sacred objects.
4. A moral code believed to be sanctioned by the gods.
5. Characteristically religious feelings (awe, sense of mystery, sense of guilt, adoration), which tend to be aroused in the presence

of sacred objects and during the practice of ritual, and which
are connected in idea with the gods.
6. Prayer and other forms of communication with gods.
7. A world view, or general picture of the world as a whole and
   the place of the individual therein. This picture contains some
   specification of an over-all purpose or point of the world and
   an indication of how the individual fits into it.
8. A more or less total organization of one's life based on the
   world view.
9. A social group bound together by the above. (1967:141–142)

Alston goes on to state that "When enough of these characteristics are present to a sufficient degree, we have a religion.
It seems that, given the actual use of the term 'religion', this is
as precise as we can be" (1967:142).

As a practical matter, however, Alston explicitly recommends
an exposition of religion in terms of what he calls a "paradigm
case" (a recommendation, as we shall see, that Southwold allows
for and that I build on in Chapter 6 by invoking a certain concept
of "prototype"). The "best way to explain the concept of religion," he says,

> is to elaborate in detail the relevant features of an ideally clear case
> of religion and then indicate the respects in which less clear cases
> can differ from this, without hoping to find any sharp line dividing
> religion from nonreligion. (Cf. Ludwig Wittgenstein's notion of
> "family-resemblances" among the things to which a term applies.)
> (Alston 1967:142)

Southwold and Polythetic Classification

Southwold (1978:370–371), who declares that his approach "seeks
to take positive advantage of the fact that the concepts we actually
have are polythetic classes," maintains that "Roughly, . . . anything
which we would call a religion must have at least some of the
following attributes:"

(1) A central concern with godlike beings and men's relations with
    them.
(2) A dichotomisation of elements of the world into sacred and
    profane, and a central concern with the sacred.
(3) An orientation towards salvation from the ordinary conditions
    of worldly existence.
(4) Ritual practices.
(5) Beliefs which are neither logically nor empirically demonstrable
    or highly probable, but must be held on the basis of faith . . .
(6) An ethical code, supported by such beliefs.
(7) Supernatural sanctions on infringements of that code.

(8) A mythology.
(9) A body of scriptures, or similarly exalted oral traditions.
(10) A priesthood, or similar specialist religious elite.
(11) Association with a moral community, a church (in Durkheim's
      sense —1912:60; 1915:43–4).
(12) Association with an ethnic or similar group.

A comparison of Southwold's list of "attributes" (which he properly claims is not exhaustive) with Alston's list of "religion-making characteristics" shows considerable overlap. There are no bibliographic citations in Southwold's 1978 paper that signal familiarity with Alston's 1967 publication or other attempts at a family resemblance characterization of religion (e.g., Edwards 1972; Hick [1978:xiv] maintains that W.C. Smith's [1962] perspectives can be accomodated by such a characterization). We may conclude that Southwold's essay was composed independently of such earlier efforts.

The overlap, however, is not surprising because Southwold and many other authors, anti-essentialist as well as essentialist, are anchored in Western cultural traditions and tend to use them as models. Their lists of features typically fit the Western monotheisms,[1] at least in their "Great Tradition" appearances.

This, generally speaking, is true of many other efforts to characterize religion. I do not think that that is ultimately compromising for cross-cultural studies. But if we implicitly or explicitly use Western cultural traditions for orientation, it behooves us to explore those traditions as they relate to our analytical interests, a matter that I emphasize in the last chapter of this work.

In any case, Southwold's interest in so-called polythetic classification partly derives from his field work among Theravada

---

[1] Spiro (Personal Communication) is uncomfortable with the expression "Western monotheisms" in that many of the adherents of one or another of those families of faiths invoke, render homage to, or otherwise take into account superhuman personages other than the One God (e.g., angels, saints, devils, etc.).

The matter is complex. Popular devotions, for one thing, may ignore or otherwise challenge monotheistic theology. Theologians bent on advancing their own vision of monotheism, moreover, may sometimes be condemned by others as subverters of monotheism (such was the fate of Arius, whom numbers of Christians list among the most prototypical of heresiarchs). And scholars do not always agree on what might be deemed most important for recognizing monotheism. Kaufmann (1972), for example, holds that the most crucial characteristic of monotheism is not numerical; rather, it is that deity is not derived from any pre-existent reality. I will not go any further in discussing this complex subject save to say that my application of the expression "Western monotheisms" should be taken as an instance of a convenient — albeit here undefended — convention.

Buddhist villagers in Sri Lanka. He claims to have found that the Buddhism of his villagers "does not manifest a central concern with godlike beings," and that "Hence, *either* the theistic definitions and conception of religion are wrong *or* Buddhism is not a religion" (1978:367). The latter possibility strikes him as an unviable option because "In virtually every other respect Buddhism markedly resembles religions, and especially the religion prototypical for our conceptions, i.e. Christianity" (*ibid.*).

Southwold concludes that "theistic definitions of religion are shown by Buddhism to be wrong, as Durkheim argued" (*ibid.*), and he opts for a polythetic approach that allows for theism as a contingent but not necessary attribute of religion. While I will not evaluate here claims about the relative unimportance of theism in certain forms of Buddhism (see Hudson 1977:238 for an analysis that recognizes theism as significant among the family resemblances of Buddhism; see also Spiro 1982 [1970]), I do want to consider some aspects of Southwold's treatment of the concept and utility of polythetic grouping.

In addition to affirming the prototypicality of Christianity for our conceptions of religion, Southwold also affirms "the near-universality in religions of a central concern with godlike beings" (1978:367). He cites that concern as the very first attribute in his list of polythetic characters (Alston specifies a belief in Gods as the first of his own "religion-making characteristics"). Such talk of prototypicality and near-universality suggests, but does not explicitly endorse, a paradigmatic centralism.

Southwold avoids unequivocal endorsement, I suspect, largely because doing so might seem to subvert a major thrust of his essay: an attack on suppositions to the effect that theism is essential to religion. In arguing his case, moreover, he holds that "The recognition that religion is a polythetic class which approaches, but does not reach, monotheticity, has a number of advantages" (1978:371). Thus, for example, he writes that such recognition is

> consistent with, and suggests, the view that a religion is not a homogeneous system responding to any single need or inclination. Rather, a religion is compounded of a variety of forms of behaviour which tend to be produced in response to diverse individual and social requirements; but these forms of behaviour, though they have in this sense diverse origins, have marked affinities one with another which tend to lead to their coalescence into a moderately coherent system. Religion is polythetic because of the diverse origins of the forms of behaviour which constitute it; it approaches monotheticity because of these affinities between them. (1978:371)

Now, as I read the above statement, it seems to say two things. First, the quotation up to the last sentence is concerned with "a religion" — presumably, each and every religion — and it asserts that any religion is a system of diverse behaviors which themselves are responses to a variety of individual and social needs. These different behaviors have something of an affinity for one another, which is why they more or less cohere in a system.

But then Southwold seems to shift levels in the last sentence, where he talks about "religion" rather than "a religion." One possible interpretation of that sentence (in light of the statement that triggers the passage that I have quoted) is the following: Religions constitute a polythetic class, a class denominated "religion," because they exhibit different but partially overlapping behavioral features, features that originate as responses to different individual and social needs among the world's peoples; yet the world's religions also come close to constituting a monothetic class because their different behavioral features show a high degree of affinity from one religion to another.

Yet why, we might ask, is there so high a degree of affinity among the behavioral attributes of the world's religions? The answer suggested by Southwold's essay is that religions are diverse but largely similar responses to diverse but parallel needs among the peoples of the world — parallel needs because, although diverse, they nevertheless evoke largely similar responses. In my reading of Southwold, religions are seen as *analogous* solutions to a variety of widely distributed human needs.

To group religions together relative to a "polythetic class" on the basis of analogies, however, — to claim, in fact, that "Religion is polythetic *because of the diverse origins* of the forms of behaviour which constitute it" (emphasis added) — begins to suggest a superficial appropriation into cultural anthropology of an interesting, empirically oriented approach to grouping phenomena in the biological sciences.

Analogy and Homology

I do not mean to suggest that all invocations of polythesis must conform as closely as possible to biological models. To the extent, however, that some biologists once conceived numerical phenetics to be a workable and promising approach — although it was also criticized (e.g., Mayr 1969:203–211, 1984:649–650; Hull 1984) and it has now been effectively supplanted by other approaches among biological systematists —, it was in part because of evolutionary connections among the "operational taxonomic units" (OTU's) that the pheneticists sought to group. This observation should sound a warning note for the anthropologist who would make use of numerical phenetics in cultural analyses. There is reason to suppose that the lesser the resemblance between the phenomena that a cultural anthropologist might attempt to group together and those that biologists group, the less suitable for anthropological purposes are constructs and methods derived from the biological sciences.

By pursuing this last point one may come to appreciate some of the contextual and other differences that distance Southwold's appropriation of the idea of polythesis from the major application of it in the biological sciences. Such appreciation, moreover, will highlight certain substantial objections to the use of what is broadly called polythetic classification for the characterization of religion.

"The basis of the classical method of establishing taxa" in the biological sciences, Sokal and Sneath (1963:22) write, "is commonly held to be the recognition of homologies. Similarly, the recognition of analogies will serve to separate artificial taxa." "The central task of evolutionary biology," Stephen J. Gould affirms, "is not the toting up of similarities but the separation of homologous from analogous likeness" (1988:26).

In 1848 Richard Owen had defined homology outside of a phylogenetic frame of reference (Simpson 1961:79–80), but with the triumph of Darwinian theory definitions reflective of that theory were widely embraced. George Gaylord Simpson's definition, "homology is resemblance due to inheritance from a common ancestry" (1961:78), is typical, and the employment of homology in that sense for taxonomic purposes is in keeping with Darwin's dictum that in grouping life forms "all true classification is genealogical" (1859:420). Darwin also remarked, however, that "genealogy by itself does not give classification" (quoted in Mayr 1984:648). Genealogy, nevertheless, is clearly deemed crucial, and descent from a common ancestor, biologists commonly maintain, is what produces homologies.

Analogies, in contrast, are resemblances that are not based on descent from a common ancestor. Rather, they are similarities produced in other ways (e.g., by convergent functional adaptations).

In phylogenetic perspective, by way of examples, the general structural similarity between human arms and the forelimbs of horses is held to be homologous while the similarity between the wings of birds and insects is analogous (insect wings probably originated as thermal regulators). Evolutionary theory disposed biologists to conceive of a "natural class" of organisms as an assemblage of individuals that are descended with modifications from a common ancestral stock, and classifications, they widely came to affirm, "are only as good as the homologies of the characters on which they are based" (Sokal and Sneath 1963:23).

The circularity of speculative phylogenetic taxonomies based on a categorical conception of homology, already alluded to, was one of a number of factors that led some biologists to attempt to base their groupings on apperceived empirical or phenotypic resemblances while excluding, ideally, phyletic inferences in the actual classificatory process. It was also a factor influencing the decision of numbers of biochemists to employ, and to continue employing, the term "homology" rather broadly in their own work, despite appeals from other biological scientists to cease doing so. Biochemists talk about percentages or degrees of homology when, for example, they sequence a large number of DNA bases in the genes of two animals in an effort to determine degrees of matching (Gould 1988:26). Such usage of the term, in Gould's vivid language, "drives evolutionary biologists right up the wall" (1988:26). Obdurate biochemists notwithstanding, Gould and many of his colleagues continue to prefer the more traditional categorical conception of homology. "Homology," Gould intones, "either is or it isn't. Homology doesn't come in degrees" (1988:26).

Pheneticists, in any event, make efforts to separate taxonomic procedure from phylogenetic suppositions (Sneath and Sokal 1973:9). But, of course, they and other biological scientists are convinced that there *are* evolutionary connections among life forms. Whatever support biologists creatively discern in nature for that conviction bankrolls, in a manner of speaking, their various classificatory strategies.

Although numerical phenetics had its critics within biology, and, according to my colleague Sally McBrearty (Personal Communication), is now "dead" as a method ("People recognize that it simply doesn't work"), in the 1950's and 1960's the pheneticists' program, in my opinion, represented something of an advance, epistemologically as well as procedurally. In those days a phylogenetic approach to grouping was decidedly speculative because of ignorance of phylogenies in the great majority of cases (Sneath and Sokal 1973:53). (Recent progress in establishing phylogenies owes much to biochemistry and molecular biology.) Further, all classificatory efforts in the biological sciences begin with phenetics. Indeed, while evolutionary branching relationships (cladistics) must be inferred from phenetic evidence, phenetic relations are not inferred from phyletic evidence but, rather, from empirical studies of the specimens themselves (Sneath and Sokal 1973:32).

But while interindividual relations in numerical phenetics are evaluated as strictly as possible on the basis of *current resemblances* among the specimens on hand, without immediately taking into account the origins of the phenetic similarities cognized, phyletic probabilities are far from being conceptually unimportant. "It is almost a truism," two of the chief advocates of numerical phenetics write, "that an intimate relation must exist between phenetic evidence and the degree of relation by ancestry" (Sneath and Sokal 1973:32). Thus considerable phenetic detail is likely to point the way to distinguishing homologies from analogies (analogous organs, for example, would be dissimilar in a large number of character states). Today, of course, data provided by biochemists and molecular biologists make possible huge sample sizes. These, as Gould points out, may finally make it possible to achieve a level of concordance so detailed as to rule out analogy in many cases and indicate homology, for the greater and more complex the similarities, the less likely it is that they arose by analogy (1988:26).

Sneath and Sokal (1973:87) suggest that we avoid a categorical distinction between homology and analogy in favor of thinking in terms of greater or lesser resemblances: thus on a conceptual continuum of relationships where total dissimilarity is at one extreme and total identity is at the other, homology is near the pole of total identity while analogy is at an intermediate point.

In any case, whether homology be conceptualized "digitally" as a matter of it-either-is-or-it-isn't, the more traditional approach, or in terms of a gradient framework of more-or-less, biological scientists continue to deem it important. There is, to be sure, continuing debate over certain issues respecting it (see Hull 1984 for a discussion of some of them). It is important, nevertheless, on microbiological levels as well as on organismic levels, as an index of genealogical relations. We read, for example, of homologous genes, homologous polypeptide chains, and the like (e.g., Zuckerkandl 1968:317, 320). "The concept of homology," Sneath and Sokal (1973:75) declare, "is central to any [scientific biological] taxonomy."

Cultural Studies and Biological Models and Metaphors

My discussion of numerical phenetics so far, and the specific criticisms of so-called polythetic classification that will soon follow, relate to an important topic: the use of biological models and metaphors in cultural studies.

I begin with a very general observation, one that connects to my discussion of anthropomorphism in Chapter 4. In that chapter I emphasized the "anthropopsychic" aspect of anthropomorphism, as (typically through the modality of religion) it constitutes a universe that contains extra-human mind, will, and purpose. Now, however, I want to consider the physical side of anthropomorphism.

In English, and in many other languages as well, there are numerous metaphoric extensions to non-human objects of terms used for the human body or for our bodily processes. We are all familiar with such expressions as "the face of the cliff," "the eye of the storm" (or needle, potato, etc.), "digesting information," and so forth. The human body, after all, is of major experiential interest and concern to us, and its use as a resource for the generation of metaphors is not particularly surprising. Nor is the metonymic use of bodily parts (e.g., "All hands on deck").

Further, recognition of the body's bilateral symmetry (two ears, two eyes, two arms, etc.) has served as a starting point for various sorts of conceptual and evaluative exercises and conventions. Sometimes the symmetry is partially transformed into meaningful disjunctions, into an "organic asymmetry," as in conventions about the right hand (or side) and the left hand (or side) (Hertz 1909 provides a seminal discussion; see also a collection of essays edited by Needham 1973). In addition, spatial relations and various other factors having to do with the body in physical and social environments are major conceptual resources (see, for example, the discussions of "conceptual embodiment" and "functional embodiment" in Lakoff 1987). The use in different kinds of tropes of expressions and images pertaining to the body, long recognized as important in human life, is very much a "hot" subject of study among some contemporary anthropologists, linguists, and psychologists.

The widespread use of biologically based tropes in ordinary speech in Western languages underwrites their various applications in the humanities and social and natural sciences. One thinks, for examples, of life-stage metaphors formulated by writers such as Spengler and Toynbee in positing developmental trajectories for civilizations. When we hear talk of the decline, senescence, and death of a civilization, it makes a certain sense to us because we recognize those stages in the lives of human beings. And when functionalist theorists suggest organic analogies — Durkheim's "organic solidarity," for example, or Radcliffe-Brown's emphasis on the contributions of "partial" activities to the "total" activities of which they form parts — they also make a certain sense, based on our understandings of the different functions of the heart, lungs, liver and other internal organs in maintaining the entire body.

Some humanists and social scientists, however, go well beyond — or, at least, imagine going well beyond — such broad associations as those mentioned above. They cultivate, or recommend cultivating, parallels to various of the *technical* models and methods of the biological sciences.

Thus, for example, some archeologists (e.g., Williams, Thomas, and Bettinger 1973) invoke polythetic classification in their technical work. This is not at all surprising, given not only the need of archeologists to sort the artifacts that they have collected, but also the fact that certain older archeological efforts at classification, such as McKern's Midwestern Taxonomic System, prefigure the polythetic cast of contemporary numerical phenetics (Dunnell 1971:179). Scholars in other disciplines, however, sometimes prefer parallels to other approaches to classification developed in the biological sciences. Stemmatics (the study of affiliations among manuscripts), for instance, cultivates parallels to cladistics (which I will describe later), a powerful approach to classification in the biological sciences, while historical linguistics, though favoring cladistics, has also developed its own versions of phenetic models (Hoeningswald and Wiener 1987:xii).

Jonathan Z. Smith, a well known student of religion, waxes enthusiastic about polythetic classification in an essay entitled "Fences and Neighbors: Some Contours of Early Judaism" (1982 [1980]). He clearly appreciates the general point of polythesis, although one might question what he says about certain of the details (e.g., he remarks that "Biologists use from fifty to one hundred . . . characteristics — the possession of *any one* of which is *sufficient* for admission to the taxon" [1982:8, emphasis added], which appears to run counter to Sokal and Sneath's dictum that "*no single feature* is either essential to group membership or is *sufficient* to make an organism a member of the group" [1963:14, emphasis added]).

In the latter part of his essay, Smith briefly describes some variations both in funerary inscriptions and in attitudes and practices relating to circumcision in early Judaism, in support of his point that "We must conceive of a variety of early Judaisms, clustered in varying configurations" (1982:14). Smith's point is well taken and important. But insofar as his treatment of *Judaism* is concerned, the invocation of polythetic classification serves only as a conceptual support for his recommendation about how we ought to conceive of early forms of that family of religions; it is not utilized as an instrument for actually sorting out those forms. Smith, that is, does not *do* a polythetic classification. He says, indeed, that "It is premature to propose a proper polythetic classification of Judaism, but it is possible to be clear about what it would entail" (1982:8).

The *raison d'être* of Smith's essay, as I read it, is to champion polythesis as a way of thinking about religion. What he says about Judaism constitutes a preliminary approximation to an example. In my opinion, Smith has taken a step in the right direction. I suspect, however, that some of the criticisms of polythetic classification given below might induce him to rethink his enthusiasm for it.

Criticisms Within the Biological Sciences

Before coming to specific criticisms of numerical phenetics, it is worth noting that there have been two major rivals to it within the modern biological sciences. These rival taxonomic approaches — sometimes dubbed, respectively, "cladistics" and "evolutionary classification" (Mayr 1984:647) — must cast doubt on numerical phenetics simply by existing as rivals to it.

Cladistics

Cladistics (or "cladism") is especially associated with Willi Hennig (see, for example, Hennig 1984 [1965]). As ideally conceived by its advocates, cladistics classifies by geneaology alone: it seeks to define monophyletic groups and to determine genealogical branches (clades) on an evolutionary tree. McBrearty (Personal Communication) puts it as follows:

> Hennig states explicitly that a) classification should reflect evolutionary relatedness; b) that valid taxa must be monophyletic groups; and c) that monophyletic groups are defined on the basis of shared derived characters (synapomorphies). Most evolutionary biologists would agree with a) and probably with b) in principle, although they might like to retain some polyphyletic groups or evolutionary "grades" (e.g., fish, pongid) for historical reasons or for convenience.

Cladists look for two daughter species whose branchings from a parent group can be identified by shared derived characters that come from their parent and are found only in those two sister groups. (The parental species as such is held to cease to exist at the time daughter species branch off even if individuals associated with it continue to live.) Two sister groups form a monophyletic group, and that unit is related in a more inclusive sisterly way to some other species by virtue of shared characters that they, and only they, have all derived from a common ancestor. Those sisters, in turn, form a phylogenetic unit that may relate even more inclusively to yet some other species or set of species in a sisterly way.

This classificatory method, like others in the biological sciences, is beset by problems that occasion difficulties in actual applications. There is, as we might well expect, the problem — indeed, the paramount problem — of determining what is a shared derived character. And when it comes to solving that problem, biologists, according to Stephen Jay Gould, "have some rough guidelines, and some seat-of-the-pants feelings, but no unerring formulas" (1983:359). Cladists, nevertheless, insist on some interesting strictures respecting similarities. To quote McBrearty once more,

> One of the major distinctions between cladistics and phenetics is that cladistics recognizes different *kinds* of similarities (shared derived vs. shared primitive). The former are useful for classificatory purposes, the latter are not. No amount of quantification of degrees of similarity will yield meaningful results if the characters selected are shared primitive traits (symplesiomorphies) or convergences (homoplasies). (McBrearty, Personal Communication).

While the general problem of deciding on similarities afflicts cladistics as well as other disciplinary approaches, the huge amounts of data made possible by molecular biology and biochemistry in recent years (and that may be anticipated in the future) enable it to address that problem in productive and exciting ways. The accomplishments of cladistics in significant measure rest on the accomplishments of the microbiological sciences.

For students of culture interested in categorization, cladistics provides some interesting lessons. Its classifications of life forms are about as non-intuitive as any in scientific biological systematics when compared to folk biological classifications. Cladistics, indeed, challenges certain of our familiar categories.

Take, for instance, a category much used in my graduate student

days: that called "ape." This category purports both to group
together our nearest living relatives (gorillas, chimpanzees,
gibbons, and orangutans) and to distinguish them as a group
from human beings. Now-a-days, however, cladists tell us that,
cladistically speaking, the category lacks warrant. Human beings,
it turns out, are genetically closer to gorillas and chimpanzees
than are either gibbons or orangutans. Genealogically, then, the
opposition between human beings and a group composed of the
four genera of our closest living relatives doesn't hold.

Cladistics shakes the confidence that some of us may have
reposed in perceptually "obvious" biological classifications that
purportedly reflect the "grounded divisions" of nature. It teaches
us some interesting lessons about the seeming "givenness" or
"naturalism" of certain old, familiar categories.

Evolutionary Classification

Evolutionary classification is the more traditional approach to
taxonomy. It goes back to Darwin, and over the years it has been
rendered increasingly sophisticated partly through its proponents'
evaluations of, disagreements with, and incorporations of, some
of the assumptions and procedures of cladists and pheneticists.

This method, most simply put, attempts to classify by similarities and differences that take on diagnostic meanings for the
classifiers by virtue of being viewed in the light of inferences
respecting their evolutionary histories. Analysis in this approach,
Mayr points out, "includes all available attributes" of the organisms it seeks to classify, including ecological and distributional
information, and it "attempts to reflect both of the major
evolutionary processes, branching and the subsequent diverging
of the branches (clades)" (1984:647).

Ideally, practitioners of this approach to taxonomy continually
test inferences about relationships by evaluating new evidence.
For this reason, according to Mayr (1984:648), evolutionary
classification constitutes "an application of the hypothetico-
deductive approach." It is by no means a mechanical or formulaic application, however. George Gaylord Simpson, one of its
proponents, affirms that its practice calls for a certain flair (cited
in Hull 1984:573), and others of its practitioners concur. Indeed,
if an outsider might hazard a guess, some biologists may be
attracted to it as much by its openness and appeal to the creative
imagination as by its scientific promise.

Some Specific Criticisms of Numerical Phenetics

Some specific criticisms of numerical phenetics voiced by biologists might be usefully entered at this point. They should serve as further considerations militating against the appropriation of that approach into cultural anthropology. In presenting these criticisms, however, fairness to the pheneticists requires acknowledgement that their approach was not static.

Pheneticists revised to some extent certain of their guiding assumptions and procedures in response both to criticisms and to problems encountered in research. Thus, for example, Hull (1984:584) points to a realization reached by pheneticists that transcends in importance its localization among that group of biological systematists, for it pertains to all efforts at classification. "Pheneticists," he writes, "seem to have gradually come to realize that the notion of a theoretically neutral phenetic classification is an illusion and have modified their position accordingly."

According to the biologist Ernst Mayr, numerical phenetics has "proved to be largely unsuccessful" (1984:649). Mayr gives two reasons why he thinks that that is so.

First, claims to the effect that numerical phenetics yields objective and repeatable results cannot always be sustained since different choices of characters used in sortings, or different choices of computational programs, conduce to different results (1984:649).

Second, claims of methodological objectivity are inconsistent, for numerical pheneticists employ "subjective biological criteria . . . in the assigning of variants (for example, sexes, age classes, and morphs) to 'operational taxonomic units'" and, at the same time, they insist that all characters be equally weighted (1984:649).

"It is now evident," Mayr states, "that no computing method exists that can determine 'true similarity' from a set of arbitrarily chosen characters." "So-called similarity," he adds, "is a complex phenomenon that is not necessarily closely correlated with common descent, since similarity is often due to convergence" (1984:649). Some characters, he remarks, provide better clues to relationships than others (1984:650). And this, it seems, necessitates careful weighting of characters.

This point and others are included in the philosopher David Hull's assessment of the phenetic approach to taxonomy. Hull evaluates that approach from a broad and multidimensional perspective.

Evolutionary theory, Hull (1984:587) notes, heightened biologists' consciousness of variation in life forms. A single specimen, that heightened consciousness affirms, can only be "typical" of the group to which it is assigned in a statistical sense. Biologists came to view a species as a polytypic rather than a homogeneous grouping. And essentialist definitions, Hull further relates, were replaced by polythetic definitions, definitions, that is, "in terms of covarying properties" (1984:587). While pheneticists, Hull remarks, resemble essentialists in believing in "the existence of natural units of overall similarity," they differ from essentialists in holding "that these units can be defined only polythetically" (1984:587).

Phenetic classification, Hull states, was originally conceived to be a matter of "look, see, code, cluster," but its champions eventually modified their views (1984:580). The notion that a phenetic classification could be theoretically neutral proved to be an illusion, albeit, in conceeding this, some pheneticists nevertheless maintained that classification could be accomplished in isolation from *evolutionary* theories (1984:580).

In later conceptualizations supported by pheneticists, Hull points out,

> Operational homologies are established utilizing any respectable scientific theory except evolutionary theory. The reasons given for permitting morphological, behavioral, physiological, serological, and DNA homologies, but forbidding evolutionary homologies, have all depended on repeated equivocations on the terms *phenetic character* and *operational homology*. Pheneticists claim that operational homologies are observed, whereas evolutionary homologies are inferred. In the first place, only characters are observed. That two instances of a character are instances of the same character (i.e., that they are operationally homologous) must be inferred. Only if operational homologies are limited to observational homologies (i.e., if they both look blue then they are blue) will these inferences be made solely on the basis of observation. All other types of inferences to operational homologies will make essential reference to a particular scientific theory, and with the introduction of theory the overly simplistc notion of observational homology must be abandoned. One cannot observe that two nucleotides are operationally homologous. Both the existence of the nucleotides and which of the nucleotides are homologous must be inferred from extremely indirect evidence in the context of current biochemical theories. (1984:584)

The above criticism relates to another. "If," Hull writes, "it is admitted that the establishment of homologies presupposes various scientific theories, then the idea of a single parameter which might be termed *overall similarity* loses much of its plausibility and all classifications become special purpose classifications" (1984:585). The notion of a general purpose classification, Hull concludes, constitutes another of the pheneticists' illusions (1984:585).

In advancing this point of view, Hull cites (as does Mayr) an influential article by Ehrlich and Ehrlich (1967), one that calls attention both to the general problem of determining similarity and the specific problem of a purportedly general purpose classification.

"Disagreements on matters of similarity are commonplace," the Ehrlichs remark, for "We bring our prejudices and purposes to judgements of similarity, and these affect our decisions even when dealing with single characters" (1967:315).

Yet even if we could somehow circumnavagate the ambiguities posed by our ideas of similarity, the Ehrlichs opine, there would still be problems. "One," they write, "is the question of which kinds of coefficients (matching, correlation, distance, etc.) properly should be used to transform similarity judgements at the individual character level to estimates of overall similarity" (1967:315). They conclude that overall similarity "cannot be dealt with in practice":

> Operationally, all phenetic classifications are special rather than general. They depend on the sampling of characters, the manner in which the characters are coded, and the coefficient selected. If a phenogram is constructed an additional factor is introduced: the selection of a clustering method. Although it is contrary to our intuition as taxonomists, we must adjust to the existence of a multitude of "valid" taxonomic arrangements of the butterflies. (1967:315)

In summary, all of the authors that I have cited above — The Ehrlichs, Mayr, Hull, Simpson, and Gould — attach great importance to the problem of determining similarities. This is indeed a vexing problem, and it troubles the reflective student of culture at least as much as it troubles reflective biological scientists. "Similarity, I submit, is insidious," says the philosopher Nelson Goodman (1972:437). It is so because of the facile assumptions that we entertain about it and about what we can do with it. Similarity is "relative, variable, [and] culture-dependent" (Goodman 1972:438). Goodman notes that while it may be "Clear enough when closely confined by context and circumstance in ordinary discourse, it is hopelessly ambiguous when torn loose" (1972:444).

Classifications, the biologists cited above agree, are built on decisions about similarities and differences and their relative importance. Classifications in the biological sciences do not just occur. They are constructed relative to interests and purposes, and are therefore always "special."

Classifications in the biological sciences, moreover, are *indexical.* Hull emphasizes that point. "Rather than being storage-and-retrieval systems themselves," he writes, classifications "serve as indexes to such storage-and-retrieval systems" (1984:576). Information, he points out, reposes in descriptive and analytical studies, in monographs, not in the classifications themselves. This is of the greatest moment for our understanding of classifications in the biological sciences. It argues persuasively against an early — and now recognized to be naive — goal of the pheneticists, the goal of constructing theory-free classifications. In the biological sciences (at least) there can be no such beasts.

I have been talking about classificatory efforts in the biological sciences. But what of folk biological classifications? Might they not be "general purpose" rather than "special purpose?" And if so, might they not be theory-free? Human beings throughout the world, after all, have much the same perceptual equipment. Are they not likely, some might ask, to see the same things in similar ways? Are there not, moreover, striking discontinuities among animals and striking discontinuities among plants in local environments? Discontinuities, one might suppose, that virtually "cry out to be named" (Berlin 1972, cited in Berlin 1978:11). In light of these considerations, might we not anticipate important, widespread resemblances in folk biological classifications?

The publications of Brent Berlin (e.g., 1976, 1978) and of Berlin, Breedlove, and Raven (e.g., 1973, 1974) lend support to a qualified affirmative answer to the question of widespread commonalities in folk biological classifications. They do not, however, support the notion that such classifications are "transcendental," that they are independent of human interests and theorizing.

Berlin, Breedlove, and Raven (1973:214) maintain that "there are a number of strikingly regular structural principles of folk biological classification which are quite general." Not only do Berlin and his associates argue for certain structural regularities in taxonomy, but, supported by impressive evidence, they conclude that different human societies throughout the world identify animals and plants in very similar ways at the taxonomic level that many of us call "genus" and that Berlin calls "folk-generic," although there is rather less similarity at other taxonomic levels.

The folk-generic rank is located in about the middle of the vertical axis of folk biological taxonomies. It is the level at which there occurs what cognitive scientists call "basic-level categorization." Basic level categories are psychologically and culturally salient. They are "basic" in four respects, as put succinctly by Lakoff (1987:47):

> Perception: Overall perceived shape; single mental image; fast identification. Function: General motor program [similar motor actions in interacting with category members]. Communication: Shortest, most commonly used and contextually neutral words, first learned by children and first to enter the lexicon. Knowledge Organization: Most attributes of category members are stored at this level.

Basic-level categories are also structurally pivotal in taxonomies, for increasing generalization occurs at taxonomic ranks above them and increasing specialization occurs at taxonomic ranks below them.

Based on his fieldwork among Tzeltal Maya in Mexico and Aguaruna Jívaro in Peru, supplemented by analyses of the publications of other students of folk biological classifications in other parts of the world, Berlin advances two broad conclusions:

> the basic principles of classification of biological diversity appear to arise directly out of the recognition by man of groupings of plants and animals formed on the basis of such visible similarities and differences as can be inferred from gross features of morphology and behavior. This is simply to say that organisms are grouped into named classes primarily on the basis of overall perceptual similarities. (Berlin 1978: 10)

and

> recognized classes of plants and animals (hereafter referred to as *taxa*) are organized into a taxonomic hierarchy whereby taxa of greater and lesser inclusiveness are related by the logical relation of class inclusion. A major substantive generalization about the nature of this organization, which is borne out by all the full-scale studies undertaken thus far, is that there exist a small number of folk biological ranks that contain mutually exclusive taxa that exhibit essentially comparable degrees of biological differentiation one from another . . . The number of ranks involved in any complete system is probably not more than six and not less than three. (Berlin 1978:11)

Berlin also relates that more than a third of the plants that are named by the Tzeltal and by the Aguaruna have no cultural utility, nor are they plants that ought to be avoided because of poisonous or other noxious properties (1978:11). This, he remarks, challenges the notion that folk classifications among so-called primitive peoples are exclusively or largely a utilitarian affair (1978:11). Scott Atran (1990) also expresses doubts about simplistic utilitarian theorizing in a book that came to my attention too late to be discussed in any depth here.

The utilitarianism deservedly put under doubt has to do with the use of plants for food, medicine, and the like and the avoiding of injurious consequences. But there is another and perhaps more subtle consequence-fraught interest that ought to be taken into account. By naming and classifying plants that otherwise might seem to have no cultural utility, the Tzeltal and Aguaruna evince an interest in them for naming and classificatory purposes. Doing so has various psychological and cultural implications with respect to rendering the world more orderly, familiar, and manageable. Naming and classifying are value-laden activities of considerable functional significance, regardless of whether or not some of the things named and classified are "utilitarian" in more narrow acceptations of that word.

There is a tradition in anthropology going back to Tylor that holds that human beings are motivated or disposed to "classify out the world." Even if there is such a disposition or motivation, however, it is unlikely that it would ever be perfectly realized. Insofar as I am aware, people do not exhaustively classify and name everything conceivable in their local environments. They are selective, and their selectivity is culturally guided, as is their choice and weighting of features.

Berlin and his associates allow that "individual societies may differ considerably in their conceptualizations of plants and animals" (Berlin, Breedlove, and Raven 1973:214). Their evidence, nevertheless, supports their claim that there are striking cross-cultural resemblances in plant and animal identifications at the taxonomic level of folk-generic categories. The interactions with the environment on which these basic-level categorizations are based may, as Lakoff (1987:38) suggests, "provide a crucial link between cognitive structure and real knowledge of the world." In evaluating, however, what we might learn from studies of folk biological classifications, it would prove useful to recognize that the regularities in structural principles described by Berlin and his associates are interpretations. They are products of certain hermeneutical maneuvers.

One such is the positing of "covert categories." These are categories for which the natives have no labels but which the analyst infers that they recognize.

Another is the translation into structural equivalences of highly diverse descriptive expressions for plants and animals. That is, various expressions in different folk biological classifications are analyzed as suggesting the same or similar taxonomic ranks. This interpretive accomplishment is all the more impressive in light of the rich use of tropes by various populations for talking about what we call plants and animals.

Mary Hesse, and Richard Rorty after her, conceptualize significant theoretical alterations or "revolutions" in Western science as metaphoric redescriptions of nature. That expression takes on intensified significance for us when we turn from one folk biological classification to another, from one metaphoric description of local nature to another.

In summary, the interpretive efforts of Berlin and his associates suggest striking structural resemblances among folk biological classifications and the operation of certain general principles that could account for the resemblances. Those efforts, moreover, have cast doubt on simplistic and narrow utilitarian interpretations of folk biological classifications. These accomplishments, however, are not equivalent to demonstrating that those classifications are theory-free or autonomous of human interests. The construction of gestalts is culturally influenced and, analytically, different populations select and weight features differently. Considerations that critics raised respecting certain suppositions of the early pheneticists, considerations that I detailed some pages ago, might be made use of, *mutatis mutandis*, in efforts to expand our understandings of folk biological classifications purportedly based on overall perceptual similarities.

Folk biological taxonomies, like those of the systematists in the biological sciences, are *indexical*. By exploring their indexicality with respect to myths and much else we might well enhance our appreciation of their theoretical groundings and commitments.

Anthropology and the Pheneticists' Methods: Needham's Objections

Needham, an influential expositor within the anthropological Republic of the idea of polythetic grouping, is sensitive to the fact that while the idea itself is innocent of any necessary phylogenetic commitment, it is applied in the biological sciences to phenomena whose relationships are held to be the products of evolutionary processes. Though he opines that "the polythetic methods developed in those sciences" are attractive in various ways, he also observes that "there are serious objections to the adoption of such methods into the study of social facts" (Needham 1975:364).

Among other things, Needham remarks,

> One very striking difference between the materials that a natural
> scientist has to classify and those which are the concern of the
> social anthropologist is the presence or absence of evolutionary
> connexions... It is doubtless the factor of phylogenetic descent
> that encourages some among even the most modern taxonomists
> to speak of 'natural' groupings of organisms, and to distinguish
> such aggregates from 'artificial' groupings. I suppose, too, that it
> is phylogeny that largely accounts for what Lockhart and Hartman
> isolate as the 'monothetic core of common properties' in polythetic
> classes of bacterial strains (1963:76). We might therefore sum up
> the situation in the natural sciences by saying that, as intrinsic
> features of the materials under comparison, common descent
> composes natural classes while natural selection variegates the
> members of such classes.

In the comparative study of social facts, however, these
conditions do not obtain. (1975:359)

Needham suggests that some forms of evolutionary reconstruction may be possible in the comparative study of social institutions. If institutions change in regular ways, one might be able
to establish regular transformations that resemble evolutionary
developments among plants and animals. He cites prescriptive
alliance systems as a potential example — but he also observes
that in a comparison of such systems one cannot posit a common
origin for them. The absence of that "crucial feature" occasions
doubt about the direct employment of the taxonomic methods
of the natural sciences in anthropology (1975:360).

A further consideration of prescriptive systems of social
classification supplies us with additional reasons for doubt.
Needham states that while the members of a zoological taxon
may be very dissimilar, prescriptive systems are so defined as to
be very similar. Their points of resemblance, however, are based
not on "culture particulars" (which would be analogous to
phenetic character states in the biological sciences), but, rather,
on analytical abstractions, which produce a monothetic class. "Even
in this quite promising line of 'evolutionary' investigation,"
Needham writes, "... the parallels with a natural science are
superficial. An abstract stipulation occupies the place of a common
ancestor; the similarity of social forms has nothing to do with
common descent; and the postulated transformations of prescriptive systems appear causally different... from the evolution of
natural species" (1975:361).

Needham also points to "a more fundamental obstacle" regarding the utilization of polythetic grouping in anthropology — an
obstacle that, if allowed to stand, must be of major concern to

students of religion, committed as we are to exploring the representations of persons whom we describe as "religious."

Needham maintains that in the natural sciences the features utilized to describe polythetic groups generally have "a real, distinct, and independent character, and they can be clearly stipulated in advance" (1975:363). In bacteriology, for instance, the reactions of micro-organisms to chemical elements and compounds permit grouping by differences, where a definite feature can be determined to be present or absent. Or in molecular biology and biochemistry, to supply another example that would seem to support Needham's argument, the presence or absence of different amino acids in protein sequences can be noted. "But in the realm of social facts," Needham states,

> this aspect of polythetic classification is hardly to be found. A main reason is that in social anthropology the determination of the constituent features of a polythetic class cannot be carried out by reference to discrete particulars, but entails instead a reliance on further features of the same character which themselves are likewise polythetic. In social life, that is, there are no established phenomena, in the form of isolable social facts for instance, which correspond to the elements and particles in nature . . . This contrast is the most marked when the materials for an anthropological classification are collective representations. (1975:364)

Two reservations, neither of which fatally challenges Needham's argument, can be noted.

First, the characters and character states used by biological pheneticists are not always as "distinct" and as "independent" as Needham's wording might imply. The reader may recall difficulties posited by Ehrlich and Ehrlich, Gould, Hull, and Mayr respecting the recognition of features and the identification and application of similarities in the classificatory pursuits of biological scientists. Still and all, character states conventionally determined by biological scientists — most notably those employed by molecular biologists and biochemists — are often more discrete than those used by cultural and social anthropologists.

Second, Needham uses the term polythetic somewhat more liberally than I prefer. Thus, for instance, while we may have good reasons to intuit that certain of our concepts are polythetic, I would prefer not to call them that until we have engaged in descriptive and analytical efforts that eventuate in substantial support for our intuitions and that facilitate the clarification of concepts for research purposes. Needham elsewhere recognizes the significance of such a reservation, for he writes that "One matter that has perhaps not been accorded its full importance is the contrast between recognising polythesis in the constitution of concepts and the deliberate (i.e. taxonomic) employment of the thesis in constructing concepts of analysis and description" (Needham, Personal Communication).

Various of our analytical constructs may perhaps be termed "polythetic" in consequence of our descriptive and analytical procedures. But many might be adequately comprehended (and more easily handled) by invoking the concept of family resemblance.

Take, for example, the case of theism as a criterial attribute of religion. When Euripides writes (*Helen* 560), "For to recognize friends is also a God" (*"theos gar kai to gignōskein philous"*), he uses the word *theos* ('God') in a way acceptable to the ancient Greeks — acceptable not merely as poetic license (Wilamowitz 1956 [1931] calls our attention to the broad usage of *theos* as a predicate term). But though we might assign 'recognizing friends' to a "polythetic class" labeled "God," so inclusive a "class," if not actually an analytical absurdity, is at least of dubious criterial utility regardless of whatever existential justification we might offer for it.

We would do better to apperceive some similarity between Euripides's use of 'God' and various other usages, and to recognize that that is what we apperceive. In any case, if we would utilize the postulation of "Gods" as one among a number of features in characterizing religion, we should acknowledge that concepts of divinity vary across cultures, perhaps to some extent (so to speak) "homologously" so among historically connected variants of an identifiable religious tradition, but, more likely than not, analogously so (and thus with greater variation in particulars) among the world's religions.

Southwold (1978:369), in an unfortunate turn of phrase, writes of "Needham's invaluable distinction between monothetic and polythetic classes" (thereby possibly misleading some readers into supposing that Needham originated the distinction). But while he thus refers to Needham's essay (and, indeed, appears to derive his understanding of polythesis largely if not entirely from Needham), he does not deal with the several difficulties that Needham sees as intervening between anthropological goals and the employment of polythetically described groups to serve them. That failure weakens his endorsement of a polythetic approach to religion.

Further, Southwold's brand of "polythetic classification" suggests a blurring of the roles that have traditionally been assigned to homology and analogy in the grouping activities of the biological sciences — if not, indeed, an actual reversal of the role of analogy. And his highly abstract approximations to the phenetic characters typically utilized in biology lend support to Needham's claim that "The disparity between the natural sciences and social anthropology, in taxonomic method as in much else, reflects a contrast of kind between natural entities and social facts" (1975:364).

Selecting Units for Comparison

In addition to the above considerations, there are others that stimulate questions about Southwold's application of "polythetic classification" to religion. One such is put well by David Aberle:

> One point . . . that always troubles me when people talk about such classifications rather than doing them has to do with insides and outsides. There has to be some criterion for deciding what units will be compared . . . Once that decision has been made, the polythetic classification applies *within* the delimited population. Now when it comes to religion, either (1) polythetic classification is just another word for a listing definition, or (2) the attributes of the variables under consideration . . . must be applied to a population of units that includes a lot of things (what things?) that are at first blush not religions or not certainly religions, to see how, or show how the religious and the non-religious units are subgrouped. (Aberle, Personal Communication)

The researcher, in other words, must first somehow establish a population of units that are to be subjected to empirical comparison for classificatory purposes. *After* that is done, the members of that population can be sorted into polythetically described groups. A bacteriologist, for example, might compare all of the bacteria in his petri dish, an entomologist all of the butterflies collected on expedition, and an archeologist all of the sherds collected from some site or set of sites.

But from where or what does Southwold get his religion and religions? He does not actually search the world for "attributes" among delimited cultural populations, engaging in systematic comparative work that might establish features that we could call "religious" and that would "show how the religious and the non-religious units are subgrouped." Nor, of course, does he support the conception of a class called "religion" structured by the intersection of specified values of certain variables (i.e., a dimensional or paradigmatic classification in which features of two or more dimensions constitute a necessary and sufficient set for defining the class, with the different religions of the world comprising the *denotata* of that class). Nor does he appear to concern himself with religion as a class defined in some described order of hierarchial inclusions (a "taxonomy" in the technical sense). Rather, like the fabled Boston matrons who do not buy their hats but "have" them, he seems to have his religions.

From what hat, then, does Southwold pull religion? Not from a hat, I think, but from the verbal conventions of his fellows, anthropologists and non-anthropologists alike: from, indeed, the way his fellows *use* the word religion, and his apperception of family likenesses among the phenomena to which the word is applied. In sum, what Southwold offers us under the rubric of "polythetic classification" might better be subsumed under another label.

Considerations Advanced by Dunnell

Further objections to asserting a "polythetic class" denominated religion can be adduced from reading the extremely technical — some might say narrow — definitions and considerations advanced by the archeologist Robert C. Dunnell in his *Systematics in Prehistory* (1971).

Dunnell restricts "definition," "classification," and "class" to what he calls the ideational realm, while associating "description," "grouping," and "group" with what he terms the phenomenal realm. So-called "polythetic classification," within his framework, belongs to the latter realm. *He does not consider it to be a kind of classification* but, rather, a form of "non-classificatory arrangement," with the consequence, of course, that the words "polythetic" and "classification" are rendered incompatible (1971:53, 87–110). (He recognizes only two sorts of classification: paradigmatic and taxonomic.)

Dunnell goes even further. Addressing himself to numerical phenetics (which, in 1971, he calls numerical taxonomy), he counsels that if it be

> treated not as a means of creating groups, but as a means of treating the *denotata* of pre-existing groups, a useful relationship with classification can be stipulated. In this case numerical taxonomy summarizes the occurrence of both distinctive and non-distinctive features over the *denotata* of a classification ... numerical taxonomy provides a valuable means of manipulating class *denotata* and formulating and testing inferences about their behavior. (1971:109)

Taking this counsel to heart, it is likely that the *idea* of polythesis could be prudently and fruitfully employed in certain clearly delimited areas in the study of religions. Where, for instance, we suppose that we can identify phenomenal entities, and where we initially hypothesize that those entities in some sense or other pertain to a group, treating them *as if* they were *denotata* of a classification and comparing them multidimensionally would seem to be methodologically sound in testing our initial hypothesis and perhaps in considering others.

"Hinduism" As a Possible Example

Numerical phenetics as Dunnell conceives it might prove useful, for example, in sorting out clusters of characters and evaluating variations among character states in cases where we have good reasons to suppose that members of some identified population of religious phenomena are historically related — in, for instance, much of that enormously complex aggregate of phenomena to which we conventionally assign the term "Hinduism." Various concepts that we associate with "Hinduism" — *karma, dharma,* and so on — could probably be established as polythetic when examined intensely in their spatio-temporal distributions. Polythetic analysis might prove useful in such cases both in coming to appreciate the span of variations and as an adjunct for accomplishing limited historical investigations.

Historical relatedness among similar cultural phenomena, after all, brings us as close as we come in the cultural sciences to what many evolutionary biologists mean by homology — although we ought not push analogies between cultural and biological phenomena too far.[2] Nirad C. Chaudhuri (1979:146), it may be recalled, writes that "Hinduism suggests certain images from the world of plants, where vegetation relentlessly proliferates and expands." That is splendid imagery, especially in light of the cross-pollination and hybridization that occur in the botanical domain. It might prove a particularly insightful image, moreover, for students of "Hinduism" who take an interest in polythesis.

---

[2] Certain social and cultural anthropologists use the term homology and various of its derivatives in other ways. Thus, for example, in applications to cultural analysis of the proportional analogy "a is to b what c is to d," some describe a and c as "homologues," and likewise b and d. In so doing, Needham (1985:21) remarks that in the study of dual symbolic classifications, "homologies depend upon context," and that, when viewed under a different aspect or in a different setting, homologies may be reversed. "Even within one tradition," for instance, "fire may be associated with the right in one context and with the left in another." E.K. Maranda (1971:117), referring to the a:b::c:d expression, observes that "Analogy is an operation of the mind. It rests on the recognition of two kinds of relations between the terms: similarity and contiguity, in other words metaphor and metonymy . . . "

Characterizing "Religion in General"

When it comes to characterizing what W.C. Smith (1962) terms
(however critically) "religion in general," I see little prospect of
making a responsible and productive use of numerical phenetics,
and we would do well to search for other options. Not only have
weighty criticisms been entered against numerical phenetics in
the biological sciences, and not only has that approach been supplanted by others, but strong reservations respecting its applicability to cultural phenomena are persuasive.

There are valuable insights and suggestions in Southwold's essay,
but they are — in actuality and in potentiality — better accomodated by Wittgenstein's family resemblances than by any of
the classificatory methods of the biological sciences. This is also
the case for Jonathan Z. Smith's appreciation of variations in
early Judaism. In my opinion, both Smith and Southwold are
heading in the right direction, but they are on the wrong train
on the wrong track.

There is another multi-factorial approach to conceptualizing
religion that we ought to consider. Viewed philosophically, it
pivots on the concept of family likeness, and it expands on that
concept in the languages of the contemporary cognitive sciences.
It is, in my opinion, not only heading in the right direction, but
it is also the right train on the right track. We board it in the
next chapter.

CHAPTER SIX

A PROTOTYPE APPROACH

To change the very concept of a category is to change not only our concept of the mind, but also our understanding of the world.
— George Lakoff, *Women, Fire, and Dangerous Things*, 1987, p. 9.

. . . selection and evaluation of predicates and variables in cognition and recognition can be explicated only in the context of purposive behavior.
— Satosi Watanabe, *Knowing and Guessing: A Quantitative Study of Inference and Information*, 1969, p. 388.

The phenomena commonly comprehended by applications of the word "religion" are too complex and variable, and often too enmeshed with other phenomena in a larger universe, to be confined analytically within sharp, impermeable boundaries. The world as we experience it is untidy — or, if you prefer, very rich in its multiplicity. If our recognition of either the world's richness or its untidyness does not actually turn us to religion, then perhaps it might make us more accepting of practical compromises in conceptualizing a category so labeled.

We begin with a word that is mouthed by millions. Like other "concept-words," religion fits the characterization made famous by Wittgenstein:

> What a concept-word indicates is certainly a kinship between objects, but this kinship need not be the sharing of a common property or constituent. It may connect the objects like the links of a chain, so that one is linked to another *by intermediary links*. Two neighboring members may have common features and be *similar* to each other, while distant ones belong to the same family without any longer having anything in common. Indeed, even if a feature is common to all members of the family it need not be the feature that defines the concept. (*Philosophical Grammar* 35).

Wittgenstein recognizes, however, that we may "wish to draw boundaries in the use of a word, in order to clear up philosophical paradoxes" (*ibid.*). When we look at the actual use of a concept-word, he tells us, "what we see is something constantly fluctuating." In our investigations, nevertheless, we may "set over against this fluctuation something more fixed, just as one paints a stationary picture of the constantly altering face of the landscape" (*Philosophical Grammar* 36). Indeed, "If for our purposes we wish to regulate the use of a word by definite rules, then alongside its fluctuating use we set up a different use by codifying one of

its characteristic aspects" (*ibid.*). Alongside, that is, the picture
of normal use in which, as it were, the colors flow into each other
"without sharp boundaries," we place another picture, one that
resembles the first in certain ways, "but is built up of colours with
clear boundaries between them" (*Philosophical Grammar* 35).

While Wittgenstein attacks "the craving for generality" and the
essentialism that it expresses and nurtures (*Blue and Brown Books*,
p. 17), his concession to defining a concept "in order," he says,
"to clear up philosophical paradoxes," can be extended, Hudson
(1977:236) observes, "so that it will cover certain more general
kinds of confusion." Wittgenstein's concession to definition,
however, by no means reduces the importance of family resemblances. The significance of the idea of family resemblances,
indeed, has been increased by some recent work on "prototypes,"
and prototype theory, in my opinion, renders it unnecessary to
avail ourselves of monothetic definitions with respect to religion.

Prototype

"Prototype," Smith and Medin (1981:2) point out, is a "label"
that "has been used to mean many different things." Perhaps the
best place to begin is with some common acceptations of the
term as described by a dictionary. While a dictionary definition
is unlikely to capture fully the range of folk uses, and although
it is decidedly inadequate for suggesting technical applications
of the term in the contemporary cognitive sciences, it is nevertheless useful in two ways. First, it has the virtue of familiarity,
a virtue at least for initial orientation, because it is based on the
most common popular usages. And, second, it suggests a temporal aspect implied by some common uses, thereby facilitating
the early introduction of an experiential dimension in what I
want to say about prototypes and how many of us begin to
conceptualize religion.

The Oxford English Dictionary (p. 1512) defines prototype as "The
first or primary type of anything; the original (thing or person)
of which another is a copy, representation, or derivative, or to
which it conforms or is required to conform; a pattern, model,
standard, exemplar, archetype." That dictionary definition is
moderately complex in that it suggests both a temporal aspect
to prototype ("the first," "the original") and a modeling or
exemplification function that focuses our attention on prototype
as a structure and standard. While the conflation of these might
sometimes promote analytical confusion, it will enhance our

understanding of common anthropological assumptions and practices to take both into account in the case of conceptualizing religion.

The Temporal Aspect: The Acquisition of Bias

The temporal dimension among anthropologists relates not to some hypothesized "first" or "original" religion, but to the acquisition of conceptual biases. Many anthropologists first learned about religion in a Western cultural setting. They came to associate religion with their particular conceptions of Judaism and Christianity, and, in time, to conceive of religion more abstractly in keeping with common contemporary Western acceptations that have their roots in the Enlightenment.

Many anthropologists eventually expanded and, to some extent, otherwise altered their understandings by reading "classic" Western theoretical accounts of religion: works, for example, by William Robertson Smith, Edward Burnett Tylor, Sigmund Freud, William James, Emile Durkheim, and Max Weber, and by authors such as Bronislaw Malinowski, Edward E. Evans-Pritchard, and so forth. All of those writers also first learned about religion in a Western cultural setting; they first associated religion with Judaism and Christianity; and they eventually added to or otherwise modified common Western conceptions of religion that stem from the Enlightenment. This is also true of such authors as Ludwig Feuerbach and Karl Marx as well as Mircea Eliade and Victor Turner.

Disagreements over specific theoretical points notwithstanding, many contemporary academic students of religion overlap in basic understandings. To an important extent, moreover, they participate in a universe of discourse with distinguished 19th century Western students of religion, although their experiences and sensitivities differ to some extent from those of their predecessors (19th century authors, for example, lived among professed religionists in societies where religion was formally accorded a greater place in public life than is generally the case today).

Many anthropologists who study religion implicitly and sometimes explicitly compare what strikes them as "religious" in non-Western societies with what they suppose to be the religious traditions of the West. Indeed, they *first recognize* "religion" among non-Western peoples by finding professed convictions and other behaviors that they interpret as analogues of those that they assign to the domain of "religion" in Western societies, past and present.

In short, ideas about the natures and histories of religions in the West serve as what the dictionary calls prototypes — as the first or original models — guiding anthropologists in their development of models of religion among non-Western peoples.

The above application of one aspect of the dictionary definition, though relevant, must be supplemented. Contemporary cognitive scientists (especially cognitive psychologists and linguists) provide us with a set of more sophisticated conceptions relating to "prototypes." In the theoretical formulations of some of them, one does not talk about "the prototype" of a category (except in special cases) but rather about "the most prototypical exemplars." For some exemplars of a natural language category, in the judgments of ordinary speakers of a language, are deemed better examples, or *more* prototypical, than others. Asymmetries in judgments about the relative goodness of fit of various exemplars of a category are known as "prototype effects."

In the approach recommended here, moreover, one can easily cope with the idea that, in the living realities of speakers and cognizers, items may pertain to two or more categories, though perhaps in different degrees of judged goodness of fit. Thus, for example, one might say that "Islam" and "communism" both exemplify the same two categories, "religion" and "political movement," while also deeming Islam to be a clearer or better example of religion than communism, and communism to be a clearer or better example of a political movement than Islam.

"Islam" and "communism" as used above, it is important to note, are literary conveniences. Islam and communism (and Christianity, Judaism, Buddhism, etc.) do not constitute monolithic and clearly bounded entities. Rather, there are numbers of Islams and numbers of communisms (Christianities, etc.) among which we recognize various sorts of family resemblances. From some persons' points of view, moreover, certain Islams are likely to be regarded as more Islamic (better, more authentic) than others, and certain communisms may be deemed more communistic (better, more authentic) than others.

Categorization

To categorize, in popular parlance, is to classify. Categorization in that sense is a judgmental act. It is a judgment of what is like what and, at least implicitly, of what is not like what. If some object, event, or process is judged to be an instance of a certain category, it is assigned in effect to a group of instances comprehended by that category and described by the category label. In a fundamental sense, as Jackendoff (1983:77) notes, categorization judgments are discriminations, and discriminations, of course, need not involve language nor need they be distinctly human. Other animals engage in discrimination tasks, and doing so is crucial to their survival as living organisms. Human category judgments, in short, evidence a certain phylogenetic continuity with the discriminatory acts of other life-forms.

The English word category probably derives from the Greek *katēgoreō*, 'to speak against', 'to accuse', 'to assert', 'to signify', 'to indicate', 'to prove'. The term has to do with *predication*. In the essentialist tradition, the elemental idea is that we can predicate something in common about the instances of a category. Thus, for example, we should be able to predicate something about all the cases that we judge to be instances of the category religion beyond their being instances.

In contravention of the essentialist tradition, the approach recommended in this chapter suggests that while there is much that we may predicate of "religion," the most interesting things that we may be able to predicate about "religion*s*" (other than that they are linked by family resemblances) might only be predicable of some rather than all. Indeed, that approach advises us to expect not a set of universal predicates for religions but, instead, a network of predicates, criss-crossing and overlapping in their applicability to phenomena that we variously deem better and less-good exemplifications of the category religion.

In the traditional, essentialist perspective that has long dominated Western thinking about categories, objects with the same essence, the same essential defining features, belong to the same class and thus pertain to the same category. Since a category, in the traditional view, is defined by a set of properties that its members commonly share, all category members equally exemplify the category. If, therefore, an individual identifies a robin as a bird but isn't sure about a penguin, this does not diminish the integrity and objectivity of the category bird; it merely testifies to the fact that a particular individual fails, for whatever reason, to endorse the opinion of those Westerners who hold that a penguin is a bird. For if commonly cited features that define the category bird are — as many essentialists suppose — representations of objective facts about birds, then a penguin (for those who endorse the prevailing classification) is as much of a bird as a robin, even if penguins don't fly. The category bird, on this view, exists as a natural fact, and human beings must work toward discovering such facts. Lakoff (1987) terms this perspective "objectivism," a perspective repudiated by what he calls "experientialism," a viewpoint supported by contemporary prototype theory.

Before proceeding any further, however, a few kind words on behalf of essentialism are in order.

First, while many of our categories can be conceptualized as family resemblance categories — that is, as categories characterizeable by a pool of features no one of which is either necessary or sufficient for assigning a candidate to a group comprehended by the category — our conventions do include genuine essentialist categories. Take, for example, the category "odd number." Odd numbers are defined as integers indivisible by two, and the essentialism of that convention is clear. In the pages that follow nothing should be construed as suggesting that there really are not any essentialist categories. Although I do not suppose that they are "purely given" by nature, they do exist as pragmatically successful conventions. My argument is that religion as an analytical category ought not to be cast in an essentialist mold. However odd the category religion might be claimed to be, we should not try to make it closely resemble the category odd number.

Second, we should not suppose that only categories organized around family resemblances may have some members that are popularly judged to be better examples of their respective categories than others. One of the key terms of contemporary prototype theorists is the expression "prototype effects," an expression used especially with reference to asymmetries in the judgments that people make respecting how well different instances of a category exemplify that category (e.g., many speakers of English would say that a robin is a better example of a bird than a penguin). But people may do something similar in the case of essentialist categories. Thus experimental subjects judge 7 to be a better exemplar of the category odd number than 23, and they are quicker in identifying the former as an example than the latter (Armstrong, Gleitman, and Gleitman 1983).

Prototype Theory

Contemporary prototype theorists have various predecessors in the raising of alternatives to classical essentialism for understanding some of the practices of speakers and cognizers. Prototype theorists themselves often single out Wittgenstein, all the more so because they have incorporated their understandings of "family resemblance" into their theory-building (e.g., Rosch and Mervis 1975, Lakoff 1987). In a recent study the linguist Karol Janicki (1990) calls our attention to the contributions of the "general semanticists" Alfred Korzybski and S.I. Hayakawa, the similar views of the philosopher Stuart Chase, and the anti-essentialist arguments of the philosopher Karl R. Popper.

Korzybski, as Janicki (1990:6–8, 33–36) describes his position, rejects the "two-valued orientation" associated with Aristotle. Indeed, he raises interesting objections to the very fundaments of Aristotelian logic, which are often described as The Law of Identity (A is A), the Law of the Excluded Middle (either A or not A), and the Law of Non-Contradiction (not both A and not A).

Hayakawa, in Janicki's treatment of him (1990:8–10, 33–36), agrees with Korzybski about the illusions that many people entertain respecting essentialist definitions. Popular opinion notwithstanding, Hayakawa maintains, such definitions "tell us nothing about things;" they should be understood, rather, "as statements about language" (Hayakawa 1939:155, quoted in Janicki 1990:9). Stuart Chase, Janicki (1990:10) notes, voices a similar idea.

Popper's anti-essentialism, as Janicki summarizes it (1990:12–17) and later enlarges on that summary (1990:37–48, passim), is broad and powerful. Popper is critical of intensional definitions not only because they inevitably involve us in infinite regress — they define selected words by using other words, and those words in turn require definitions, and the words that we use to define them need to be defined, and so on, in principle endlessly — but for additional reasons as well. In criticizing "What is questions" (e.g., "What is religion?," "What is a piano?"), for example, Popper not only refers to the matter of infinite regress in definitional chains, but he criticizes Aristotle's endorsement of intellectual intuition as a way of establishing truth in the posing and answering of ontological questions (Janicki 1990:14). Popper, indeed, broadly attacks Aristotle's idea that by identifying the essence of something we establish the meaning of the word that we apply to that thing.

In reading Popper, Janicki (1990:15) suggests, we should always distinguish between "precision" and "clarity." While Popper holds that definitions cannot provide us with precision, he allows that they may sometimes promote clarity, and that they are welcome when they do.

This matter of precision and clarity touches on the discussion of vagueness and ambiguity broached in Chapter 3. Vagueness, it may be recalled, has to do with uncertainty about what a word covers, what it may include or exclude. Criteria relating to boundaries may be soft, as when, for example, we come upon a reference to an "old" book and are uncertain as to the applicable criterion for establishing what is old. Ambiguity, in distinction, relates to terms having more than one meaning because they simultaneously participate in two or more semantic classes. Examples include expressions such as "civic religion" and "secular religion."

The term religion, my colleague David Murray points out (Personal Communication), is sometimes used vaguely, sometimes ambiguously (though I think it likely that vagueness has been a greater goad to definition-making than ambiguity). The latter case, Murray notes, is professionally troubling to the anthropologist who encounters categories in other cultures that appear to straddle the normal ranges of two or more category terms available to us in English for describing them (e.g., a category in some culture that appears to be both "religious" and "economic" and cannot easily be described as one or the other). Wittgenstein helps us to treat with seeming boundary problems, with vagueness, but we must also, Murray argues, handle the matter of ambiguity.

Anthropologists and others have sometimes attempted to alleviate if not obviate problems of both vagueness and ambiguity by stipulating definitions. But even if such definitions might seem to dampen the problem of ambiguity, they are less successful in giving the appearance of doing so in the case of vagueness. Precision, as the first four chapters of this work suggest, is a chimerical goal in defining religion. The prototype approach recommended here recognizes that that is so. That recognition, moreover, contributes to clarifying what is involved in conceptualizing religion. It does so especially with respect to the problem of boundaries, the problem of vagueness, and in so doing it helps to defuse the problem of ambiguity.

Coleman and Kay, in describing what they mean by "prototype semantics," state that "our PROTOTYPE view of word meaning attempts to account for the obvious pretheoretical intuition that semantic categories frequently have blurry edges and allow degrees of membership." "On this view," they continue, "applicability of a word to a thing is in general NOT a matter of 'yes or no' but rather of 'more or less'" (1981:27; capitalizations in original).

That is, the appeal to prototypes eschews the sort of approach that pivots on what Fillmore (1976:24) calls "a checklist of criterial properties," a list of features that an object supposedly must satisfy if it is to be deemed properly labeled by some word.

In ordinary discourse we sometimes treat certain referents of category terms as sharper or more conventional or more reasonable exemplars of their categories than others. As speakers of English and participants in North American culture, for instance, we are likely to regard apples and oranges as better exemplars of fruit than olives, and a chair as a more clear-cut exemplar of our category furniture than a radio (Rosch and Mervis 1975:573). Some chairs, moreover, may be deemed better exemplars than others (*ibid.*).

This fact of common, every-day experience is of great importance for our understanding of certain possibilities in categorization. Various authors build on it in such idioms as "primary types," "core types," "focal types," "focal points," and the like. In anthropology, for example, we find sensitivity to it incorporated into genealogical extensionist views of the distribution of kinship terms (e.g., Malinowski 1929, Lounsbury 1964, Scheffler and Lounsbury 1971), into the analysis of the distribution of color terms (Berlin and Kay 1969), and into much else.

The recognition of more clear-cut exemplars implies, of course, that some referents of the category terms under consideration are less clear-cut. Rosch, who has explored this possibility in her research, denies, however, that scalar differences in the ratings that people make of goodness of example necessarily mean that membership in a group comprehended by a category is also scalar. There may be scalar memberships in some cases and non-scalar memberships in others.

In sum, prototype effects, or judgments that some things that pertain to a category better exemplify that category than other things that pertain to it, do not prove that membership in the category is graded and that the structure of the category is given by the prototype effects. A category such as "tall man" has graded membership, for some tall men are taller than others and the category has no sure boundaries. Prototype effects here, Lakoff (1987:45) remarks, "may result from degree of category membership, while in the case of *bird*, which does have rigid boundaries, the prototype effects must result from some other aspect of internal category structure.""Exemplariness," Gleitman, Armstrong, and Gleitman (1983:102) observe, "is not the same as class membership." Goodness of example, nevertheless, is not only important for the learning of categories but probably figures importantly into the very development of many categories. Categories, Rosch (1975:179) suggests, "develop around potential prototypes."

In any event, our appreciation of the significance of differential goodness of fit is heightened when we couple it with Wittgenstein's insight that many of our categories are unlikely to have sharp boundaries. Yet, as Rosch (1978:35) points out, "cognitive economy" (the provision of maximal information with minimal cognitive effort) dictates that our categories be viewed as distinct from one another as possible.

One way to achieve this, or to give the impression of achieving it, in the fashioning of our analytical categories is by means of monothetic definitions: we formally stipulate for each category some set of individually necessary and jointly sufficient criteria that govern membership in the group comprehended by that category. This excludes candidates for membership that are deficient in one or more of the required features.

But there is another way to achieve a certain separation among our analytical categories and thus promote clarity. That other way enables us to serve our cognitive needs while abandoning indefensible demands for sharply bounded categories with clear-cut discontinuities between them. We may explicitly conceive of categories *with reference to* clear cases that best fit them rather than conceptualizing categories monothetically, which implicates stipulated limits. This approach obviates the sort of problems that have plagued essentialists in arriving at categorical judgments, for such problems, as Wittgenstein notes, tend to arise when one is concerned with category boundaries (Rosch 1978:35–36).

Our understanding of what might be meant by "prototypes" with reference to how people actually employ them in daily life owes much to the work of the cognitive psychologist Eleanor Rosch and her associates. "By prototypes of categories," Rosch writes, "we have generally meant the clearest cases of category membership defined operationally by people's judgements of goodness of membership in the category" (1978:36).

Yet even so general and seemingly innocent a conceptualization can be distorted and lead us back to the very essentialism that we may wish to escape. For, as Rosch observes (*ibid.*), this notion of prototype can be reified: treated, that is, as if it referred to some one specific exemplar of a category or mental structure. Questions are then likely to arise about whether or not some phenomenon is "the" prototype or a part of the prototype, just as in naked essentialism digital or "categorical" (yes or no) questions are raised about category boundaries. "Such thinking," Rosch writes, "precisely violates the Wittgensteinian insight that we can judge how clear a case something is and deal with categories on the basis of clear cases in the total absence of information about boundaries" (*ibid.*).

The general concept, moreover, may be obfuscated by another confusion: empirically grounded substantive claims about proto-typicality can sometimes be conflated with theories about cog-nitive processing. In effect, one might sometimes fail to distin-guish clearly between the structures of categories and our theories about the uses of those structures in processing information (*ibid.*).

Rosch suggests that when we speak of a prototype, we are engaging in "a convenient grammatical fiction" (1978:40). What we are really referring to, she states, are *judgments about degrees of prototypicality*. While some "artificial categories" (of the sort, say, that are designed by psychologists for experimental purposes) may by definition have some literal, single prototype, this is not the case, Rosch maintains, in "natural-language categories." To speak as if a single entity were the prototype "is either a gross misunderstanding of the empirical data or a covert theory of mental representation" (*ibid.*).

Not all cognitive scientists, however, are averse to positing a stereotypic representation. Casson, for example, characterizes a prototype as "a stereotypic, or generic, representation of a concept that serves as a standard for evaluating the goodness-of-fit be-tween schema variables and elements in the environment" (1983:434). But Jackendoff (1983:142), although supplying a reason why it might be intuitively appealing to suppose that the meaning of a category word is to be found in an image of a stereotype that instances the category, summarizes and endorses arguments against the stereotype theory.

Jackendoff notes that Fodor (1975) in effect maintains that "there are terrible problems in stating how one relates the stereotype to anything else," and that one cannot use the stereo-type to achieve categorization judgments (1983:142). Further, Jackendoff credits Rosch et al (1976) with undermining "the generality of a stereotype theory by pointing out that one does not form an image of a stereotype for every catgeory" (1983:142). Thus, for example, people are not likely to image "furniture," although they may image "chairs," a class of "basic objects" that have similar shapes. While stereotype theory has a certain plau-sibility for basic object categories that may be imaged by means of default values for typicality, that theory is less plausible for a category such as furniture, where the commonality of members, such as it may be, is more a matter of function than of shape (Jackendoff 1983:142–143).

Now, the anthropologist Martin Southwold, using a somewhat different conception of prototype, does in effect talk about "the prototype" when he refers to Christianity as "the religion prototypical for our conceptions" of religion (1978:367). He does so, moreover, while emphasizing functional aspects of religions. His usage is in line with dictionary senses of prototype as "a pattern" or "model" and, with respect to the learning experiences of most professional anthropologists, "The first or primary type of anything," the experiential "original" to which other religions more or less conform.

Most anthropologists, as I suggested earlier in this chapter, probably began to think of religion largely by recourse to their conceptualizations of Christianity and Judaism, conceptualizations based on impressions of those religions formed as they grew up in Western societies. And however abstracted or otherwise modified their early models may have become in the effort to accommodate Theravada Buddhism or some other "religion," the literature suggests that for Southwold and others Christianity and Judaism remain chief exemplars of the category. This affects in important ways anthropological efforts to characterize religion and to employ the category in research, for, as Rosch and Mervis point out (1975:599), "the extent to which members are conceived typical of a category appears to be an important variable in the cognitive processing of categories."

While I think that what Southwold says is understandable, I advocate that we move from talk of Christianity (and Judaism) as "the prototype" to a discourse that describes them as "among the most prototypical" examples of what we mean by religion. We commonly think of them as being typical of the category despite some important considerations relating to them, considerations that have some interesting consequences for how many of us conceptualize religion.

Judaism and Christianity: Some Considerations

First, it is important to remember a point made earlier in this work. There is no "Judaism" or "Christianity" if by those terms we mean monolithic entities. There are numerous Judaisms and Christianities, and the singulars of those terms are best thought of as referring to *families* of religions. Whenever I use a singular term such as Judaism or Christianity, I mean a family of religions.

Second, it is unlikely that any two persons have exactly the same ideas and feelings about Judaism or Christianity (or any other family of religions). While two people may carry on a mutually satisfying conversation about a denominated family of religions, they ought not to be expected to share precisely the same understandings and attitudes. This relates to an important point about language. Rather than supposing that the function of language is to describe the world, a more sophisticated view holds that, as Jackendoff (1983:94) puts it, "the purpose of language is to make one's internal structures projectable to others . . . i.e., to express thought."

Third, any person's ideas and feelings about Judaism, Christianity, or some other denominated family of religions are likely to change over time. This is true of the proponent of some faith, the scholar who studies that faith, and the occasional onlooker.

Fourth, at the same time that professional anthropologists are disposed to treat "Judaism" and "Christianity" as very typical (very prototypical) of the category religion, many of them view those faiths, at least in their contemporary settings in Western countries, as *atypical* in certain respects among the world's religions. Conceptual problems are thus clouded by something of an irony: the recognition of both the typicality or "prototypicality" of Judaism and Christianity for the category religion and the peculiar, apparently atypical contemporary existential situation of those families of religions.

How atypical? Briefly put, religions in the West, unlike religions in many other settings, have become marked off in various ways — *by the natives themselves!* — from other aspects of cultural life. One of the chief ways of marking them off, of course, is to label them: the very term "religion" serves to distinguish them, however imprecisely in some cases, from much else. Religion, moreover, has become increasingly optional in the West, and being "religious" tends to be foregrounded by virtue of its contrast with not being religious. The historical crystalization of religion in the West constitutes a long-term, complex process of bounding and clarification in tandem with shrinkage and weakening (pockets of resistance and contemporary florescences of "fundamentalism" and/or theistic militancy notwithstanding). That process is not replicated in various other societies, or so many ethnographies affirm.

The very diffuseness of religion in some non-Western societies

in comparison to what we find in Western societies has doubtless
reinforced the disposition of Western anthropologists to treat
their understandings of Judaism and Christianity as convenient
models of religion: convenient because they are close at hand,
and convenient because, comparatively speaking, they are sharply
etched within their cultural settings.

Early in life, moreover, many who became anthropologists
became aware of religious differences. Ironically enough, while
much theory in the social sciences stresses the functions of religion
in promoting social solidarity and contributing to the persistence
of the social order, social scientists growing up in Western societies
could hardly avoid being conscious of religious differences and
the divisiveness of social classifications based on religion. Thus,
for example, Durkheim, who is probably our most famous theorist
respecting the social eufunctions of religion, was himself an-
occasionally-discriminated-against descendant of rabbis in a mainly
Catholic France that was still troubled by the Dreyfus Affair.
Awareness of religious differences, indeed, probably heightened
nascent social scientists' impressions of the reality, saliency, and
importance of religion.

The diversity and peculiar place of religion in the contemporary West when compared to what appears to be the case in many
small-scale, non-Western societies, and the typical experiences of
Western anthropologists in their own societies, help us to
understand why some anthropologists are likely to describe a
ritually observant American Jew or Christian as "very religious"
whereas they may treat a ritually observant Nuer or Hopi as an
unexceptional Nuer or Hopi.

Anthropological sophistication, some anthropologists suppose,
enters in when we explicitly recognize that familiar contemporary Western religions are in certain respects peculiar or atypical
among the world's religions, and that the category religion must
be flexible enough not only to accommodate *them* (our original
models, after all!) but also others. How to do this, of course, constitutes the nub of the analytical problem.

Progress might be made by refining a multi-factorial conceptualization of religion by working toward a distributional understanding of prototypicality. In doing so, moreover, theism, a
prevalent bias in Western folk conceptions of religion, ought to
be recognized as a "default assignment" that relates to, and is
often given explicit expression in, numbers of scholarly efforts
to crystalize religion as an analytical category. I deal with these
points below. In doing so it will prove useful to pay attention

to some work on natural language categories. By attending to certain conclusions drawn from research on the ways that people use every-day categories, we are better prepared to address the problem of conceptualizing prescriptive analytical categories.

A Distributional Understanding of Prototypicality

Rosch and her associates have assembled experimental data that support certain conclusions about the judgments that people make among the referents of natural-language category terms. The referents adjudged most prototypical are usually those that are deemed (1) to "bear the greatest family resemblance to other members of their own categories" and (2) to "have the least overlap with other categories" (Rosch and Mervis 1975:599).

Building on this finding, Rosch and Mervis suggest a productive approach to prototypes that is guided by Wittgenstein's insights respecting family resemblances. This approach would not only measure the frequencies with which elements occur among the referents of the category terms studied, but it would also investigate the distribution of those elements over the referents of terms pertaining to contrasting categories (adapted from Rosch and Mervis 1975:600). A distributional approach as distinguished from a simple enumeration of frequencies within categories, they state, "is most relevant to prototypes in natural categories" (ibid.).

Translating that suggestion into language apposite to our interest in conceptualizing "religion" as an analytical category, one can say the following. In considering "features" — or, as I prefer to say on reading Coleman and Kay (1981:28, n.5), elements — that many anthropologists associate with religion, we ought to look at those elements as they may occur *outside* of the purview of what we conventionally take to be religion as well as within it. This advice applies to, among other things, "theism," which some authors regard as the very hallmark of religion. Before addressing theism, however, another matter deserves attention.

Striking a Balance

A problem worthy of some discussion at this juncture is the problem of striking some practical compromise between an appreciation of family resemblances and prototypicality on the one hand and the dispositions and needs of anthropologists on the other.

Some anthropologists call for an explicit characterization of what it is that one studies when one studies religion. I have argued, moreover, that numbers of anthropologists use their understandings of those families of religions denominated "Judaism" and "Christianity" as, at the very least, initial orienting models for the category religion. (The demand verbalized by Spiro [1966:91] that our definition of religion must not be "counter-intuitive" reflects, *inter alia*, an awareness of the historical association between the folk term and those religions.)

Now, despite the weakening and contraction of religion in various Western countries in post-Enlightenment times, the "Judaism" and "Christianity" described in text-books in comparative religion remain among the clearest cases, the best examples, of what many anthropologists mean by religion. It is hardly an accident that the lists of religious attributes furnished by Alston and Southwold (quoted in Chapter 5) totally fit "Judaism" and "Christianity," whereas we are correctly given to understand by those same authors that they fit some other religions less completely.

I propose that we formally acknowledge what many of us do informally: that we explicitly recognize our individual idealizations of 'mainstream' Judaisms and Christianities as "prototypical" in the highest degrees of the category religion. I suggest, moreover, that we enlarge this set of eminently category-fitting phenomena to include that family of religions called "Islam."

Although "Islam" is an object of study among Western scholars who are sometimes called "orientalists," a designation of layered connotations (Said 1978), we may regard it as fundamentally Western. Its theologies, anthropologies, eschatologies, and rituals are clearly related to (albeit, in the Qur'an and elsewhere, sometimes openly contrasted to) those of "Judaism" and "Christianity;" certain of the personages referred to in its scriptures are also found in the canonized literatures of one or both of the other Western monotheisms (e.g., Abraham, Joseph, Moses, Mary, Jesus), though given a distinct significance; and, as was the case for Judaism and Christianity, Islam also had its significant (and variegated) confrontations with elements in the span of Greek thought.

Conceptualizing Religion

I first present my viewpoint in relatively compacted form and then elaborate on some of its elements in the pages that follow.

Religion is an abstraction. It is an abstraction promulgated in our culture and supported by our experiences, including our experiences in reading. While many of us illumine our thinking about religion through recollections and a diversity of mental images — the smell of incense, perhaps, or snatches of hymns, or whatever —, religion is an intellectual abstraction, a concept, and not a concrete particular.

Numbers of Westerners, I suspect, if asked to describe at length what they understand by the word religion, might do so in terms of a pool of elements. Faced with analytical questions, they might reply with analytical answers. On other occasions, however, many of them might cognize religion metonymically (in terms, that is, of beliefs in God or Gods).

In any case, I recommend that academic students of religion explicitly conceptualize religion for analytical purposes in terms of a pool of elements that often cluster together but that may do so in greater or lesser degrees. Further, elements that we so associate with religion may be said to be in association with other things that are not deemed religions.

Our pool of elements includes belief in and communion with God, Gods, and "spiritual beings" as variously conceived; a moral code to which religious persons attribute an extra-human reference or warrant; ideas about the possibilities of transcending human suffering; rituals with extra-human and/or eschatological references; and all of the other things in the lists drawn up by Alston and Southwold, along with some of the suggestions made by persons cited in the first four chapters of this work.

Different religions relate to that pool differently. We predicate many religion-constituting elements of "religion in general," but not all of them are predicable of all religions. This logic also applies to denominated families of religions. While, for instance, some branches or members of the family "Buddhism" may be deemed "atheistic," as Durkheim, Southwold, and others claim, others are not. Hence, as Hudson (1977:238) argues, theism is among the family resemblances of Buddhism and can be predicated of Buddhism even if it cannot be predicated of all Buddhisms. To supply another and more particularized example, the doctrine of the dual nature of Christ, the doctrine that Jesus Christ is both fully human and fully divine, is specifically predicable of Christianity even though it is rejected by many members of monophysite Christian churches and by numbers of other Christians who are members of non-monophysite churches.

The best exemplars of what I mean by religion are the Western monotheisms. They are the most prototypical examples of the category, for they clearly include all of the elements cited by Alston and Southwold in the lists that I quoted in Chapter 5. While we ought not to say that by religion we mean Judaism, Christianity, and Islam — we ought not to say it because by religion we mean a conceptual model that can be described analytically in terms of abstracted elements that we more or less relate together —, those religions are, for most Westerners, the clearest examples of what is normally meant by religion. They can be used as such for reference and for comparative purposes.

My proposal, then, is that we self-consciously conceptualize "religion" as an analytical category with reference to, but not in actual terms of, our personal and changeable understandings of Judaism, Christianity, and Islam — that we regard our understandings of those familial cases as foregrounding what is notably prototypical of the category *without attempting to draw sharp boundaries around that category.* In doing so, we recognize, of course, that those families of religions, as comparatively understood by knowlegeable persons, differ in various important respects from each other as well as from other religions, and that the members of each family differ in interesting respects from one another.

Some religions will express most of the elements that we utilize in conceptualizing religion. Others will express less. And any element expressed in different religions is likely to be elaborated on differently in those religions.

We may often opine that phenomena that we are reluctant to call religions contain elements that we elsewhere deem to be religious elements. We are reluctant to call these cases religions largely for one or both of two reasons. First, they strike us as containing too few of the elements that we associate with religion. Second, the contexts in which the elements occur, and the ways the elements are elaborated within those contexts, do not remind us strongly enough of other phenomena that we have no hesitation in calling religions. In such cases, then, we identify religious elements that pertain to instantiations of what we regard as other categories — and such cases are legion! So identifying religious elements facilitates going beyond religion and attending to "the religious dimension" of much of human life. It is important to note in that regard that religious elements are not bounded by the category religion because I conceptualize that category without reference to boundaries.

Precedents

At least some of the elements in my recommendations have precedents in the scholarly literature dealing with religion.

In Chapter 5, for example, I quoted the philosopher William Alston's suggestion that we "elaborate in detail the relevant features of an ideally clear case of religion and then indicate the respects in which less clear cases can differ from them, without hoping to find any sharp line dividing religion from non-religion."

Wilfred Cantwell Smith, to cite another precedent, remarks that "the term 'religious' designates those matters in Western history that have generally been called religious there — specifically, Christian and Jewish tradition and faith — plus anything else on earth that is significantly similar" (1984:257).

And in a complex essay that evinces a multi-disciplinary appreciation of analogy, metaphor, family resemblance, and polythesis, the anthropologist Fitz John Porter Poole envisions an approach to conceptualizing religion that, as he explicitly puts it (1986:427–428), "readily accommodates a prototype theory of meaning and the nature of categories (Rosch 1978; Rosch and Mervis 1975)." In explicating Wittgenstein, indeed, Poole observes that "Explanation of a concept by examples is comparable to indicating a place by pointing, and not to delimiting it by drawing a boundary" (1986:427).

The Exemplar View

Conceptualizing and explicating a concept with reference to examples, it must be noted, is not the same thing as actually representing a category in the mind in terms of its best example(s). Lakoff (1987:136–152) argues against a view of prototype theory that (1) regards a prototype as a representation of a category's structure (with the membership of other entities computed on the basis of similarity to the properties of the prototype) and that (2) holds that prototype effects directly reflect degree of membership in a category.

As for (2), membership in groups comprehended by categories may or may not be scalar, and Lakoff, I think, is right to argue against the generalization that goodness of example is (always) a direct reflection of degree of membership. In the case that concerns us, however, Western analysts and comparativists might safely and productively follow their biases and conceptualize religion as a category that comprehends a group with graded membership.

Various biases do suggest the possibility of graded membership. Thus, for example, Paul Tillich writes of "quasi-religions,"

religions that are religions according to his experiential criteria but that are based on concerns that are falsely ultimate. Jill Dubisch conceptualizes the health food movement as religion-like and she deems it productive to analyze it in religious terms. And while Ward Goodenough and B.K. Smith treat communism or Marxism as fully fitting their respective monothetic definitions of religion, some of us are likely to maintain that although communism and Marxism resemble religions in certain important respects (even though many of their adherents claim to be anti-religious), they are not 'full' religions, or they are less of a religion than something else. For certain analytical purposes, however, it can make sense to treat them as religions.

As to point (1) above: Considerations that relate to our analytical and comparative interests in religion can be foregrounded by looking at certain aspects of that point as treated by Smith and Medin (1981:143–161) in their discussion of what they call "the exemplar view."

According to Smith and Medin (1981:144), "There is probably only one assumption that all proponents of the exemplar view would accept: The representation of a concept consists of separate descriptions of some of its exemplars (either instances or subsets)." This has been criticized as, among other things, leaving little or no room for abstractions.

Smith and Medin (1981:143) attempt to counter that criticism by arguing that we can use a subset of a concept as exemplification rather than a specific instance (e.g., for the category clothing, a subset corresponding to blue jeans in general rather than some specific pair of blue jeans). The exemplar view in such cases, Smith and Medin (*ibid.*) argue, permits abstractions. In the case that concerns us, however, representation of the concept of religion by a separate description of some exemplar — "Christianity," say — would require (for anyone who knows a fair amount about the Christian family of confessions, past and present) mind-boggling complexities and subtleties that go well beyond any that I can imagine for blue jeans as an exemplar of clothing — and I do not suppose "blue jeans in general" to be unproblematical.

A second and even more arresting problematic has to do with the disjunction of exemplars associated with a conceptual category. As Smith and Medlin (1981:157) put it, on the view that "exemplars tend to be represented separately, . . . how can we represent something that pertains to all exemplars?" A possible solution, they suppose, might be that "knowledge about a correlation between properties is *computed* from an exemplar-based representation when needed, rather than *prestored* in the representation" (1981:157). They go on to say that

> For the best-examples model, . . . there may be a need to specify
> some necessary features, or some sufficient ones, for each exemplar
> represented in a concept; otherwise we are left with problems such
> as the exemplar permitting too great a degree of disjunctiveness.
> (1981:158)

A different — and, I think, better — solution with respect to the case that concerns us specifically is one that seeks to make statements about religion as an analytical category rather than attempting (and failing!) to specify necessary or sufficient conditions for what we deem our most prototypical examples of that category. I have two major reasons for preferring that solution.

First, I don't think that it is productive to posit necessary and/ or sufficient conditions of exemplars when dealing with an analytical category such as religion. While biological pheneticists may often hold that there are monothetic cores in polythetic taxa, anthropologists and other students of religion ought not to suppose something analogous for religions and for "religion" as an analytical instrument. Our most prototypical exemplars of religion are themselves richly polythetic.

Second, my preferred solution — one that calls attention to the importance of contingency-sensitive predicates — has much to recommend it in its own right.

I deal with both of these reasons below.

Necessity, Sufficiency, and Boundaries

It is not enough to point to "Judaism," "Christianity," and "Islam" as being, for persons brought up in Western societies, our clearest examples of religion. We must also come to terms with the understanding that Judaism, Christianity, and Islam must themselves be approached with reference to prototypicality. Each of those families exhibits considerable synchronic as well as diachronic variety. While knowledgeable proponents of one or another may tell us what they suppose to be the distinguishing features of their faith, such talk is valuable not as decisive insider authority — especially if we reject essentialist distinguishing features! — but as data that requires evaluation in our efforts to determine degrees of prototypicality.

A fair amount of information has been gathered by the compilers of textbooks in comparative religion. We can turn to them, but not for statements of what properties are necessary and sufficient for each family of religions. Rather, we find in such compilations descriptions of elements that canonical texts and various respected commentators have emphasized as being most important in constituting prototypes that we respectively identify with the rubrics Judaism, Christianity, and Islam.

Explicitly conceiving of a category "religion" with reference to (but not in concrete terms of) what we individually and variously take to be some of its clearest (though not unproblematical) exemplars, the Western monotheisms, does not by any means exclude less clear-cut cases from our analytical purview. We need initial orientation, and our most clear-cut examples of religion provide it. They allow us initially to organize our analytical efforts with reference to type cases, comparing the elements of other cases to their elements and rendering judgments with regard to the respective degrees of typicality of those other cases. It is worth reiterating in that connection that, as Rosch (1978:40) puts it, "To speak of a *prototype* at all is simply a convenient grammatical fiction; what is really referred to are judgements of degree of prototypicality."

But where, then, essentialist diehards may nevertheless ask, does the category give out? Where is the line that separates religion from non-religion? *There is no hard and fast line.* This admission, however, prompts me to raise and attempt to answer two questions. First, is there no test of "sufficiency" that will enable us to include and exclude candidates with some facility, to deal expeditiously with, say, "civil religion" (Bellah 1967, Bellah and Hammond 1980) or Goodenough's claim that "communism" is "one of the great religions of modern times" (1989:6)? And, second, if there is not, does that not pose serious practical problems for our research and teaching?

The prototype approach sketched here can be construed as a variant of the "multi-factorial" approaches discussed in Chapter 5. Advocates of "family resemblance" and "polythetic" conceptualizations of religion, it may be recalled, propose a list of "attributes" (Southwold 1978:370) or "religion-making characteristics" (Alston 1967:141), where no single one of them is necessary to establish the existence of religion. Authors who compile such lists, however, generally suppose that some combination of attributes, variable from case to case, is sufficient to do so, although no precise formula specifying what might constitute a sufficient conjunction is usually supplied.

Rem Edwards, who attempts a family resemblance approach to religion, remarks that "There are many sufficient but no necessary conditions for calling something religion" (1972:38). Jonathan Z. Smith, who advocates "polythetic classification," applauds Edwards's remark (1982:136–137, n.15). And, as noted earlier, Alston (1967:142) states that when "enough" of his nine "religion-making characteristics" are "present to a sufficient degree, we have a religion," and that "given the actual use of the term 'religion', this is as precise as we can be."

All of the authors cited above appear to operate with a notion of sufficiency that requires very few factors. Doing so, however, is not mandated by a strict application of either Wittgenstein's concept of family resemblance or the biologists' numerical phenetics. With respect to the latter, it may be recalled, Sokal and Sneath remark that "no single feature is either essential to group membership or is sufficient to make an organism a member of the group" (1963:14), and they advocate using at least forty characters, each with its own character states, in classificatory procedures. And Wittgenstein is concerned with meaning as use rather than analytical criteria of sufficiency.

The student of religion, however, generally operates with a smaller number of characters and character states than does the numerical pheneticist in biology. Scholars of religion, moreover, are less likely than biologists to agree empirically on character states, for the establishment of some of them (as in the study of "belief systems") requires relatively high order interpretations. And the higher the order of interpretation, the less widespread agreement may tend to be. Nor can the comparatively oriented student rest content with the analysis of natural language usages; cross-cultural studies demand analytical categories developed within the framework of a carefully thought out — indeed, teleological — "language-game."

But Alston, Edwards, and J.Z. Smith, in addition to allowing for sufficiency, exhibit slippage between religion as a folk category and religion as an analytical category. Their conceptual structures appear to be weighted by considerations bearing on what Alston describes as "the actual use of the term 'religion'." Those authors, in effect, supply us with prescriptions about conceptualizing religion that are connected to an appreciation of natural language usages, the prescriptions consisting, fundamentally, in the rejection of a demand for necessity and an allowance for sufficiency. The approach that I recommend, however, differs with respect to the matter of sufficiency and in its self-consciousness about analytical categories.

It is worth noting that prototype semantics as construed by

Coleman and Kay for the analysis of natural language categories
dispenses with sufficiency as well as necessity. In their gradient
framework, they write, "the bivalent concepts of the 'necessity'
and 'sufficiency' of properties do not apply" (1981:28). If we
commit ourselves to prototype semantics, then, a *descriptive*
approach to the category religion, an approach constituted by
the investigation and analysis of *how people actually use* the category label, can presumeably be accomplished without invoking
sufficiency. But does that mean that we might do without it
in *prescriptive* statements about religion — in statements, that is,
that stipulate what anthropologists *should* mean by religion as an
analytical category?

Operating without the concepts of necessity and sufficiency
would seem to pose practical problems for our research and
teaching. The researcher may understandably desire explicit
criteria that would serve to govern admission to, and exclusion
from, some collectivity of phenomena that are to be assembled
for cross-cultural exploration. Similarly, the teacher would find
it useful to enunciate clear standards that mark off the field of
religious scholarship.

Yet the approach recommended here does operate without
universal criteria for inclusion and exclusion in conceptualizing
religion as an analytical category. The best that I can do — some
will find it unsettling! — is to trace diminishing degrees of
typicality, and to offer arguments as cogent as I can make them
for my decisions in assigning or failing to assign specific candidates to the group comprehended by the category. In stipulating a research category explicated with reference to the clearest
examples, I commit myself to the rendering and defending of
analytical judgments respecting less clear cases.

Contingency-Sensitive Predicates

In an exposition of polythesis that accomodates prototype theory,
Poole writes that

> Following Campbell (1965), Needham (1975) has argued that a
> polythetic category formed on the basis of the similarities of family
> resemblance must have a list of "basic predicates." Rather than
> circumscribing the boundary of a category on the basis of shared
> characteristics in the manner of monothetic classification, a poly-
> thetic categorization directs attention to the interpretation of basic
> predicates as the principles that enable the connection of phenom-
> ena in family resemblance chains. Such predicates, therefore, are
> not empirical properties of the phenomena, but are formal aspects

of the model of classification. The use of formal predicates of analytic models rather than empirical properties of phenomena as the basis of categories is largely inimical to any single-factor similarity definitions of a class. (1986:427)

Assimilating this to a prototype approach to conceptualizing the category religion, I would add that individual predicates associated with the model of classification are contingency-sensitive respecting *particular instantiations* of the category. That is, they may or they may not apply in particular cases. I choose predicates about "theism" as an example, both because they illustrate this point nicely and because they are important in related ways.

Theism

Martin Southwold, it may be recalled, treats theism (which we may broadly identify as the postulation of Gods) as a contingent but not necessary element in religion. In my opinion, he is right to do so. Yet theism, I believe, not only fascinates many anthropologists, but it also constitutes a set of default values for them in their conventional conceptualizations of religion. I explore each of these points in turn.

While I cannot cite much in the way of supporting data, it is my impression that many anthropologists who study religion are not themselves conventionally religious. Although some may occasionally attend religious services in their own societies, sizeable numbers of them, or so it seems to me, do not personally endorse theism or the mythic and soteriological understandings that are distinctly associated with religion in their cultures. Distanced from religion, many are intrigued by (if sometimes critical of) religious persons. What is it about religious persons that fascinates them the most? Probably, I suspect, the several sorts of investments that religious persons in Western and in many other societies make in what anthropologists conventionally label Gods.

While numbers of non-religious anthropologists accept the reality of beliefs in deities, they tend to suppose that deity as such is unreal. Yet many religious persons (numerous Theravada Buddhists included) not only affirm the existence of Gods, but they often describe them as being invisible or otherwise un-observable much of the time (in many traditions, however, it is affirmed that the Gods may become sensible to their worshippers in certain ways). Further, they generally maintain that the Gods are powerful enough to affect human life in several important respects and that they are inclined to enter into communion with humans. Many religious persons, moreover, expend valued resources on the Gods. Often enough in human history, indeed, they have sincerely and fatally pledged their lives, their fortunes, and their sacred honors in the service or propitiation of beings that, in the opinion of many anthropologists, have no reality independent of the imaginations and assertions of human beings and the cultural traditions that those human beings have created.

Should the non-theist analyst reflect on the apparent proclivity for theism suggested by human history, he or she may feel a certain estrangement from humanity's teeming theistic multitudes. The analyst's sense of his/her own 'otherness' may itself become a factor inspiring and coloring research, rendering theism a scholarly problem deemed "tremendous and fascinating" — a mystery that we do not embrace but probe.

Theism, of course, is not a simple matter. There are various problems relating to what might be meant by "God" and the comparability or incomparability of postulations made in different societies respecting the wide range of beings that we conventionally gloss as 'Gods'. Furthermore, while what we call theism occurs within the compass of many cultural traditions that we conventionally term religions, it also occurs outside of that compass.

Theism, most of us would agree, is an element or complex of elements typically encountered in "religions." Yet we can also discern it among what we regard as instantiations of other categories. It occurs sometimes, for example, in association with the category "science," a category that numbers of Western authors have opposed or contrasted to religion. We could argue, of course, that when scientists such as Newton, Kepler, and Boyle invoked God in their scientific theories, they did so because they were themselves religious. But to say that and no more is to miss much of interest. While it is true that Newton, Kepler, and Boyle were socialized and enculturated to be religious, it is also the case that their styles of science required God for theoretical reasons, and that they persisted in being theists partially because they were scientists of a certain sort.

In analyzing religions in the way recommended here, theism, as already pointed out, is to be considered contingent. It can be highly visible and important in some cases, absent in others, and in still others discernable though perhaps neither salient nor, on analysis, crucially important. Yet for numbers of participants in Western cultures, most anthropologists included, theism is quite probably more important for pattern recognition and the study of religion than any other elements. This occasions no problems in principle for prototype theory for, as Coleman and Kay note, "properties may be of differential importance in constituting the prototype" (1981:27).

But while employing theism for pattern recognition and subsequent thinking about religion is not a problem in principle, it may well prove to be a problem in practice. For many contemporary Westerners, theism may constitute a metonym for religion. For some persons, indeed, the identification of theism is tantamount to the discovery of religion.

In the analytical approach recommended here, the conventionally determined 'part', theism, is neither necessary nor sufficient for the identification of all cases of religion, regardless of any folk metonymic cognitive models to the contrary and their celebration in academic monothetic definitions. Theism can and should be predicated of religion as a category. We should have no trouble in regarding it as an aspect of our analytical model. It may not, however, be predicable of various cases that, on other (i.e., non-theistic) grounds, some analysts deem religions (e.g., "communism"). Or it may be predicable in certain cases in troubling, problematic ways. Aristotle's Unmoved Mover, for example, takes no notice of humankind and any sort of communion with it is entirely out of the question. Does Aristotle's God suggest religion?

In my opinion, which is weighted significantly by considerations of communion, Aristotle's Unmoved Mover does not point to religion; rather, it forms part of a theistic metaphysical system. But those analysts who emphasize religion's roles in posing and answering questions about "ultimate reality" may wish to include Aristotle's God under the rubric religion. Disagreements of this sort should be expected. One hopes, however, that analysts make serious efforts to state explicitly the reasons for their respective positions.

Predications of theism, in short, are contingency-sensitive. For most Westerners, however, certain cases that prominently include theism (e.g., "Judaism," "Christianity") are very likely to seem significantly better exemplars of the category religion than those that do not (e.g., "communism") or that do not accord it crucial cosmogenic and soteriological significance (e.g., "canonical Theravada Buddhism").

Default Values

Frequently encountered presumptions and expectations about the association of theism and religion suggest that for numbers of Westerners, some anthropologists included, theism often functions as a "default assignment" in the schematization of religion.

Many readers are probably familiar with the expression default assignment as utilized with respect to computers and software programs. A word processing program, for example, is likely to have various prefigured — "default" — values for such things as the sizes of right and left page margins, the number of lines that will be accepted on a page of a certain size, and so forth. If the operator does nothing, those are the values that s/he must operate with. Typically, however, those preset values can be overriden by the operator: changed, that is, within a restricted range of possibilities.

In natural language use, default assignments tend to be associated with "unmarkedness." Numbers of language terms may be marked or unmarked. Thus, for example, in English "dog" is an unmarked term, applying both to a male and a generalized animal, but the term "bitch," a female dog, is a marked term. Default assignments are usually the unmarked elements of categories. Lakoff (1987: 60–61) remarks that the marked/unmarked distinction is employed by linguists for describing a sort of "prototype effect," an asymmetry, where one element or subcategory pertaining to a category is taken to be "somehow more basic" than any other.

In the contemporary cognitive sciences, a default assignment is broadly characterized as an attribution not directly and fully specified by knowledge of the situation at hand. In the absence of specific knowledge of actual situational values, assignment is made on the basis of a knowledge of, and expectations derived from, other cases that are apperceived to resemble the one at hand.

So, too, do anthropologists sometimes invoke default values on first apperceiving what appear to be theistic variables in the field. The most widely invoked default values are probably those of the Judeo-Christian God conceived of as a supernatural creator, sustainer, law-giver, judge, and savior. Those values, however, may not always serve us well.

In practice, close attention to specific situations may require the detachment of various default values from our interpretive structures. Critical attitudes and a high capacity for critical thought are of crucial significance for doing so. As Minsky points out,

" 'Schematic' thinking, based on matching complicated situations against stereotyped frame structures, must be inadequate for some aspects of mental activity. Obviously," he continues, "mature people can to some extent think about, as well as use their own representations" (1975:230).

Critical thought about religion can be advanced by fashioning an explicit analytical approach that both allows for our conventional Western schemata and their default assignments and at the same time prepares us to detach (override) whatever values we may need to discard or supplant in our particularized attentions to the world. I argue in the next (and concluding) chapter that this would contribute to the development of our interpretive approximations to alter's understandings by facilitating progressive, self-conscious distanciation from our conventional exemplars while preserving and utilizing them as points of comparison. In short, we might profit from our prototypical biases by critically recognizing and employing them as such, and probing them in the process.

In Summary

My suggestion for conceptualizing religion is this: Religion is an abstraction. For analytical purposes we may conceptualize it in terms of a pool of elements that more or less tend to occur together in the best exemplars of the category. While all of the elements that we deem to pertain to the category religion are predicable of that category, not all of them are predicable of all the phenomena that various scholars regard as instantiations of religion. Those instantiations, called religions, include the Western monotheisms, our most prototypical cases of religion. They also include whatever else we deem to participate in the pool of elements to the extent of resembling the Western monotheisms in significant respects. And how do we establish what is significant? By cogent analytical arguments about elements that we deem analogous to those that we associate with our reference religions, the Western monotheisms.

We decide by reasoned arguments the question of whether or not to include under the rubric religion candidates that strike us as representing lesser degrees of prototypicality. We do so in the absence of certitude about, and firm commitments to, boundaries. Ideally, moreover, our reasoned arguments will include some statement of what we hope to accomplish by designating phenomena "religions" or by pointing out that they contain elements that we identify as "religious." Our procedures can be most cogently explicated when they are related to an open consideration of our purposes (cf. Watanabe 1969:388).

Each candidate must be examined as thoroughly as possible when considered with reference to our analytical model and when compared and contrasted to our clearest cases. While this approach is not entirely open-ended, it is relatively so in comparison to typical monothetic approaches.

The reader may object that the approach recommended here does not actually resolve the problem of identifying religions other than the Western monotheisms but only defers it. That complaint is justified. Case by case analysis must still be accomplished and accompanying arguments constructed about candidates, arguments perhaps in some cases (e.g., "civil religion" or "communism") relevant to the construction of a gradient framework by means of which we hope to order them. I have suggested the general direction that the analyst should take, but genuine progress depends on detailed, imaginative analysis.

In the approach recommended here, there are no clear boundaries drawn about religion. Rather, elements that we may apperceive as "religious" are found in phenomena that numbers of us, for a variety of reasons, may not be prepared to dub religions. But if our ultimate purpose as scholars is to say interesting things about human beings rather than about religions and religion, appreciation of the pervasiveness of religious elements in human life is far more important than any contrivance for bounding religion.

CHAPTER SEVEN

ETHNOCENTRISM AND DISTANCIATION

Whereas the traditional accounts of concept application seek to avoid the chaos of wide-open texture by the idea that we can grasp properties or essences, Wittgenstein avoids it by assuming that language-users are trained in a body of conventionalised practice. The concept-user must learn how a similarity here trades off against a difference there.
— David Bloor, *Wittgenstein: A Social Theory of Knowledge*, 1983, pp. 34–35.

Some readers may judge the approach to conceptualizing religion that I recommend in the preceding chapter to be egregiously ethnocentric. They may hold that that is the case because they suppose that I privilege the Western monotheisms.

Now, I confess to being "ethnocentric" in a certain sense, but I contend that I am productively rather than outrageously so. And I do not privilege the Western monotheisms because I personally deem them superior to other religions, or the most evolved forms of religiosity, or anything of the sort. Rather, those families of religion are connected in complex ways to the development of religion as a Western category, and ideas about them continue to influence how Westerners and persons educated in the West use the term religion. Because of that, the Western monotheisms might be used — if critical monitoring is employed — as markers that map a productive starting place.

Ethnocentrism: A Starting Place

An oft-noted irony afflicting those who would start life anew by escaping from present circumstances is that no matter where they might flee, they bring themselves with them. They bring, that is, a dynamic jumble of culturally mediated understandings, sensibilities, and dispositions that powerful Western analytical traditions, traditions now questioned by numbers of anthropologists, encourage us to sort into boxes labeled "cognitions," "affects," and "conations." Those understandings, sensibilities, and dipositions are baggage that we carry with us. While we may lighten their peculiar loads by altering or even discarding some of them and changing the mix, doing so is likely to take time.

That is also the case for the ethnographer who goes into the field. The ethnographer may make heroic efforts to bracket himself/herself in order to advance research, but such efforts, barring death or some extreme form of insanity, can only be partial.

One's understandings, sensibilities, and dispositions do not simply evaporate at will. New experiences may conduce to their alteration, but that is an on-going process. In the meantime, one confronts novelties with categories and sensitivities — and insensitivities — developed or shielded through participation in some other cultural order. Those categories, sensitivities, and insensitivities constitute launching pads in our efforts to construct understandings of newly encountered categories, sensitivities, and insensitivities: those of the natives.

The ethnographer's journey toward novel understandings begins in culturally formatted personal space and the multiple language-games in which s/he has participated. These include some that are especially associated with formal training in anthropology.

Anthropology departments and curricula are pointed toward the cultivation of certain perspectives and critical dispositions. They generally attempt to encourage professionally approbated research interests, awarenesses, and behaviors. In doing so, they sensitize students to the discipline's categories and various of its methodological, analytical, and theoretical traditions. And, often enough, they stimulate critical attitudes towards the foregoing as they relate to the ethnographic enterprise and other professional concerns.

The ethnographer, in short, does not arrive in the field a mythical "blank slate." And, as I put it elsewhere, "The ethnographer's mind, though possibly boggled by the field situation, is rarely if ever blown clean by it" (Saler 1977:50). This means, among other things, that the categories that the ethnographer brings into the field do not silently slip away. They remain, and they play important roles. They relate, indeed, to other factors in complex motivational and awareness structures, all of which are more than tinged by ethnocentrism. Let us explore certain of their facets.

Research

I begin with the high valuation placed on research. Research might be broadly characterized as organized efforts to acquire and assimilate information. As such, it is, of course, by no means distinctly Western. Indeed, it is not even distinctly human, since other animals exhibit connected efforts to probe and utilize their environments. But while we can infer that curiosity and information processing are widely distributed phylogenetically, and that others of the world's culturally organized human societies have institutionalized research agendas and programs, different cultures are likely to sponsor different research styles and emphases.

Human social orders promote various foci of interests, goals, and methods, and each is to some extent distinctive in those regards. The West's distinctiveness resides in significant measure in the abstractness and critical reflexivity of its culturally motivated and organized research efforts. That is the case not only in contemporary academic disciplines and their predecessors, but in much else beside. Those features, indeed, are well marked in literary and other artistic pursuits.

Leszek Kolakowski affirms what he regards as "a distinctive feature of European culture at the peak of its maturity:" namely, "its capacity to step outside its exclusivity, to question itself, to see itself through the eyes of others" (1990:18). The seeing of one's civilization through the eyes of others in order to attack it, he notes, "became a literary mannerism prevalent in the writings of the Enlightenment" (1990:18). Indeed,

> This capacity to doubt herself, to abandon — albeit in the face of strong resistance — her self-assurance and self-satisfaction, lies at the heart of Europe's development as a spiritual force. She made the effort to break out of the closed confines of ethnocentricity, and the ability to do so gave definition to the unique value of her culture. Ultimately we may say that Europe's cultural identity is reinforced by her refusal to accept any kind of closed, finite definition, and thus she can only affirm her identity in uncertainty and anxiety. And although it is true that all sciences, social and natural, either were born or reached their maturity (maturity in a relative sense, of course, from the perspective of what they are today) within European culture, there is one among them which, because of its very content, is the European science par excellence: anthropology. (1990:18–19)

As "the European science par excellence," contemporary anthropology's research program is "to penetrate as far as possible into the viewpoint of another and assimilate his way of perceiving the world" (1990:19). Kolakowski supposes that to this end the anthropologist must make efforts to suspend his/her own judgments, norms, and "mental" as well as moral and aesthetic habits. But he acknowledges that total success in achieving the goal of anthropological research "would presuppose an epistemological impossibility — to enter entirely into the mind of the object of inquiry while maintaining the distance and objectivity of a scientist" (1990:19). The effort, however, is not in vain.

"We," writes Kolakowski, "cannot completely achieve the position of an observer seeing himself from the outside, but we may do so partially" (1990:19). And though the anthropologist may in some ways suspend judgment, "the very act of suspending is culturally rooted: it is an act of renunciation, possible only from within a culture which, through learning to question itself, has shown itself capable of the effort of understanding another" (1990:19).

Because of its cultural rootedness, however, "the anthropologist's stance is not really one of suspended judgment" (1990:19). Rather, Kolakowski suggests, the anthropologist's attitude is grounded in the idea that description and analysis unencumbered by the spirit of superiority or fanaticsm are better than those so encumbered. And this, he adds, is as much of a value judgment as its contrary. *"There is no abandoning of judgments,"* Kolakowski declares, and "what we call the spirit of research is a cultural attitude, one peculiar to Western civilization and its hierarchy of values" (1990:19, emphasis added).

Kolakowski's allusions to anthropological (more particularly, ethnographic) research, though welcome to me as an anthropologist, are decidedly abstract. So, too, are a number of other treatments that situate that research culturally. Cultural situation, however, involves a diversity of factors, some of them so prosaic and seemingly obvious that we may not say much about them. If, however, they are important, then attention should be called to them. So at the risk of sounding more obvious and less high-minded than some other authors, I want to say something about the anthropologist's career concerns.

In the field, the ethnographer is under the judgment, and sometimes the consistent scrutiny, of the natives. And, to be sure, some cooperation from them is of crucial importance for the successful outcome of field research. Further, the ethnographer's encounters with the natives may well have powerful and lasting effects on various facets of his or her personal development. But while the natives are of proximate importance to the achievement of various research goals, other persons also strongly affect the ethnographer's career. The natives, after all, do not normally award research grants or serve as referees for journal articles and books. Nor do they usually certify what needs to be certified for the conferring of academic degrees, or institute hiring procedures at universities, or write letters of recommendation, or sit on tenure and promotion committees.

Ultimately, the anthropologist must impress a different audience, an audience, for the most part in most cases, of academics. And no matter how well the ethnographer has learned the natives' language, no matter how assiduously s/he has worked to master the natives' categories and to understand their points of view, much more is required. The ethnographer must convey whatever understandings s/he has constructed in a language other than that of the natives, through categories and analogies that are creatively figured and cogently interwoven.

The ethnographer must ultimately return to the intellectual community from which s/he was launched and be favorably received by it. That is the case, at any rate, for those who seek conventional career advancements. For them — the overwhelming majority of anthropologists — a journey to the field is normally a round-trip affair, and the return is no less important than the departure.

Objectivity

In what sense, if any, might an ethnographer be said to be objective? Numbers of anthropologists would probably agree that if by "objective" we mean apprehending and reporting the natives' understandings or points of view as they "really are," there are good reasons for supposing that the ethnographer cannot be objective.

In approaching this topic, we would do well to recognize that it is an over-generalization to talk about "the" natives' understandings or "point of view." The natives hardly constitute a homogeneous population with a monolithic world view. Unfortunately, however, numbers of anthropologists have been given to over-generalizing in this and in other ways, sometimes with ludicrous abandon. (Cora DuBois, for instance, studied a small "pagan" population in the radjahship of Alor on the island of Alor in what is now Indonesia. Although that population was culturally and linguistically distinct from the island's coastal Muslims and many of the other "pagans" in the island's other three radjahships, she entitled her study of them *The People of Alor*, and gave it an odd subtitle, *A Socio-Psychological Study of an East Indian Island*.)

Not only are human populations likely to be more heterogeneous than the generalizing tendencies of some of their

ethnographers suggest, but any one native is unlikely to constitute a cultural agent distinguished by entirely harmonious and
stable understandings. There is no experientially founded reason
to expect that of the native. A moment's reflection ought to
convince us that the understandings of people with whom we
have a profound acquaintance in our own society — our spouses,
children, and parents, for instance — are sometimes conflicted
and changeable.

Since we begin to understand newly encountered others largely
by constructing analogies that link their expressed ideas and other
behaviors to those of persons whom we already know, why have
anthropologists in past years downplayed (without entirely
neglecting) intra-individual as well as inter-individual dynamism
and diversity? Why in significant measure did they construct their
ethnographies as if the natives supported a monolithic culture?
And why, when they encountered what they took to be paradox
or inconsistency, did they often make serious efforts to explain
it away?

The answers to those questions are complex. Broadly put, it
was the style to do those things, in keeping with regnant paradigms. The ethnographer was concerned with describing "a
culture," either as a worthwhile task in itself or as a necessary
step in testing hypotheses. And a culture, it was often supposed,
could best be described as if it were integral and timeless.

Anthropologists realized, of course, that what they called
cultures have histories and are dynamic. But the convention was
to fix a culture as the ethnographer came to know it in a brief
span of months or years, the ethnographer's special time, "the
ethnographic present."

Since cultures, moreover, were conceptualized as systems, as
structured wholes, emphasis was devoted to positing organizational principles and themes. Whatever struck the ethnographer
as internally discordant had to be accounted for in one fashion
or another. One tactic was to claim that certain sorts of discordancies are structured oppositions that are transcended at some
higher level of organization. Other tactics included assertions to
the effect that the natives are unaware of the discordancies, and/
or that apparent paradoxes can sometimes be explained away as
metaphorical figures, or artifacts of ellipsis, or something else.

Today, in contrast, increasing numbers of anthropologists are
disposed to posit culturally motivated paradoxes without trying
to explain them away — or, at least, they do not attempt to do
so clothed in the fashions of yesteryear. The natives, they suggest,

may be aware of discordancies but live with them nonetheless. Paradox and inconsistency, these anthropologists maintain, are part and parcel of human life, and ethnographic theories and research strategies ought to allow them importance (see, for example, Shore 1983).

This shift in emphasis, greatly simplified in the above description and by no means endorsed by all anthropologists, can be related to our question about "objectivity."

When theoretical emphasis is put on structural principles and functional relationships that work to maintain cultural and social order, ethnographies tend to depict internal harmony and stability in ethnographically particularized examples of human life (often with allowances to the effect that exogenous factors may sometimes promote change). Considerable "data," moreover, is often furnished in support of such portraits.

Those anthropologists — postmodernists and others — whose perspectives lead them to emphasize paradox and inconsistency as normal human conditions also furnish "data" in support of their point of view. The ethnographies that they produce, moreover, tend to pivot on, or otherwise give prominence to, paradoxes or conflicts presented as perduring.

These positions are relative, not absolute. Virtually all anthropologists apperceive both centripetal and centrifugal forces at work in human life. But veering toward one dimension rather than the other will produce an ethnography of a distinctive sort. The important point respecting our interest in objectivity is that a theoretical slant tends to generate an ethnography bent in the direction of that slant. If we were to insist on regarding an ethnographer as a recording instrument, then we would be well advised to realize that *all* recording instruments exhibit biases and, to the extent that we might calibrate and measure them by using other instruments, greater or lesser distortion curves.

Objectivity can be thought of as a matter of performance to tolerance. It is relative and not absolute and its locus is not a person or a work. Objectivity has to do with a relationship. That is, an ethnographer's work can be adjudged more or less "objective" to the extent that it conforms to the expectations and canons that anthropologists affirm as practitioners of a discipline. In a manner of speaking, objectivity attaches to agency but not to an agent. And it is not merely relational but normatively so.

On this account the ethnographer is under the judgment of an intellectual community. That community, of course, is not monolithic. What the ethnographer does may be deemed

commendable by some professionals at the same time that it is
severely criticized by others. The point is, however, that the
ethnographer *qua* ethnographer is accountable to some set of
standards.

Conceptualizing objectivity as a positive relation between
research and disciplinary canons affirms immanence and suggests a positive role for ethnocentrism.

Immanence

Immanence is the quality of being immanent, of "remaining or
operating within a domain of reality or realm of discourse"
(*Webster's Ninth New Collegiate Dictionary*, 1983, p. 601). Anthropologists are "immanent" in that sense. Even though they may
sometimes selectively operate in different realms of discourse,
and bracket some of their usual beliefs and disbeliefs — attempting to do so is one of the great challenges and, for many of us,
one of the great pleasures, of fieldwork — they nevertheless
typically operate within professionally approbated realities and
discourses throughout their careers.

I speak of domains and realms in the plural, for while there
is considerable overlap in anthropological discourses/reality
commitments, there are significant differences as well. Anthropologists, moreover, might deservedly boast that their domains
and realms tend to be fairly accomodative to some sorts of
experimentation (see, for example, Crapanzano 1980). Nevertheless, not everything is acceptable.

Claims that strike other anthropologists as wild or otherwise
dubious invite criticism. And statements that other anthropologists deem contrary to their moral canons — statements, for
example, that some judge to be racist or sexist — are likely to
be condemned severely. But in addition to these examples, there
are claims and suggestions that are discounted by some — and
exalted by others — because of their apperceived theoretical and
analytical slants.

At this point some consideration of what may be implicated
by the term "discourse" might prove useful in exploring the
anthropologist's immanence. In Chapter 3 I referred to discourse
as an organizing concept, and in discussing Talal Asad's criticisms of Geertz I mentioned Foucault's uses of it, particularly as
they have been situated for us by Bové.

Bové (1990:53) suggests that in light of the uses of "discourse"
in poststructuralist discourses, one cannot easily answer essential-

izing questions about the "meaning" or "identity" of the concept called by that term. "To attempt to do so," he remarks, "would be to contradict the logic of the structure of thought in which the term 'discourse' now has a newly powerful critical function" (1990:53). Poststructuralists, he continues, "hold that these essentializing questions emerge from the very interpretive models of thought which the new focus on 'discourse' as a material practice aims to examine and trace" (1990:53). The importance of terms such as discourse, he advises us, is ultimately to be found in their function, "their place within intellectual practices," rather than in what they might abstractly be said to "mean" (1990:51).

Bové's points are well taken, but perhaps mainly for those who already participate in his brand of postructuralist discourse. For other persons some additional remarks about discourse might prove informative and welcome. I shall later discuss certain aspects of Paul Ricoeur's conceptualizations of it, particularly as they relate to what he calls "text" and "distanciation." Here, however, it will suffice to think of it as a referential framework having to do with — some poststructuralists would say "constitutive of" — objects, classes of objects, and truths. The basic formative units of a discourse may be thought of as sentences or "statements." As Bové (1990:57) puts it, "Not unless a statement is about an 'object' and can be judged in its truthfulness does it enter into a discourse; but once it does, it furthers the dispersal of that discourse and enlarges the realm of objects and statements which produce knowledge that can be judged legitimate or illegitimate."

The sense of discourse given above is quite sweeping, all the more so when an understanding of it is enhanced by the ancillary notion of "power" touched on in Chapter 3. The power of discourse not only legitimates certain questions and answers and invalidates others, but it facilitates the conception of certain sorts of identities on the part of those who participate in the discourse, identities that render them effective agents of that discourse and the institutional structures it empowers. The sweeping character of discourse so conceived can be better appreciated if we contrast it with the different — and less global — concept of language-games that I invoked in preceding chapters.

Wittgenstein apparently first developed the idea of language-games as a *technique* for doing philosophy, philosophy, as he envisioned it, being a series of techniques aimed at clarification (Monk 1990:330). The technique known as language-games is intended to help free our intelligence from bewitchments such as essentialism and notions to the effect that the meaning of a

word can be determined by noting the object(s) for which it
stands.

The technique is to imagine a situation in which some language is *used* in specified ways. We are to think of the language
in a language-game as complete in itself, imagining it as if it were
the "entire system of communication of a tribe in a primitive
state of society" (Wittgenstein, *The Blue and Brown Books*, p. 81).
Thus, for example, we are asked to

> Imagine a people in whose language there is no such form of
> sentence as 'the book is in the drawer' or 'water is in the glass',
> but whenever we should use these forms they say, The book can
> be taken out of the drawer', 'The water can be taken out of the
> glass.' (*The Blue and Brown Books*, p. 100)

Language-games, as Wittgenstein conceived them, are exercises
through which we can rid ourselves of the "mental mist" which
tends to enshroud our ordinary uses of language. That is because
of their relative simplicity. They are ways of using signs that are
typically simpler, and thus more transparent, than the ways of
using them in our more complicated everyday languages.

In addition to their utility in leading us to appreciate language
in new ways, these exercises also provide grounds for making
sharp points — it would not be inappropriate from a Wittgensteinian perspective to speak of moral points — about our
conceptual apparatus. Thus, for example, Wittgenstein imagines
a tribe that "has two concepts, akin to our 'pain'," each applied
in a distinctive way. To the question, do the tribesmen "really
not notice the similarity" between their two concepts?, he point-
edly replies with questions that might provoke us to think about
our own concepts in ways that could shake smug ethnocentrism:

> Do we have a single concept everywhere there is a similarity? The
> question is: Is the similarity *important* to them? And need it be so?
> And why should their concept 'pain' not split ours up? (*Zettel* 380)

From early formulations of language-games as analytical techniques, language-games became a way of conceptualizing language as a dynamic phenomenon the speaking of which is part
of a form of life:

> But how many kinds of sentences are there? Say assertion, question,
> and command? — There are *countless* kinds: countless different
> kinds of use of what we call "symbols," "words," "sentences." And
> this multiplicity is not something fixed, given once for all; but new
> types of language, new language-games, as we may say, come into
> existence, and others become obsolete and get forgotten. (We can
> get a *rough picture* of this from the changes in mathematics.)

> Here the term "language-*game*" is meant to bring into promi-
> nence the fact that the *speaking* of a language is part of an activity,
> or of a form of life. (*Philosophical Investigations* I:23)

Language-games become conceptualized as created (and, of
course, alterable) social realities, so that Bloor, on a close reading
of Wittgenstein, can write that "Introducing a child to an existing
language-game involves shaping spontaneous behaviors by example, rewards and punishment... The relative uniformity of
the responses that children make to training provides the
foundation of all language-games" (1983:26).

For Wittgenstein, words are tools, and their meanings come
from the uses to which they are put. "Only in the stream of
thought and life," he tells us, "do words have meaning" (*Zettel*
173). From the Wittgensteinian perspective, Bloor points out, it
is an illusion to suppose

> that meaning determines subsequent usage, and that these future
> applications are already implicit in what has gone before. This is
> an idea that would derive support from the assumption that
> language-users *already* possess a language in advance of the crea-
> tion of language-games: as if all our unknown, future experiences
> had already been linguistically processed. Then we would just read
> off the correct applications of our concepts as our experience
> unfolds. Our response to the world would be a response to a text,
> and our verbal rendering of experience would be a process of
> translation. But, insists Wittgenstein, 'words are not a translation
> of something else that was there before they were' (Z[*ettel*], 191).
> The point is not that there is nothing in the world but words. The
> point is that words are ultimately connected to the world by training,
> not by translation. (Bloor 1983:27–28)

Wittgenstein's "language-game," then, serves a different intellectual strategy than that suggested by poststructuralist uses of
"discourse" as we encounter them in the writings of Foucault,
Bové, and like-minded others. While consideration of the former
contributes to remedy against certain forms of bewitchment,
consideration of the latter helps us relate the construction of
meaning-discriminating selves to empowerment. Foucault and
Wittgenstein, however, complement each other in their allowance for creativity and creative potential, as when the one, among
his various uses of "power," sees it as "a making possible," and
the other stresses that meaning is created by use. In their grappling
with creativity they are joined by Ricoeur. Thus, for example,
while Wittgenstein views language as an instrument or tool,
Ricoeur treats it as a material to be worked upon and shaped
and realized in discourse (see below).

Bové asks how "discourse," as he and various other postructuralists conceive it, is "key to more than a politics of abstract language games?" The answer, he tells us, "lies in the materiality of discourse. That is, 'discourse' makes possible disciplines and institutions which, in turn, sustain and distribute those discourses. Foucault has shown how this works in the case of prisons and medical clinics" (1990:57). Indeed,

> "Discourse" is one of the most empowered ways in modern and postmodern societies for the forming and shaping of humans as "subjects." In a now-famous play on words, we might say that "power" through its discursive and institutional relays "subjects" us: that is, it makes us into "subjects," and it "subjects" us to the rule of the dominant disciplines which are empowered in our society and which regulate its possibilities for human freedom — that is, it "subjugates" us. (Bové 1990:58)

It is in those senses that we may conceptualize anthropologists as "immanent." More is involved than "operating . . . within a . . . realm of discourse."

Anthropological "discourses" (in poststructuralist senses of discourse) make possible the discipline of anthropology, and that discipline sustains and distributes those discourses. Those discourses are empowered ways of shaping professionals who, subjected to rules, operate in ways more or less approbated by their fellow anthropologists and who conceive of themselves as professionals. Their self-identity as anthropologists, as "subjects" who are practitioners of what Kolakowski calls "the European science par excellence," is shaped by their discourses. The human self, as Rorty (1989:7) puts it, "is created by the use of a vocabulary rather than being adequately or inadequately expressed in a vocabulary." And the anthropologist's professional vocabulary, the anthropologist's analytical categories, are for the most part warmed-over Western folk categories, categories that are perpetually debated and refined in the unending process of creating modified discourses, newly conceptualized goals, and re-situated professionals.

The dynamism of which I speak is notable. Among the factors promoting and supporting it are careerist considerations. These relate to situational and other variables affecting the apperception of career goals and problematics and the strategies and tactics that might be employed with respect to them.

The members of every generation of academic anthropologists face a similar career problem: how to make a place for themselves in the academic world. Making a place means more than getting an academic appointment and being given tenure. In a larger sense, it implies recognition from peers and, perhaps, fame of a sort. Different anthropologists handle this problem in different ways. Some drop out or are forced out. Others settle for limited recognition in the form of tenure and then, so to speak, retire early. Still others address their efforts largely to the great public beyond anthropology. But the largest number cultivate their anthropological gardens as best they can and for as long as they can, now and then winning modest recognition within their own discipline.

For those in the early stages of laboring within the discipline, there is the problem of achieving respect and power comparable to that enjoyed by senior generations. There are two major ways of doing so, and both are employed in one fashion or another. One is to succeed the elders, largely as their disciples. The other is to displace them as rivals. Those who opt for displacement need not be as crude as Freud's parricidal brothers, nor need they experience the guilt that Freud attributes to his imagined founders of human society. Rather than physically terminating the elders, it may suffice to call into question or discredit key elements in their discourses and to champion others.

I do not want to exaggerate the importance of such careerist maneuvers. They are merely one of several sorts of factors that support the development of a shifting mix of overlapping and competitive discourses. Nor do I want to imply that the champions of newer discourses are insincere. Many, insofar as I can tell, are convinced that the perspectives that they extoll, their conceptualizations of problems, their framing of questions, their research strategies, are genuinely superior to those of differently committed anthropologists.

A consideration of careerist concerns, nevertheless, may well enlarge our understandings of both the loyalty that some show to a discourse in which they have invested their careers and the apparent ease with which others embrace newer perspectives and vocabularies. This, however, is by no means a simple matter of younger versus older despite what I said earlier about younger generations desiring to replace older ones. It is not all that rare for older, established anthropologists to announce their conversion to what numbers of their own age-mates call a new and foolish fad. And still others may be conflicted, especially if they view the competition as being what Rorty (1989:9) describes as "a contest between an entrenched vocabulary which has become a nuisance and a half-formed new vocabulary which vaguely promises great things."

Some consideration of careerist concerns is one of a number

of considerations likely to add to our appreciation of the anthropologist's immanence: operating within a disciplinary discourse and all that that implies. And if the available overlapping discourses are competitive, and if the anthropologist has the liberty to shift allegiance, those circumstances attest to a "form of life" within which such competitions and career manuevers are possible and intelligible.

Transcendent Natives

In Chapter 1 I alluded to a long-standing tradition among Western theologians: the attempt to render intelligible a deity said to be infinite and beyond human experience by drawing analogies between such a being and finite human beings. More particularly, I referred to Gordon Kaufman's version of that tradition and F. Michael McLain's criticisms of certain of Kaufman's specifics.

Although Kaufman later altered his opinion in certain respects (1972:xi-xx), he originally maintained that other human beings are "transcendent" for each and every one of us. They are such, he said, because their thoughts and feelings are inaccessible except for moments of 'revelation' in which they manifest them. An experientially-based model of human interpersonal relations that accords prominence to alter's transcendence and revelations, Kaufman suggested, can thus serve for analogically comprehending the divinity's transcendence and self-disclosures in history.

McLain, I pointed out, did not fully agree with Kaufman's original point of view. Human alters, he argued, are not radically transcendent realities known to us only through their self-disclosures, and they therefore are not suitable models for comprehending the deity's radical transcendence. Human selves, he maintained, are embodied realities that have public and observable aspects. These public and observable aspects are not adventitious but intrinsic to our very conception and understanding of human persons. Yet although other human beings are not radically transcendent, McLain wrote, they are nevertheless "relatively occult," for it is "a contingent fact" that we know some things about other persons only because those persons choose to reveal them (1969:167).

In discussing other persons, neither McLain nor Kaufman draws a distinction between "us" and "the natives." Kaufman's and McLain's others are *all* others, those close to us and those not, those who share our discourses and participate in our language-games and those who do not. I suspect that many of us would agree that all those others are "relatively occult" in McLain's sense. I imagine, moreover, that some would also argue that in certain respects each of us is relatively occult, or in some ways opaque, even to our own understandings, and that the Delphic Imperative, "Know thyself!," is perhaps the most difficult of all commandments to obey.

In any case, Kaufman and McLain have made an anthropological point that anthropologists could well take under advisement. A crucial thing about any alter, they suggest, is that in at least some respects alter's thoughts, feelings, and motivations are veiled from us. In saying "Amen!" to that, the anthropologist might add that this is true regardless of whether alter is flesh of our flesh or some denizen of a distant forest whom we have encountered in fieldwork.

The complement to that point is that while we cannot know or understand everything about alter, there is much that we can come to know and understand if alter is accessible. And this is true regardless of who alter happens to be. If alter speaks a language with which we are initially unfamiliar, we will have to work hard to master it. And if alter's expressed convictions initially strike us as far-fetched, we shall have to suspend or arrest our disbelief in the interest of gaining greater comprehension.

In short, we may have to struggle more in the case of the forest denizen than in the case of a compatriot. In light, however, of the many family resemblances among human beings, we can expect to learn much about both. Sometimes, indeed, we might be more discerning about a newly encountered forest dweller than about one of our own cousins in our own home town. That is because we are likely to take less for granted in the case of the forest dweller. S/he strikes us as more exotic than our cousin, and we feel less confident about understanding his/her language. Understanding our cousin, nevertheless, is hardly unproblematic.

Throughout this work, however, I have followed a convention among anthropologists and emphasized questions about coming to understand "the native's point of view." Anthropologists, if asked, would almost certainly acknowledge that problems attendant on attempting to understand the views of our spouses, parents, children, cousins, and other compatriots are in some cases rather much the same as, or otherwise overlap with, problems encountered in ethnographic fieldwork. But anthropologists professionally focus on what they call — sacrificing precision of expression on the altar of convenience — "the natives" and their "points of view."

Now, despite the likelihood that we can understand a great

deal about the natives, there is nevertheless warrant to call them "transcendent." They are not, however, radically transcendent, in analogy to the God of many theologians. Those theologians claim that their God is quite beyond our experiences. But that, of course, cannot be claimed of the natives.

The natives *act* in numerous ways that are public and observable, and the ethnographer not only observes the natives but *interacts* with them. The ethnographer constructs understandings of native actions (those actions include the production of accessible sentences). S/he does so by interpreting impressions of them, and making inferences about less accessible matters, in the light of theories that s/he has already built up about human beings. Experiences of, and inferences about, the natives are assimilated to first-hand experiences of other persons, to inferences about them, and to vicarious experiences of still others as well as second-hand inferences about them gained through reading (including the reading of literary and other sorts of works as well as the anthropological literature).

The ethnographer, in brief, not only has numerous direct experiences of the natives as public, observable realities, but s/he typically understands the natives as a variety of, not a deviation from, humankind. Yet although the natives on this account cannot be construed as radically transcendent, there is a sense in which even their observed behavior might be said to be "transcendent." This is so over and above designating them (as well as people in our own society) "relatively occult" because we may come to know certain things about them only in consequence of their choosing to reveal those things.

The natives are transcendent for us not only because their language-games and discourses are initially beyond our experiences and competence in various important respects, but also because we must ultimately expect distance between our understandings of their form of life and their understandings of it. No matter how competent we may eventually seem to be — even to the point of attaining a cherished ambition of many field workers, congratulations from the natives themselves on how well we speak and otherwise maneuver in their world —, the natives' understandings are still 'beyond' our own. That is so if by "understanding" we mean "to grasp the meaning of" or "to interpret" in quite the same ways as the natives do. This is because of the complex and dynamic experiential dimensions of both native understandings and the anthropologist's understandings.

Understandings are developed within a shifting matrix of experiential associations. These go back to infancy and are often quite complex. While a native may tell an ethnographer what some activity or event means to him or her, that report is likely to be a pallid abstraction, perhaps pointed to some matter at hand but otherwise divorced from a mass of other personal associations. It is, moreover, a contingent understanding, subject to alteration.

The exquisitely difficult task of the ethnographer is to construct an understanding of the native's understandings that relates as much as possible to the native's associations, old and new, remembered and perhaps half-forgotten. While sensitive and energetic ethnographers can do much in the way of learning about these experiential associations, their knowledge and appreciation of them are vicarious and incomplete.

That point was explicitly made to me on various occasions among the Wayú (Guajiro) of the Guajira Peninsula of northeastern Colombia and Venezuela. It was emphasized, for instance, one afternoon during the course of a discussion about herding and herders that I had with five adult men. Those men claimed that by the time a Wayú boy is ten, they and other adult Wayú can predict with great accuracy whether or not the boy will develop into a successful adult caretaker of livestock. They related predictions about success in handling livestock, moreover, to predictions about success in certain sorts of adult social negotiations, though not with as much apparent confidence as they claimed in the case of predictions about herding.

My informants maintained that responsibility, dilligence, and energy, although of great importance for successful herding, are not enough. They mentioned other factors, and speculated that some of them are innately based and differently distributed. Thus, for example, they mentioned eyesight and memory, and linked them. Boys often drive sizeable herds and flocks to public wells and rain-catchments, and the animals may mingle with animals from other herds and flocks. A good herder will not only have a keen eye, but will remember the physical and behavioral characteristics of each and every one of his sheep, goats, or other animals, and will be able to retrieve them.

When I suggested that a boy could rely on the brands with which each animal is marked, my informants replied that an *alijuna*, a non-Indian, might think so, but that a Wayú would not. Not all Wayú brand all livestock, so that even if a herder wanted to rely on the brands he might not be able to do so. But even more important, a Wayú herder, whether boy or man, would be embarassed in interactions with other Wayú if he had to depend on marks put on animals (except in serious disputes in which theft is alleged and in certain other cases). A Wayú herder should depend on his familiarity with each animal in his care. Other Wayú will not esteem him highly if he does not.

My informants went on to say that while they could tell me much about livestock raising — they could, for example, correct such errors as my assumption that all animals are branded — they could not tell me enough to enable to know what it is actually like to be a Wayú boy put in charge of his kinsmen's livestock. Nor could they convey all that a mature Wayú herder, with his multiple responsibilities and tasks, thinks and feels as he cares for his animals. If I wanted to learn more, then in addition to writing down what they told me (as I was then doing), I ought to purchase flocks and herds and take care of them myself. I could then come closer to understanding what it is like to be a Wayú herder, although, they declared, I would never become a Wayú for, among other things, I could never become a Wayú boy!

I agree with my Wayú informants. That very agreement, indeed, suggests a bridge between the Wayú and me: we did not regard each other as totally alien and inaccessible beings. In fact, I eventually came to construct substantial understandings of "*skwaipa wayú*," Wayú custom. On the basis of case studies and other ethnographic activities designed to generate information, I produced a fair amount of "data." And, in accordance with certain canons of anthropology, I posited social and cultural organizing principles that rendered Wayú practices intelligible on a level of abstraction not voiced to me by the Wayú themselves (see Saler 1988). Despite, however, my global and particular understandings, many Wayú experiences are different than mine, and some of them are forever beyond my reach.

Although I made progress in coming to know Wayú lifeways (without ever settling down as a livestock raiser or doing many of the other things that many Wayú do), I do not grasp their understandings in quite the same ways that they do. Their understandings are constituted and colored by a multiplicity of experiential associations that are not mine and that, to the extent that I know about them, I can only fathom second-hand. Although I made efforts to learn their language, to penetrate their language-games, and to comprehend their discourses, those efforts earned me only limited approximations to their understandings. My appreciations of their language-games and discourses are at best distanced and abstracted.

I think that numbers of contemporary anthropologists would agree that what we call beliefs, ideas, or concepts have meaning by virtue of being related to other beliefs, ideas, or concepts. They have contextualized meanings. And as uses of "concept words" alter in onflowing streams, so do their immediate contexts and meanings. But how wide and deep are such streams? As wide, we might say, as the experiences of one's life, and as deep as one's attitudes and feelings.

There is change, to be sure. "When I was a child," Paul tells us, "I spake as a child, I understood as a child, I thought as a child: but when I became a man, I put away childish things" (*I Corinthians* 13:11). Yet the putting away of childish things, the genius of Freud advises, is imperfect, and consequentially so. "The child is father of the man," Wordsworth says (*My Heart Leaps Up*), and my Wayú friends would quite agree. Our experiences from infancy on, including the many that fall from conscious recollection, are themselves contextualizing even as we try to make sense of some of them, and they are likely to leave traces.

The natives are in this sense transcendent: their experiences, and thus their understandings, their points of view, are beyond, which is to say elusive to, our full grasp. They transcend our powers to know and describe them in their totality. The natives in that regard constitute a special case of all alters. Their transcendence differs in content and degree from, say, the transcendence of one's colleagues and other society mates. And, of course, there is mutuality, for the anthropologist is transcendent to the natives. (The native anthropologist who conducts research among his natal group can also be described with reference to this mutual transcendence. S/he has distanced himself/herself from compatriots in the process of becoming an anthropologist and now pursuing research as one. Native life, moreover, flows on relative to positively cathected goals that are not important to the distanced native in the same ways that they are to other natives.)

If we accept mutual experiential transcendence as a condition of the ethnographic enterprise, then we might productively ask how we can *bridge* the perspectival gaps between natives and anthropologists without ever expecting to *close* them. We might begin to conceptualize a workable solution to the problem of bridging, it seems to me, by considering the matter of distanciation, and then the pragmatic attractions of unbounded analytical categories.

Distanciation

Distanciation has to do with distance, with separation. Most social scientists and humanists, I think, would agree that distance is important for perspective, and that distancing, in the sense of conceptually creating distance, is integral to the various analytical tasks that they engage in. (This is also the case, but rather less of a problem, in the simpler sciences — physics and chemistry, for example, — which deal with subject matters but not additionally with sentient subjects. Except in attending to colleagues and themselves, physicists and chemists *qua* physicists and chemists do not have to puzzle over consciousness and intentionality, nor interpret interpretations.)

Our appreciation of the importance of distance, I think, can benefit from certain ideas offered us by Paul Ricoeur, who makes distanciation an important concept in his hermeneutical philosophy. I turn now to some of what he says. In order, however, to understand his treatment of distanciation, it will be necessary to explicate various of his other concepts.

Addressing himself to what he conceptualizes as a fundamental and pervasive hermeneutical problem, Ricoeur posits, and then seeks to overcome, an antinomy that establishes what he deems untenable alternatives, those of "alienating distanciation and participatory belonging" (1981:131).

Ricoeur describes the antinomy as follows:

> on the one hand, alienating distanciation is the attitude that renders possible the objectification which reigns in the human sciences; but on the other hand, this distanciation, which is the condition of the scientific status of the sciences, is at the same time the fall that destroys the fundamental and primordial relation whereby we belong to and participate in the historical reality which we claim to construct as an object. Whence the alternative underlying the very title of Gadamer's work *Truth and Method*: either we adopt the methodological attitude and lose the ontological density of the reality we study, or we adopt the attitude of truth and must then renounce the objectivity of the human sciences. (1981:131)

In rejecting that antinomy by attempting to overcome it, Ricoeur's strategy is to adopt "a dominant problematic" that seems to escape from the alternatives posed. That problematic is the "text," which reintroduces distanciation, but in a positive and productive way. In Ricoeur's view, the text is "the paradigm of distanciation in communication. As such, it displays a fundamental characteristic of the very historicity of human experience, namely that it is communication in and through distance" (1981:131).

The text, Ricoeur makes clear, "cannot . . . be purely identified with writing," and writing does not constitute "the unique problematic of the text" (1981:132). He gives several reasons.

First, it is the dialectic of speaking and writing rather than writing itself that gives rise to the hermeneutical problem. Second, the dialectic is built on a "dialectic of distanciation" which is already part of oral discourse as such and is therefore more primitive than the opposition of speaking and writing. We must therefore look to discourse itself for the fundaments of subsequent dialectics. Third, the idea of "the realisation of discourse as a structured work" needs to be inserted "between the realisation of language as discourse and the dialectic of speaking and writing" (1981:132).

Although Ricoeur's theory of textuality is directed to texts as literary works, his discussion can be generalized to other phenomenal orders. These can be analogously conceptualized as texts, as works of discourse, and "materialized" as such in keeping with the hermeneutical function of distanciation (a complex function that will be treated later). Ricoeur's theorizing, together with allied though different efforts made by other authors, have inspired some anthropologists to conceptualize culture as text. Ricoeur and other poststructuralists have also inspired them to use the term "discourse" in ways that resemble usages in contemporary literary criticism.

For Ricoeur, discourse, "even in an oral form," exhibits a primitive kind of distanciation that contains the possibility of much else. A dialectic of event and meaning helps us to understand it.

Discourse is to be appreciated as an *event*, for when someone speaks, something happens. This understanding is crucial "when we take into consideration the passage from a linguistics of language or code to a linguistics of discourse or messages" (Ricoeur 1981:133).

Taking into account Ferdinand de Saussure's distinction between 'language' and 'speech', Louis Hjelmslev's discrimination between 'schema' and 'use', and Émile Benveniste's distinction between a linguistics of language built upon the 'sign' and a linguistics of discourse constructed with the 'sentence' as its basic unit, Ricoeur goes on to draw distinctions between language and discourse that support the conceptualization of discourse as an event: discourse is realized in a time frame, that of the present, while language as a system is outside of time; language has no subject whereas discourse is self-referential in that it refers back to its speakers by means of personal pronouns and other indicators; while the signs of a language system refer only to other signs in that system, so that language "no more has a world than it has a time and a subject," discourse, being about something, is an event in the sense of "the advent of a world in language [*langage*] by means of discourse;" and, finally, though language provides the codes for communication and is thus a prior condition of communication, "it is in discourse that all messages are exchanged" (1981:133). These features of discourse collectively constitute it as an event, and "they appear only in the realisation of language in discourse, in the actualisation of our linguistic competence in performance" (1981:134).

Discourse's eventful character, however, is but one of two "constitutive poles." The other pole is meaning. And "it is the tension between the two poles which gives rise to the production of discourse as a work, the dialectic of speaking and writing, and all the other features of the text which enrich the notion of distanciation" (1981:134). Discourse is realized as an event and understood as meaning, and we wish to understand the meaning that endures rather than the fleeting event.

Event and meaning are articulated in the linguistics of discourse. "This articulation," Ricoeur declares, "is the core of the whole hermeneutical problem. Just as language, by being actualised in discourse, surpasses itself as system and realises itself as event, so too discourse, by entering the process of understanding, surpasses itself as event and becomes meaning" (1981:134).

Speaking and writing are creative activities. They are both ways of realizing discourse. Fundamental to the creativity of both is the polysemy, the different but related meanings, of words. Speakers and writers creatively opt for some meanings at the expense of others by contextual deployments, and auditors and readers characteristically make context-related decisions about meaning — interpretations, starkly conceived. But while speaking and writing are in these respects alike, writing in certain important ways distances the texts produced from what is characteristic of oral realizations of discourse. Ricoeur's concept of distanciation has to do with what is involved in that distancing.

Ricoeur describes several sorts of distanciation. The first is "the distanciation of the saying in the said" (1981:134). In distinction to the meaning that we associate with speaking, in writing meaning is intentionally exteriorized, and this "renders possible the exteriorisation of discourse in writing and in the work" (1981:136).

Another distanciation relates to a certain autonomy created by the passage from speaking to writing. The text produced by writing can be said to be autonomous "with respect to the intention of the author" (1981:139). What a text signifies need not be assumed to coincide with what its author may have meant. A major significance of the autonomy of the text vis-à-vis the intentions of the author is that "henceforth, textual meaning and psychological meaning have different destinies" (1981:139).

The distancing of textual meaning from psychological meaning has a sociological parallel. In speaking there is a dialogical relationship between speaker and auditor. But a text — Ricoeur writes of "a literary work, and of a work of art in general" — "transcends" the psychological and sociological conditions of its production for it is open to "an unlimited series of readings, themselves situated in different socio-cultural conditions" (1981:139). This distanciation of the text from the psycho-sociological conditions of its production constitutes a 'decontextualization' of the text that supports a 'recontextualization' in some new situation, a recontextualization accomplished by the very act of reading (1981:139).

What Ricoeur calls the "emancipation" of the text from its author, he suggests, has a parallel with respect to the readership of the text. Unlike the dialogical situation, where there is an immediacy of speaker and auditor, written discourse in principle creates an audience that extends to anyone who can read. This distanciation of the text from "the dialogical condition of discourse is the most significant effect of writing" (1981:139).

The autonomy of the text, Ricoeur maintains, has certain hermeneutical consequences. Suffice it for my purposes to point to the first that he gives, and to quote his words:

> distanciation is not the product of methodology and hence something superfluous and parasitical; rather it is constitutive of the phenomenon of the text as writing. At the same time, it is the condition of interpretation . . . We are thus prepared to discover a relation between *objectification* and *interpretation* which is much less dichotomous, and consequently much more complementary, than that established by the Romantic tradition [of hermeneutics]. (1981:139-140)

The Romantics, Ricoeur relates, emphasized the expression of genius and sought to render genius contemporary. And Dilthey, whom he sees as close to the Romantics in that respect, emphasized 'understanding' in his concept of interpretation — that is, as Ricoeur puts it, understanding understood as "grasping an alien life which expresses itself through the objectification of writing" (1981:140). But the psychologizing and historicizing of Romantic and Diltheyan hermeneutics, Ricoeur maintains, no longer form a route open to us "once we take distanciation by writing and objectification by structure seriously" (1981:140).

Nor is the alternative of structuralism open to us, based as it is on an approach to language, on a linguistics of language, that is concerned with a closed system of mutually dependent signs in which the signs are defined by their differences alone. Interpretation, in Ricoeur's view, is not to be reduced to "the dismantling of structures" (1981:141).

What, then, is to be interpreted? According to Ricoeur, "to interpret is to explicate the type of being-in-the world unfolded *in front of* the text" (1981:141). Here Ricoeur adopts a suggestion made by Heidegger in *Being and Time* regarding 'understanding' (*Verstehen*). Understanding, as Ricoeur puts it, "is no longer tied to the understanding of others, but becomes a structure of being-in-the-world . . . For what must be interpreted in a text is *a proposed world* which I could inhabit and wherein I could project one of my ownmost possibilities. That is what I call the world of the text, the world proper to *this* unique text" (1981:142).

This world of the text, Ricoeur continues, "is therefore not the world of everyday language" (1981:142). It constitutes, indeed, "a new sort of distanciation which could be called a distanciation of the real world from itself" (1981:142). Narratives, folktales, and poems have their referent, but it is a referent that is discontinuous with that of everyday language. "Through fiction and poetry," says Ricoeur, "new possibilities of being-in-the-world are opened up within everyday reality" (1981:142).

The reader, indeed, may appropriate texts, appropriation being (to begin its characterization) "understanding at and through distance" (1981:143). Interpretation of a text understood as appropriation "culminates in the self-interpretation of a subject who thenceforth understands himself better, understands himself differently, or simply begins to understand himself" (1981:158). Ultimately, Ricoeur tells us, what one appropriates is a proposed world. And that world is not behind the text, in the sense of a presumed hidden intention, but, rather, in front of it, "as that which the work unfolds, discovers, reveals" (1981:143). To understand, then, "*is to understand oneself in front of the text.* It is not a question of imposing upon the text our finite capacity of understanding, but of exposing ourselves to the text and receiving from it an enlarged self . . ." (1981:143).

What Ricoeur says about poetry and fiction opening up new possibilities of being-in-the-world ought to strike a responsive chord among many anthropologists, *for we have long said rather much the same thing about ethnography.* The idea, moreover, of exposing ourselves to "texts," broadly conceived to include diverse cultural works, and receiving from them enlarged selves resonates not only with the hopes of many anthropologists but with their experiences as well. For not only has the doing of ethnography proven to be challenging and self-enlarging for many of those who engaged in it first hand, but the close reading of ethnographic monographs sometimes has.conduced to similar results.

Many anthropologists, I think, have been prepared by their own experiences to find value in at least some of what Ricoeur says about the hermeneutical function of distanciation, including his claim that "distanciation is the condition of understanding" (1981:144). At the same time, however, some anthropologists see something regrettable in distanciation.

What I interpret to be regret is involved, for example, in claims that writing down a myth "destroys" that myth. While talk of destruction may seem to be something of an exaggeration, it does make a supportable point.

Among many of the world's peoples myths are not handled in ways analogous to our practice of casually taking a book down from the shelf and reading it when we deem it convenient to do so. In numbers of societies myths are told at certain times of the year and/or on specific occasions. Their telling, moreover, is sometimes hedged about with considerable protocol. Further, "telling" a myth is often more than a verbal production, and certainly more than the dispassionate articulation of a narrative. The myth-performer — a more accurate term in many cases than "myth-teller" — may exhibit various sorts of bodily movements and facial expressions that are integral to the performance. Words may be given selective emphases and modulations. And the engagement of the audience in the performance can be important and take diverse forms.

In short, there is likely to be far more to a myth than a written transcription of its story might suggest. Our usual notational systems are inadequate to capture even the stresses and modulations given to words, let alone the other complexities and subtleties involved in the performance. Making a myth into a text by writing down only its narrative elements can be regarded as a veritable exsanguination, the production of a corpse, and thus a subversion of the truth of the myth for its usual constituency, the natives. We have good reason to entertain reservations about the value of focusing largely or exclusively on the analysis of myth as narrative structure, even if the analyst be as brilliant as Claude Lévi-Strauss.

What is said of myth can also be said, *mutatis mutandis,* of much else that we write about the natives, their competencies, and productions. For the general public these writings are best known in the form of ethnographic monographs, the major works of the anthropological discipline. Anthropologists have long viewed them as opportunities and means to do what Ricoeur, Heidegger, and others have put so elegantly: to expand our awareness of new possibilities of being-in-the-world, possibilities of human existence that we can apprehend without sundering our everyday reality. Yet an "understanding at and through distance" of alternative forms of life may at the same time stimulate us to question the seeming givenness of our own.

Without further belaboring the point that Ricoeur's insights and those of authors from whom he draws are applicable to ethnographic monographs, I want to turn to a related matter. For while the ethnographic monograph is indeed a writtten work, it would be more accurate in many cases to describe it as a *re-writing.* That is, the published monograph is usually dependent to a great extent on field notes and can be regarded as a re-thinking of them. Although field notes are not usually published (except as re-written), and although much less has been written about them than about the monograph *qua* monograph, they are of great importance as first writings, as early and palpable distanciations.

Field notes are typically fragmentary. They are partial accounts of the ethnographer's experiences and interpretive efforts, and they may sometimes self-consciously express puzzlement and other reactions to the vagaries of the field. They imply distanciation, for, as texts, they are "discourse fixed by writing" (Ricoeur 1981:145). There is, to be sure, much else that could be said about the making and use of them. But I limit myself to an observation that relates to my interest in categories: field notes are generally written with some concern for the eventual retrieval of information.

The notes are usually written sequentially, as the fieldwork develops over time. They typically cover a wide diversity of topics, so that it is of practical value to so arrange them as to facilitate the retrieval of information specific to different interests. There is, of course, a variety of ways of organizing one's notes. Today, indeed, ethnographers who have computers in the field (perhaps run by solar-charged batteries) can enter their notes directly into a data-base manager that allows considerable flexibility in coding and retrieval. But however it is done, information is sorted by categories. In the great majority of cases they are probably those of the ethnographer, though perhaps with some admixture of native categories, especially when the ethnographer deems them handy indexes, and particularly where there is no parsimonious way of translating the category terms into the ethnographer's language.

Field notes are notes for something. As, in effect, responses to general and particular questions that frame research, they are initial interpretations. Already distanciated from the living immediacy of the situations that inspired them, they will later be re-worked in the monograph. Their organization, influenced by the ethnographer's research aims, and intended to facilitate retrieval as well as understanding, is itself a predisposing analytical structure. It is, indeed, largely an ethnocentric one. This is so not only with respect to many (probably most) of its categories but also their arrangement. Were we to analyze it as a classificatory apparatus we would be likely to discern familiar taxonomic and thematic schemas.

And yet, while congruent (or so we hope) with assumptions about the perspectival independence of the natives, classificatory apparatuses for field notes also serve to facilitate interpretation in Ricoeur's sense of "making one's *own* what was initially *alien*" (1981:159). How, if it can be done at all, might interpretation in that sense be done with least insult to the cultural integrity of both the natives and ourselves? By what magic of categories? By, I suggest, the analogical powers of unbounded analytical categories. The thaumaturgy of such categories resides in their relative openness compared to extreme essentialist alternatives.

By "extreme" essentialist alternatives I mean categories explicitly defined so that we are obliged to treat all members of the groups comprehended by the categories as equal members, even if doing so contradicts our intuitions. Various scholarly definitions of religion that render "communism" a religion — Goodenough's and B. K. Smith's different definitions, for example — are cases in point. Most of us, I suspect, would tend to say that if communism is a religion at all, it is less so than many other religions. A saving grace of many operant essentialist categories is that the people who give them meaning through use also in effect attribute differential significance to their instantiations, for some exemplars of a category are more readily brought to mind or given preference over others. But that saving grace can be jeopardized through the distanciation produced by the very fixity of essentialist definitions. Such a possibility can be factored into arguments in favor of abjurring any sort of definition. There are, however, alternative strategies, the most promising of which, I have argued, are suggested by the idea of family resemblances and its elaboration in prototype theory.

Unbounded Analytical Categories

"One of the aims of all hermeneutics," Ricoeur (1981:159) declares, "is to struggle against cultural distance." That struggle is inevitably conducted through categories, and our conceptualizations of them can retard or advance the goal — and sometimes, alas, contribute to false impressions of victory.

Categories are not only devices for re-cognizing, for sorting out and thus taking notice of in some definite way, 'objects' (whatever we cognize) and organizing and retrieving information about them, but they facilitate and routinize the extension of our understandings. If we suppose that two objects pertain to the same category and one is better known to us than the other, we tend to make inferences about the lesser known on the basis of our acquaintance with the better known. Doing so is doubtless advantageous to us in coping with the existential press of life, our confrontations with a multitude of problems that tax our capacities and competencies.

Attending to the world through categories and organizing categories into classificatory structures is thus an urgent matter for human beings, one that cannot be postponed until a sabbatical year. "Even average 3-year-olds, who are years away from the logical and symbolic operations postulated by Piaget and Bruner," Ellen Markman (1989:7) tells us, "have quite thoroughly classified their world. They have formed hundreds of categories of vehicles, clothes, food, toys, . . . and so on."

The idea that "The child is father of the man" applies to categorization and the arrangement of catgeories as well as to much else. As individuals develop, they normally become more sophisticated in learning and applying categories. But although there are discontinuities, they also build on early experiences and competencies, and they do not entirely put away childish things.

According to Markman (1989:161), very young children tend to assume that categories are mutually exclusive. Mutual exclusion is one way of relating categories to one another. But while such an assumption can facilitate in certain ways learning how to use words, it makes it difficult to learn class inclusion, which is another way of relating categories. In class inclusion hierarchies subordinate categories are included in superordinate ones, and the names or labels of the superordinates can be applied to their subordinates. Thus, for example, we call a dog an animal as well as a dog. On the same taxonomic level (which we graph horizontally in two-dimensional space) we expect exclusion rather than inclusion (we deem dog and cat, for instance, to be mutually exclusive). Vertical ascension, however, emphasizes inclusion of categories (dog and cat, by way of an example, are both animals).

Children, of course, typically do learn and operate with class inclusion hierarchies, despite their earlier attachments to mutual exclusivity. Such attachments, however, do not go away. Rather, they are eventually incorporated into more sophisticated understandings and manipulations of catgeories.

The early childhood emphasis on mutual exclusivity may betoken more than a constraint that marks the young child's handling of language. It may derive, Markman (1989:212) suggests, from a belief entertained by children about objects — that each object has but one identity, and that its identity is revealed by its label. A key assumption about objects would thus be paralleled by a key assumption about object labels. Markman notes that "Flavell (in press) argues that young children assume that each thing in the world has only one nature — an assumption that adults may sometimes share. Unlike adults, however, children do not understand that each thing may, nevertheless, be mentally represented in more than one way" (1989:212).

Adult proclivities toward mutual exclusivity and the idea of distinct natures tend to be quite marked in the case of so-called "natural kind" categories. While philosophers and others have debated what we might understand by that expression, suffice it for my purposes to observe that many persons in our society suppose that numbers of categories closely correspond or correlate to what is actually "out there" in nature. In this view, by way of an example, dogs and cats "naturally" exist, they are different and mutually exclusive animals, and our categories called "dog" and "cat" reflect those facts.

Not only are "natural kind" categories widely employed as correlational structures, as structures of attributes that are treated as given by nature, but the members of groups comprehended by such categories are popularly assumed to share the same natures. Westerners conventionally assume that these natures find expression in stereotypic behavior. Thus, for example, to paraphrase (in academese) a song from a musical drama well known

in North America, fish of necessity must swim, and birds of
necessity must fly.

That some birds do not really fly, and that not everything that
flies or swims is, respectively, either a bird or a fish, poses little
or no problem for most adults. Flying, to restrict myself to one
case in point, is a default value in popular abstract conceptualizations of the category bird. Penguins and ostriches, if thought
of at all, and if thought of as birds, are merely rather peculiar
birds (less typical birds because a major default value of the
category must be dropped in describing them specifically). Bats,
however, are not classed with birds (in many societies, at any
rate) even though they fly. The Germans perhaps express Western
folk opinions about the nature of the bat best: they call it *die
Fledermaus*, the 'fluttering' and therefore 'flying' mouse (rodent),
a term imitated by the rarely voiced English expression "flitter-
mouse."

Making such distinctions, and grading typicality of examples
while subscribing intellectually to essentialism, facilitates continued endorsement of natural categories. Such endorsement,
moreover, does not greatly trouble the endorsers when dealing
with what some engineers call "real world phenomena" — at least
not when dealing with finches and salmon and, on a more
inclusive level, birds and fish. Biological systematists may raise
problems (see, for example, Gould 1983:363 on why "fish" is not
a cladistic group), but many other people who use those categories seem to do so with few or no misgivings.

So-called natural kind categories, as best exemplified by familiar
species of animals, are attractive to many persons in our society
in two ways. First, they are deemed non-arbitrary. That is, they
are supposed to correlate with the natural order, to reflect what
is, and one can draw comfort from being in step with reality.
Second, they are deemed mutually exclusive, and thus they serve
to obviate the sort of confusion that some might experience were
an object to pertain simultaneously to two categories when one
is not conceptualized as including the other.

Now, without involving myself in arguments pro and con
respecting the warrant and worth of natural kind categories, I
do want to argue that they are unsuitable as models for analytical
categories such as religion. This is not to suggest that religion
is an arbitrary category. It is certainly not that for a Westerner,
for it suggests a pool of elements that has an historical reality
in Western experiences. Categories that correlate with historical
particularities and that are warranted in a discourse are hardly

arbitrary. I do want to suggest, however, that analytical categories such as religion ought not to be deemed mutually exclusive with other such analytical categories (e.g., economics, politics, law, and so forth).

Some discussion of what I mean by "analytical categories" and what I mean by religion as such a category is now required.

I conceive of analysis as the grasping of a whole and then intellectually decomposing it into the elements and relations that might be said to constitute it. We do this in an effort to understand the whole better. We can apprehend a complex holistically, and doing so is a form of understanding. Analysis, however, can enrich such an understanding. In an analysis the posited constituencies and relations are intellectually ordered by subsuming them under category labels. The categories with which we conduct our analysis thus can be described as analytical categories.

Of what, or for what, is religion an analytical category? As used by many members of anthropology departments and departments of religious studies, religion is a category for advancing our understandings of culture or, more broadly, the human condition. Hence the talk of religion as a cultural system and the talk of a religious dimension of human life. Culture, unlike grace in some Christian theologies (all of which contain anthropologies), is not "sup.eradded" to human nature. If we suppose that there is an intrinsic human nature, culture is integral to its realization: one cannot imagine human forms of life without culture. And, if we reject the notion of an intrinsic human nature and/or contemporary acceptations of the term culture, we must still posit a complex of realized capacities that approximates to what we now call culture in our efforts to achieve a global perspective on what it means to be human.

To say that religion is one of a number of analytical categories for comprehending culture or the human condition does not commit us to the notion that religion is a human universal. It may well be the case that elements that we conventionally think of as "religious" occur in all human societies. Whether or not, however, we want to call some aggregation of such elements "religion" is another matter.

In any case, I think that, with certain possible exceptions (e.g., "implicational universals" in linguistics), we would be better off if we talked about resemblances rather than universals. I suggested earlier in this work that the conceptual benefits that might accrue from positing universals can be gleaned in most cases by establishing resemblances, and without the problematic ontological commitments or baggage that the assertion of universals tends to entail. Talk of resemblances suggests that they are resemblances in someone's apperception — that resemblances are constructed according to some principle or canon, in accordance with some schema.

In constructing likenesses in preference to positing universals, however, we would be well advised to particularize resemblances: to describe, that is, apperceived resemblances between the members of pairs of particulars, and apperceived resemblances between pairs of resemblances, and so on (Woozley 1967:205). This caution, though a concession to regress, is none-the-less desireable, lest in careless efforts to construct a more sophisticated comparative discipline we inadvertently apotheosize resemblance into a universal.

In establishing resemblances, we are not without guidance on how to go about it. What guides us? In a manner of speaking, our lives guide us. Our lives are not preparations for making discriminations and sorting out resemblances and differences. They are, in fact, the very doing of those things, and we might well take notice of what Rorty terms "the blind impress all our behavings bear" (1989:34).

In our daily lives we encounter countless stimuli, and we take notice of, or otherwise respond to, only some. We are sensitized and desensitized in various ways, and we conceptualize and attend to the world selectively. To conceptualize and attend to the world is to make discriminations, to sort differences and similarities. Our language-games and discourses are powerful instruments in guiding us, but they do not lock out creativity. We can and do make analogical leaps, develop tropes, and come to see the world in fresh ways.

Regardless, however, of how creative we may be, we operate with and through categories. Our categories, indeed, are discriminatory devices for sorting out the world. And it is understandable, I think, that people would want their discriminations to be as clean and as orderly as possible. Hence one of the attractions of essentialist categories.

But instead of following essentialist canons and deeming certain conditions as *necessary* to a category, we could simply mark them as *typicality* conditions (Jackendoff 1983:139). Thus stripeless animals that otherwise look like typical tigers, that sound like typical tigers, and that hunt and kill like typical tigers can be called tigers, even if untypical in a certain respect. If an important interest in discriminating tigers is to avoid being eaten by them, this would seem to be an especially sensible procedure, since it is not the stripes that would do us in. But even if we suppose that tigers constitute a "natural kind category" independent of our utilitarian concerns, there is still good reason to distinguish such a category in terms of typicality rather than necessity of elements. For the world as we experience it often bulges in and out through the boundaries that we establish by positing necessary and sufficient conditions.

The point just advanced with respect to tigers can also be advanced — and enhanced! — in the case of religions. Even those who proffer essentialist definitions of religion generally admit that the religions of the world are quite variable, certainly in content and to some extent in form. Were those definers explicitly asked to make a comparison, I suspect that most of them would emphatically agree that religions are more variable than tigers, and that religion is a more abstract conceptual category than tiger. Further, I suspect that at least some proponents of "natural kind categories" would be significantly less sanguine about — or perhaps distinctly opposed to — a suggestion to the effect that religions constitute such a category.

Religion is an abstraction, and one not formed into a category and conjured with by various of the world's peoples. As a Western analytical category, moreover, it is not now, and never has been, "neutral." Its operant logic has always been the logic of the discourses that legitimate it as a category. As an analytical instrument, indeed, its shapes and specifics are expressions of research goals and strategies and more encompassing perspectives that include suppositions about the possibilities and desireabilities of knowledge.

In extending the category religion and applying the category label to certain phenomena among non-Western peoples, we are claiming some similarity to what we deem an important aspect of human life in the West. We generally claim or imply, moreover, that we do so because of apperceived similarity: that is, that we do not create the similarity simply by extending the term, but that we apply the term because we discern some similarity.

The positing of resemblances is, of course, an act of judgment. Whether we initially configure resemblances by attending to newly encountered phenomena holistically, or whether we engage in analytical procedures that foreground certain elements and weight their importance, we are engaged in making judgments. And judgments do not occur in voids. They are context-related and based on something. To repeat what has been said earlier, we

determine what is similar and what is different relative to our
conceptual biases as expressed in and influenced by our conventions, our discourses, and our language-games. This renders similarities and differences relevant in the very act of establishing
them.

In pursuing their ethnographic research, anthropologists must
also work out from their conventions, discourses, and language-
games. What they do cannot be entirely "open-textured," and in
significant measure it can be accounted "ethnocentric." At the
same time, however, anthropologists can distance themselves to
varying extents from their conventions, discourses, and language-
games, partially through an increasing understanding and
"appropriation" (in Ricoeur's sense) of the conventions, discourses, and language-games of the natives. What anthropologists
do is ineluctably comparative, and comparative judgments of
similarities and differences can be well served, I think, by
unbounded analytical categories.

Conceiving of our type case, religion, as an unbounded
analytical category provides an example of how we might bridge
the immanence of anthropologists and the transcendence of the
natives. As an unbounded category based on our apperceptions
of family resemblances, religion serves as a two-way analytical
bridge that facilitates back-and-forth travel in the establishment
and contemplation of analogies. By traveling this bridge in both
directions, indeed, we distance ourselves from its poles as we
compare them. Comparison, the establishment of what we take
to be similarities and differences and the weighting of them
relevant to some purpose, promotes distanciation.

We begin an intellectual journey nurtured by our understandings of what, for us, are the most prototypical cases that exemplify the category religion. We go on to posit by analogy, and
to explore, different and perhaps rather more peripheral cases.
These other cases are deemed religions to the extent that they
remind us of our most clear-cut exemplars of the category.

In doing all this, we are not only enabled to establish analogies
(instead of searching for identities of essence), but the differences that we apperceive can be aligned with the similarities
without threatening the integrity of our classificatory schemas.
Co-classification, indeed, can occur on the basis of analogies even
when the phenomena brought together — those of the natives
and those of the West — are deemed to pertain to other categories as well as to the category religion.

The notion that something may be more or less of a religion

than something else complements what most of us already take for granted: that some persons may be more or less religious than other persons. That this, in effect, can also be the case for religions requires us to readjust our thinking about categories and how we conceptualize them.

Some may say that comparing religions in this way is invidious as well as ethnocentric.

I have already discussed the matter of ethnocentrism, but it is worthwhile, I think, to recapitulate my sense of the matter here, and in terse, bottom-line terms: Yes, it is ethnocentric, at least initially, but how could it be otherwise? We must start with our own categories, our own language-games, our own discourses, for how else can we start? We have not yet learned those of the natives, and we cannot make our minds into blank slates. And long after we start, when we sit down to write our ethnographies, we must also resort to the categories, language-games, and discourses of anthropology. Even if we write in the native language — which hardly ever happens unless the native language is an Indo-European one — we cannot fully escape the impress of our discipline, the impress of what Kolakowski aptly characterizes as "the European science par excellence." But ethnocentrism can be tempered by making native categories and classifications central to our analyses. And ethnocentrism can be tempered by distanciation.

The charge of being invidious is, of course, related to the charge of being ethnocentric. There are some contemporary anthropologists who seem to suppose that virtually any use of Western categories in the ethnographic enterprise is "hegemonic," at the very least a vestige or hint of intellectual imperialism or neo-colonialism. Those who hold such a point of view have attempted to suggest ways out, such as, for example, a dialogical approach whereby the ethnographer and the natives mutually forge a fresh discourse. In light, however, of the general considerations that I stated earlier respecting ethnocentrism, I deem such ways out to be of limited value and to be ultimately inadequate insofar as avoiding ethnocentrism is concerned.

In any case, those who decry "hegemonic" ethnography are likely to be especially disturbed by my up-front advocacy of treating many religions as less good examples of religion than the Western monotheisms. Does this not, some are likely to ask, claim explicitly that various religions, including many of those in the non-Western world, are "inferior" to the Western monotheisms? And, despite the lengthy arguments presented in the preceding chapters of this work, why should we privilege the Western monotheisms in the first place? I will not answer the second question here, for I believe that I have answered it elsewhere, especially in Chapters 5 and 6. But the first question, although touched on elsewhere, deserves explicit answer here.

To claim that some religions are less good examples than others of how we conceptualize the category religion is not in any way to claim that one is inferior to the other except as an example for purposes of categorization. It is easier to categorize some than others, but other judgments relative to that fact are personal value judgments that are not endorsed by the approach to categorization recommended here. Some persons, indeed, may feel that the less "religious" a religion appears to be, so much the better. And others may entertain a contrary opinion.

The real problem has to do with comparison. Making comparisons is a process of discriminating and organizing similarities and differences, and it is always guided by assumptions that include standards. Judging that some phenomena approximate more closely to our standards than other phenomena need not implicate moral judgments, but in our society it often does. There is sometimes an associative chain of thought, at the very least connotative, that runs from "more" (elements or features) to "more complete," and from thence to "integral" and then to "integrity," and finally to "good."

It need not be that way but it often is. Which is why, in part, some contemporary anthropologists shy away from the old disciplinary claim that anthropology is and should be a comparative science. Comparison, some suggest, is inevitably ethnocentric and hegemonic, and they hold out the hope that a non-comparative hermeneutical anthropology, in comparison to (!) a purportedly scientific anthropology, will escape — or (to capture another irony) better escape — ethnocentrism and hegemony.

I regard that hope as vain. We cannot fully escape ethnocentrism, but we can temper and tame it. And we cannot avoid comparisons. Our minds to a significant extent operate by making comparisons in our constant monitoring of the world, as do the minds of other life-forms.

When an anthropologist studies a culturally-organized human society, s/he compares it in various ways to other culturally-organized societies, those in which s/he has lived and those that s/he has read about in a diversity of literatures. These comparisons ineluctably play important roles in working toward understandings. That comparisons may be poorly done, or that they may mislead, or that they may be used to support conclusions now deemed "politically incorrect" are other matters. But the idea that we can avoid comparisons entirely is absurd. Anthropology is and will remain a comparative discipline. Hence the great importance of how we go about conceptualizing our analytical categories.

Two Suggestions

(1) If we continue to use refinements of such Western categories as religion, economics, law, and so forth as analytical categories, then the study of the development of those categories and their labels in the West could be very useful to us. By coming to know more about their context-relatedness and their complexities and subtleties in the history of the West, we are very likely to enrich the intellectual resources that we marshal and deploy for transcultural research. An enhanced appreciation of our Western categories, obtained by scholarly attentions to their histories, might well heighten our sensibilities and sensitivities for the study of other peoples' categories. So I recommend that my fellow anthropologists do what they can to increase their intellectual groundings in Western traditions.

(2) While anthropologists normally devote much attention to native categories in ethnographies of the peoples who utilize those categories, the time has come, I think, to borrow selectively from such categories and experiment with them as transcultural tools. That is, we might try to use them for probing and describing the cultures of peoples who do not employ them, just as we now use religion as a category for probing and describing the cultures of people who have no word and category for religion.

To do this most effectively, of course, requires as profound an appreciation as possible of the relevant cultural contexts and uses of those categories among the people who support them. The sorts of categories that would best serve our interests are likely to be rather abstract and complex, and the category terms are very likely to be polysemous. These terms and categories, moreover, will cut across various of our own.

We can best experiment with selected non-Western categories by conceptualizing them as organized by family resemblances and as unbounded. Viewed analytically, that is, we deem each such category to be constituted by a pool of elements no one of which is either necessary or sufficient to include something in a group comprehended by the category. We expect the greatest number of elements to cluster in certain sorts of usage among the people from whom we borrow the category. It is very likely, moreover, that those people will in effect weight the elements with respect to how well they predict probable inclusion in any group comprehended by the category.

As we attempt to apply such a category to the analysis of other cultures, we expect the applicable elements in the original pool to decrease and the weightings to shift. This, of course, will provide us with interesting opportunities to study applicable elements in novel contexts and so enrich our comparative appreciation of the significance and power of contextualizations. An example that readily comes to mind is *dharma* in Hindu traditions (see Fitzgerald 1990): I deem it a potentially interesting tool for the construction of understandings of some non-Hindu societies — and such understandings, I have argued, are ineluctably comparative.

The purposes of so experimenting with other people's folk categories and converting them into analytical instruments are twofold: First, to increase the intellectual resources at our disposal and so enrich our options for engaging in the ethnographic enterprise. Second, to help us go beyond, as well as utilize, the Western framework that has hitherto guided and constrained us in attending to the possibilities of being-in-the-world. By so doing, we can hope to produce a more polyphonic and multicultural anthropology than would otherwise be possible.

REFERENCES CITED

Aaron, Richard I. 1967. *The Theory of Universals*, 2nd edition. Oxford: The Clarendon Press.

Aberle, David F. 1986. Personal Communication.

Adams, James Luther. 1969. Introduction to *What Is Religion?* by Paul Tillich, 9–24. New York: Harper and Row.

Alston, William P. 1967. Religion. In *The Encyclopedia of Philosophy*, vol. 7, ed. Paul Edwards, 140–145. New York: Macmillan and The Free Press.

Appell, George N. 1983. Ethnic Groups in the Northeast Region of Indonesian Borneo and Their Social Organizations. *Borneo Research Bulletin* 15:38–45.

Argyll, The Duke of. 1884. *The Unity of Nature*. London: John B. Alden.

———. 1896. *The Philosophy of Belief, or Law in Christian Theology*. London: John Murray.

Aristoteles. 1941. *The Basic Works of Aristotle*, ed. Richard McKeon. New York: Random House.

Armstrong, Sharon Lee, Lila R. Gleitman and Henry Gleitman. 1983. On What Some Concepts Might Not Be. *Cognition* 13:263–308.

Asad, Talal. 1983. Anthropological Conceptions of Religion: Reflections on Geertz. *Man* 18(2):237–259.

Atran, Scott. 1990. *Cognitive Foundations of Natural History: Towards an Anthropology of Science*. Cambridge: Cambridge University Press.

Bambrough, J. Renford. 1960/61. Universals and Family Resemblances. *Proceedings of the Aristotelian Society* 61:207–222.

Beattie, John H.M. 1964. *Other Cultures: Aims, Methods, and Achievements in Social Anthropology*. New York: The Free Press.

———. On Understanding Ritual. In *Rationality*, ed. Bryan R. Wilson, 240–268. Oxford: Basil Blackwell.

Beckner, Morton. 1959. *The Biological Way of Thought*. New York: Columbia University Press.

Bell, Catherine. 1989. Religion and Chinese Culture: Toward an Assessment of 'Popular Religion'. *History of Religions* 29(1):35–57.

Bellah, Robert N. 1967. Civil Religion in America. *Daedalus* 96(1):1–21.

Bellah, Robert N. and Phillip E. Hammond. 1980. *Varieties of Civil Religion*. San Francisco: Harper and Row.

Benveniste, Émile. 1969. *Le Vocabulaire des Institutions Indo-Européennes*, Vol. 2. Paris: Éditions de Minuit.

———. 1971 [1956]. Remarks on the Function of Language in Freudian Theory. In *Problems in General Linguistics*, trans. Mary Elizabeth Meek, 65–75. Coral Gables, FL: University of Miami Press.

Berlin, Brent. 1976. The Concept of Rank in Ethnobiological Classification: Some Evidence from Aguaruna Folk Botany. *American Ethnologist* 3: 381–399.

———. 1978. Ethnobiological Classification. In *Cognition and Categorization*, ed. Eleanor Rosch and Barbara B. Lloyd, 9–26. Hillsdale, NJ: Lawrence Erlbaum Associates.

Berlin, Brent, Dennis E. Breedlove and Peter H. Raven. 1973. General Principles of Classification and Nomenclature in Folk Biology. *American Anthropologist* 75(1):214–242.

———. 1974. *Principles of Tzeltal Plant Classification*. New York: Academic Press.

Berlin, Brent and Paul Kay. 1969. *Basic Color Terms: Their Universality and Evolution*. Berkeley: University of California Press.

Bloor, David, 1983. *Wittgenstein: A Social Theory of Knowledge*. New York: Columbia University Press.

Bochenski, Innocentius M. 1956. The Problem of Universals. In *The Problem of Universals: A Symposium*, 35–54. Notre Dame: University of Notre Dame Press.

Bock, Philip K. 1969. *Modern Cultural Anthropology: An Introduction*. New York: Alfred A. Knopf.

Bové, Paul A. 1990. Discourse. In *Critical Terms for Literary Study*, ed. Frank Lentricchia and Thomas McLaughlin, 50–65. Chicago: The University of Chicago Press.

Bushnell, Horace. 1910 [1858]. *Nature and the Supernatural As Together Constituting the One System of God*. New York: Charles Scribner's Sons.

Caesar, Gaius Iulius. 1898. *De bello gallico*. Boston: Ginn and Company.

Campbell, Keith. 1965. Family Resemblance Predicates. *American Philosophical Quarterly* 2(3):238–244.

Casson, Ronald W. 1983. Schemata in Cognitive Anthropology. In *Annual Review of Anthropology*, Vol. 12, ed. Bernard J. Siegel et al., 429–462. Palo Alto: Annual Reviews Inc.

Chaney, Richard Paul. 1978. Polythematic Expansion: Remarks on Needham's Polythetic Classification. *Current Anthropology* 19(1):139–143.

Chaudhuri, Nirad C. 1979. *Hinduism: A Religion To Live By*. Oxford: Oxford University Press.

Christian, William A., Jr. 1981. *Person and God in a Spanish Valley*. Princeton: Princeton University Press.

Clifford, James. 1983. On Ethnographic Authority. *Representations* 1:118–146.

———. 1988. Comment on "Rhetoric and the Authority of Ethnography: 'Postmodernism' and the Social Reproduction of Texts" by P. Steven Sangren. *Current Anthropology* 29(3):425.

Clifford, James and George E. Marcus (eds.). 1986. *Writing Culture: The Poetics and Politics of Ethnography*. Berkeley: The University of California Press.

Cohen, Werner. 1964. What is Religion? An Analysis for Cross-Cultural Comparisons. *Journal of Christian Education* 7(2/3):116–138.

———. 1967. "Religion" in Non-Western Cultures? *American Anthropologist* 69(1):73–76.

Coleman, Linda and Paul Kay. 1981. Prototype Semantics: The English Word Lie. *Language* 57:26–44.

Comrie, Bernard. 1989. *Language Universals and Linguistic Typology*, second edition. Chicago: The University of Chicago Press.

Copi, Irving M. 1961. *Introduction to Logic*, second edition. New York: Macmillan.

Crapanzano, Vincent. 1980. *Tuhami: Portrait of a Moroccan*. Chicago: The University of Chicago Press.

Culler, Jonathan. 1982. *On Deconstruction: Theory and Criticism after Structuralism*. Ithaca, NY: Cornell University Press.

Darwin, Charles. 1859. *On the Origin of Species*. A Facsimile of the First Edition (1964). Cambridge, MA: Harvard University Press.

Davis, Natalie Zemon. 1974. Some Tasks and Themes in the Study of Popular Religion. In *The Pursuit of Holiness in Late Medieval and Renaissance Religion*, ed. Charles Trinkaus and Heiko A. Oberman, 307–336. Studies in Medieval and Reformation Thought 10. Leiden: E.J. Brill.

———. 1982. From 'Popular Religion' to Religious Cultures. *In Reformation Europe: A Guide to Research*, ed. Steven Ozment, 321–341. St. Louis: Center for Reformation Research.

Dawson, Lorne L. 1987. On References to the Transcendent in the Scientific Study of Religion: A Qualified Idealist Proposal. *Religion* 17:227–250.

———. 1988. *Reason, Freedom, and Religion: Closing the Gap Between the Humanistic and the Scientific Study of Religion*, Toronto Studies in Religion. New York: Peter Lang.

———. 1990. *Sui Generis* Phenomena and Disciplinary Axioms: Rethinking Pals' Proposal. *Religion* 20:38–51.

Despland, Michel. 1979. *La religion en occident: évolution des idées et du vécu*. Montreal: Éditions Fides.

Diels, Hermann. 1951. *Die Fragmente der Vorsokratiker*, vol.1. Berlin: Weidmannsche Verlagsbuchhandlung.

Dorsey, James Owen. 1884. *Omaha Sociology*. In Third Annual Report of the Bureau of Ethnology to the Secretary of the Smithsonian Institution, 1881:1882, 205–370. Washington: Government Printing Office.

Dreyfus, Hubert L. and Paul Rabinow. 1983. *Michel Foucault: Beyond Structuralism and Hermeneutics*, second edition. Chicago: The University of Chicago Press.

Dubisch, Jill. 1989 [1981]. You Are What You Eat: Religious Aspects of the Health Food Movement. In *Magic, Witchcraft, and Religion: An Anthropological Study of the Supernatural*, second edition, ed. Arthur C. Lehman and James E. Myers, 69–77. Mountain View, CA: Mayfield Publishing Company.

Du Bois, Cora. 1944. *The People of Alor: A Socio-Psychological Study of an East Indian Island*. Minneapolis: The University of Minnesota Press.

Dumont, Louis. 1980 [1966]. *Homo Hierarchicus: the Caste System and Its Implications*, completely revised English edition, trans. Mark Sainsbury, Louis Dumont, and Basia Gulati. Chicago: The University of Chicago Press.

———. 1982. A Modified View of Our Origins: The Christian Origins of Modern Individualism. *Religion* 12:1–27.

———. 1986. *Essays on Individualism: Modern Ideology in Anthropological Perspective*. Chicago: The University of Chicago Press.

Dumont, Louis and David F. Pocock. 1957. Village Studies. *Contributions to Indian Sociology* 1:23–41.

———. 1959. On the Different Aspects or Levels in Hinduism. *Contributions to Indian Sociology* 3:40–54.

Dunnell, Robert C. 1971. *Systematics in Prehistory*. New York: Macmillan.

Durkheim, Émile. 1965 [1912]. *The Elementary Forms of the Religious Life*, trans. Joseph Ward Swain. New York: The Free Press.

Eck, Diana L. 1985 [1981]. *Darśan: Seeing the Divine Image in India*, second revised and enlarged ed. Chambersburg, PA: Anima Books.

Edgerton, Franklin. 1942. Dominant Ideas in the Formation of Indian Culture. *Journal of the American Oriental Society* 62:151–156.

Edwards, Rem B. 1972. *Reason and Religion: An Introduction to the Philosophy of Religion*. New York: Harcourt Brace Janovich.

Ehnmark, Erland. 1935. *The Idea of God in Homer*, trans. O. von Feilitzen. Uppsala: Almqvist and Wiksells.

Ehrlich, Paul R. and Anne P. Ehrlich. 1967. The Phenetic Relationships of the Butterflies: I. Adult Taxonomy and the Nonspecificity Hypothesis. *Systematic Zoology* 16(4):301–317.

Eisenstadt, S.N. 1983. Transcendental Visions — Other Worldliness — and Its Transformations: Some More Comments on L. Dumont. *Religion* 13:1–17.

Eliade, Mircea. 1958. *Patterns in Comparative Religion*, trans. Rosemary Sheed. New York: World.

Evans-Pritchard, Edward E. 1954. *The Institutions of Primitive Society, A Series of Broadcast Talks*. Glencoe, IL: The Free Press.

———. 1956. *Nuer Religion*. Oxford: Oxford University Press.

Fillmore, Charles J. 1976. Frame Semantics and the Nature of Language. *Annals of the New York Academy of Sciences* 280:20–32.

Firth, Raymond. 1959. Problem and Assumption in an Anthropological Study of Religion. *Journal of the Royal Anthropological Institute* 89(Pt.II): 129–148.

Fitzgerald, Timothy. 1990. Hinduism and the 'World Religion' Fallacy. *Religion* 20:101–118.

Fodor, Jerry A. 1975. *The Language of Thought*. Cambridge, MA: Harvard University Press.

Foucault, Michel. 1972 [1969]. *The Archeology of Knowledge and the Discourse on Language*, trans. A.M. Sheridan Smith. New York: Harper and Row.

———. 1980. *Power/Knowledge: Selected Interviews and Other Writings, 1972–1977*, ed. Colin Gordon. New York: Pantheon Books.

Fowler, W. Warde. 1908. The Latin History of the Word "Religio." *Transactions of the Third International Congress for the History of Religions* 2:169–175.

Frankfort, H and H.A. Frankfort. 1946. Introduction. In *The Intellectual Adventures of Ancient Man: An Essay on Speculative Thought in the Ancient Near East*, ed. H. Frankfort and H. A. Frankfort et al., x–xx. Chicago: The University of Chicago Press.

Frazer, James George. 1890. *The Golden Bough: A Study in Magic and Religion*, 2 vols. London: Macmillan.

Freud, Sigmund. 1955 [1919]. The Uncanny. In *The Standard Edition of the Complete Psychological Works of Sigmund Freud*, Vol. 17, ed. James Stracher, trans. Alex Strachey, 219–252. London: Hogarth Press and the Institute for Psycho-Analysis.

———. 1957 [1910]. The Antithetical Meaning of Primal Words. In *The Standard Edition of the Complete Psychological Works of Sigmund Freud*, Vol. 11, ed. James Stracher, trans. Alan Tyson, 155–161. London: Hogarth Press and the Institute for Psycho-Analysis.

Gadamer, Hans Georg. 1975. *Truth and Method*, trans. William Glen-Doepel, ed. John Cumming and Garrett Barden. London: Sheed and Ward.

Geertz, Clifford. 1966. Religion as a Cultural System. In *Anthropological Approaches to the Study of Religion*, ed. Michael Banton, 1–46. Edinburgh: Tavistock Publications.

———. 1968. *Islam Observed: Religious Development in Morocco and Indonesia*. New Haven: Yale University Press.

———. 1973. *The Interpretation of Cultures*. New York: Basic Books.

Gillespie, Neal C. 1979. *Charles Darwin and the Problem of Creation*. Chicago: The University of Chicago Press.

Gilson, Étienne. 1938. *Reason and Revelation in the Middle Ages*. New York: Charles Scribner's Sons.

Gleitman, Lila R., Sharon Lee Armstrong and Henry Gleitman. 1983. On Doubting the Concept 'Concept'. In *New Trends in Conceptual Representation: Challenges to Piaget's Theory?*, ed. Ellin Kofsky Scholnick, 87–110. Hillsdale, NJ: Lawrence Erlbaum Associates.

Goodenough, Erwin R. 1965. *The Psychology of Religious Experience*. New York: Basic Books.

Goodenough, Ward H. 1970. *Description and Comparison in Cultural Anthropology*. Chicago: Aldine Publishing Company.

———. 1974. Toward an Anthropologically Useful Definition of Religion. In *Changing Perspectives in the Scientific Study of Religion*, ed. Alan W. Eister, 165–184. New York: John Wiley & Sons.

———. 1989. The Nature of Religion as a Human Phenomenon. *Institute on Religion in an Age of Science Newsletter* 37(3):6–7.

Goodman, Nelson. 1956. A World of Individuals. In *The Problem of Universals: A Symposium*, 15–31. Notre Dame, IN: University of Notre Dame Press.

———. 1972. *Problems and Projects*. Indianapolis: Bobbs-Merrill.

Goody, Jack. 1961. Religion and Ritual: The Definitional Problem. *British Journal of Sociology* 12:142–164.

Gould, Stephen Jay. 1983. *Hen's Teeth and Horse's Toes*. New York: W.W. Norton and Co.

———. 1986. Evolution and the Triumph of Homology, or Why History Matters. *American Scientist* 74:60–69.

———. 1988. The Heart of Terminology. *Natural History* 97(2):24–31.

Goulet, Jean-Guy. 1982. Religious Dualism among Athapaskan Catholics. *Canadian Journal of Anthropology* 3(1):1–18.

Greenberg, Joseph H. 1966. *Language Universals, with Special Reference to Feature Hierarchies*. The Hague: Mouton.

———. 1990. Two Approaches to Language Universals. In *On Language: Selected Writings of Joseph H. Greenberg*, ed. Keith Denning and Suzanne Kemmer, 702–720. Stanford, CA: Stanford University Press.

Guthrie, Stewart. 1980. A Cognitive Theory of Religion. *Current Anthropology* 21(2):181–203.

Hallowell, A. Irving. 1960. Ojibwa Ontology, Behavior, and World View. In *Culture in History: Essays in Honor of Paul Radin*, ed. Stanley Diamond, 19–64. New York: Columbia University Press.

Harris, Marvin. 1975. *Culture, People, Nature: An Introduction to General Anthropology*, second edition. New York: Thomas Y. Crowell.

Harvey, David. 1989. *The Condition of Postmodernity: An Enquiry into the Origins of Cultural Change*. Oxford: Basil Blackwell.

Hassan, Ihab Habib. 1985. The Culture of Postmodernism. *Theory, Culture and Society* 2(3):119–132.

Hayakawa, S.I. 1939. *Language in Thought and Action*. London: George Allen and Unwin.

Heidegger, Martin. 1962. *Being and Time*, trans. John Macquarrie and Edward Robinson. New York: Harper and Row.

Hennig, Willi. 1984. Phylogenetic Systematics. In *Conceptual Issues In Evolutionary Biology*, ed. Elliott Sober, 603–622. Cambridge, MA: The MIT Press.

Hertz, Robert. 1909. La Prééminence de la main droite: étude sur la polarité religieuse. *Revue philosophique* 68:553–580.

Hesse, Mary. 1980. *Revolutions and Reconstructions in the Philosophy of Science*. Bloomington, IN: Indiana University Press.

Hick, John. 1978. Foreward to *The Meaning and End of Religion* by Wilfred Cantwell Smith, ix–xviii. San Francisco: Harper & Row.

Hocart, Arthur Maurice. 1932a. Natural and Supernatural. *Man* 32:59–61.

———. 1932b. Letter: Natural and Supernatural. *Man* 32:246–247.

Hoenigswald, Henry M. and Linda F. Wiener. 1987. *Biological Metaphor and Cladistic Classification: An Interdisciplinary Perspective*. Philadelphia: The University of Pennsylvania Press.

Horton, Robin. 1960. A Definition of Religion, and Its Uses. *Journal of the Royal Anthropological Institute* 90 (Pt.2):201–226.

———. 1962. The Kalabari World View: An Outline and Interpretation. *Africa* 32(3):197–220.

———. 1964. Ritual Man in Africa. *Africa* 34(2):85–104.

———. 1967. African Traditional Thought and Western Science. *Africa* 37: 50–71, 155–187.

———. 1971. African Conversion. *Africa* 41(2):85–108.

———. 1973. Lévy-Bruhl, Durkheim and the Scientific Revolution. In *Modes of Thought: Essays on Thinking in Western and Non-Western Societies*, ed. Robin Horton and Ruth Finnegan, 249–305. London: Faber.

———. 1982. Tradition and Modernity Revisited. In *Rationality and Relativism*, ed. Martin Hollis and Steven Lukes, 201–260. Cambridge, MA: The MIT Press.

Hudson, W.D. 1974. *A Philosophical Approach to Religion*. New York: Barnes and Noble.

———. 1977. What Makes Religious Beliefs Religious? *Religious Studies* 13: 221–242.

Hull, David L. 1984. Contemporary Systematic Philosophies. In *Conceptual Issues in Evolutionary Biology: An Anthology*, ed. Elliott Sober, 567–602. Cambridge, MA: The MIT Press.

Hultkrantz, Åke. 1979 [1967]. *The Religions of the American Indians*, trans. Monica Setterwall. Berkeley: University of California Press.

———. 1983. The Concept of the Supernatural in Primal Religion. *History of Religions* 22(3):231–253.

Hunt, Robert C. 1989. Personal Communication.

Jackendoff, Ray. 1983. *Semantics and Cognition*. Cambridge, MA: The MIT Press.

Jaeger, Werner. 1947. *The Theology of the Early Greek Philosophers*. Oxford: The Clarendon Press.

James, William. 1929 [1902]. *The Varieties of Religious Experience: A Study in Human Nature*. New York: The Modern Library.

Janicki, Karol. 1990. *Toward Non-Essentialist Sociolinguistics*. Contributions to the

Sociology of Language 56. Berlin: Mouton de Gruyter.

Jaspers, Karl. 1945. *Vom Ursprung und Ziel der Geschichte.* Zurich.

Johnson, William Alexander. 1974. *The Search for Transcendence: A Theological Analysis of Non-Theological Attempts to Define Transcendence.* New York: Harper and Row.

Kaufman, Gordon D. 1965. Two Models of Transcendence: An Inquiry into the Problem of Theological Meaning. In *The Heritage of Christian Thought: Essays in Honor of Robert Lowry Calhoun,* ed. R.E. Cushman and E. Grislis, 182–196. New York: Harper and Row.

———. 1972. *God the Problem.* Cambridge, MA: Harvard University Press.

Kaufmann, Yehezkel. 1960 [1937–1956]. *The Religion of Israel: From Its Beginnings to the Babylonian Exile,* trans. and abridged by Moshe Greenberg. New York: Schocken Books.

Kenny, Anthony. 1973. *Wittgenstein.* Cambridge, MA: Harvard University Press.

Kerferd, G.B. 1967. Xenophanes of Colophon. In *The Encyclopedia of Philosophy,* Vol. 8, ed. Paul Edwards, 353–354. New York: Macmillan and the Free Press.

Kim, Choong Soon. 1990. The Role of the Non-Western Anthropologist Reconsidered: Illusion versus Reality. *Current Anthropology* 31(2): 196–201.

Kluckhohn, Clyde. 1953. Universal Categories of Culture. In *Anthropology Today: An Encyclopedic Inventory,* ed. Alfred L. Kroeber, 507–523. New York: Columbia University Press.

Kolakowski, Leszek. 1990. *Modernity on Endless Trial.* Chicago: The University of Chicago Press.

Kurtz, Stanley N. 1989. Personal Communication.

Lakoff, George. 1987. *Women, Fire, and Dangerous Things: What Categories Reveal about the Mind.* Chicago: The University of Chicago Press.

Lange, Friedrich Albert. 1876/1877 [1865]. *Geschichte des Materialismus und Kritik seiner Bedeutung in der Gegenwart,* 2 vols. Iserlohn: Verlag von J. Baedeker.

Lawson, E. Thomas and Robert N. McCauley. 1990. *Rethinking Religion: Connecting Cognition and Culture.* Cambridge: Cambridge University Press.

Leach, Edmund R. 1961. *Rethinking Anthropology.* London School of Economics Monographs on Social Anthropology, No. 22. London: The Athlone Press.

———. 1965 [1954]. *Political Systems of Highland Burma: A Study of Kachin Social Structure.* Boston: Beacon Press.

———. 1966. Virgin Birth. *Proceedings of the Royal Anthropological Institute* 39–49.

———. 1968. Introduction. In *Dialectic in Practical Religion,* ed. E.R. Leach, 1–6. Cambridge Papers in Social Anthropology. Cambridge: Cambridge University Press.

Lessa, William and Evon Z. Vogt. 1958. *Reader in Comparative Religion: An Anthropological Approach.* New York: Row, Peterson and Co.

Lévi-Strauss, Claude. 1961 [1955]. *Tristes Tropiques,* trans. John Russell. New York: Atheneum.

———. 1969 [1964]. *The Raw and the Cooked,* trans. John and Doreen Weightman. New York: Harper and Row.

Lévy-Bruhl, Lucien. 1936 [1931]. *Primitives and the Supernatural,* trans. Lilian A. Clare. London: Allen and Unwin.

Lienhardt, Godfrey. 1961. *Divinity and Experience: The Religion of the Dinka.* Oxford: The Clarendon Press.

Lloyd, G.E.R. 1966. *Polarity and Analogy: Two Types of Argumentation in Early Greek Thought.* Cambridge: Cambridge University Press.

Lockhart, W.R. and P.A. Hartman, 1963. Formation of Monothetic Groups in Quantitative Bacterial Taxonomy. *Journal of Bacteriology* 85:68–77.

Lounsbury, Floyd G. 1964. A Formal Account of the Crow- and Omaha-type Kinship Terminologies. In *Explorations in Cultural Anthropology: Essays in Honor of George Peter Murdock,* ed. Ward H. Goodenough, 351–393. New York: McGraw Hill.

Lubac, Henri de. 1934. Remarques sur l'histoire du mot "Surnaturel." *Nouvelle Revue Théologique* 61:225–249.

——. 1946. *Le surnaturel: études historiques.* Paris: Aubier, Éditions Montaigne.

MacIntyre, Alasdair. 1970 [1964]. Is Understanding Religion Compatible with Believing? In *Rationality*, ed. Bryan R. Wilson, 62–77. Oxford: Basil Blackwell.

Malinowski, Bronislaw. 1929. *The Sexual Life of Savages.* London: G. Routledge and Sons.

Mandelbaum, David G. 1966. Transcendental and Pragmatic Aspects of Religion. *American Anthropologist* 68(5):1174–1191.

Maranda, Elli Kongas. 1971. IV. 'A Tree Grows'. Transformations of a Riddle Metaphor. In *Structural Models in Folklore and Transformational Essays*, by Elli Kongas Maranda and Pierre Maranda, 116–139. *Approaches to Semiotics*, Vol. 10, ed. Thomas A. Sebok. The Hague: Mouton.

Marcus, George E. and Michael M.J. Fischer. 1986. *Anthropology as Cultural Critique: An Experimental Moment in the Human Sciences.* Chicago: The University of Chicago Press.

Marett, Robert Ranulph. 1909. *The Threshold of Religion*, London: Methuen and Co.

Markman, Ellen M. 1989. *Categorization and Naming in Children: Problems of Induction.* Cambridge, MA: The MIT Press.

Marmorstein, Arthur. 1968 [1937]. *The Old Rabbinic Doctrine of God*, Vol. 2 (*Essays in Anthropomorphism*). London: H. Milford.

Marriott, McKim. 1955. Little Communities in an Indigenous Civilization. In *Village India: Studies in the Little Community*, ed. McKim Marriott, 171–222. Chicago: The University of Chicago Press.

Maybury-Lewis, David. 1989. Introduction: The Quest for Harmony. In *The Attraction of Opposites: Thought and Society in the Dualistic Mode*, ed. David Maybury-Lewis and Uri Almagor, 1–17. Ann Arbor: The University of Michigan Press.

Mayr, Ernst. 1969. *Principles of Systematic Zoology.* New York: McGraw Hill.

——. 1984. Biological Classification: Toward a Synthesis of Opposing Methodologies. In *Conceptual Issues in Evolutionary Biology: An Anthology*, ed. Elliott Sober, 646–662. Cambridge, MA: The MIT Press.

McBrearty, Sally A. 1991. Personal Communication.

McKinney, John C. 1966. *Constructive Typology and Social Theory.* New York: Appleton-Century-Crofts.

McLain, F. Michael. 1969. On Theological Models. *Harvard Theological Review* 62:155–87

Mensching, Gustav. 1964. Folk and Universal Religion. In *Religion, Culture and Society*, ed. Louis Schneider, 254–255. New York: Wiley.

Minsky, Marvin. 1975. A Framework for Representing Knowledge. In *The Psychology of Computer Vision*, ed. Patrick Henry Winston, 211–277.New York: McGraw Hill.

Monk, Ray. 1990. *Ludwig Wittgenstein: The Duty of Genius.* New York: The Free Press.

Morgan, John. 1977. Religion and Culture as Meaning Systems: A Dialogue between Geertz and Tillich. *The Journal of Religion* 57(4):363–375.

Munson, Henry Jr. 1986. Geertz on Religion: The Theory and the Practice. *Religion* 16:19–32.

Murdock, George P. 1945. The Common Denominator of Cultures. In *The Science of Man in the World Crisis*, ed. Ralph Linton, 123–141. New York: Columbia University Press.

Murray, David W. 1989. Personal Communication.

Nadel, S.F. 1954. *Nupe Religion.* London: Routledge and Kegan Paul.

Needham, Rodney. 1971. Remarks on the Analysis of Kinship and Marriage. In *Rethinking Kinship and Marriage*, ed. Rodney Needham, 1–34. London: Tavistock Publications.

———. 1972. *Belief, Language, and Experience.* Oxford: Basil Blackwell and Mott; Chicago: The University of Chicago Press.
———. 1975. Polythetic Classification: Convergence and Consequences. *Man* 10 (3):349–369.
———. 1980. *Reconnaissances.* Toronto: University of Toronto Press.
———. 1981. *Circumstantial Deliveries.* Berkeley: University of California Press.
———. 1983. *Against the Tranquility of Axioms.* Berkeley: University of California Press.
———. 1985. *Exemplars.* Berkeley: University of California Press.
———. 1986. Personal Communication.
Needham, Rodney (ed.). 1973. *Right and Left: Essays on Dual Symbolic Classification.* Chicago: The University of Chicago Press.
Obeyesekere, Gananath. 1981. *Medusa's Hair: An Essay on Personal Symbols and Religious Experience.* Chicago: The University of Chicago Press.
O'Neil, Mary R. 1986. From 'Popular' to 'Local' Religion: Issues in Early Modern European Religious History: Reviews of *Religion in Sixteenth Century Spain* by William Christian, Jr. and *Apparitions in Late Medieval and Renaissance Spain* by William Christian, Jr. *Religious Studies Review* 12(3/4):222–226.
Oxford Latin Dictionary. 1968–1982. Oxford: The Clarendon Press.
Pagels, Elaine H. 1979. *The Gnostic Gospels: A New Account of the Origins of Christianity.* New York: Random House.
Pals, Daniel L. 1986. Reductionism and Belief: An Appraisal of Recent Attacks on the Doctrine of Irreducible Religion. *Journal of Religion* 66:18–36.
———. 1987. Is Religion a Sui Generis Phenomenon? *Journal of the American Academy of Religion* 55:259–282.
———. 1990a. Autonomy, Legitimacy, and the Study of Religion. *Religion* 20: 1–16.
———. 1990b. Autonomy Revisited: A Rejoinder to Its Critics. *Religion* 20: 30–37.
Parsons, Talcott. 1937. *The Structure of Social Action.* New York: McGraw Hill.
———. 1963. Introduction to *The Sociology of Religion* by Max Weber, xix–lxvii. Boston: Beacon Press.
Penner, Hans H. 1989. *Impasse and Resolution: A Critique of the Study of Religion.* Toronto Studies in Religion Vol 8. New York: Peter Lang.
Poole, Fitz John Porter. 1986. Metaphors and Maps: Towards Comparison in the Anthropology of Religion. *Journal of the American Academy of Religion* 54(3):411–457.
Popper, Karl R. 1957. *The Poverty of Historicism.* Boston: The Beacon Press.
———. 1962. *Conjectures and Refutations: The Growth of Scientific Knowledge.* New York: Basic Books.
Preus, J. Samuel. 1987. *Explaining Religion: Criticism and Theory from Bodin to Freud.* New Haven: Yale University Press.
Price, Henry Habberley. 1969a [1953]. *Thinking and Experience,* second edition. London: Hutchinson.
———. 1969b. *Belief.* London: Allen and Unwin.
Radin, Paul. 1937. *Primitive Religion: Its Nature and Origin.* New York: Dover.
———. 1960 [1953]. *The World of Primitive Man.* New York: Grove Press.
———. 1970. Introduction to the Torchbook Edition of *Religion in Primitive Culture* by Edward Burnett Tylor, ix–xvii. Gloucester, MA: Peter Smith.
Redfield, Robert. 1941. *The Folk Culture of Yucatan.* Chicago: The University of Chicago Press.
———. 1955. *The Little Community: Viewpoints for the Study of a Human Whole.* Uppsala: Almqvist and Wiksells; Chicago: The University of Chicago Press.
Redfield, Robert and Alfonso Villa Rojas. 1934. *Chan Kom: A Maya Village.* Washington: The Carnegie Institution.
Reese, William A. 1980. *Dictionary of Philosophy and Religion: Eastern and Western Thought.* Atlantic Highlands, NJ: Humanities Press.
Ricoeur, Paul. 1981. *Hermeneutics and the Human Sciences, Essays on Language, Action and Interpretation,* ed., trans, and introduced by John B. Thompson. Cambridge: Cambridge University Press.

Rivière, Peter. 1971. Marriage: A Reassessment. In *Rethinking Kinship and Marriage*, ed. Rodney Needham, 57–74. London: Tavistock Publications.

Rorty, Richard. 1979. *Philosophy and the Mirror of Nature*. Princeton: Princeton University Press.

———. 1989. *Contingency, Irony, and Solidarity*. Cambridge: Cambridge University Press.

———. 1991a. *Objectivity, Relativism, and Truth*, Philosophical Papers Vol.1. Cambridge: Cambridge University Press.

———. 1991b. *Essays on Heidegger and Others*, Philosophical Papers Vol. 2. Cambridge: Cambridge University Press.

Rosch, Eleanor. 1975. Universals and Cultural Specifics in Human Categorization. In *Cross-Cultural Perspectives on Learning*, ed. Richard W. Brislin, Stephen Bochner, and. Walter J. Lonner, 177–206. New York: John Wiley & Sons.

———. 1978. Principles of Categorization. In *Cognition and Catgorization*, ed. Eleanor Rosch and Barbara B. Lloyd, 27–48. Hillsdale, NJ.: Lawrence Erlbaum Associates.

Rosch, Eleanor and Carolyn B. Mervis. 1975. Family Resemblances: Studies in the Internal Structure of Categories. *Cognitive Psychology* 7 (4): 573–605.

Rosch, Eleanor and Carolyn Mervis, Wayne Gray, David Johnson, and Penny Boyes-Braem. 1976. Basic Objects and Natural Categories. *Cognitive Psychology* 8:382–439.

Russell, Bertrand. 1912. *The Problems of Philosophy*. London: Galaxy Book.

Sahlins, Marshall. 1976a. *Culture and Practical Reason*. Chicago: The University of Chicago Press.

———. 1976b. *The Use and Abuse of Biology: An Anthropological Critique of Sociobiology*. Ann Arbor: The University of Michigan Press.

Said, Edward W. 1978. *Orientalism*. New York: Vintage Books.

Saler, Benson. 1974. Review of *Belief, Language, and Experience* by Rodney Needham. *American Anthropologist* 76:861–866.

———. 1977. Supernatural as a Western Category. *Ethos* 5(1):31–53.

———. 1980. Comments on "A Cognitive Theory of Religion" by Stewart Guthrie. *Current Anthropology* 21(2):197.

———. 1987. *Religio* and the Definition of Religion. *Cultural Anthropology* 2(3):395–399.

———. 1988. Los Wayú (Guajiro). In *Los aborígenes de Venezuela*, Vol. 3, ed. Walter Coppens, Bernarda Escalante, and Jacques Lizot, 25–145. Caracas: Fundación La Salle de Ciencias Naturales/Monte Avila Editores.

Saliba, John A. 1976. Religion and the Anthropologists, 1960–1976, Pt.1. *Anthropologica* 18(2):179–213.

Sapir, Edward. 1949 [1929]. The Status of Linguistics as a Science. In *Selected Writings of Edward Sapir in Language, Culture and Personality*, ed. David G. Mandelbaum, 160–166. Berkeley: University of California Press.

Scheffler, Harold W. and Floyd G. Lounsbury. 1971. *A Study in Structural Semantics: The Siriono Kinship System*. Englewood Cliffs, NJ: Prentice–Hall.

Schleiermacher, Friedrich. 1958 [1799]. *On Religion: Speeches to its Cultured Despisers*, trans. John Oman. New York: Harper and Row.

Schneider, David. 1984. *A Critique of the Study of Kinship*. Ann Arbor: University of Michigan Press.

Schwartz, Benjamin I. 1975. The Age of Transcendence. *Daedalus*, 104(2): 1–7.

Seeger, Anthony. 1989. Fuzzy Thinking or Fuzzy Sets? In *The Attraction of Opposites: Thought and Society in the Dualistic Mode*, ed. David Maybury-Lewis and Uri Almagor, 191–208. Ann Arbor: The University of Michigan Press.

Segal, Robert A. 1983. In Defense of Reductionism. *Journal of the American Academy of Religion* 51:97–124.

Segal, Robert A. and Donald Wiebe. 1989. Axioms and Dogmas in the Study of Religion. *Journal of the American Academy of Religion* 57(3):591–605.

Shore, Bradd. 1983. Anthropology: A Quaint Science. *American Anthropologist* 85(4):919–929.

Simpson, George Gaylord. 1961. *Principles of Animal Taxonomy.* New York: Columbia University Press.

Skorupski, John. 1976. *Symbol and Theory: A Philosophical Study of Religion in Social Anthropology.* Cambridge: Cambridge University Press.

Smith, Brian K. 1987. Exorcising the Transcendent: Strategies for Defining Hinduism and Religion. *History of Religions* 27(1):32–55.

Smith, Edward E. and Douglas L. Medin. 1981. *Categories and Concepts.* Cambridge, MA: Harvard University Press.

Smith, Jonathan Z. 1982 [1980]. Fences and Neighbors: Some Contours of Early Judaism. In *Imagining Religion: From Babylon to Jonestown,* by J.Z. Smith, 1–18. Chicago: The University of Chicago Press.

Smith, Morton. 1968. Historical Method in the Study of Religion. In *On Method in the History of Religions,* ed. James S. Helfer Middletown: Wesleyan University Press.

Smith, Wilfred Cantwell. 1963 [1962]. *The Meaning and End of Religion.* New York: The Macmillan Co.

——. 1979. *Faith and Belief.* Princeton: Princeton University Press.

——. 1984. Philosophia, as One of the Religious Traditions of Humankind: The Greek Legacy in Western Civilization, Viewed by a Comparativist. In *Différences, valeurs, hiérarchie: textes offerts à Louis Dumont,* ed. Jean-Claude Galey, 253–279. Paris: Éditions de l'École des Hautes Études en Sciences Sociales.

——. 1988. Transcendence. *Harvard Divinity Bulletin* 18(3):10–15.

Sneath, Peter H.A. and Robert A. Sokal. 1973. *Numerical Taxonomy: The Principles and Practices of Numerical Classification.* San Francisco: W. H. Freeman and Company.

Sokal, Robert R. and Peter H. A. Sneath. 1963. *Principles of Numerical Taxonomy.* San Francisco: W. H. Freeman and Company.

Southwold, Martin. 1978. Buddhism and the Definition of Religion. *Man* 13: 362–379.

Spiro, Melford E. 1961. Social Systems, Personality, and Functional Analysis. In *Studying Personality Cross-Culturally,* ed. Bert Kaplan, 93–127. Evanston: Row, Peterson and Company.

——. 1966. Religion: Problems of Definition and Explanation. In *Anthropological Approaches to the Study of Religion,* ed. Michael Banton, 85–126. London: Tavistock Publications.

——. 1968. Virgin Birth, Parthenogenesis and Physiological Paternity: An Essay in Cultural Interpretation. *Man* (n.s.) 3:242–261.

——. 1978 [1967, 1974]. *Burmese Supernaturalism: A Study in the Explanation and Reduction of Suffering,* expanded edition. Philadelphia: Ishi Publications.

——. 1982 [1970]. *Buddhism and Society: A Great Tradition in Its Burmese Vicissitudes,* second, expanded edition. Berkeley: University of California Press.

——. 1987. Personal Communication.

Staal, Frits. 1988. *Universals: Studies in Indian Logic and Linguistics.* Chicago: The University of Chicago Press.

Staniland, Hilary. 1972. *Universals.* Garden City: Doubleday & Co.

Stevenson, Charles. 1944. *Ethics and Language.* New Haven: Yale University Press.

Strawson, P.F. 1963. *Individuals: An Essay in Descriptive Metaphysics.* New York: Doubleday.

Tambiah, Stanley J. 1970. *Buddhism and the Spirit Cults in North-east Thailand.* Cambridge: Cambridge University Press.

Tedlock, Barbara. 1983. A Phenomenological Approach to Religious Change in Highland Gautemala. In *Heritage of Conquest: Thirty Years Later,* ed. Carl Kendall and John Hawkins, 235–246. Albuquerque: University of New Mexico Press.

Temple, William. 1934. *Nature, Man and God.* London: Macmillan.

Tertullianus, Quintus Septimius Florens. 1954 [c.206]. *De carne Christi. Tertulliani Opera* II, *Corpus Christianorum.* Rome: Typographi Brepols.

Tillich, Paul. 1953. *Systematic Theology*, Vol. 1. Chicago: The University of Chicago Press.
———. 1957. *Dynamics of Faith*. New York: Harper and Row.
———. 1963. *Christianity and the Encounter of the World Religions*. New York: Columbia University Press.
———. 1969. *What Is Religion?*, ed. James Luther Adams. New York: Harper and Row.
Towler, Robert. 1974. *Homo Religiosus: Sociological Problems in the Study of Religion*. London: Constable.
Turner, Victor. 1962. *Chihamba, the White Spirit*. Rhodes-Livingstone Papers 33. Manchester: University of Manchester Press.
Tylor, Edward B. 1871. *Primitive Culture*, 2 vols. London: John Murray.
———. 1970 [1958]. *Religion in Primitive Culture* (chapts. 11–29 of Tylor 1871). Gloucester, MA: Peter Smith.
Vrijhof, Pieter H. 1979. Introduction; Conclusion. In *Official and Popular Religion: Analysis of a Theme for Religious Studies*, ed. Pieter Vrijhof and Jacques Waardenburg, 1–7; 668–699. Religion and Society 19. The Hague: Mouton.
Waghorne, Joanne Punzo and Norman Cutler (eds.) in association with Vasudha Narayanan. 1985. *Gods of Flesh/Gods of Stone: The Embodiment of Divinity in India*. Chambersburg, PA: Anima Publications.
Wagner, Roy. 1981 [1975]. *The Invention of Culture*, revised and expanded edition. Chicago: The University of Chicago Press.
Wallace, Anthony F.C. 1966. *Religion: An Anthropological View*. New York: Random House.
Watanabe, Satosi. 1969. *Knowing and Guessing: A Quantitative Study of Inference and Information*. New York: John Wiley and Sons.
Wax, Murray L. 1984. *Religion* as Universal: Tribulations of an Anthropological Enterprise. *Zygon* 19(1):5–20.
Weber, Max. 1963 [1922]. *The Sociology of Religion*, trans. Ephraim Fischoff. Boston: Beacon Press.
Wiebe, Donald. 1981. *Religion and Truth: Toward an Alternative Paradigm for the Study of Religion*. The Hague: Mouton.
———. 1983. Theory in the Study of Religion. *Religion* 13:283–309.
———. 1984. Beyond the Sceptic and the Devotee: Reductionism in the Scientific Study of Religion. *Journal of the American Academy of Religion* 52:156–165.
———. 1988. Postulations for Safeguarding Preconceptions: The Case of the Scientific Religionist. *Religion* 18:11–19.
———. 1990. Disciplinary Axioms, Boundary Conditions and the Academic Study of Religion: Comments on Pals and Dawson. *Religion* 20:17–29.
Wilamowitz-Möllendorff, Ulrich von. 1956 [1931]. *Der Glaube der Hellenen*, Vol. 1. Basel: Benno Schwabe and Co.
Williams, Leonard, David Hurst Thomas and Robert Bettinger. 1973. Notions to Numbers: Great Basin Settlements as Polythetic Sets. In *Research and Theory in Current Archeology*, ed. Charles L. Redman, 215–237. New York: John Wiley and Sons.
Wilt, Henry Toomey. 1954. *Religio: A Semantic Study of the Pre-Christian Use of the Terms Religio and Religiosus*. Unpublished Ph.D dissertation, Columbia University (New York) and University Microfilms (Ann Arbor, Michigan).
Winch, Peter. 1958. *The Idea of a Social Science and its Relation to Philosophy*. London: Routledge and Kegan Paul.
———. 1970 [1964]. Understanding a Primitive Society. In *Rationality*, ed. Bryan R. Wilson, 78–111. Oxford: Basil Blackwell.
Wissler, Clark. 1923. *Man and Culture*. New York: Thomas Y. Crowell.
Wittgenstein, Ludwig. 1958 [1953]. *Philosophical Investigations*, third edition, trans. G. E. M. Anscombe. New York: Macmillan.
———. 1966 [1938]. Lectures on Religious Belief. In *Lectures and Conversations on Aesthetics, Psychology, and Religious Belief*, ed. Cyril Barrett, 53–72. Oxford: Basil Blackwell.

——. 1969 [1958]. *The Blue and Brown Books*. Oxford: Basil Blackwell.
——. 1974. *Philosophical Grammar*, trans. Anthony Kenny, ed. Rush Rhees. Berkeley: University of California Press.
——. 1981 [1967]. *Zettel*, second edition, trans. G.E.M. Anscombe, ed. G.E.M. Anscombe and G.H. von Wright. Oxford: Basil Blackwell.
Wolterstorff, Nicholas. 1970. *On Universals: An Essay in Ontology*. Chicago: The University of Chicago Press.
Woozley, A.D. 1967. Universals. In *The Encyclopedia of Philosophy*, ed. Paul Edwards, Vol. 8, 194–206. New York: Macmillan and Free Press.
Wyschograd, Edith. 1981. The Civilizational Perspective in Comparative Studies in Transcendence. In *Transcendence and the Sacred*, ed. Alan M. Olson and Leroy S. Rauner, 58–79. Notre Dame, IN: University of Notre Dame Press.
Yinger, J. Milton. 1970. *The Scientific Study of Religion*. New York: Macmillan.
Zuckerlandl, Emile. 1968 [1965]. The Evolution of Hemoglobin. In *The Molecular Basis of Life: An Introduction to Molecular Biology*, 316–324. San Francisco: W. H. Freeman and Company.

INDEX

Aaron, Richard I., 152; and problem of universals, 153
Abel, Karl, 66–67
Aberle, David F., and classification, 193
Absolute universals, 155
Ad hoc definitions, 81–84; initial development of, 80
Adams, James Luther, 106
Agent-act model, 56
Aguaruna Jívaro (Peru), 187–88
Almagor, Uri, 10, 16
Alor (Indonesia), 231
Alphas, and nominalist approach, 162–63
Alston, William P., 212, 213, 214, 219; and family likeness, 170–71; as precedent for prototype theory, 215; and religion-making characteristics, 170–71; and Southwold, 172; and theism, 173
Ambiguity, in definitions, 204; and monothetic definitions, 87–88
Analog scales, 13
Analogical approach, advantages of, 20
Analogical processes, and Lévi-Strauss, 15
Analogies, 175–76; establishment of, 260
Analogy, 215; and structuralism, 15
Analytical categories, conceptualization of, 263–64
Analytical concepts, use of, 125
Animatism, 126
Animism, 36, 37, 89–91, 92, 126
Anthropological research, and ethnocentrism, 228–31; and goal of, 229–30
Anthropologists, and attitudes toward religious persons, 221–22; and awareness of religious differences, 210; career concerns of, 230–31; and ethnographic research, 260; and immanence, 6, 234–40; and the natives' point of view, 241–42; and shifting allegiances, 239–40; transcendence of, 245
Anthropology, as category, 8; as comparative science, 262–63; and concept of the transcendent, 53–55; and development of community studies, 34; discipline of, and discourse, 238; and effect on analyses by transcendence, 61–62; as Euro-

pean science par excellence, 229–30; formal training in, and ethnocentrism, 228; major concern of, 4; and paradox, 232–33; and pheneticists' methods, 189–93; and polythetic grouping, 189–93; and taxonomic methods, 190; and Western-derived categories, 10
Anthropomorphic Gods, 60
Anthropomorphism, 131–37, 150; physical side of, 178–79
Anthropopsychism, 133, 134
Anti-nominalist theory, 11
Ape, as category, 181–82; and cladistics, 181–82
Apostolic creed and Christianity, 42
Apotropaic Buddhism, 36
Appel, George N., and digital and non-digital modalities, 12
Appropriation, 146
Aranyakas, 43
Archeologists, and polythetic classification, 179
Argyll, The Duke of, on anthropomorphism and anthropopsychism, 133–34; and Mind, 47
Aristotle, 162; objections to, 203; and religion, 223; and universals, 152, 153, 154; and Xenophanes, 132
Aristotelian logic, 203
Arius, 172*n*
Armstrong, Sharon Lee, Lila R. Gleitman, and Henry Gleitman, 202
Artha (profit or worldly success), 48
Asad, Talal, 89, 100, 104, 147, 234; and critical evaluation of Geertz, 94–102; criticisms of, 97–102; evaluation of, 96–97; and faith, 97; and poststructuralist views, 102; and religious symbols, 101; and use of term power, 99
Association of Third World Anthropologists, goal of, 8
Athapascan faith, 37
Atran, Scott, 187
Augurs, 66
Augustine, St., 96
Autonomy, idea of, 2–3
Axial age, 50–51
Aztec pantheon, 29

Bambrough, J. Renford, and alphas, 162–63; and exposition of

Wittgenstein, 160–64; and Wittgenstein, 154
Barth, Karl, 55
Basic-level categorization, 187
Beattie, John H. M., and modified symbolist approach, 144–45; and use of term religion, 143
Being, human problems of, and Goodenough, 116
Being and Time, 250
Belief, 130–31; conceptualization of, 91
Belief, Language, and Experience, 92
Beliefs, and behavior, 139; and intellectualist program, 138; symbolic analysis of, 139
Bell, Catherine, and popular religion, 40
Bellah, Robert N., 218
Bellah, Robert N. and Phillip E. Hammond, 218
Benveniste, Émile, and etymology of religio, 65; and Freud, 66–67; and meaning of superstitio, 65–66, 67; and Ricoeur, 247
Berkeley, George, and universals, 152
Berlin, Brent, and folk biological classifications, 186–89
Berlin, Brent, Dennis E. Breedlove, and Peter H. Raven, and folk biological classification, 186–88
Berlin, Brent, and Paul Kay, 205
Bettinger, Robert, 179
Bible, 42, 56, 111; dualism found in, 52
Biological sciences and polythetic grouping, 167–69
Bloor, David, and words, meaning of, 237
Bochenski, Innocentius M., and universals, 151
Bock, Philip K., criticisms of, 29; and omission of religion as a separate category, 28–29
Boundaries, 78; question of, 126; see also Ch. 6
Bové, Paul A., 101, 124; and discourse, 237, 238; on poststructuralist discourse, 234–35; and power, conceptualization of, 99–100
Boyle, The Hon Robert, and theism, 222
Brahmanas, 43
Brahmanical authority, and relationship to Vedas, 45
Brahmins, and the Vedas, 44
Bricoleur, 134
Bruner, Jerome, S., 254
Brunner, H. Émile, 55

Buddhism, 31, 33, 35–36, 43, 49, 131, 200; and the axial age, 51; in Burma, 36; and doctrine of karma, 37; and theism, 173, 213; view of, by Western scholars, 38–39
Buddhism and Society, 36
Buddhists, 45
Bultmann, Rudolf Karl, 55
Burma, religious practices in, 36–37, 38; religious traditions in, 36
Burmese Supernaturalism, 138
Bushnell, Horace, and the supernatural, 58

Caesar, Gaius Julius, and use of religio, 67
Calvin, John, 110
Campbell, George Douglas, see Argyll, The Duke of
Campbell, Keith, 220; and Bambrough, 164; and criticism of family resemblance approach, 164–67; and Wittgenstein, 164–65
Canon, characteristics of, 47; discussion of, 45–46
Canonical authority approach, and B.K. Smith, 44
Canonical reflexivity, 46–47
Casson, Ronald W., and stereotypic representation, 207
Caste system, 45, 82, 84; and Hinduism, 43
Categories, analytical, and relationship to folk categories, 1; application of, 254; and class inclusion hierarchies, 254–55; as discriminatory devices, 258; extreme essentialist, 253–54; importance of, 1; mutually exclusive, 254–55, 256; natural kind, 255–56; non-Western, and family resemblance conceptualization, 263–64; purpose of, 254; and typicality conditions, 258–59; unbounded analytical, 253, 254–63; as unsuitable models for religion, 256–57
Categorization, 200–2; and core types, 205; and focal points, 205; and focal types, 205; possibilities in, 205; and primary types, 205
Categorizing, analogical approach to, 20; digital approach to, 20
Category, 25; etymology of, 201; natural kind, 259
Cathected goals, 245
Chaney, Richard Paul, and family resemblance and polythetic classification compared, 170; and multifactorial approaches, 159

Chase, Stuart, 203
Chaudhuri, Nirad C., criticism of, 48; and main object of Hinduism, 47–48; and notion of salvation, 47; and polythesis, 195; and view of Hinduism, 49; natural kind, 259
Cherbury, Edward, Lord Herbert of, 96
Christ, 31, 110; as religious symbol, 110
Christian faith, object of, 30–31
Christianity, 42, 47, 49, 72, 199, 200, 214; and diversity in cumulative traditions, 42–43; and dualistic approach, 39; and the exemplar view, 216; and interaction with Mayan tradition, 37–38; and nature of Christ, 213; basic premises of, 42; prototypicality of, 173, 217–18; as religion prototype, 208; and religious symbols, 110–11; and theism, 223
Christmas tree, 29; see also syncretism
Cicero, Marcus Tullius, and etymology of religio, 65
Circumcision in early Judaism, 180
Clades, 180, 182
Cladism, see cladistics
Cladistics, 177, 179, 181–82; problem, 181–82
Clarity in definitions, 204, 206
Classification, paradigmatic, 194; and similarities, 191; taxonomic, 194
Classifications, in the biological sciences, 185–86; folk biological, 186–89; and utilitarian theorizing, 187–88; 189
Classifying, as value-laden activity, 188
Clement of Alexandria, and Xenophanes, 132
Clifford, James, 147–48; and postmodernism, 5
Clifford, James and George E. Marcus, 42, 147
Cognitive economy, and monothetic definitions, 206
Cognitive processing and prototypicality, 207
Cohen, Werner, 8
Coleman, Linda and Paul Kay, 211; on necessity and sufficiency, 220; and prototype semantics, 204–5; and prototype theory, 223
Communal symbolic idioms, 112
Communion-manipulation polarity, 129, 130
Communism, 200; anthropological conceptualization of, 19–21; and essentialist categories, 253; as religion, 19–20, 223, 216, 253
Communists, 46

Community study approach, 34
Comparative analytic categories, 82
Comrie, Bernard, 155
Comte, Auguste, 89
Conceptual polarity, and Leach, 38–39
Conceptualism, 154; and problem of universals, 152
Conceptualization of religion: Alston and religion-making characteristics, 218, 219; family resemblance, 218; polythetic, 218; solution to problem of, 24–25; Southwold and attributes, 218; more recent strategy for, 24; see also Chs. 5 and 6
Conceptualizations, and essentialist theory, 21; multiple existence of, 21
Concept-words, 197–98
Confucianism, and the axial age, 51
Copi, Irving M., 73, 79
Corpus Inscriptionum, 65
Counter-Reformation, and conceptions of religion, 22
Crapanzano, Vincent, 234
Culler, Jonathan, 17
Cultural analogues, and study of religion, 72
Cultural anthropologists, orientations of, 2; contrasted to religious studies colleagues, 3–4; and grounded divisions of nature, 166–67
Cultural anthropology, and criteria for terms and concepts, 119; as interpretive discipline, 4–5
Cultural phenomena, and interpretivists, 148
Cultural studies, and use of biological models and metaphors, 178–96
Cultural unity and popular religion, 40
Cultural universals, 155; see also universals
Culture, analysis of, 114; as category, 8, 42; change in, and structuralism, 17; and human nature, 257; and imposition of human laws, 15–16
Cultus, 22; and theistic belief, 22
Cumulative tradition, as major construct, 32

Darwin, Charles, 182
Darwinian theory, 133; and classification, 175
Das Unheimliche, ('The Uncanny'), 67
Davis, Natalie Zemon, and construct religious cultures, 40; and popular religion, 39–40
Dawson, Lorne L., 2, 85
De Bello Gallico, 67
Death, and Buddhist practice, 39

Deconstruction, and structuralism, 17
Default assignments, and schematization of religion, 224–25; and unmarkedness, 224
Defined predicates and border problems, 165
Definitional controversies, 76, 77
Definiendum, 79
Definiens, 79
Definitional approaches in the social sciences, and Jack Goody, 125–26
Definitional tasks, productive approaches to, 79
Definitions: *ad hoc*, 81–84; and controversies, 77; essential, 77; essentialist, 80–81, 120; implicit/explicit, 84–85; monothetic, 79–81, 85, 87–121; ostensive, 77–78, 79; precision and clarity of, 203–4, 206; real, 77; universalist, 95–96; vagueness and ambiguity of, 204; and vocabulary required, 78–81
Deity, transcendence of, 62; and Western theologians, 240; *see also* Transcendence
Dene-tha, 37, 38
Description and comparison in Cultural Anthropology, 119
Despland, Michel, 8
Determinacy, and modernism, 5
Dharma, 43, 48, and non-Hindu societies, 264; and polythesis, 195
Dialectic of distanciation, 247
Digital, *see* digitizing
Digitize, *see* digitizing
Digitism, and homology, 177
Digitizing, 12–13; and author's extended use of term, 12; and essentialist definitions, 120; and monothetic definitions, 87; moral overtones of, 13; questions about, 16; and religious practices, 41; and structuralism, 13–15
Dilthey, Wilhelm, and interpretivists, 146; and opposition between explanation and interpretation, 4; and the Romantics, 249
Dinka, 123
Discourse, 146–47, 234–35; linguistics of, 248; power of, 235; usages of, 100; ways of realizing, 248
Distanciation, 235, 245–54; and autonomy of the text, 248–49; disapproval of, 251; and ethnocentrism, 261; and exteriorization of discourse, 248; and field notes, 252, 253; hermeneutical function of, 247, 249–51; and partici-

patory belonging, 25; promotion of, 260; of the real world from itself, 250; *see also* Ricoeur
Divine revelation, interpretation of, 57
Dorsey, James Owen, and synchronic variability, 33
Dreyfus, Hubert L. and Paul Rabinow, 99
Dualism, conceptual content of, 13; elite/non-elite, 40; Great Tradition/Little Tradition, 40; justification for, 16; and religious diversity, 40
Dubisch, Jill, and analogical approach to categorizing, 20; and health-food movement, 18–20, 216
Du Bois, Cora, and over-generalization, 231
Dumont, Louis, 51; and category "hierarchy," 83; and comparative analytic categories, 82; and use of term "religion," 83–84
Dumont, Louis and David F. Pocock, and Hindu religiosity, 35
Dunnell, Robert C., 179; and numerical phenetics, 194, 195; and polythetic classification, 194
Durkheim, Émile, 29, 77, 84, 131, 172, 173, 199, 213; criticism of, 125; and theoretical definition of religion, 71, 72–73; discrimination against, 210; and Horton, 126; and organic solidarity, 179; and the supernatural, 122–23

Easter Bunny, 29; *see also* syncretism
Eck, Diana L. 43
Edgerton, Franklin, on dualism in Hinduism, 48
Edwards, Rem B., 172; and family resemblance approach, 218–19
Ego problems, and W.H. Goodenough, 116–17
Ehnmark, Erland, and Homer's description of the Gods, 137
Ehrlich, Paul R. and Anne P. Ehrlich, 191; and criticism of numerical phenetics, 185
Eisenstadt, S.N., and transcendence, 51
Elements of religion, 211, 213–14
Eliade, Mircea, 2, 102, 199
Embodiment, conceptual and functional, 178
Empirical transcendence, 54
Encompassing/encompassed, 83
Enlightenment, 199; and conceptions of religion, 22; and development of meaning of religion, 30

Epicurus, and nature of the soul, 90
Eschatology, 213
Esoteric Buddhism, 36
Essays on Individualism, 83
Essence, commitment to idea of, 30; definition of, 10–11; quest for, 30–31
Essential definitions, 77
Essentialism, 206–7; and language-games, 235; and nominalism 10–12
Essentialist categories, 202
Essentialist definitions, 80–81, 120
Ethical code, 172
Ethnocentrism, 8–10; and comparison of religions, 261, 262–63; defense against, 25; meaning of, 8–9; and objectivity, 162; as starting place, 227–28; tempering of, 261; *see also* Ch. 7
Ethnographers, caveats for, 57; criticism of, 57; and ethnocentrism, 227–28; and experiential associations, 243–44; and fieldwork, procedures of, 112; and natives, 57, 230–31; methods of, compared with theologians', 57–58; monographs of, as rewriting, 252; objectivity of, 231–34; and over-generalization, 231–32; and writing, 82
Ethnography, 25, 145; and *ad hoc* definitions, 81–82; and conceptualization of religion, 18; and creation of analogies, 18; hegemonic, defense of, 261–62; difficulties of, 17–18, 75; and informants, 124; and the invention of culture, 18; production of, 147; and religious practices, 41; and study of religion, 17–18; and transcendence, 84; weaknesses of, 16
Ethos, and world view, fusion of, 104
Euripides, 192
Euro-American cultural phenomena, 18–21
Evans-Pritchard, Edward E., 84, 199; on definition of religion, 71–72; and intellectualist approach, 138; and Tylor, 126
Event and discourse, 248; *see also* discourse
Evolutionary classification, 182
Evolutionary theory and numerical phenetics, 184
Exemplification, and use of general terms, 163; *see also* Ch. 6
Existentialism, and Lévi-Strauss, 14
Experientalism, 80
Explicit definitions, disadvantages of, 74–75

Faith, 97, 106, 172; as category, 42, 64; as major construct, 32; and W.C. Smith, 32, 50; research strategies of, 231–34
Family resemblance, 192, 198, 201, 203, 215, 220; and Alston, 170–71; and applications to religion, 42, 170–71; categories of, 202; idea of, 24, 25; and polythetic classification compared, 170; and prototype theory, 254; *see also* Religion, multi-factorial approaches to
—— predicates, and border problems, 165; and natural grounds problems, 166
"Fences and Neighbors: Some Contours of Early Judaism," 179–80
Feuerbach, Ludwig, 199
Field notes, categorization of, 252–53; ethnocentric structure of, 253; and ethnography, 252–53; interpretation of, 25
Fillmore, Charles J., and criterial properties, 205
Firth, Raymond, and multi-factorial approach, 158
Flatus vocis, 147, 155
Flavell, John H., 255
Fodor, Jerry A., and stereotype theory, 207
Folk accretions, and Buddhism, 39
Folk approaches, meaning of, 21
Folk categories, as analytical instruments, 264; transformation of, 1
Folk-generic categories, 188–89; rank in taxonomies, 186–87
Formal universals, 155
Foucault, Michel, 99, 100, 234, 237; and discourse, 238; and interpretivists, 146
Fowler, W. Warde, 65; and *religio* as scruple, 64–65
Frankfort, H. and H.A. Frankfort, 135
Frazer, James George, and intellectualist approach, 137
Freud, Sigmund, 199, 239, 254; and Benveniste, 66–67
Freudianism, and canonical authority, 44; contrasted with Hinduism and Christianity, 47; as religion, 43, 46
Freudians, 46
Funerary inscriptions in early Judaism, 179–80

Gadamer, Hans Georg, 246
Gallup, George Jr., and poll of Christians, 42–43

Geertz, Clifford, 19, 89, 150, 155–56, 234; and anthropological study of religion, 101–2; and anthropomorphism, 134; and conceptual analysis of religion, 103; and construct religious cultures, 40; critical evaluation of, 95–102; and early forms of interpretivism, 5; and individual differences, 102–4; and religion as a cultural system, 93–95; and religious behavior, 103–4, 105

Gegensinn der Urworte ('The Antithetical Sense of Primal Words'), 66

Genealogy, concept of, 100

Genre/boundary and modernsim, 5

Geschichte des Materialismus, 133

Gifford Lectures, 50

Gillespie, Neal C., 133

Gilson, Étienne, 96

Gleitman, Lila R., Sharon Lee Armstrong, and Henry Gleitman, 205

God, as agent, 63; as agent-act model, 56; Euripides's use of, 192; manipulation of, 128; personalistic conception of, 55, 135; as the transcendent, 52, 61, 62; as the Unconditional, 110

Gods, 170, 171; anthropomorphic, 60; belief in, 213; as religious objects, 136–37; view of, by religious persons, 221–22; see also Supernatural, Theism, Transcendent

Goodenough, Edwin R., 115

Goodenough, Ward H., 131, 150; and characterization of religion, 46; and concept of communism as a religion, 19–20, 216, 218; and criteria for cultural comparisons, 119; criticism of, 117–21; and digital approach to categorizing, 20; and emphasis on believer, 115–16; and essentialist categories, 253; and expansionist view of religion, 116–17, 120; and kinship definition, 119; and overly-inclusive category, 121; and Tillich, 117; and ultimate concern approach, 115–21

Goodman, Nelson, and nominalism, 152; and similarity, 185

Goody, Jack, 88, 125–26, 131, 134; and definitional approaches in the social sciences, 125–26; and Durkheim, rejection of, 125; and homology, 177; and intellectualist approach, 137

Gould, Stephen Jay, 181, 185, 191, 256; on analogy and homology, 175; on usage of homology, 176

Goulet, Jean-Guy, and concept of dualism, 38; and religious dualism, 37

Great Tradition concept, 43; and Christianity, 42

Great Tradition/Little Tradition: problems with, 34–35; and religious dualism, 34–38, 40; and social diversity, 41; and use of, outside anthropology, 39

Greek conceptual distinctions and Lévi-Strauss, 16

Greenberg, Joseph H., 155

Guajira Peninsula (Colombia and Venezuela), 243

Guajiro, see Wayú

Guthrie, Stewart, and anthropomorphism, 134–137; criticisms of, 135, 137; and intellectualist approach, 137; and Mind, 47; and universals, 150, 151

Hallowell, A. Irving, on natural/supernatural dichotomy, 122

Hariolus ('seer'), 66

Harris, Marvin, 123; and criticism of Geertz, 93

Harvey, David, and explanation of postmodernism, 5

Hassan, Ihab Habib, and explanation of postmodernism, 5

Hayakawa, S.I., and essentialist definitions, 203

Health food movement, anthropological conceptualization of, 18–21; as religion, 19, 216

Hegel, Georg Wilhelm Friedrich, and criticism of Schleiermacher, 118

Heidegger, Martin, 250, 252

Hennig, Willi, and cladistics, 180

Hertz, Robert, and organic asymmetry, 178

Hesiod, 132

Hesse, Mary, 166; and redescriptions of nature, 189

Hick, John, 172

Hierarchy, 82; as category, 83; etymology of, 83

Hinduism, 35, 42, 47; and the axial age, 51; convictions attributed to, 43; and diversity in cumulative traditions, 43–50; and dualistic practices of, 48; and Great Tradition/Little Tradition distinction, 33–34; life stages of, 49; and numerical phenetics, 195; and quest for salvation, 47; and resolution of dualistic paradox, 48–49; variable nature of, 31; view of, by Hindus, 44; and worldly prosperity, 47

Hippolytus, 132

Historical linguistics and phenetic models, 179
Hjelmslev, Louis, and Ricoeur, 247
Hocart, Arthur Maurice, 123; and Lévi-Strauss, 16
Hoeningswald, Henry M. and Linda F. Wiener, 179
Holism, 82
Holistic orders, 51
Holy, the 64
Homer, 132; and description of the Gods, 137
Homo Hierarchicus, 83
Homological relations, 15
Homology, 195n, 175–76; and numerical phenetics, 184; and taxonomies, 176–77; *see also* Ch. 5
Homoplasies, 181
Hopi, 210
Horton, Robin, 88, 131, 134; and boundary problems, 136; on Durkheim, 123; and evolutionary fate of religion, 129–30; and intellectualist approach, 137, 145; and James, 128–29; on Leach, 143; and religion, definitional approaches to, 126–30; and universals, 150, 151
Hudson, W.D., 63; and logical transcendence 54; and theism 173; and Wittgenstein, 142, 198
Hull, David L., 175, 177, 182, 191; and criticisms of numerical phenetics, 183–85; and evaluation of phenetic approach to taxonomy, 183–85; on pheneticists, modified position of, 183
Hultkrantz, Åke, and non-Western supernaturalism, 123
Human alters and transcendence, 6, 55–58, 240–41; *see also* Transcendence
Human behavior, interpretation of, 6
Human beings, religious dimension of, 29–30
Human body, bilateral symmetry of, 178
Human nature and Geertz, 95
Human religiosity, semiotic approach to, 134–35
Hume, David, and universals, 152
Hundred schools and the axial age, 51
Hunt, Robert C., and universals, reasons for allegiance to, 119
Huxley, Sir Julian Sorell, and religion, evolutionary fate of, 130
Hypothetico-deductive approach, 182

Immanence, 62; of anthropologists, 260; definition of, 234; and postmodernism, 5
Immanent, definition of, 6
Immanent anthropologists, 25, 234–40; *see also* Immanence
Impingement, 63, 64
Implicational universals, 155
Incest tabu, 15
Indeterminacy and postmodernism, 5
Indexicality and folk biological taxonomies, 186, 189
India, analysis of, 82; and hierarchy, 83; rural religiosity in, 35
Indic religions, 43; *see also* Buddhism, Hinduism, Jainism
Individuals: An Essay in Descriptive Metaphysics, 56
Indologists, difficulties of, 83–84
Indonesia, 97
Intellectualists, and comparative studies, 145; more inclusive outlook of, 145
Interior prayer and James, 128
Interpersonal transcendence, 55
Interpretation, 146–47, 249, 250; and explanation, relationship of, 4–7; and postmodernism, 5; reading and modernism, 5
Interpretivists, 139, 146–50; approach of, 143; criticisms of, 148–50; point of view of, 5
Intuitivity, 76, 77
Islam, 33, 46, 49, 200, 214; as prototypical and Western, 212; and protot ypicality, 217–18; and similarities to Judaism and Christianity, 212
Jackendoff, Ray, 258; and categorization, 201; and language, purpose of, 209; and stereotype theory, 207–8
Jaeger, Werner, and Xenophanes, 132
Jainism, 43; and the axial age, 51
Jains, 45
James, William, 199; and communion, 128–29; and multi-factorial approach, 158; on personal religious experience, 50; and religious behavior, 104
Janicki, Karol, on Hayakawa, 203; on Korzybski, 203; on Popper, 203
Jaspers, Karl, 50
Jesus, 29, 110
Job, 61
Johnson, William Alexander, and transcendence, 60; and the transcendent, 53
Judaism, 49, 72, 110, 199, 200, 214; and the axial age, 51; and polythetic

classification, 179–80; as prototype, 208; and prototypicality, 217–18; and theism, 223

Judaism and Christianity, as models of religion, 212; as prototypical examples of religion, 208–11

Judeo-Christian God, default values of, 224

Judgments of centrality, 169–70, · 173

Kachin (Burma) and symbolism, 139

kama (love), 48

Kammatic Buddhism, 36

karma, 37, 43; and polythesis, 195

Karmic Buddhism, *see* Kammatic Buddhism

Kaufmann, Gordon D., 172*n*; and dualism in the Bible, 52; and experiential limits, 56; and idea of God, 53; and interpersonal transcendence, 55; and McLain, 55–56; and teleological transcendence, 55; and transcendence, 240–41; and transcendent being, 6

Kenny, Anthony, 169–70

Kepler, Johann, and theism, 222

Kierkegaard, Sören Aabye, 109

Kinship, 69, 82, and categorization terms, 205; and universality, 77

Kluckhohn, Clyde, 150

Kolakowski, Leszek, 238, 261; and ethnocentricity, European rejection of, 229; and goal of anthropologist, 229–30

Korzybski, Alfred, and the two-valued orientation, 203

Kurtz, Stanley N., on comparative analytic categories in Dumont, 82

Lactantius, and etymology of *religio*, 65

LaFleche, Frank, and Joseph LaFleche, 33

Lakoff, George, and basic-level categorization, 187; and embodiment, conceptual and functional, 178; and experientialism, 80, 202; and folk-generic categories, 188; and marked/unmarked distinction, 224; and objectivism, 202; and prototype effects, 205; and prototype theory, 215; and Wittgenstein, 203

Lange, Friedrich Albert, criticism of, 133

Language, and discourse, 247–48; nominalist's view of, 69; universals, 155; *see also* Discourse

Language-game(s), 141–42, 219; and discourse, 235–36; and the ethnographer, 228; and family resemblance approach, 159–60; and general terms, 167; and language, conceptualization of, 236–37

Lawson, E. Thomas and Robert N. McCauley, and explanatory theory, 5–6

Leach, Edmund R., 143; on Buddhism 38–39; and conceptual polarity, 38–39; and dualism, 38–39; and practical religion, 39, 47; and pure/impure distinction, 39; and ritual, 144; and symbolism, 139–40

"Lectures on Religious Belief," 141

Lessa, William, and ultimate concerns, 109

Lessa, William and Evon Z. Vogt, 107; criticism of, 106–7; and ultimate concern, 106

Lessa, William, Evon Z. Vogt, and J. Milton Yinger, criticisms of, 114–15; and search for ultimate concerns, 111–12, 114–15

Lévy-Bruhl, Lucien, 103; on Durkheim, 123

Lévi-Strauss, Claude, 134, 251; and digital processes, 13–14; and existentialism, criticisms of, 14; and nature/culture opposition, 15–16; and phenomenology, criticisms of, 14; and structuralism, 14–16

Lienhardt, Godfrey, and natural/supernatural distinction, 123

Life-stages, of Hinduism, 43; metaphors of, 178–79

Literalism, 140; and intellectualist approach, 138–39

Lloyd, G.E.R., 12

Locke, John, and universals, 152

Lockhart, W.R. and P.A. Hartman, and phylogeny, 190

Logical transcendence, 54

Lounsbury, Floyd G., 205

Lubac, Henri de, 123

Lucretius and etymology of *religio*, 65

Lumping/splitting approach, 41–42

McBrearty, Sally A., and cladistics, 150; and numerical phenetics, 176; and similarities, kinds of, 181

MacIntyre, Alasdair, 97, 142, 143

McKern's Midwestern Taxonomic System and numerical phenetics, 179

McLain, F. Michael, and criticisms of Kaufman, 55–56; and modified teleological model, 56; and relatively occult being, 6; and transcendence, 240–41

Magic and religion, distinction between, 144

Malinowski, Bronislaw, 103, 199, 205

Mana, 64; and health food movement, 19

Mandelbaum, David G., 47

Manichaeanism, 13

Maranda, Elli Kongas, and analogy, 195n

Marcus, George E. and Michael M.J. Fischer, 17

Markman, Ellen M., 254; and mutually exclusive categories, 254–255

Marett, Robert Ranulph, and animatism, 126

Marmorstein, Arthur, 135

Marriage, 69

Marriott, McKim, and village religion in India, 35

Marx, Karl, 19, 199

Marxism, and canonical authority, 44; contrasted with Hinduism and Christianity, 47; as religion, 43, 46, 116–17

Mary, 29

Maya pantheon, 29

Mayan tradition and Christianity, interaction with, 37, 38

Maya-Quiché, 37

Maybury-Lewis, David, 11, 16

Mayr, Ernst, 175, 180, 191; and evolutionary classification, 182; and numerical phenetics, criticism of, 183, 185

Meaning and discourse, 248; see also Discourse

The Meaning and End of Religion, 30

Melanesians and religion, 71, 72

Mensching, Gustav, and dualistic approach, 39

Mervis, Carolyn B., 12

Metaphors, 215; generation of, and human body, 178

Mexico and syncretism, 38

Mind, 47

Minsky, Marvin, and schematic thinking, 224–25

Misreading and postmodernism, 5

Modernism, emphasis of, 5

Mokṣa (release), 43, 49

Monk, Ray, 235

Momosteco catechumens and necessity for choice, 38

Momostenango (Guatemala), 37

Monism in Hindu thought, 48

Monophyletic groups, 180, 181

Monothetic classifications, problems posed by, 168

Monothetic definitions of religion, 79–81, 85, 87–121; and cognitive economy, 206; functional, 80; mixed, 80; substantive, 79–80; and supernaturalism 122–25; weaknesses of, 135–36; universal functional, elasticity of, 121

—— Asad and evaluation of Geertz, 95–102

—— Geertz and individual differences, 102–4; and religion as cultural system, 93–95

—— Goodenough, W.H., 115–21

—— Goody, 125–26

—— Guthrie, 134–37

—— Horton, 126–30

—— Lessa and Vogt, and Yinger, 111–15

—— Radin, and types, 104–5

—— Spiro, 130–31

—— Tillich and ultimate concern, 105–11

—— Tylor and minimum definition, 88–91

Monotheticity and Southwold, 173–74

Moral code, 213

Moral community, 171, 172

Morgan, John, on Tillich and Geertz, 111

Morocco, 97

Municipios and lack of isolation, 34

Murdock, George P., 150

Murray, David, and term religion, vagueness and ambiguity of, 204; on Winch, 142

Muslims, 45

Myth, subversion of truth of, 251

Mythology, 172

Myth-performer, 251

Myths, and nature of thought, 14; and religion, 44; structural analysis of, 14–15; unproductive analysis of, 17

Nadel, S.F. and the Nupe, 128, 129

Nat cultus, see Nats

Native categories, and ethnography, 147; use of, as transcultural tools, 263

Natives, as relatively occult, 242; transcendence of, 240–45

Nats (malevolent beings), 36, 37

Natural language: categories, 207, 219–20; category terms, 211; usage, 25

Natural/supernatural dichotomy, 122–23

Nature, de-Godding of, 133; grounded divisions of, 166–67

Nature and the Supernatural as Together

Constituting the One System of God, 58

Nature/culture opposition, misuse of, 16

Needham, Rodney, 44, 69, 96; and belief, 91–92; and the concept of religion, 27; criticisms of, 191–93; and homologies, 195*n*; and multi-factorial approach, 159; and numerical phenetics, criticisms of, 189–93; and organic asymmetry, 178; and polythetic category, 220–21; and social institutions, comparative study of, 190

New Testament, 42

Newton, Sir Isaac, and theism, 222

Nibbanic Buddhism, 36

Niebuhr, Reinhold, 55

Nietzsche, Friedrich Wilhelm, 100

Nirvanic Buddhism, *see* Nibbanic Buddhism

Nominalism, and universals, problem of, 152; and resemblance theory, 153

Nominalist theory, 11

Nominalists, and classification, principles of, 163–64; and contrast to Wittgenstein, 161–62

Non-being, anxiety over, 113

Non-implicational universals, 155

Nuer, 210

Nuer Religion, 126

Numerical phenetics, 167–68, 174–77, 219; criticisms of, 183–96; and Dunnell, 194; early goal of, 186; and Needham, 189–93; and religion in general, 196; and rival taxonomic approaches, 180–82; and subjective biological criteria, 183

Nupe and view of God, 128, 129

Obeyesekere, Gananath, 112

Objectification, 249, 250

Objectivism, 80

Ojibwa, 122, 166

O'Neil, Mary R., and popular religion, 40

Operational taxonomic units (OTU's), 175

Oral tradition, 44

Origen, 90

Ostensive definitions, 77–78, 79

Other Cultures, 144

Outline of text, 23–26

Owen, Richard, and homology, 175

The Oxford Latin Dictionary and *religio*, 67

Pali Canon, 36; *see also* Buddhism

Pals, Daniel L., 3, 85

Paradigm and modernism, 5

Parmenides of Elea, 132

Parochialization, 35

Parsons, Talcott, and common ultimate-value attitudes, 107; on religious motivation, 59

Participatory belonging and alienating distanciation, 25

Paul, St., 245

Peircean semiotics, 17

Penner, Hans H., 2; criticisms of, 85

Personal religious experience, the transcendent in, 50–64

Phenetics, 24, 167; *see also* Numerical phenetics

Phenomena, 25; and causal connections, 139

Phenomenological approach, 37

Phenomenology and Lévi-Strauss, 14

Philosophical religion/practical religion, 39

Philosophic theology and dualism, 38

Phusus (nature), and *nomos* (usage), 16; and *technê* (art), 16

Phylogenetic unit, 181

Phylogeny, 190

Piaget, Jean, 254

Pietas, 65

Plato, 155–56; and universals, 152

Pluralism, growing acceptance of, 22

Pocock, David F., *see* Dumont and Pocock

Polysemy, 248

Polythesis, and the biological sciences, 175

Polythetic classification approach, and Southwold, 171–74

Polythetic grouping, 189–90; utility of, 173–74

Polythetic taxa, construction of, 168–69

Poole, Fitz John Porter, and prototype theory, 215, 220–21

Popper, Karl R., 148; and anti-essentialism, 203; and classification of objects, 81; on definitions, 79; and term essentialism, 11

Popular religion and Little Tradition, 40

Postmodernism, 5

Postmodernists, 147

Poststructuralism and conceptualization of power, 99–100

Poststructuralists, 147; and discourse, 234–35; 238, 247

Practical religion and dualism, 38–39

Prayer, 171

Predicates, basic, and classification, 220–21

Predication, 201

Pre-Socratic philosophy and the axial age, 51

Preus, J. Samuel, 8; and criticism of Tylor, 89; and explanatory theory, 5–6

Price, Henry Habberley, and resemblance theory, 153–54; and subject of belief, 92

Priesthood, 172

Protestant principle and Tillich, 111

Prototype, definitions of, 198–99; temporal aspect, and the acquisition of bias, 199–200

—— approach, as multi-factorial, 218

—— effects, 200, 202, 205–6

—— theory, 25, 42, 198–99, 202–8; and contingency-sensitive predicates, 220–21, 223; and natural language usage, 25; research basis of, 25; see also Ch. 6

Prototypes, productive approach to, 211; and religion, 199–200

Prototypicality, degrees of, 207; a distributional understanding of, 211–12, 214, 215, 217–18, 220–21, 225–26; and need for balanced view, 211–12

The Psychology of Religious Experience, 115

Pure/impure distinction, 83; and Leach, 39

Putnam, Hilary, on "God's-eye view," 57

Quaker tradition, 89

Quasi-religions and Tillich, 108, 109

Radcliffe-Brown, Alfred Reginald, 179

Radin, Paul, and religious behavior, 104–5; and synchronic variability, 41; on Tylor, 89

Raw and cooked, 15–16

Reading and Ricoeur, 146–47

Real definitions, 77

Realism: Aristotelian, 154; and problem of universals, 152; and recurrence theory, 153

Realists, and contrast to Wittgenstein, 161–62; and principles of classification, 163–64

Recurrence theory and problem of universals, 153

Redfield, Robert, and community study approach, 34

Reese, William A., 154

Reformation and conception of religion, 22

Reincarnation, Hindu concept of, 29

Relationships: pure communion, 127–28; pure manipulation, 128; religious, 128

Relative occultism of the natives, 56–58

Relativism and ethnography, 147, 148–49

Religio, 30; etymology of, 65; opposable uses of, 67; in sense of obligation, 64; semantic history of, 64–69; semantic suppleness of, 67; usages of, 64–68

Religion, as abstraction, 212–13, 225; attributes of, 171–72; and autonomy, argument over, 2; and belief, 21–22

—— as analytical category, 68–69, 220, 257; conceptualization of, 211; dubious, 27–30; transformed from folk category, 1; unbounded, 163, 260; use of, 25; Western, 259; see also Ch. 6

—— as category, 7–8, 64, 85; and essentialism, 10; and family resemblance approach, 85; folk, in contemporary U.S., 21–23; as research tool, 24; Western, 77

—— conceptualization of, 1, 17–18, 212–26; approaches in, 21–23; ideal, 18; multi-factorial, 24 and Ch. 5; problems in, 22–23, 24; unbounded, 78

Religion, and cultural anthropologists, 3–4, 210, 221–23; as cultural creation, 7–8; as cultural institution, 131; as cultural system, 3

—— and definition: abjuring of, 27–69; aesthetic perspective in Geertz's view, 93–94; arguments for postponing, 70; a case for, 70, 76–78; and Christian historical processes, 95–96; common-sense perspective of, 103; common-sense perspective in Geertz's view, 93; conceptual options in, 74–76; controversies concerning, 77–78; deferring, advantages of, 70–72; difficulties in formulating, 73–74; disadvantages of, 70–71; essentialist, 24; examples of, 22; holding in abeyance, 74–76; implicit, sources of, 71–72, Ch. 6; implicit/explicit, 84–85; need for, 21, 23–24, Ch. 2; popular definition of, 21–22; reasons for, 85; and relation to problems of human existence, 119–20; religious perspective, 103; religious perspective in Geertz's view, 93–94, 96, 97; scientific perspective in Geertz's view, 93–94; substantive definitions of, 24

Religion, diffuseness of, 209–10; dispensing with term of, 31–32;

evolutionary fate of, 129–30; exemplar view of, 215–17; expansionist view of, 116–17, 118; and fixed canon, 44; in general, characterizing, 196; and language, use of, 134; larger cultural/social context of, 8–9; intellectualist approach to, 137–39; intellectualist and symbolist approaches compared, 139–40; interpretation of, 2; and matter of sufficiency, 218–20; and natural/supernatural distinction, 28–29; as pool of elements, 213–14, 225, 226, 256; and principles of exclusion/inclusion, lack of, 218–19, 226; and non-Western analogues, 17–18; in non-Western societies, and Western anthropologists, 209–10; —— monothetic definition of: benefits and costs of, 156–57, intellectualist approach, 143; literalist approach, 143; symbolist approach, 143; symbolists and efforts at clarification of, 143–45; a Wittgensteinian approach, 140–43
—— multi-factorial approaches to, 158–96; analogy and homology, 174–80; and Keith Campbell, 164–67; cultural studies and use of biological models and metaphors, 178–96; family resemblance, 159–60, 163; polythetic classification, 159; a prototype approach, 197–26; phenomenological autonomy of, 28; and polythesis, 194–95; and polythetic grouping, 167–69; prototypes of, 260; and power, relationship to, 98; and resemblances, positing of, 259–60; and semantic inclusiveness of word, 23; and social relationships, extension of, 127; study of, and cultural analogues, 72; superior, according to Tillich, 111; superiority as determined by central symbols, 110–11; as system of symbols, 93, 94–95; and tacit understanding, advantages of, 72–73; ultimate concern of, 105–7; universal-essentialist conceptions of, 96, 98–99; and universality, 77; in West, historical crystalization of, 209; and Western bias of, 208; and Western cultural setting, 199

Religion: An Anthropological View, 122
"Religion and Ritual: The Definitional Problem," 125
Religiones, as ritual ceremonies, 64
Religion-making characteristics, 170–71
Religion/non-religion boundary, 135–36

Religious behavior, 103–4, 131 motivations, of 105; and ritual activities, 105; *see* Ch. 6
Religious commitment, study of, 103
Religious cultures as construct, 40
Religious dimension: and evaluation of W.C. Smith's approach, 32–33; of human life, 32; study of, 60–61; term used by Philip Bock, 28–29
Religious diversity, analysis of, 34–38; and dualism, 34–38
Religious dualism, and Leach, 39; and religious syncretism, 38; and Spiro, 37
Religious factionalism, 41
Religious feelings, 170
Religious geniuses, and William James, 128
Religious persons, 130
Religious statements, meanings of and Wittensteinian approach, 140–41
Religious studies, and attitudes to the discipline, 2
Religious symbols, 98, 101
Religious types, 104–105
Religions, comparison of, 260–61; families of, 209; historical, 33; as monothetic class, 174; as polythetic class, 174; and predicates, 201; primal, 33; primitive, 33; ranking of, by Tillich, 110–11; reasons for study of, 114; and relationships, communion aspect of, 130; as response to human needs, 174; tribal, 33; variability of, 259; world, 33
"Remarks on the Function of Language in Freudian Theory," 66
Resemblance theory, 156; and establishment of resemblances, 257–258; and problem of universals, 153; and Wittgenstein, 154
Rhetoric and postmodernism, 5
Ricoeur, Paul, 25, 252, 260; and antinomy respecting distanciation, 246; and cultural distance, struggle against, 54; and discourse, 235; and distanciation, 246–53; and interpretation, 253; and interpretivists, 146; and language, 237; on language and discourse, 247–48; and ramifications for ethnography, 250–51; and theory of textuality, 246–47; and understanding, 250; and the world of the text, 250
Ritual: acts, 170, 171; and belief, 129; and symbolists, 143–44
Rituals, 213; of Hinduism, 43
Rivière, Peter, 69

Roman Catholics and hierarchy, 83
Romantics, 249
Rorty, Richard, 69, 147, 166, 258; and matter of vocabulary, 238, 239; and nominalism 152; and redescription of nature, 189; on universals, 155
Rosch, Eleanor, 206, 215; and cognitive economy, 206; and digitizing, 12; and prototype, 218; and prototypicality, degrees of, 207; and· prototypes, 206–7; and scalar memberships, 205; and stereotype theory, 207
Rosch, Eleanor and Carolyn B. Mervis, 208, 211, 215; on categories, 205; and Wittgenstein, 203
Russell, Bertrand Arthur William, 3rd Earl Russell, and universals, 153

Sacred, the, 64, 74, 77; consciousness of, 102
Sacred literature, of Hinduism, 43; as unifying factor, 43
Sacred/profane, 170, 171; and Durkheim, 125
Said, Edward W., 212
Saler, Benson, 91; and anthropomorphization, incompleteness of, 136; on ethnography, 228; and supernaturalism 123–4; and the Wayú, 243–4, 245
Saliba, John A., 29
Salvation, 171; and W.H. Goodenough, 116; quest for, and Hinduism, 47
Samsara, 13
Sanctitas, 65
Sanskritic tradition, see Great tradition/ Little Tradition
Sapir, Edward, and nominalist theory, 11
Saussure, Ferdinand de, and Ricoeur, 247
Saussurian semiotics, 17
Scalar membership in groups, 215–16
Scheffler, Harold W. and Floyd G. Lounsbury, 205
Schiller, Johann Christoph Friedrich von, 133
Schleiermacher, Friedrich, and autonomy of religion, 118; and Horton, 127; and interpretivists, 146
Schneider, David, and criticism of Goodenough, 119
Schwartz, Benjamin I., and the axial age, 51; and meaning of transcendence, 50
Scriptures, 172
Secular humanism as a religion, 22–23
Seeger, Anthony, 16
Segal, Robert A., 2

Semantics and modernism, 5
Semiotics, Peircean, 17; Saussurian, 17
Shore, Bradd, 233
Signified and modernism, 5
Signifier and postmodernism, 5
Similarity, problems of determining, and numerical phenetics, 185
Simpson, George Gaylord, 175, 185; and evolutionary classification, 182; and homology, 175
Single field, 37
Skorupski, John, and description of intellectualist program, 138–39; and literalism 138–39, 140; and symbolism, 139; and Wittgensteinian approach, 140–41
Smith, Brian K., and Hinduism, definition of, 43; and Marxism, 216; and conceptual approach to religion, 43–47; criticism of, 46–47; and essentialist categories, 253; on Hinduism, unity of, 44; on religious unifying process, 43–47; and the Vedas, 43–44
Smith, Edward E. and Douglas L. Medin, and the exemplar view, 216–17; and prototype, 198
Smith, Jonathan Z., 196; and multifactorial approaches, 159; and polythetic classification, 179–80
Smith, Jonathan Z. and Rem B. Edwards, and necessity and sufficiency, 219
Smith, Wilfred Cantwell, 8, 37, 43, 172, 196; and approach to the religious dimension, 32–33; challenge to, 59; and construct of cumulative tradition, 32; and construct of faith, 32, criticisms of, 63–64; and definition of religion, 30–33; and diversity in traditions, 49–50; evaluation of, 23, Ch. 1; on faith, 52; and Great/Little Traditions, 34; and idea of essence, 30; and personal religious experience, 50; as precedent for prototype theory, 215; on religious diversity, 42; and semantic history of religio, 64; and B.K. Smith, 44; and term religion, 68; and Tillich, 108; and transcendence, 62–63; and the transcendent, 52–55
Smith, William Robertson, 199
Smriti (remembered) literature, 43
Sneath, Peter H.A. and Robert R. Sokal, 168, 169; and homology, 177; and phenetics, 176–77
Social institutions, evolutionary reconstruction of, 190
Social scientists, concern of, 112

Sokal, Robert R. and Peter H.A. Sneath, 87, 176, 179; and classificatory procedures, 219; on establishing taxa, 175; and grouping in numerical phenetics, 168–169

Souls, nature of, 90

Southwold, Martin, 131, 195, 212, 213, 214; and Alston, 172; and Christianity as prototype, 208; on Needham, 192; and polythetic approach to religion, 192–93; and polythetic classification, 171–75; and source of attributes, 193–94; and theism, 221

Spengler, Oswald, and life-stage metaphors, 178

Spiritual beings as category, 90

Spiritual/material dualism, 89–90

Spiro, Melford E., 79, 80, 88, 130–31, 134; and boundary problems, 136; and Buddhism, 36; and concept of dualism 38; criticisms of, 78; and definition of religion, 212; and intellectualist approach, 137–38; on Leach, 143; on need for a definition of religion, 76–78, 85; and real definitions, 77; rejection of, 157; on religion, implicit definition of, 71; and religious behavior, 131; and religious dualism 37; and syncretism, 36–37; and Tambiah, differences in approach and Tambiah's solutions, alternative to, 35–36; and theism, 173; and theory about theistic commitments, 7; and two religions thesis, 36; and universals, 150–51; and Western monotheisms, 172n

Śruti (heard) literature, 43

Staal, Frits, and universal, usage of, 155

Staniland, Hilary, 152

Status/power, 83

Stemmatics, 179

Stevenson, Charles, and persuasive definitions, 110

Strawson, P.F., 55–56

Structuralism, 13–17, 250; and analysis of myths, 14; and binary opposites, 14–15; and categorization, 14; contributions, of, 16; criticisms of, 16; and diminished enthusiasm for, 16–17; as theory about communication, 15

Substantive universals, 155

Superhuman beings, 151; and Spiro, 130–31

Supernatural, 74, 126; as category, 122–25; etymology of, 123; and non-/Westerners, 123, 124; premise and F.C. Wallace, 122; as Western category, 24; and Westerners, 123, 124

Supernaturalism, 129

Supernatural/natural dualism, questionnaire on, 124

Superstitio as contrary of religio, 65–66

Symbolic analysis and Geertz, 101–2

Symbolism, 139–40

Symbolists, and comparative studies, 145; and decoding, 145; more inclusive outlook of, 145–46

Symbols, conceptualizations of, 97; religious, 111

Symplesiomorphies, 181

Synapomorphies, 180

Synchronic variability, 33–50

Syncretism, 36, 38; examples of, 29

Syntagm and postmodernism, 5

Systematics in Prehistory, 194

Systems of beliefs, 64

Taboo, concept of, and health food movement, 19

Tabu, 64

Tambiah, Stanley J., and Great/Little distinction, 34; and single field solution, 35, 37; and Spiro, differences in approach with, 35–36; and study of religion in north-east Thailand, 35–36

Taoism, 31; and the axial age, 51

Taxa, exemplars of, 169–70; and folk biological ranks, 187

Taxonomy, structural regularities in, 186–87

Tedlock, Barbara, and concept of dualism, 37–38; and dialectical perspective, 37

Teleological world view, 171

Telos, 47

Temple, William, on divine revelation, 57

Ten Commandments, 42

Tertullian, Quintus Septimius Florens, 90; on Christ's resurrection, 123; and etymology of religio, 65

Text, 146, 235; autonomy of, 248–49; and distanciation, 246–51; decontextualization of, 249; emancipation of, 249; recontextualization of, 249; and relationship to reader, 250

Text/intertext and postmodernism, 5

Textual concerns, ranking of, 113–14

Thailand, religious traditions in, 35–36

Theism, 210, 211; as attribute of religion, 173; and Buddhism, 213; as central to conceptions of religion, 21–22; as contingency-sensitive predicate of religion, 222–23; as critical attribute of religion, 192; and default values, 221, 224–25; and disbelieving anthropologists, 7; predicates of, 221–23; reduced affirmations of, 22; repudiation of, 131; and science, 222; study of, 6–7

Theistic definitions of religion and Southwold, 173

Theologians, methods of, compared with ethnographers', 57–58

Theology, insinuation of, into religion studies, 3

Theravada Buddhism, 35, 208, 221, 223; and Southwold, 173

Thomas, David Hurst, 179

Tillich, Paul, 55, 103, 117; and Calvin, 110; and W.H. Goodenough, 115, 116; influences on, 107; and Lessa and Vogt, and Yinger, 111, 115; and positions on ultimate concern, 107–11; and quasi-religions, 108, 109, 215, 216; and religious behavior, 105–7; and superiority of some religions, 109, 110; and ultimate anxiety, 113

"Toward an Anthropologically Useful Definition of Religion," 115

Towler, Robert, and dualistic approach, 39

Toynbee, Arnold Joseph, and life-stage metaphors, 178–179

Transcendence, 44, 45; and the axial age, 50–51; elusiveness of, 58; empirical, 54; epistemological problem of, 54; general sense of, 60–61; interpersonal, 55; logical, 54; and modernism, 5; mystery of, 63; of the natives, 56–58, 260; and religion, 59–64; role of, in human experience, 31; semantic problem of, 54; special sense of, 61; teleological, 55; third sense of, 62; two senses of, and effect on anthropologists' analyses, 61–62; as useful topic for study, 60–61; and W.C. Smith's view of, 30–31

Transcendent, authority functions of, 53; elemental meaning of, 60; and natives, 25; in postmodernist criticism, 51–52; and W.C. Smith, 50; as universal constant, 53; in Western religious tradition, 52–53

Transcultural theories, 149–150

Tristes Tropiques, 14

Two Crows, 33

Trukese (Micronesia) and W.H. Goodenough, 116

Truth and Method, 246

Turner, Victor, 145, 199

Tylor, Edward Burnett, 122, 126, 144, 188, 199; and animism, 90, 92; criticism of, 89–93; and Goody, 125–26; and Guthrie, 131–37; heirs of, 125–38; and Horton, 126–30; and intellectualist approach, 137, 139; and minimum definition of religion, 88–93; and mystical experience, 89; and spiritual beings, 90–91; and spiritual/material dualism, 89–90; and Spiro, 130–31

Tzeltal Maya (Mexico), 187–88

Ultimate concerns of the individual, 111–12, 113–14

Ultimacies, false, and Paul Tillich, 108

Unbounded categories, usefulness of, 25, Ch. 7; see also Categories

the Unconditional, 108–10

Units for comparison, 193–94

Universal categories, 150–56; boundaries of, 120

Universal functional definition, elasticity of, 121

Universalism, 76–77; in Greek theology, 132

Universalist definitions, 95–96

Universalization, 35

Universals, allegiance to, 118–19; assumptions concerning, 154; definition of, 155; implicational, 257; lists of, 155; problem of, 147, 151–56, 257–58; search for, 127; suggested approach to, 155–56; see also cultural universals

Upanishads, 43

Vagueness, in definitions, 204; and monothetic definitions, 87–88

Vedas, 43–44

Vedic tradition and Hindu orthodoxy, 43

Villa Rojas, 34

Vogt, Evon Z., criticism of, 106–7; and ultimate concerns, 106, 109; see also Lessa and Vogt, and Yinger

Vrijhof, Peter H., and dualistic approach, 39

Waghorne, Joanne Punzo and Norman Cutler, 43

Wagner, Roy, on ethnographers, 57

Wallace, Anthony F.C., 88; and evolutionary fate of religion, 129; and the supernatural premise, 122; and supernaturalism as distinguishing feature of religion, 122, 125; and thirteen minimal categories of behavior, 122

Watanabe, Satosi, 226

Wax, Murray L., 8

Wayú (Guajiro), custom, and limited understanding of, 244, 245; and predictions about herding, 243–44

Weber, Max, 84, 104, 199; on definition of religion, 71, 72; on religious motivation, 59

Western categories, privileging of, 8

Western folk categories, as anthropological vocabulary, 238; as sources for analytical categories, 25–26

Western individualism in contrast with India, 82

Western logic as essence, 11

Western monotheisms, 172, 172n; and ethnocentrism, 227; as exemplars of religion, 213–14, 217–18, 225, 261, 262

Western religions as atypical, 210

Western traditions and need for increased grounding in, 263

Wiebe, Donald, 2–3

Wilamowitz-Möllendorff, Ulrich von, 192

Williams, Leonard, 179

Wilson, Bryan R., 142

Wilt, Henry Toomey, and meaning of religio, 65

Winch, Peter, and Wittgensteinian approach, 142

Wissler, Clark, 150

Wittgenstein, Ludwig, 75, 101, 112, 140–43, 170, 171, 196, 203, 207, 215; and advantages of Wittgensteinian approach, 141; and boundaries, 206; and boundary problems, 204; and classificatory procedures, 219; and concept words, 197–98; and family resemblance approach, 159–60, 211; and language-games, 235–36, 237; perspectives of, 24, Ch. 5; and polythetic classification, 24, Ch. 5; and problem of universals, 160–62

Wolterstorff, Nicholas, 151

Wordsworth, 245

Woozley, A.D., 152, 258; and Aristotelian universal, 153; and resemblance theory, 153–54

Words, authority of, 68

World views, non-Western, 60

Worldly prosperity, as goal of Hinduism, 47–48

Worship, religion and, 22

Wyschograd, Edith, and transcendence, 58

Xenophanes of Colophon, and criticism of anthropomorphism, 131–33

Yin and yang, 13

Yinger, J. Milton, criticism of, 106–7; and ultimate concerns, 106, 109; see also Lessa and Vogt, and Yinger

Zettel, 236, 237

Zoroastrianism and the axial age, 51

Zuckerkandl, Émile, 177